STRATEGIC MANAGEMENT:

A Framework for Decision Making and Problem Solving

STRATEGIC MANAGEMENT:

A Framework for Decision Making and Problem Solving

A.J. Almaney
DePaul University

Sheffield Publishing Company

Salem, Wisconsin

For information about this book, write or call:
Sheffield Publishing Company
P.O. Box 359
Salem, Wisconsin 53168
(414) 843-2281

Cover: The cover depicts how strategic management is not static, rather it is a process consisting of interrelated phases. The circles represent the different phases involved in this dynamic and ongoing process. The phases involved include environmental analysis, classification of internal and external conditions, strategic match, strategy formulation, strategy implementation and strategy control.

To Kathleen

For Kathleen

CONTENTS

Preface xv

Chapter 1 A Framework for Strategic Decision-Making and Problem-Solving: An Overview 1
The Case Method: A Decision-Making and Problem-Solving Tool 1
    Popularity of the Case Method 1
    Rationale of the Case Method 2
    Strategic Management Cases 2
Introducing a Strategic Decision-Making and Problem-Solving Framework 3
The Descriptive Phase 3
    Purpose of the Descriptive Phase 6
    Benefits of the Descriptive Phase 6
The Diagnostic Phase 7
    Diagnostic Labels 7
The Prescriptive Phase 9
    The Prescriptive Phase and Healthy Organizations 9
The Framework and the Decision-Making Process 10
The Framework and the Problem-Solving Skills 10
Objectives of the Framework 11
Review Questions 14

Chapter 2 The Descriptive Phase: Profiling the Internal Environment 16
Fundamentals of the Profiling Process 16
The Concept of Factoring 16
Profiling the Organization's Environments 18
Profiling the Internal Environment 19
Profiling the Corporate/Business Level 21
    Profiling the Major Components of the Corporate/Business Level 23
    Checklists on the Subcomponents of Strategic Managers 25
        The Board of Directors 25
        Top Management 25
    Checklists on the Subcomponents of Environmental Analysis 25

Internal Analysis 25
External Analysis 26
Checklists on the Subcomponents of Strategy
Formulation 26
Mission 26
Corporate Objectives 26
Grand Strategies 26
Competitive Strategies 26
Checklists on the Subcomponents of Strategy
Implementation 27
Organizational Structure 27
Policies 27
Budgetary Allocations 27
Leadership 28
Corporate Culture 28
Communication 28
Motivation 28
Checklists on the Subcomponents of Strategy
Control 28
Establishment of Standards 28
Evaluation of Performance 29
Correction of Deviations 29
Profiling the Functional Level 29
Profiling the Major Components of the Functional
Level 32
Checklists on the Subcomponents of Marketing 32
Products/Services 32
Marketing Research 32
Target Market 32
Sales 33
Market Share 33
Pricing 33
Distribution 33
Advertising and Promotion 33
Checklists on the Subcomponents of Production 34
Location of Facilities 34
Newness of Facilities 34
Layout of Facilities 34
Checklists on the Subcomponents of Research and
Development 35
Focus 35
Posture 35
Budget 35

Checklists on the Subcomponents of Human
  Resources 35
    Succession Planning 35
    Recruitment and Selection 36
    Training and Development 36
    Performance Appraisal 36
    Compensation 36
Checklists on the Subcomponents of Public Affairs . . 36
    Ethics 36
    Social Responsibility 36
    Crisis Management 37
Checklists on the Subcomponents of Finance/
  Accounting 37
    Management of Cash 37
    Management of Inventories 37
    Management of Accounts Receivable 37
    Management of Total Assets 38
    Management of Debt 38
    Capital Budgeting 38
    General Profit Picture 38
Appendix A: The Board of Directors 39
Appendix B: Top Management 40
Appendix C: Scanning the External Environment 41
Appendix D: Mission 42
Appendix E: Corporate Objectives 43
Appendix F: Grand Strategies 43
Appendix G: Competitive Strategies 46
Appendix H: Organizational Structure 47
Appendix I: Policies 57
Appendix J: Leadership Style 58
Appendix K: Corporate Culture 60
Appendix L: Target Marketing 60
Appendix M: Advertising Budget 61
Appendix N: Quality Control Techniques 62
Appendix O: Research and Development 62
Appendix P: Succession Planning 63
Appendix Q: Public Affairs 63
Appendix R: The Meaning and Computation of Ratios 64
Appendix S: Sources of Information on Industry Ratios 66
Review Questions 69

Chapter 3 The Descriptive Phase: Profiling the External
            Environment 72
    Steps of Profiling the External Environment 72
    Profiling the Task Environment: Checklists 72
            Industry 75
            Competitors 75
            Suppliers/Raw Materials 75
            Suppliers/Capital 76
            Suppliers/Labor 76
            Customers 76
            Labor Unions 76
            Government Regulators 76
    Profiling the General Environment 77
            Demographics 77
            Culture 77
            Economy 77
            Politics 78
            Technology 78
            Pressure Groups 78
    Checklists and Factors 78
            The Meaning of Factor 79
            Favorable and Unfavorable Factors 80
    Observations on the Descriptive Phase 80
    Appendix A: Entry and Exist Barriers 82
    Appendix B: Sources of Information on Industry 83
    Appendix C: The Experience Curve 84
    Appendix D: Sources of Information on Competitors 84
    Appendix E: Sources of Information on Labor Availability . . 85
    Appendix F: Sources of Information on Government
        Regulators 85
    Appendix G: Sources of Information on Demographics 86
    Appendix H: Sources of Information on Culture 86
    Appendix I: Sources of Information on the Economy 86
    Appendix J: Sources of Information on Politics 87
    Appendix K: Sources of Information on Technology 87
    Appendix L: Sources of Information on Pressure Groups . . . 88
    Review Questions 89

Chapter 4 The Diagnostic Phase 90
    The Link between Diagnosis and the Descriptive Phase 90
    Objective of the Diagnostic Phase 90
    Steps of the Diagnostic Process 91
            Diagnosing the Strengths 91

Strengths of the Corporate/Business Level . . . 93
Strengths of the Functional Level 96
The Organization's Distinctive Competency . . 96
Diagnosing the Weaknesses 96
Weaknesses of the Corporate/Business Level . 98
Weaknesses of the Functional Level 98
The Organization's Key Weakness 98
Diagnosing the Opportunities 99
Opportunities in the Task and General
Environment 101
The Organization's Key Opportunity 101
Diagnosing the Threats 102
Threats in the Task and General Environment 103
The Organization's Key Threat 104
Observations on Strengths, Weaknesses,
Opportunities, and Threats 105
Diagnosing the Major and Subordinate Problems with
Their Symptoms and Probable Causes 105
The Meaning of Symptom 105
The Meaning of Cause 105
The Difference Between Symptoms and
Causes 106
Intermediate Factor 107
Intermediate Factors and the Cause-Tracking
Question 108
A One-Level Intermediate Factor 109
A Two-Level Intermediate Factor 109
The Root Cause and the Prescriptive Phase . 110
The Percolation Effect 112
Causal Treatment and Symptomatic Relief . . 116
The Meaning of Problem 116
The Difference between Major and
Subordinate Problems 118
Statement of the Problem 119
The Process of Diagnosing Major and
Subordinate Problems 121
Review Questions 127

Chapter 5 The Diagnostic Phase 128
Determining the Strategic Match 128
Dimensions of the Strategic Match 128
Constraint 128
Leverage 131

Maintenance   132
Vulnerability   132
Value of the Strategic Match Dimensions   133
Determining the Primary Strategic Match Position   133
Portfolio Planning Techniques   133
The BCG Growth/Share Matrix   135
Question Marks   137
Stars   137
Cash Cows   137
Dogs   138
The GE Planning Grid   138
The Three Zones of the Planning Grid   140
Adopting the GE Planning Grid as a Strategic
Match Matrix   141
Positioning a Firm on the Matrix   141
Diagnosing the Distinctive Competency and the Major
Weakness of the Competitors   150
Review Questions   151

Chapter 6 The Prescriptive Phase   154
Functions of the Prescriptive Phase   154
Formulating a Strategic Plan   154
Writing a New Mission Statement   156
Setting Corporate Objectives   156
Making the Strategic Choice   156
Generating Alternative Grand Strategies . . .   157
Evaluating Alternative Grand Strategies . . .   159
Selecting a Strategy   163
Observations on the Strategy-Evaluation
Approaches   163
Combination Strategy   164
Contingency Strategy   164
Selecting a Competitive Strategy   165
Formulating Functional Objectives and Strategies   165
Establishing the Conditions Necessary to Implement the
Strategic Plan   171
A Concluding Observation: The Communication Dimensions
of the Case Method   173
Appendix A: Policies   174
Appendix B: How to Handle Criticism   177
Appendix C: How to Express Criticism   178
Appendix D: How to Overcome Nonparticipation   179
Appendix E: How to Avoid Overparticipation   180

Appendix F: How to Prepare a Written Report 180
Appendix G: How to Make an Oral Presentation 184
Review Questions 186

Chapter 7 An Illustrative Case A: Profile of United States Gypsum Corporation, 1990 188

Chapter 8 An Illustrative Case B: Analysis of United States Gypsum Corporation, 1990 223

Strategic Management Cases

Case 1.   Mary Kay Cosmetics, Inc. 264

Case 2.   Harley-Davidson, Inc.: The Eagle Soars Alone 293

Case 3.   Apple Computer, Inc., 1987 ... The Second Decade 314

Case 4.   Deere and Company: Into the 1990s 345

Index 363

PREFACE

This book deals with the skills of making decisions and solving problems in a strategic management context. It is designed for use in the business strategy and policy course which, in many schools, is offered as a capstone course for undergraduate and graduate business students.

The Strategy Course and the Case Method

In a capstone strategy course, students are afforded the opportunity to integrate the various strands of their previously acquired knowledge in solving problems and making decisions in a broad range of organizations. By far, the most popular and most widely used pedagogical tool in the capstone strategy course is the case method which heavily relies on the use of case studies. The case method turns the classroom into a decision-making laboratory where students gain experience by practicing the theoretical concepts they have accumulated during the prior years of their educational programs. Thus, rather than playing the passive role of listening to lectures and taking notes, students become active participants in the learning process. They analyze companies, diagnose problems, debate issues, and propose solutions. And in so doing, they practice more than the art and science of strategy making. They also have the opportunity to hone their logical reasoning, written and interpersonal communication skills, and public-speaking ability. Further, they come to see first-hand how different individuals arrive at different conclusions even though all start out with the same pieces of information. And when students work in teams, as they often do in the case method, they are exposed to the real-life problems that are inherent in group interaction, which can put to the test their conflict-resolution adeptness as well as their leadership and persuasion skills.

Because of its effectiveness as an instructional tool, the case method has been used in a wide assortment of business courses including finance, marketing, human resources, operations management, and so on. However, the case method as applied in the strategy course has two distinctive features. First, whereas in the other, typically non-capstone, courses, the case method focuses on only one function of the organization; in a strategy course, the approach emphasizes the organization's operations in all their variety. Hence, the students examine not only such functional areas as production, R&D, marketing, finance, human resources, and so on but transcend that by evaluating the ways in which the organization formulates, implements, and controls its strategies.

Second, in the non-capstone courses, students typically play the role of functional managers concerned with issues of interest to a particular department. In a strategy course, however, the student assumes the role of the chief executive officer (CEO) or owner of the organization. In this capacity, he or she is responsible for the welfare of not only one functional unit but of the entire organization and is charged with the task of charting a strategic vision of not only one department but of the enterprise as a whole. Clearly, to be successful in his or her endeavor, the CEO needs to possess a good understanding of the interrelationships existing among the various organizational units and to view such units as equally significant contributors to the organization's viability and long-term prosperity. The CEO, in other words, is required to embrace a system view of the corporation where all the parts affect one another and all contribute in pivotal ways to the attainment of the organization's mission and objectives. In this sense, the strategy course equips students with the skills that will prepare them for that day when they themselves become the captains of their own corporate ship.

An Analysis Framework

There are perhaps as many tools for analyzing strategy cases as there are professors of strategic management courses. No tool can be said to be good or bad. Each tool is useful for achieving certain learning objectives, and, as a consequence, each is reflective of the professor's desire to accentuate certain dimensions of the strategy process.

The analysis framework discussed in this text represents one approach to the enhancement of students' ability to solve problems and make decisions in a strategic management context. The framework is characterized by two unique features: it is thorough as well as exceedingly practical.

The framework is comprehensive by virtue of the fact that it is constructed to closely follow the strategic management process. It begins with the initial stage of gathering information about the organization's internal and external environments and concludes with the implementation of strategy. As can be seen below, the entire framework consists of several steps, all of which constitute critical elements of the strategy process:

1. Profiling the internal environment (Part A).
2. Profiling the external environment (Part B).
3. Diagnosing the strengths of the corporate/business level and the functional level and the organization's distinctive competency (Part C.1, 2, and 3).
4. Diagnosing the weaknesses of the corporate/business level and the functional level and the organization's key weakness (Part D.1, 2, and 3).
5. Identifying the external opportunities and diagnosing the key opportunity (Part E.1, 2, and 3).
6. Identifying the external threats and diagnosing the key threat (Part F.1, 2, and 3).

7. Determining the major and subordinate problems with their symptoms and probable causes (Part G).
8. Establishing a strategic match between the internal strengths and weaknesses on the one hand and the external opportunities and threats on the other (Part H).
9. Identifying the organization's primary strategic match position through the application of portfolio planning (Part I).
10. Formulating a strategic plan by:
    a) writing a mission statement for the organization (Part K.1).
    b) setting long and short-term corporate objectives (Part K.2).
    c) making the strategic choice by selecting the most effective grand strategy (Part K.3).
    d) selecting a competitive strategy (Part K.4).
    e) formulating functional objectives and strategies (Part K.5).
11. Establishing the conditions necessary to implement the strategic plan (Part L). This is accomplished through effective:
    a) organizational structure
    b) policies
    c) leadership
    d) corporate culture
    e) communication
    f) motivation

The second principal unique feature of the analysis framework presented in this text is its practical orientation. The framework provides students with hands-on-experience in strategic management. When the framework is applied in its entirety, it allows students to gain valuable knowledge of the process involved in researching cases and sorting out information on their own for purposes of strategic analysis. The framework also furnishes students with the opportunity to practice their strategic management knowledge by, for instance, writing a mission statement, setting long and short-term objectives, and formulating detailed functional strategies complete with time table, cost, and benefit (or savings). Additionally, the framework challenges the students' creative thinking and imagination by requiring them to formulate policies for the corporation as a whole and for each of the functional areas of marketing, production, R&D, human resources, finance/accounting, and public affairs.

Because of its pragmatic bent, the framework is of value not only to strategic management students who need a systematic and coherent approach to analyzing textbook cases. It can be equally beneficial to strategic management practitioners whose success hinges on their deftness in tackling complex strategic issues and solving organization-wide problems in a methodical and practical fashion.

How to Use the Framework

The analysis framework may be used in its entirety or only partially. This depends on the professors' preference. The thoroughness of the framework endows it with a considerable measure of flexibility.

In courses where students are required to analyze actual (live) companies, the Descriptive Phase of the framework is most critical. This phase serves as a roadmap guiding students to the organizational dimensions they need to focus on and the type of information they should be looking for. This phase, however, might not be so crucial when textbook cases are relied upon as the principal learning tool.

The application of the Diagnostic Phase and the Prescriptive Phase varies with the number of cases the professor would like analyzed during the academic term. For instance, only certain parts of these two phases may be used on a consistent basis in analyzing cases, or different parts of the two phases may be applied alternatively with different cases. In a highly truncated application, only Part G (diagnosing the major and subordinate problems) and Part K.3 (making the strategic choice by selecting the most effective grand strategy) may be included in the analysis. In a broader application of the framework, Parts C (diagnosing strengths), D (diagnosing weaknesses), E (diagnosing opportunities), and F (diagnosing threats) may be added. Each one of these two approaches may, of course, be combined with a large project in which students are required to apply the entire analysis framework to a case and then submit the results of the analysis at the end of the term in the form of a major research undertaking.

Cases

Although the book contains some cases, it is clearly not a case book. Rather, it is a book that presents an analysis framework which can be used with a case book. The four cases included in the text--Mary Kay Cosmetics, Inc., Harley-Davidson, Inc., Apple Computer, Inc., and Deere and Company--are intended for use as practice cases by those professors who, like this writer, might require their students to analyze actual companies. One or all of the four cases may be utilized for this end to make sure that the students have a good handle on the analysis process before they embark on their major project of analyzing a "live" corporation.

A Note to the Students

Your ability to perform effectively in a case-oriented class is predicated on more than your knowledge of the analysis process. It also depends on how well you understand the concepts that underlie the discipline and how successful you are in interacting with other members of the class and in communicating your ideas orally and in writing. In this book, you are provided with appendixes designed to enhance both your conceptual and communicative skills.

Appendixes on Concepts. Chapters 2, 3, and 6 contain numerous appendixes dealing with concepts fundamental to your ability to apply the analysis framework. Actually, you will not be able to conduct the analysis without first acquainting yourself thoroughly with these concepts. Some of these appendixes list key sources from which you can obtain information if you are asked to research actual companies.

Appendixes on Communication. Communication plays a vitally significant role in case-oriented courses. It is virtually intertwined with every aspect of case analysis. Whether students probe issues, ask questions, respond to criticisms, make oral presentations, or write reports, they find themselves constantly engaged in a critically important communication activity. Consequently, their effectiveness to play these diverse roles depends on how well versed they are in the art of communication. In Chapter 6, you will find several appendixes aimed at providing you with important tips on how to become an effective communicator or a good participant in group deliberations. Read these appendixes carefully before making your class presentation or engaging in your first class discussions.

An Illustrative Case. Chapters 7 and 8 contain an illustrative case. In Chapter 7, the Descriptive Phase of the analysis framework is used in generating a profile of United States Gypsum Corp. In Chapter 8, the Diagnostic and Prescriptive Phases are applied in analyzing this company. Take a look at the analysis to get an idea on how to apply the framework and how to present the results of your analysis.

Acknowledgement

The strategic decision-making and problem-solving framework described in this book represents the culmination of several years of refinement. It has undergone numerous modifications and embellishments as a result of the evolving nature of the strategic management field and the exceedingly useful inputs from my students. I would, therefore, like to take this opportunity to express my appreciation to all my students who helped either directly or indirectly in fine-tuning the framework. Some students made specific recommendations for change. Others indirectly inspired me with ideas for change as they struggled with the initial "coarse" versions of the framework. And still others made useful suggestions after applying the framework in their own jobs. I am grateful to all of them for helping me smooth out many of the rough edges of the framework.

In the Department of Management at DePaul University, I would like to express my appreciation to my dear friend and unique human being, the late Professor Karen Emig, for her support and valuable suggestions. I would also like to thank my colleagues, Professors James Belohlav and Kenneth Thompson, for their helpful observations and recommendations.

My special thanks go to my wife, Kathleen, who patiently and valuably served as a sounding board for my ideas and whose unwavering support and encouragement were instrumental in the birth of this book.

A. J. Almaney

Chapter 1

A FRAMEWORK FOR
STRATEGIC DECISION-MAKING AND PROBLEM-SOLVING:
AN OVERVIEW

Strategic management is basically a decision-making and problem-solving process. In mapping out a future direction for their firm, strategists make a whole range of critical decisions. They determine the business domain in which the firm should operate; set long and short-term objectives; analyze, evaluate, and select grand and competitive strategies; create an organizational structure appropriate for the strategy; allocate financial, human, and technological resources; draw up fair and consistent policies; create a corporate culture that supports the chosen strategy; institute effective motivation and communication systems; establish a workable control system; and so on.

In the process of formulating, implementing, and controlling such decisions, strategists grapple with an endless stream of problems. Among these are low industry growth rate; aggressive competitors; unreliable suppliers; shrinking customer base; anti-business legislation; labor strikes; unfavorable demographic, cultural, and political shifts; product obsolescence; and hostile special interest groups.

Whether a corporation succeeds or fails in achieving its strategic aims depends primarily on how skillful its strategists are in making decisions and solving problems.

THE CASE METHOD:
A DECISION-MAKING AND PROBLEM-SOLVING TOOL

The skill to make sound decisions and solve problems is not an innate quality. Rather, it can be learned.[1]

A variety of tools can be used to teach decision making and problem solving. Prominent among these is the case method which involves analysis of cases. Case analysis is viewed as a "proven educational method that is especially effective in a strategic management course."[2]

Popularity of the Case Method

The case method has become one of the most popular instructional tools. It is being used by a growing number of schools and in a wide array of disciplines.

One reason for the popularity of the case method is that it confers realism on the classroom setting. By analyzing cases involving actual organizations,

1

students are given the chance to act as executives with the responsibility to make strategic decisions and solve problems. The case method, therefore, permits students to apply their knowledge in tackling real-life problems. It also enables them to "try out new ideas, plans, and operations without taking the actual risks involved in such decisions in actual organizations."[3]

Another reason underlying the popularity of the case method is that it fosters the student's independent thinking and initiative. In the case method, students are expected to do the thinking themselves rather than have someone do the thinking for them, as is normally the situation in listening to a lecture or reading a textbook. This point is emphasized by a leading scholar of the case method who said, while addressing his students: "Learning by participating in discussion, where a large part of the burden is on you to discover the central lessons and insights, is far more effective than learning by the more traditional academic methods."[4]

The case method, then, creates an environment where the student plays an active rather than a passive role in the learning process.

Rationale of the Case Method

The case method is based on the concept of "learning by doing." That is, to be able to swim, play tennis, or fly an airplane, you need more than theoretical knowledge. You need to practice what you know. Similarly, you cannot be a strategic manager by merely reading a textbook or listening to lectures. Practice is the best teacher. The case method serves as a "valuable means of providing aspiring managers with an important daily practice in wrestling with management problems."[5]

Strategic Management Cases

It is worthwhile to observe that the cases used in a strategic management course differ in some significant ways from those used in other more focused courses such as marketing, finance, operations, or human resources. In these courses, the cases typically involve issues of particular relevance to one functional area. In analyzing such issues, the student usually assumes the role of a functional area manager.

By contrast, strategic management cases tend to be more comprehensive, encompassing the organization's operations in their variety. Not only do the cases furnish information on marketing, production, R&D, human resources, finance, and so on; they also provide information on the the board of directors, top-management, and the manner in which strategies are formulated, implemented, and controlled. Further, strategic management cases often contain information on such external environmental conditions as the industry, competitors, government regulators, suppliers, economy, demographics, culture, and the like.

Another difference between strategic management cases and functionally centered cases is that in the former, students play the role of a chief executive officer rather than a functional manager. In this capacity, they are required to treat the organization as a total entity and formulate strategies for the entire corporation rather than for one functional unit.

In the above context, case analysis in a strategic management setting is designed to equip students with the skills they need to function effectively as future chief executive officers. At a minimum, strategic case analysis helps students to become informed members of their organizations, capable of understanding why top management chooses certain strategies and not others and why some strategies (or companies) succeed while others fail.

INTRODUCING A STRATEGIC DECISION-MAKING AND PROBLEM-SOLVING FRAMEWORK

In this segment of our discussion, we will introduce a framework that serves as a tool for making decisions and solving problems within a strategic management context.

Portrayed in Exhibit 1-1, the framework is closely tied to the strategic management process and covers all the principal concepts of the process. Thus, when students use the framework in analyzing cases, they are bound to apply all of these principles.

As can be seen in the exhibit, the framework is composed of three phases: a descriptive phase, a diagnostic phase, and a prescriptive phase. Each of these phases is, in turn, made up of smaller elements calculated to focus on specific aspects of strategic management. As a whole, the framework serves as a road map, guiding students from one phase of the case analysis to the next in a logical and systematic fashion.

It is worth observing that the framework is not only useful for purposes of analyzing textbook cases. Its conceptual underpinnings are practical enough to be used by practitioners in conducting actual strategic analysis.

THE DESCRIPTIVE PHASE

Delineated in Chapters 2 and 3, the descriptive phase (often called the situational audit) represents the information-gathering phase of the analysis process. As can be seen in Exhibit 1-2, this phase involves profiling (or collecting data about) the internal and external environments of the organization under study.

Exhibit 1-1   A FRAMEWORK FOR STRATEGIC DECISION MAKING AND PROBLEM SOLVING

THE DESCRIPTIVE PHASE

A. Provide a profile of the organization's internal environment
   1. Profile the corporate/business level in terms of:
      a. strategic managers
      b. environmental analysis
      c. strategy formulation
      d. strategy implementation
      e. strategy control
   2. Profile the functional level in terms of:
      a. marketing
      b. production
      c. research and development
      d. human resources
      e. public affairs
      f. finance/accounting

B. Provide a profile of the organization's external environment
   1. Profile the task environment in terms of:
      a. industry
      b. competitors
      c. suppliers
      d. customers
      e. government regulators
      f. labor unions
   2. Profile the general environment in terms of:
      a. demographics
      b. culture
      c. economy
      d. politics
      e. technology
      f. pressure groups

THE DIAGNOSTIC PHASE

C. Diagnose the strengths:
   1. Identify the strengths of the corporate/business level
   2. Identify the strengths of the functional level
   3. Identify the organization's distinctive competency

D. Diagnose the weaknessess:
   1. Identify the weaknesses of the corporate/business level
   2. Identify the weaknesses of the functional level
   3. Determine the key weakness

E. Diagnose the opportunities:
   1. Identify the opportunities in the task environment
   2. Identify the opportunities in the general environment
   3. Determine the key opportunity

F. Diagnose the threats:
   1. Identify the threats in the task environment
   2. Identify the threats in the general environment
   3. Determine the key threat

G. Diagnose the major and subordinate problems with their symptoms and probable causes

H. Determine the organization's strategic match

I. Determine the organization's primary strategic match position

J. Diagnose the distinctive competency and the major weakness of the key competitors

THE PRESCRIPTIVE PHASE

K. Formulate a strategic plan:
   1. Write a new mission statement for the organization
   2. Set corporate objectives
   3. Make the strategic choice by selecting the most effective grand strategy
   4. Select a competitive strategy
   5. Formulate functional objectives and strategies

L. Establish the conditions necessary to implement the strategic plan

Exhibit 1-2 **The Descriptive Phase of the Analysis Framework**

A. Provide a profile of the organization's internal environment

    1. Profile the corporate/business level in terms of:
        a. Strategic managers
        b. Environmental analysis
        c. Strategy formulation
        d. Strategy implementation
        e. Strategy control

    2. Profile the functional level in terms of:
        a. Marketing
        b. Production
        c. Research and development
        d. Human resources
        e. Public affairs
        f. Finance/accounting

B. Provide a profile of the organization's external environment

    1. Profile the task environment in terms of:
        a. Industry
        b. Competitors
        c. Suppliers
        d. Customers
        e. Government regulators
        f. Labor unions

    2. Profile the general environment in terms of:
        a. Demographics
        b. Culture
        c. Economy
        d. Politics
        e. Technology
        f. Pressure groups

Purpose of the Descriptive Phase

The purpose of the descriptive phase is to generate a comprehensive and coherent profile of the organization's environmental conditions. As its name suggests, the phase seeks to "describe" the forces operating within and outside the organization. In this phase, the analyst's task involves observing and reporting all the internal and external variables that can impact the firm's performance either in a positive or a negative fashion.

Benefits of the Descriptive Phase

Incorporation of the descriptive phase in case analysis has several benefits. For example:

1. The descriptive phase permits students to select and classify the available information in terms of its relevance to the analysis.

Most strategic management cases are long and complex, containing a wide variety of qualitative and quantitative data. The descriptive phase serves as an aid to students in their effort to extract those pieces of information that focus on the vital signs of the enterprise. Such information can more readily reveal the extent to which the organization is sick or healthy.

In illustrating the importance of this dimension of the descriptive phase, Glueck and Jauch observe:

> When you get your mail, some of it is important, some useless, some of minor interest. At work, managers are bombarded with information. It too consists of a mix of the relevant, the partially relevant, and the useless. So it is with cases. When the case writer gathers information, some of it will become crucial to the analysis. Other pieces of information are not especially useful. Since you are training to be a manager, it is your job to do the manager's job, to separate the wheat from the chaff.[6]

2. The descriptive phase prompts students to conduct research to fill in any missing information.

While some cases provide a great deal of unusable data, others often omit certain critical pieces of information. On such occasions, students will have to conduct their own research to collect the missing information. In this manner, the descriptive phase offers students the opportunity to acquire the highly valued skills of gathering first-hand information. It also underscores the notion that scanning the current and future conditions in the external environment is a crucial aspect of strategic management.

It is important to point out that omission of the descriptive phase implies that the students-to-be-managers will always have a "case writer" to furnish them with the information they need for making decisions. Of course, this is not always the case. At certain junctures in their careers, managers will have to rely on their own skills to generate information for their own use or for use by their superiors.

3. The descriptive phase allows students to probe fully, and to accord equal weight to, all facets of the organization's strategic posture.

By requiring students to take a comprehensive look at the diverse aspects of an organization's operations, the descriptive phase helps in ensuring the generation of a complete profile of the enterprise. It prevents students from skipping or glossing over events in obscure areas, which might prove to be vital to understanding the reasons behind the firm's successes or failures.

4. The descriptive phase serves as a useful guide for reading cases.

Due to its structural specificity, the descriptive phase makes it easier for students to read a case purposefully. It directs them not only to the dimensions of the organization that need to be examined, but also to the types of information that ought to be gathered within each dimension. Experience in applying the framework shows that after analyzing only one case, students become quite proficient in reading cases and extracting the needed information without getting lost in the maze of seemingly unrelated issues.

THE DIAGNOSTIC PHASE

The second phase of the analysis framework is the diagnostic phase which will be explored in Chapters 4 and 5.

The term "diagnosis" is used here in reference to the process of examining a particular observation or piece of information and passing judgment on its meaning. Diagnosis represents the conclusion or verdict we arrive at after carefully scrutinizing the available data.

Diagnostic Labels

The judgment we make or the conclusion we draw concerning a particular observation is typically articulated in the form of a label or an evaluative statement. In the context of our framework, eight major labels are exclusively reserved for use in the diagnostic phase. As depicted in Exhibit 1-3, the labels are strengths, weaknesses, opportunities, distinctive competency, threats, problems, symptoms, and causes. We may, for instance, say that a certain piece of information gathered in the descriptive phase indicates a "strength" in the organization. Or, it indicates a "weakness." And within the latter context, we may say that it represents a "symptom" of a "problem" or a "cause" of the "symptom."

Exhibit 1-3 The Diagnostic Phase of the Analysis Framework

A. Diagnose the organization's strengths:

   1. Identify the strengths of the corporate/business level.
   2. Identify the strengths of the functional level.
   3. Determine the organization's distinctive competency.

B. Diagnose the organization's weaknesses:

   1. Identify the weaknesses of the corporate/business level.
   2. Identify the weaknesses of the functional level.
   3. Determine the key weakness.

C. Diagnose the organization's opportunities:

   1. Identify the opportunities in the task environment.
   2. Identify the opportunities in the general environment.
   3. Determine the key opportunity.

D. Diagnose the organization's threats:

   1. Identify the threats in the task environment.
   2. Identify the threats in the general environment.
   3. Determine the key threat.

E. Diagnose the organization's major and subordinate problems with
   their symptoms (weaknesses) and causes (weaknesses/threats).

F. Determine the organization's strategic match by relating the
   strengths and weaknesses to the opportunities and threats.

G. Determine the organization's primary strategic match position.

H. Diagnose the distinctive competency and the major weakness of the key
   competitors.

In general, then, whenever we begin to attach labels such as "strengths," "weaknesses," "opportunities," or "threats," to an observation, we are engaged in a diagnostic activity.

THE PRESCRIPTIVE PHASE

The final phase of the strategic decision-making framework is the prescriptive phase. This will be covered in Chapter 6.

To prescribe is to advise or recommend the adoption of a set of actions and behaviors while avoiding others. Hence, the prescriptive phase involves the analyst's views concerning the future direction in which the organization must move, in light of the knowledge gained in the descriptive and diagnostic phases.

In the prescriptive phase, students have the opportunity to apply their knowledge of strategic management concepts in constructing a comprehensive plan for an organization. They formulate a new mission statement; set corporate objectives; generate, evaluate, and select grand strategies; determine competitive strategies; and formulate functional objectives and functional strategies. They are also provided with the chance to apply their knowledge of factors that determine the effectiveness of strategy implementation. This entails the establishment of the conditions that facilitate the execution of strategy.

The Prescriptive Phase and Healthy Organizations

Customarily, students are asked in the prescriptive phase to solve or eliminate problems identified in the diagnostic phase. As you can see in Exhibit 1-4, no mention is made in the prescriptive phase of the word "problem." This omission is deliberate. It is intended to render this phase applicable to all organizations whether they are prosperous or sick.

Some of the cases students analyze involve highly successful business concerns with no evidence of glaring difficulties. As a result, many students become frustrated because they think that the sole purpose of case analysis is to identify and solve problems. This is not necessarily so. The primary purpose of case analysis, particularly in a strategic management course, is to permit students to use their conceptual skills in understanding the workings of an organization and in charting a future strategic plan.

Consequently, whether they are engaged in analyzing successful or troubled businesses, students will have to go through the same steps in devising a comprehensive plan. Their purpose in this endeavor is to turn a sick firm into a healthy one and to ensure that a strong firm remains strong or becomes even stronger.

To summarize, the prescriptive phase may be seen as having two objectives. First, it provides students with the practical skills necessary to draw up an effective strategic plan. And second, it emphasizes the notion that formulating good strategy is not enough and that strategic success depends on the establishment of the conditions necessary for the smooth implementation of the chosen strategy.

Exhibit 1-4 The Prescriptive Phase of the Analysis Framework

A. Formulate a strategic plan:
  1. Write a new mission statement for the organization.
  2. Set corporate objectives.
  3. Make the strategic choice by selecting the most effective
     grand strategy.
  4. Select a competitive strategy.
  5. Formulate functional objectives and strategies.

B. Establish the conditions necessary for the implementation of the
   strategic plan.

THE FRAMEWORK AND THE DECISION-MAKING PROCESS

The three phases of the analysis framework as described above parallel, in some important respects, those pursued by virtually all decision makers when confronted with a new or an unfamiliar situation.

Physicians, coaches, army generals, attorneys, psychiatrists, as well as business executives, all begin the decision-making process by gathering data on the situation demanding decisions (the descriptive phase).

Once the information has been gathered, it is subjected to a careful examination. The purpose behind the scrutiny is to discern the favorable and unfavorable dimensions inherent in the situation (the diagnostic phase).

The third stage is the action or intervention stage. At this point, the decision makers seek to influence the status quo. They do so by selecting from among several possible alternatives the course of action that will most effectively allow them to capitalize on the favorable conditions. They must also avert the damaging effects of the unfavorable conditions (the prescriptive phase).

THE FRAMEWORK AND PROBLEM-SOLVING SKILLS

One of the useful dimensions of the strategic decision-making framework is that it fosters the problem-solving skills in students. In Part G of the diagnostic phase, students are required to recognize the difference between major and subordinate problems, then diagnose their symptoms and causes. In the process of making such diagnosis, students reap several benefits. They learn the difference between symptom, cause, and problem. These can be quite confusing at times. They also acquire the skill of establishing causal relationships between symptoms and their causes and to differentiate between symptomatic relief and causal treatment.

The Importance of Problem-Solving Skills

It is well to recognize that problem solving represents a crucial part of the manager's job. In their day-to-day activities, managers spend a substantial amount of time grappling with a continuous flow of organizational issues. Their ability to deal with these problems affects not only their subordinates' perception of their managerial competence, but can impact significantly their chances of advancement in the organization. Typically, managers who exhibit problem-solving skills "gain a good reputation with peers as well as with their bosses and tend to move up the ladder faster than those who do not."[7]

Although of value to all managers, problem-solving skills are of particular importance to strategic managers. By virtue of their broad responsibilities, strategists tend to wrestle with issues of far-reaching implications to the survival and long-term success of the enterprise as a whole. By acquiring these problem-solving skills, strategists can add another powerful tool to their storehouse of analytical instruments, thereby enhancing the quality of the strategy-making process.

Problem Solving Is a Learned Skill

Problem-solving skills can be learned. What is required is a good understanding of the basic concepts, knowledge of the problem-solving process, and some measure of logical reasoning. With practice, not only can the concepts and process be acquired but also the ability to think logically. In emphasizing this point, one chief executive officer said: "Good business school training, I would think, would strive to develop this kind of practical problem-solving ability ... It is clear that such problem-solving can be developed--we do it in business all the time."[8]

OBJECTIVES OF THE FRAMEWORK

The overall objective of the strategic decision-making framework is to equip students with both analytical and conceptual skills. That is, as the students engage in examining textbook cases, they not only learn sound analytical skills, but are also afforded the opportunity to practice their multidisciplinary knowledge in general and their knowledge of the strategic management concepts in particular.

Translating this overall objective into more focused terms, the framework is designed to accomplish the following specific ends:

1. *Instill into students the basic analytical principle that knowledge of any system as a whole can best be acquired through knowledge of its individual parts.*

Dividing a complicated mass into simpler elements can be helpful in understanding any complex situation.[9] Individuals who separate a larger whole into smaller components, address each component separately, and then combine the results at the end tend to perform better as problem solvers and as decision makers.[10]

This is the approach upon which the descriptive phase of the framework is based. In this phase, students are exposed to the procedure of factoring an organization into the smallest possible components as a means of developing a comprehensive picture of the organization's strategic posture.

2. *Equip students with the information-gathering skills.*

Once individual components of the strategic posture have been identified, students are required to gather information about each component.

The case under analysis constitutes an important source of information. But, as was pointed out earlier, cases do not furnish all the data essential for gaining a comprehensive picture of an organization's conditions. This is especially true with regard to the organization's external environment. Hence, students need to conduct research to gather information on such matters as industry outlook and competitors, as well as the anticipated demographic, cultural, and economic trends that must be considered in drawing up a strategic plan for the subject firm.

One significant by-product of this exercise is that students become well-acquainted with the sources of information necessary for conducting strategic management research in actual business settings.

3. *Sharpen students' logical thinking.*

Logical thinking is interwoven in virtually every phase of the analysis framework. Students use logic in deciding what types of information to gather and report, what types of future strategies to propose, and how to defend their decisions if they are challenged by other students or the instructor.

The need for logical skills, however, is nowhere more manifest than in the diagnostic phase. Here, students use logical reasoning in distinguishing between strengths and weaknesses or opportunities and threats. They also apply logic in matching opportunities with threats and strengths with weaknesses. The students' logical skills are further put to the test as they endeavor to establish linkages between causes, symptoms, and problems, and as they attempt to separate major problems from subordinate problems.

4. *Foster students' creativity.*

The prescriptive phase of the framework is primarily oriented toward the enhancement of students' creative ability.

Whether they are engaged in formulating a mission statement, setting objectives, devising functional strategies, or recommending new policies, students find themselves in a constant search for novel ideas or different approaches. Such an exercise serves to stimulate their imagination and unlock their creative potentials.

5. *Allow students to apply the strategic management concepts.*

Finally, the framework enables students to apply their knowledge of strategic management throughout the analysis process. Actually, unless the students have a good grasp of these concepts, they will be unable to apply the framework meaningfully.

For instance, students must first know what a mission statement is before they can analyze the firm's current mission or develop a new mission for the future. Likewise, unless they are thoroughly familiar with the different types of grand strategies, they will be unable to identify and analyze the firm's current strategies. Nor will they be able to develop, evaluate, and select future strategies for the enterprise being analyzed.

REVIEW QUESTIONS

1. Define each of the three phases of the analysis framework.

2. List the benefits that accrue to students by going through the descriptive phase prior to diagnosing the case issues.

3. Discuss the following statement: "The prescriptive phase is primarily designed to alleviate an organization's problems."

4. What are the two objectives of the prescriptive phase?

5. How are the three phases of the analysis framework related to the decision-making process?

6. Identify the five objectives of the analysis framework.

References

1. W.M. Bright, "Are Innovators Born or Made?" *Research Management*, Vol. 12, No. 3, May 1969, p. 125.

2. John A. Pearce II, Richard Robinson, Jr., and Shaker A. Zahra, *An Industry Approach to Cases in Strategic Management* (Homewood, IL.: Irwin, 1989), p. 1.

3. R.M. Hodgetts and M.S. Worthman, Jr., *Administrative Policy: Text and Cases in Strategic Management* (N.Y.: John Wiley and Sons, 1980), p. 146.

4. Quoted in C. Argyris, "Some Limitations of the Case Method in a Management Development Program," *The Academy of Management Review*, Vol. 5, No. 2, April 1980, p. 297.

5. G.I. Gregg, "Because Wisdom Can't be Told," in M.P. McNaire, ed., *The Case Method at Harvard Business School* (N.Y.: McGraw-Hill Book Co., 1954), p. 11.

6. William F. Glueck and Lawrence R. Jauch, *Business Policy and Strategic Management* (N.Y.: McGraw-Hill Book Company, 1984), p. 422.

7. Waldron Berry, "Group Problem Solving: How to Be an Effective Participant," *Supervisory Management*, June 1983, p. 14.

8. Fred C. Foy, "A Businessman Looks at Business Education," in American Association of Collegiate Schools of Business, *Views on Business Education* (Chapel Hill, N.C.: University of North Carolina, 1960), p. 15.

9. William H. Newman and James P. Logan, *Strategy, Policy, and Central Management*,8th ed., (Cincinnati, Ohio, 1981), p. 8.

10. C. W. Hofer and D. Schendel, *Strategy Formulation: Analytical Concepts* (St. Paul, Minn.: West Publishing Company, 1978), p. 20.

Chapter 2

THE DESCRIPTIVE PHASE:
PROFILING THE INTERNAL ENVIRONMENT

In the preceding chapter, we introduced a three-tiered strategic decision-making framework, consisting of a descriptive phase, a diagnostic phase, and a prescriptive phase. In this chapter and the next, we will explore the first phase which, as portrayed in Exhibit 2-1, involves the descriptive phase.

As you recall, the descriptive phase was defined in the previous chapter as the process of gathering information on the internal and external environments of the organization under study. It has as its sole purpose the generation of a comprehensive and coherent profile of the dynamics prevailing inside and outside the organization. The information collected in the descriptive phase serves, later, as the basis for diagnosing issues and making critical strategic decisions.

FUNDAMENTALS OF THE PROFILING PROCESS

Before we discuss the procedure involved in profiling an organization's internal and external conditions, let us attempt to gain an understanding of the basic principles underlying the profiling process. Such understanding is useful in two ways.

First, it will show that the profiling principles are universal in their application. That is, they can be used in analyzing any type of system, be it social, biological, or mechanical. Further, the same principles can be applied not only to the system as a whole, such as a business concern, but also to any one of its subunits such as marketing, production, human resources, or finance. The second benefit to be gained from understanding the rationale behind the profiling process is that it enables us to conduct the analysis in an enlightened and purposeful manner rather than in a mechanical fashion.

THE CONCEPT OF FACTORING

The effort to generate a profile of an organization's conditions cannot be left to chance. It should not be based on a haphazard or hit-and-miss approach that could very well mislead us into focusing only on the most salient strategic features. Rather, it should embody a systematic process, calculated to direct our search for all the relevant information.

To fully understand the conceptual underpinnings of the profiling process, it is useful to consider the meaning of the term "analysis." Analysis can be

Exhibit 2-1   A FRAMEWORK FOR STRATEGIC DECISION MAKING AND PROBLEM SOLVING

THE DESCRIPTIVE PHASE

A. Provide a profile of the organization's internal environment

1. Profile the corporate/business level in terms of:

   a. strategic managers
   b. environmental analysis
   c. strategy formulation
   d. strategy implementation
   e. strategy control

2. Profile the functional level in terms of:

   a. marketing
   b. production
   c. research and development
   d. human resources
   e. public affairs
   f. finance/accounting

B. Provide a profile of the organization's external environment

1. Profile the task environment in terms of:

   a. industry
   b. competitors
   c. suppliers
   d. customers
   e. government regulators
   f. labor unions

2. Profile the general environment in terms of:

   a. demographics
   b. culture
   c. economy
   d. politics
   e. technology
   f. pressure groups

THE DIAGNOSTIC PHASE

C. Diagnose the strengths:

1. Identify the strengths of the corporate/business level
2. Identify the strengths of the functional level
3. Identify the organization's distinctive competency

D. Diagnose the weaknessess:

1. Identify the weaknesses of the corporate/business level
2. Identify the weaknesses of the functional level
3. Determine the key weakness

E. Diagnose the opportunities:

1. Identify the opportunities in the task environment
2. Identify the opportunities in the general environment
3. Determine the key opportunity

F. Diagnose the threats:

1. Identify the threats in the task environment
2. Identify the threats in the general environment
3. Determine the key threat

G. Diagnose the major and subordinate problems with their symptoms and probable causes

H. Determine the organization's strategic match

I. Determine the organization's primary strategic match position

J. Diagnose the distinctive competency and the major weakness of the key competitors

THE PRESCRIPTIVE PHASE

K. Formulate a strategic plan:

1. Write a new mission statement for the organization
2. Set corporate objectives
3. Make the strategic choice by selecting the most effective grand strategy
4. Select a competitive strategy
5. Formulate functional objectives and strategies

L. Establish the conditions necessary to implement the strategic plan

defined as the process of breaking a whole into its individual parts with an eye toward understanding the nature and function of each part separately and in relation to the other parts. This process is commonly referred to as "factoring."

Commenting on the usefulness of factoring, Newman and Logan state: "...as with any complex situation, a tested approach that divides the complicated mass into simpler elements can be very helpful."[1] On the same point, McCarthy, Minichiello, and Curran note that in order to generate a coherent picture of an organization as a totality "... one must first examine all the parts of the company, then observe the interrelationships between the parts, and synthesize the parts into a profile of the whole company."[2]

In summing up the research findings supporting the value of factoring for decision-making and problem-solving purposes, Hofer and Schendel observe:

> Research on structured problem-solving and decision making processes has indicated that most persons perform far better when they separate these processes into distinct components, address each component separately, and then combine the results at the end. While we are unaware of similar evidence regarding unstructured problem-solving and decision-making processes, we believe the result would be the same.[3]

Factoring is a widely used tool in understanding processes, events, and objects. For example, in an effort to comprehend the process of management, we typically break it down into the components of planning, organizing, staffing, directing, and controlling. Studying each component separately and in relation to the other components can facilitate the development of a full picture of the process of management as a whole. Similarly, in seeking to understand the workings of the human body, scientists subdivide it into the smallest possible parts. By examining the nature of each part separately and then as it relates to the other parts, scientists are able to gain a picture of how the entire body functions.

Factoring is rooted in the notion that it is easier, more practical, and eventually more fruitful to investigate the smallest parts of a system individually than it is to tackle the system as a totality. And it is this approach that we have selected to use as a basis for the descriptive phase of our strategic decision-making framework.

PROFILING THE ORGANIZATION'S ENVIRONMENTS

In applying the concept of factoring as a profiling tool, we will rely on the meaning of strategic management as a starting point. Strategic management is defined as the process of analyzing the internal and external environments of an organization as a basis for selecting a course of action (i.e., strategy) designed to achieve the organization's long-term objectives. This definition provides us with an important clue as to how to profile an organization from a strategic management perspective. It tells us that before making a strategic decision, the strategist needs to conduct an analysis, or develop an understanding, of the organization's internal and external conditions.

Utilizing this line of reasoning, our effort to generate a profile of the organization as a whole begins by first separating the organization's conditions into two major targets of investigation. As depicted in Exhibit 2-2, the targets consist of an internal environment and an external environment.

Exhibit 2-2   **Reducing the Organization's Environments to Two Major Targets of Investigation**

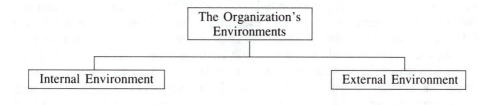

PART A: PROFILING THE INTERNAL ENVIRONMENT

Having sliced up the organization's environments into two principal targets of examination, internal and external, the task at hand becomes one of seeking to understand the nature of each target. In this chapter, our concern will center only on providing a profile of the internal environment which is Part A of the analysis framework. In the next chapter, we will reflect on the external environment or Part B of the framework.

Dealing with the internal environment as a focal point of investigation is certainly more manageable than an effort to tackle the organization's environmental conditions as a whole. It is a narrower target. The internal environment, in itself, represents a broad area that can be quite cumbersome and unwieldy to probe with any degree of effectiveness. Unless we manage to separate it into smaller components, our endeavor to gain an in-depth view of its various dimensions will be heavily attenuated. This results in fragmented and transparent images.

In an effort to gain a penetrative look at the internal environment, we will break it down into still smaller targets of examination. As shown in Exhibit 2-3, the targets consist of the corporate/business level and the functional level.

Why Combine the Corporate and Business Levels

Before we proceed with our description of the profiling process, let us pause here for a moment to explain our decision to lump the corporate and business levels together. To do that, we need to briefly discuss the strategy-making hierarchy concept.

In large, multi-business organizations, strategic decisions are formulated, implemented, and controlled at three levels: a corporate level, a business level, and a functional level. The corporate level consists of the board of directors and the top management team. These executives are primarily responsible for determining the businesses in which the company should or should not operate. The business level is made up of strategic business units (SBUs). At this level, executives are charged with the task of deciding how best to compete in their respective markets. Finally, the functional level executives are concerned with formulating strategies aimed at achieving their own departmental objectives, and in the process contribute to the attainment of the business-level objectives.

There are three reasons why the corporate level and business level may be combined for purposes of case analysis:

1. In a single-business firm, the business level does not exist. Hence, in this type of company, Hofer states, "the business and corporate levels would be the same."[4] That is, the responsibility for determining the company's competitive strategy is carried out by the corporate-level executives. Many of the textbook cases which students analyze involve this type of enterprise.

2. Frequently, a strategic business unit (SBU) is set up as an autonomous company with its own president and board of directors. In such a situation, the SBU's managers perform functions similar to those of corporate-level executives. According to Jauch and Glueck: "Essentially, the SBU strategists perform similar roles to those of top managers for their business and attempt to get best results in their business segment given their resources and corporate objectives."[5]

Exhibit 2-3 **Reducing the Internal Environment to a Corporate/Business Level and a Functional Level**

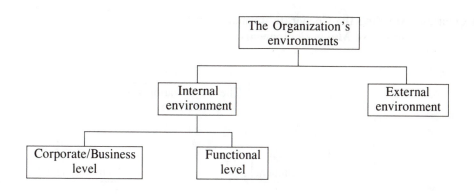

Thus, the SBU's strategists make decisions not only about how to compete most effectively in their own market. They also formulate grand strategies including product development, market expansion, and the acquisition of a supplier, a distributor, or a competitor, which normally fall within the scope of the top management team.

3. Combining the corporate and business levels helps in achieving structural simplicity in analysis.

PART A.1: PROFILING THE CORPORATE/BUSINESS LEVEL

Having reduced the organization's internal environment to a corporate/business level and a functional level, we will now endeavor to generate a separate profile of each level. We will begin by examining the former.

As noted previously, the corporate/business level consists of the highest strategy-making groups in the organization. These are the board of directors and the top management team. In light of the type of strategists who staff this level and the type of decisions they make, the corporate/business level may be divided into five components. For future reference, these will be referred to as *major components*. As depicted in Exhibit 2-4, the major components include strategic managers, environmental analysis, strategy formulation, strategy implementation, and strategy control.

Exhibit 2-4   **Dividing the Corporate/Business Level
into Five Major Components**

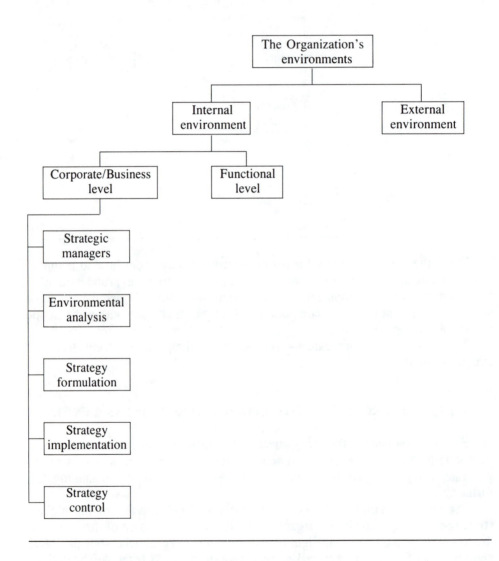

PROFILING THE MAJOR COMPONENTS
OF THE CORPORATE/BUSINESS LEVEL

Thus far, we have narrowed our focus from the organization's internal environment as a whole to five major components. Although each one of these major components is narrower in scope than the corporate/business level, they are still not narrow enough to produce the in-depth view we seek of this level. So, in the interest of achieving a more thorough investigation, the major components should further be broken down into smaller elements.

The process of profiling the major components of the corporate/business level consists of two basic steps:

1. Subdivide each major component into smaller targets of investigation which we will call *subcomponents*.

2. Compile checklists aimed at gathering information on each of the subcomponents.

Subcomponents

The first step of profiling the major components is illustrated in Exhibit 2-5 which shows the various subcomponents comprising each major component.

This step is valuable in that it permits us to zero in on some crucial dimensions of the corporate/business level. These dimensions could very well be overlooked or ignored if we tried to focus our attention on the major components only. For instance, if we center our analysis on strategic managers as the smallest unit of investigation, we are likely to emphasize top management to the neglect of the board of directors, and vice versa. Likewise, if we treat strategy formulation as the lowest level of scrutiny, there is a good chance that we would fail to take a good look at the mission, corporate objectives, or grand strategies.

If some critical strengths or weaknesses happen to exist in any of the overlooked subcomponents, they will remain hidden and, thus, will not be used in the diagnostic phase of the framework. This can have an important bearing on the prescriptive, or the recommendation, phase. For if we are unaware of the organization's strengths and weaknesses, we cannot reasonably be expected to formulate a strategy capable of exploiting the strengths and eliminating the weaknesses.

Checklists

The next step in profiling the major components of the corporate/business level of the internal environment entails the preparation of a separate checklist on each subcomponent. By checklist, we simply mean a questionnaire consisting of a set of questions aimed at collecting information on the various subcomponents.

The checklist represents a central element in the process of profile generation. Our success in forging an accurate and complete picture of all the significant variables inherent in every subcomponent is predicated on the type of questions we pose and the consequent information we manage to glean.

Exhibit 2-5   **The Major Components and Subcomponents of the Corporate/Business Level of the Internal Environment**

Major Components	*Subcomponents*
Strategic managers:	Board of directors
	Top management
Environmental analysis:	Internal analysis
	External analysis
Strategy formulation:	Mission
	Corporate objectives
	Grand strategies
	Competitive strategies
Strategy implementation:	Organizational structure
	Policies
	Budgetary allocations
	Corporate culture
	Communication
	Motivation
Strategy control:	Establishment of standards
	Evaluation of performance
	Correction of deviation

Checklists on the Subcomponents of Strategic Managers

In the following pages, we will provide a set of sample questions designed to develop a good understanding of the subcomponents that underlie strategic managers, environmental analysis, strategy formulation, strategy implementation, and strategy control. It is important to emphasize that the checklists presented in this text are by no means comprehensive. You are likely to come up with many more questions that might prove helpful in painting a clearer picture of each subcomponent.

We will begin with a checklist on the subcomponents of strategic managers, namely, the board of directors and top management.

The Board of Directors

1. What qualifications--in terms of skills, experience, education, etc.--do the board members possess?
2. Can the members of the board be described as management directors, affiliated nonmanagement directors, or independent directors?
3. Would you characterize the board as a constitutional, rubber stamp, oversight, or catalyst board?
[For a definition of terms,]
[see Appendix A.]

Top Management

1. What are the qualifications of top executives in terms of skill, experience, and education?
2. How long have they been with the firm? Who, among them, was brought from the outside and who was promoted from within?
3. What managerial mode characterizes the chief executive officer (CEO)? Is it entrepreneurial, adaptive, or strategic planning?
4. What decision-making style best describes the CEO?
[For a definition of terms,]
[see Appendix B.]

Checklists on the Subcomponents of Environmental Analysis

Internal Analysis

1. Does management periodically conduct internal analysis to identify the firm's strengths and weaknesses?

2. Which of the following methods does management utilize in scanning the internal environment: personal contacts, observations, interviews, survey questionnaires, periodic reports, audits?

External Analysis

1. Does management conduct periodic external analysis to identify environmental opportunities and threats?
2. Has management missed out on some important opportunities or has it been faced with serious threats due to the lack of external scanning?
3. Which of the following tools does management use in scanning the external environment: commercial intelligence, industrial espionage, or forecasting?

[For a definition of terms,]
[see Appendix C.]

Checklist on the Subcomponents of Strategy Formulation

Mission

1. Does the company have a mission statement? If so, does it spell out the business domain, products or services, distribution channels, customers, and management's beliefs and philosophy?
2. If a mission statement is not provided, is there sufficient information in the case to enable you to shed light on the concepts upon which a mission statement is usually built (such as business domain, products or services, etc.)?

[For a definition of the mission and its components,]
[see Appendix D.]

Corporate Objectives

1. Does the company have explicit long-term and short-term objectives?
2. If so, what are they? Are they stated in measurable terms, and do they have a specific time horizon?

[For a good statement of objectives,]
[see Appendix E.]

Grand Strategies

1. Which of the following grand strategies has the firm employed in achieving its objectives: (a) concentration, (b) market development, (c) product development, (d) product innovation, (e) vertical integration, (f) horizontal

integration, (g) concentric diversification, (h) conglomerate diversification,(i) joint venture, (j) retrenchment/turnaround, (k) harvest, (l) divestiture, or (m) liquidation?
2. Before making its strategic choice, does management rely on the unstructured approach, the semi-structured approach, or the structured approach in evaluating alternative grand strategies?

[For an explanation of grand strategies]
[and strategy evaluation methods, see Appendix F.]

Competitive Strategies

1. Which of the following competitive strategies has the firm used: (a) cost leadership, (b) product differentiation, or (c) focus?
2. Has the strategy produced its desired results?

[For an explanation of competitive strategies,]
[see Appendix G.]

Checklists on the Subcomponents of Strategy Implementation

Organizational Structure

1. What type of organizational structure exists? Is it entrepreneurial, functional, geographic, product, strategic business unit, or matrix?
2. Does the structure follow the firm's grand strategy?
3. Is the structure centralized or decentralized?

[For an explanation of organizational structures,]
[see Appendix H.]

Policies

1. Are appropriate policies established to ensure consistency and uniformity of action throughout the organization?
2. Have any organizational difficulties emerged due to a lack of clear policies?

[For an explanation of policies,]
[see Appendix I.]

Budgetary Allocations

1. Has top management been willing to commit the necessary financial resources to carry out its strategies?
2. Has the firm's strategic efforts ever faltered due to insufficient funds?

Leadership

1. What type of leadership style characterizes members of the top management team? Is it authority-compliance, impoverished management, country-club management, team management, or middle-of-the-road management?
2. Are the right managers placed in the right positions?
   [For a definition of terms,]
   [see Appendix J.]

Corporate Culture

1. What type of culture characterizes the organization? Does the culture emphasize product quality, customer service, innovation, job security, family feelings, respect for the individual, open communication, informality, or decentralization?
2. Is the culture functional or dysfunctional? Does it support corporate strategy?
   [For an explanation of corporate culture,]
   [see Appendix K.]

Communication

1. Does top management make an effort to communicate the firm's mission, objectives, strategies, and policies to employees throughout the organization?
2. Which of the following tools does management utilize in communicating with the organization's members: public speeches, meetings, employee publications, or informal contacts?

Motivation

1. Are employees loyal to the firm? Are they committed to its objectives and strategies?
2. Is there a high rate of employee turnover and absenteeism? Is employees' morale high or low? Have there been any cases of employees' sabotage?
3. What tools does management most heavily rely upon in motivating employees: participative management, financial rewards, nonfinancial rewards (i.e. recognition), sanctions, or a combination of these?

Checklists on the Subcomponents of Strategy Control

Establishment of Standards
1. Are profitability standards established with regard to return on investment, return on equity, earnings per share, growth in sales, net profit, stock price, dividend rates, and asset growth?

2. Are performance standards established in other key result areas such as productivity, competitive position, technological leadership, and social responsibility?

Evaluation of Performance

1. Does management periodically monitor the actual implementation of strategy and compare the obtained results against the planned standards?
2. What methods are used in evaluating strategy implementation: personal observations, periodic reports from subordinates, computerized printouts, internal and external audits, executive information system, or a combination of these?
3. Does the evaluation mechanism swiftly and accurately detect any discrepancies between the expected and the actual results?
4. Is the information generated by the monitoring system timely? Does it reach the right person at the right time?

Correction of Deviations

1. Do significant deviations frequently occur between the firm's actual accomplishments and its desired results?
2. Does management usually take corrective actions immediately after a deviation has been discovered?

PART A.2: PROFILING THE FUNCTIONAL LEVEL

In the preceding pages, our discussion has been concerned with the development of a profile of one of the two levels comprising the internal environment, namely, the corporate/business level. To be able to gain a complete picture of the internal conditions of an organization, we should endeavor to form a profile of the other level which is the functional.

The functional level represents a broad dimension of the operations of any medium-sized or large organization. As such, it would be quite naive as well as futile to attempt to investigate this level without disassembling it into its individual parts. Using the factoring approach, we will break the functional level down into six major components. Shown in Exhibit 2-6, the major components include marketing, production, research and development (R&D), human resources, public affairs, and finance/accounting.

Exhibit 2-6   **Dividing the Functional Level
into Six Major Components**

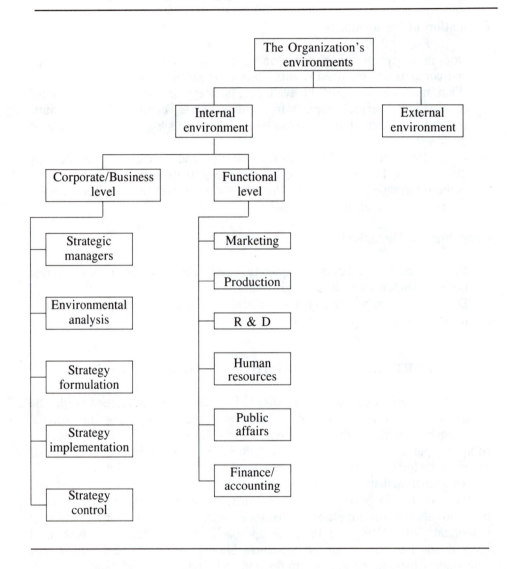

Exhibit 2-7 **The Major Components and Subcomponents of the Functional Level of the Internal Environment**

Major Components	*Subcomponents*
Marketing:	Products
	Marketing research
	Target market
	Sales volume
	Market share
	Pricing
	Distribution
	Advertising and promotion
Production:	Location, newness, and layout of facilities
	Quality control
	Production capacity
	Inventory
Research and Development:	Focus
	Posture
	Budget
Human Resources:	Succession Planning
	Recruitment and selection
	Training and development
	Performance appraisal
	Compensation
Public Affairs:	Ethics
	Social responsibility
	Crisis management
Finance/Accounting:	Management of cash
	Management of inventories
	Management of accounts receivable
	Management of total assets
	Management of debt
	Capital budgeting
	General profit picture

PROFILING THE MAJOR COMPONENTS
OF THE FUNCTIONAL LEVEL

Reducing the functional level to six major components is a decidedly helpful step in our quest to gain a full understanding of this level. As you might suspect, the major components are still too broad to permit a rigorous inquiry and must, therefore, be broken down into smaller elements.

The process involved in providing a profile of the major components of the functional level is identical to the one we pursued in profiling the major components of the corporate/business level. The process requires us to:

1. *Break each major component into subcomponents.* Exhibit 2-7 details the subcomponents that make up each major component of the functional level. These subcomponents may be viewed as reasonably narrow enough in scope to allow us to conduct a sound examination.

2. *Compile checklists aimed at gathering information on each of the subcomponents.*

In the following section, we will offer several checklists that serve as tools seeking to illuminate the nature of each subcomponent.

Checklists on the Subcomponents of Marketing

Products

1. Does the company provide related or unrelated products and services? What are they?
2. Is the quality of products or services high, average, or low as compared with competitors? Is the quality uniform throughout all its products or services, or does it vary with each type of product or service?

Marketing Research

1. Does the firm conduct any marketing research? If not, what effects has this had on the firm's competitive market position?
2. If marketing research exists, is it conducted on a continual or sporadic basis?
3. How effective has management been in utilizing the results of marketing research in formulating its marketing objectives and strategies?

Target Market

1. Does the firm have a well-defined target market?

2. What type of target marketing does the company use? Is it undifferentiated marketing, concentrated marketing, or differentiated marketing?
    [For a definition of terms,]
    [see Appendix L.]

Sales Volume

1. What is the firm's current annual sales volume?
2. Has the trend of the sales volume been stable, growing, or receding over the past five years?
3. Is the sales volume seasonal? If so, how does the firm deal with slow seasons?

Market Share

1. What is the firm's current share of the market?
2. Has the firm's market share been growing, remaining stable, or declining within the past five years?

Pricing

1. Are the firm's prices of products or services higher or lower than those of the competitors?
2. Are the prices realistic given the quality of the firm's offerings?

Distribution

1. Is the distribution of products or services local, regional, national, or international in its coverage?
2. Does the firm have outlets of its own, or does it sell through intermediates such as jobbers, retailers, or wholesalers? What is the firm's rationale for selecting its distribution channels?

Advertising and Promotion

1. What is the size of the advertising budget?
2. Which of the following methods is used in determining the advertising budget: percentage of sales, competitive matching, or affordability?
3. Is the firm known for its innovative advertising techniques? Are the copy and themes of advertising effective?

4. Are any promotional devices used to support the advertising campaign? Does the firm participate in trade shows and exhibits? Does it provide store demonstrations? Does it offer premiums or special discounts?
    [For a definition of terms,]
    [see Appendix M.]

Checklists on the Subcomponents of Production

Location of Facilities

1. Where are the production facilities located? Are they centrally located, or are they geographically dispersed?
2. Are production facilities located close to the firm's sources of raw materials, labor, suppliers, and customers?

Newness of Facilities

1. Is the production equipment modern or outmoded? How old is the equipment, and what is its average life?
2. Is the equipment well maintained, properly used, and regularly inspected for potential trouble?

Layout of Facilities

1. What is the general layout of the production process? Are similar operations, equipment, personnel, and materials grouped together?
2. Is the present arrangement of facilities conducive to efficient work flow? Does it maximize the utilization of equipment, personnel, and materials?

Quality Control

1. Does the firm experience a high rate of defective products?
2. Which one of the following quality-control techniques does the firm use: acceptance sampling or in-process sampling?
    [For the meaning of quality-control methods,]
    [see Appendix N.]

Production Capacity

1. Does the company have adequate, excess, or inadequate production capacity?
2. Does it often fail to meet customers' demands on time? Does it often get stuck with a lot of unsold products?

Inventory

1. Does the firm maintain a satisfactory level of inventory?
2. Has the firm experienced any difficulties due either to a high or a low level of inventory?

Checklists on the Subcomponents
of Research and Development

Focus

1. Does the firm primarily focus on basic or applied research?
2. Has the R&D focus helped or hurt the firm's competitive position?

Posture

1. Is the firm's R&D posture innovative, protective, catch-up, or a combination of the three?
2. Has the R&D posture been effective in turning out new products or in significantly improving the firm's existing products?

Budget

1. What is the size of the R&D budget, and how does it compare with the firm's competitors?
2. Is the budget large enough to enable the firm to acquire state-of-the art research facilities and attract high-caliber scientists?

[For a definition of terms,]
[see Appendix O.]

Checklists on the Subcomponents of Human Resources

Succession Planning

1. Does the firm conduct any forecasts of its future needs for personnel?
2. Are junior managers coached and groomed to fill higher executive positions as they become vacant?

[For an explanation of succession planning,]
[see Appendix P.]

Recruitment and Selection

1. What recruiting methods are ordinarily used? Newspaper ads, employment agencies, in-house announcements, union channels, personal contacts, college visits, or a combination of these?
2. How heavily does the firm rely on recruiting outsiders as opposed to promoting insiders to fill vacant positions?

Training and Development

1. What types of training and development programs exist in the company?
2. Have the training and development programs been effective? Have they led to cost reduction, high morale, or improved performance?

Performance Appraisal

1. Is there a formal system of evaluating employee performance? What specific evaluation methods are used?
2. Are the results of the evaluation system used as a basis for decisions pertaining to promotions, pay increases, layoffs, and transfers?

Compensation

1. Are employees' wages and benefits competitive?
2. Do employees perceive the firm's compensation policy as fair?

Checklists on the Subcomponents of Public Affairs

Ethics

1. Has the firm ever been involved in unethical behaviors?
2. Does it require all its employees to engage in ethical behavior?

Social Responsibility

1. Does the firm engage in socially responsible actions? Does it contribute to the betterment of the community where it operates?
2. Which one of the following methods does the firm use in carrying out its social responsibility program: direct contributions, matching employee contributions, or cause-related marketing?

Crisis Management

1. Does the firm have a crisis management plan to promptly deal with emergencies as they occur?
2. Has the company ever been involved in a crisis that affected its public image? How did it deal with the crisis?
3. In general, is the company effective in its external communications?
    [For an explanation of ethics, social responsibility]
    [and crisis management, see Appendix Q.]

Checklists on the Subcomponents of Finance/Accounting

Management of Cash

1. Does the firm have enough cash on hand to conduct its ordinary business such as making purchases?
2. Does the firm have a strong credit rating? Can the firm borrow additional cash on short notice whenever the need arises? Does the firm have a "line of credit" that obligates a bank to provide future credit if requested?
3. What is the firm's current ratio?
    [For the meaning and computation of all the]
    [ratios referred to in the checklists,]
    [see Appendix R.]
4. How does it compare with the industry average?
    [For sources of information on industry ratios,]
    [see Appendix S.]
5. What is the firm's quick (acid-test) ratio?
6. How does it compare with the industry average?

Management of Inventories

1. Do inventories contain too many slow-moving items?
2. How large is the size of inventory that is subject to obsolescence due to the competitors' modification or improvement of a product?
3. What is the firm's inventory-turnover ratio?
4. How does it compare with the industry average?

Management of Accounts Receivable

1. Does the firm permit sales on credit? What standards does it use in extending credit privileges?

2. Does the firm have a lax collection procedure? If so, has the procedure encouraged strong customers to be slow payers and weak customers to default?
3. What is the firm's collection-period ratio?
4. How does it compare with the industry average?

Management of Total Assets

1. What is the firm's total-assets ratio?
2. How does it compare with the industry average?

Management of Debt

1. What is the firm's debt-to-total-assets ratio?
2. How does this ratio compare with the industry average?
3. What is the firm's times-interest-earned ratio?
4. How does it compare with the industry average?

Capital Budgeting

1. What proportion of the firm's funds has been allocated to the capital budget (i.e., long-term investment) within the past five to ten years?
2. Was the capital budget used to: (a) replace worn-out or obsolete equipment? (b) expand production facilities? (c) purchase land and buildings? (d) diversify the firm's product line to reduce the risk of failure resulting from operating in a single market?, or (e) launch a long-term advertising and promotion campaign?
3. What are the firm's future plans relative to the use of capital budget?

General Profit Picture

1. What is the firm's general profit picture? Have profits been increasing, decreasing, or stagnant?
2. What is the firm's profit-margin ratio?
3. How does this ratio compare with the industry average?
4. What is the firm's return-on equity ratio?
5. How does it compare with the industry average?
6. As a whole, would you say that the company is in a poor or sound financial position?

Appendix A
THE BOARD OF DIRECTORS

The board of directors represents, at least in theory, the highest rung in the strategy-making hierarchy. Its members are chosen by shareholders to carry out two basic responsibilities: (1) protect the interests of the stockholders and (2) safeguard the assets of the company.

BOARD COMPOSITION   In general, boards may be seen as composed of three types of directors: management directors, affiliated nonmanagement directors, and independent directors.[6] Whereas management directors are insiders, the latter two categories are composed of outside directors.

Management Directors   Management directors are full-time executives of the company and may be referred to as "officer directors." A management director could be the president of the corporation, the vice president of finance, or the manager of the manufacturing division.

Affiliated Nonmanagement Directors   An affiliated nonmanagement director may be a former company executive, a relative of a company executive, an investment banker dealing with the firm, a customer, a creditor, or any other individual with some type of involvement with the company.

Independent Directors   The independent director is one who fits neither of the first two categories. He or she may be an active or a retired executive from another company, a community leader, a university professor, a minister, or any other individual with no company affiliation.

TYPES OF BOARDS   In terms of their degree of involvement in strategic planning, boards of directors can fall into one of four categories: constitutional, rubber stamp, oversight, and catalyst boards.

Constitutional Boards   These boards exist primarily to satisfy the legal requirement that every corporation must be governed by a board. Constitutional boards rarely, if ever, meet. They play no role whatsoever in strategic decision making which is centered in the hands of the chief executive.

Rubber Stamp Boards   Rubber-stamp boards are similar to constitutional boards. However, rubber-stamp boards do meet, though not on a regular basis. And they do engage in deliberations of the issues. But their deliberations are so flimsy that the boards almost always wind up rubber stamping the chief executive's decisions.

Oversight Boards   These boards measure up to their intended purpose; that is, to act as an overseer or as a governing body. In this capacity, oversight boards serve as a powerful countervailing force in the organization. Unlike the previous two types, oversight boards play an active role in reviewing, approving, modifying, or rejecting management's decisions concerning the company's mission, objectives, strategies, and policies.

Catalyst Boards   Rather than just being a watchdog, as oversight boards in some respects are, catalyst boards go one step further. They become an initiator of action. Aside from having a very assertive strategy committee, catalyst boards take "the leading role in establishing and modifying the mission, objectives, strategy, and policies."[7]

Appendix B
TOP MANAGEMENT

THE CEO'S MANAGERIAL MODES   Managerial mode is the tendency of CEOs to be either risk-averse or risk prone, particularly in terms of the way they respond to changes in the external environmental conditions. Viewed in this way, CEOs may be characterized as having (1) an entrepreneurial mode, (2) an adaptive mode, or (3) a strategic planning mode.[8]

The Entrepreneurial Mode   The entrepreneurial mode is a proactive, risk-prone approach. The principal objective of the entrepreneurial CEO is the hunt for and exploitation of environmental opportunities. And the means, most frequently utilized in achieving it, involves bold, often risk-fraught, decisions.

The Adaptive Mode   In the adaptive mode, CEOs assume a reactive, risk-averse posture. Normally having conservative tendencies, the adaptive CEOs are more concerned with survival and stability than with growth and change. The adaptive CEOs, however, are not totally averse to exploiting external opportunities. They are willing to do so, but only after other companies have proved that taking advantage of an opportunity is virtually risk-free.

The Strategic Planning Mode   The strategic planning mode is a blend of both the entrepreneurial and the adaptive modes. This mode involves a systematic and thorough analysis of the company's external as well internal conditions. Depending on what the external environmental analysis reveals and in light of the firm's internal capabilities, a CEO may either take a carefully calculated risk or pursue an adaptive, conservative approach.

THE CEO'S DECISION-MAKING STYLE   In a broad sense, decision-making styles can be placed into two categories: autocratic and participative styles. Although there are some CEOs who consistently use one of these two styles, most CEOs tend to fall somewhere along the autocratic-participative style continuum.

Autocratic Style   Also called authoritarian, the autocratic style involves the unilateral decision making by the CEO. The CEO formulates strategies and expects others to carry them out without criticism or modification.

Participative Style   In the participative, alternatively called democratic, style, CEOs strive to consult with their subordinates before reaching a final decision. Even though the participative CEOs possess the formal authority to make decisions unilaterally, they nonetheless make a concerted effort to seek input from their subordinates.

Appendix C
SCANNING THE EXTERNAL ENVIRONMENT

Competitor Intelligence   Competitor intelligence involves the use of legal methods of gathering "information about competitor capabilities and intentions that provides a basis for planning long-term strategy."[9] About 80 percent of the Fortune 1000 companies maintains an intelligence department.[10]

Competitor intelligence assumes a variety of forms. These include reading published material, questioning competitors' technicians at conferences and trade shows, hiring people away from competitors, debriefing competitors' former employees, encouraging key customers to talk, analyzing labor contracts, and taking plant tours.

Industrial Espionage   Industrial espionage refers to the illegal use of information-gathering tools. It is the act of stealing the trade secrets of competitors.

Forecasting   Forecasting is the process of developing assumptions about probable future events. Some of the commonly used forecasting techniques include executive opinions, delphi, brainstorming, scenarios. trend analysis, time-series analysis, regression analysis, econometric models, cross-impact analysis, and leading indicators.

Appendix D
MISSION

A mission is a broad statement that, at a minimum, seeks to describe the organization's purpose or reason for being. The mission defines the company's business.

ELEMENTS OF THE MISSION   A good mission statement typically embodies five elements: business domain, products or services, distribution channels, customers, and management's beliefs and values.

Business Domain   The basic question that ought to be answered in the mission statement is: "What business are we in?" In other words, the mission must first seek to define the company's business.

Products and Services   The second element of the mission is closely linked to the first. It provides a description of the company's various products or services.

Distribution Channels   The third element of the mission is designed to specify the type of channels used in distributing the products or services and the geographic areas where they are distributed. In its mission statement, General Motors Acceptance Corporation, for example, describes its distribution channels in this way: "GMAC offers its financing services through 349 offices in the United States and many other countries in which General Motors sells its products."

Customers   Identifying the customers targeted by the company's products or services constitutes the fourth building block of a mission. Product users may be classified as governments, institutions, industries, or individual consumers.

Management's Beliefs and Values   The mission statement provides top management with an excellent forum for articulating its beliefs and values. Top management can utilize the mission to clearly enunciate its stance toward the company's stakeholders, namely, customers, employees, shareholder, and the community in which it operates.

[For a statement of mission, see the illustrative]
[case analysis in Chapter 8.]

Appendix E
CORPORATE OBJECTIVES

An objective is typically defined as the result to be accomplished by a specific time. Hence, corporate objectives refer to the results pursued by the organization as a total entity.

A good statement of objective must satisfy two minimal requirements: (1) the objective must be measurable, and (2) it must have a time frame (i.e., planning horizon). Below is an example of a good and poor statement of objectives.

Good Objective: Our objective is to increase sales from $100 million to $150 million in five years.
Poor Objective: Our objective is to increase sales substantially.

Appendix F
GRAND STRATEGIES

A grand strategy is the general course of action through which an enterprise seeks to accomplish its corporate objectives.

Grand strategies include: (1) concentration, (2) market development, (3) product development, (4) innovation, (5) vertical integration, (6) joint venture, (7) horizontal integration, (8) concentric diversification, (9) conglomerate diversification, (10) retrenchment/turnaround, (11) harvest, (12) divestiture, and (13) liquidation.

Concentration   Concentration is a strategy that emphasizes the firm's current business; it concentrates on vigorously marketing current products in today's market. For many years, Coors Brewing Co. followed this strategy by marketing its beer in the western states. This technique is also called market penetration.

Market Development   Whereas concentration involves an effort to penetrate today's market with current products, market development is calculated to expand the geographic coverage of current products. The decision by Coors Brewing Co. to market its product nationally rather than regionally represents a market-development strategy.

Product Development   Product development involves an improvement of the company's current product. It is designed to extend the life cycle of the product rather than starting a new product life cycle. This explains why such products are commonly referred to as line extensions. Line extensions, then, are not new but modified products. An example of a product development is Liquid Tide which is an extension of regular Tide.

Innovation   Innovations are products that mark the advent of a new product life cycle, thereby making any existing similar products obsolete. An example of an innovative product is the hand-held calculator which ended the slide-rule business.

Vertical Integration   Vertical integration is a strategy that permits a company to become involved in the different phases of manufacturing a product and marketing it to the ultimate user.

Vertical integration is of two types: backward and forward. Backward integration occurs when a company acquires, or increases its control of, another firm that supplies it with raw materials. It also occurs when a company establishes its own sources of supplies. The benefits of backward integration include: (1) assuring a steady supply of raw materials, (2) maintaining the desired quality of supplies, and (3) increasing the firm's control of the costs of the supplies.

Forward integration refers to the acquisition by a company of the distributors of its products or the establishment of its own distribution outlets. This strategy has the advantages of enabling the company to: (1) cut the costs of its products by eliminating intermediaries, (2) increase product sales through better customer service or improved advertising, and (3) develop a better feel for changes in customers' needs and preferences.

An oil refining company that acquires an oil drilling firm is an example of backward integration. On the other hand, an oil refining company that establishes its own service stations or acquires existing service stations is viewed as engaging in a forward integration strategy.

Horizontal Integration   Horizontal integration is a strategy in which a firm acquires one of its competitors, provided the action does not violate the antitrust laws. In recent years, the acquisition by the top ten advertising firms of many smaller agencies is an illustration of horizontal strategy.

Concentric Diversification   The word "concentric" means having a common center. Hence, concentric diversification involves a strategy where one company acquires another with related or complementary products. Put differently, the two companies, though not operating in the same market, create a "strategic fit" by sharing some common thread. The thread may relate to the make-up of the product, technology, distribution, customers, sales force, and so on. An illustrative case is Anheuser-Busch's acquisition of Saratoga Springs Mineral Water Co.

Conglomerate Diversification   This strategy involves the acquisition of firms with unrelated products. Unlike concentric diversification where management is primarily concerned with a strategic fit between the companies' products, conglomerate diversification is principally driven by profit considerations. The failed acquisition of Columbia Pictures by Coca-Cola Co. was driven not by a "strategic fit" but by profit maximization.

Joint Venture   Also called a strategic alliance, joint venture is a strategy in which two or more firms enter into a partnership to undertake a mutually beneficial project. All participants in the venture continue to maintain their separate identities. The alliance between General Motors Corp. and Toyota Corp., for example, to manufacture a new car (Nova) in the U.S. held certain benefits to both companies. The venture provided GM with useful insight into Toyota's much touted production and managerial techniques. On the other hand, it enabled Toyota to implement its long-term strategy of establishing plants in the U.S.

Retrenchment/Turnaround   This strategy is used when a company experiences a critically steady decline in profitability and is considered to be in exceedingly poor health. The purpose of the retrenchment/turnaround strategy is to reverse the profit slide and restore the company to good health. Implementation of the retrenchment/turnaround strategy often calls for bringing in a new CEO and invariably entails drastic cost-reduction measures.

Harvest   A harvest strategy is designed to milk the maximum possible cash from a poor-performing strategic business unit (SBU) that cannot be sold for profit.

Divestiture   Divestiture is the strategy of selling off one of the corporation's SBUs. The divested SBU might be unprofitable or it might not fit neatly into the company's portfolio. The decision by Coca-Cola Co. to shed its motion picture, cutlery, and instant tea and coffee businesses to concentrate on its soft-drink business is an example of a divestiture strategy.

Liquidation   Liquidation is a last-resort strategy when all other measures fail to turn an ailing company around. The strategy involves selling the company in parts or as a whole to recover its tangible asset value. Under this strategy, then, the firm ceases to exist as a going concern.

EVALUATING ALTERNATIVE GRAND STRATEGIES

Approaches to evaluating alternative grand strategies may be grouped into three categories: unstructured, semi-structured, and structured approaches.

The Unstructured Approach   This approach is highly informal and does not follow a specific step-by-step procedure. Rather, and at best, it involves a general discussion of the comparative benefits of the available strategic options. Managers who use the unstructured approach tend to rely heavily on intuition in determining the superiority of a particular strategic option.

The Semi-Structured Approach   Unlike the unstructured approach which primarily relies on "gut feeling", the semi-structured approach is more formal and involves the use of a rather specific procedure. In this approach, a particular set of evaluative criteria are first agreed upon by the strategizing team. It is then followed by group discussions aimed at determining how each strategic option fares in respect to its potential to satisfy each criterion.

The Structured Approach   The structured approach involves a specific step-by-step procedure designed to enhance the objectivity of the strategic choice process. In this approach, an effort is made to quantify the discussions, thus forcing strategists to scrutinize more closely the viability of each strategy.

Appendix G
COMPETITIVE STRATEGIES

Michael Porter classifies competitive strategies into three categories: cost leadership, product differentiation, and focus.[11]

Cost leadership is designed to make an SBU (or a single-business firm) a cost leader in its market through such measures as the construction of efficient facilities, tight overhead control, and avoidance of marginal customer accounts. Product differentiation involves differentiating the firm's product or service in some fashion. This may be accomplished through brand image, technology, features, or dealer network. The focus strategy seeks to carve out a special niche for the company. The niche may take the form of a specific group of customers, a narrow geographic area, or a particular use of the product.

Appendix H
ORGANIZATIONAL STRUCTURE

A variety of organizational structures are in use. The major structures include: (1) entrepreneurial, (2) functional, (3) geographic, (4) product, (5) strategic business unit, (6) matrix, and (7) project management.

Entrepreneurial Structure   Representing the first stage in the growth of a business concern, the entrepreneurial structure typifies a small firm whose operations are focused on one line of business. In this most simple structure, shown in Exhibit 2-8, the owner/manager runs the show nearly single handedly.

Functional Structure   A functional structure is the grouping of the same or similar tasks into one department or functional unit. For example, and as illustrated in Exhibit 2-9, all tasks pertaining to production are grouped within the production department, all tasks relating to finance are grouped within the finance department, and so on.

Geographic Structure   A geographic structure is suitable for any organization whose operations are geographically dispersed. In this structure, all tasks needed to manufacture a product or provide a service are organized on the basis of territory. Thus, and as portrayed in Exhibit 2-10, there could be an eastern division, a mid-western division, and a western division. Headed by a general manager, each one of these divisions may then be structured along functional or product lines.

Exhibit 2-8　**Entrepreneurial Structure**

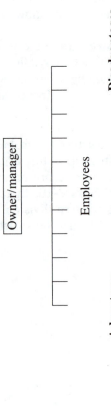

Owner/manager

Employees

Advantages

1. It facilitates a prompt response to environmental opportunities and threats.

2. It facilitates effective coordination of the various tasks.

3. It fosters effective face-to-face communication between the owner and employees.

Disadvantages

1. Survival of the firm depends on the decision-making skills of one person.

2. The owner might not have enough time to chart future strategies.

3. The firm is not likely to attract competent and ambitious employees.

Exhibit 2-9 **Functional Structure**

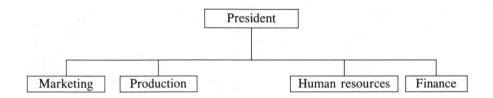

Advantages

1. It fosters the efficiency that comes with specialization, since each department is staffed with specialists.

2. It reduces the risks of making poor decisions as the chief executive now has the expert advice of functional managers.

3. It eases the heavy work load of the chief executive who can focus more closely on long-term strategies.

Disadvantages

1. It might spawn unhealthy rivalries among the various functions for more resources.

2. Face-to-face communication between the CEO and employees becomes difficult.

3. The CEO might lose control of the organization.

Exhibit 2-10   **Geographic Structure**

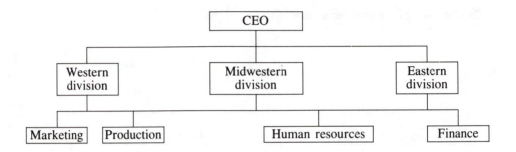

Advantages	Disadvantages
1. It permits divisional managers to be more responsive to the needs of local customers.	1. It lessens the CEO's control over regional divisions.
2. It facilitates the establishment of profit centers where each division is evaluated on its profit-generation ability.	2. It can be costly as it requires the hiring of general managers and involves duplication of the same functions.
3. It allows for the development of general managers with the skills required to coordinate and control various functional units.	3. It might promote divisional myopia if divisional managers place their interests ahead of the company's.

Product Structure   When a company diversifies its offerings into related and/or unrelated products and services, it enters a fourth stage of business growth. Here, the firm is structured along a product line. In a product structure, all the activities necessary to manufacture a product or provide a service are grouped together in one division. Like the geographic structure, each division is made up of a number of pertinent functional units. For an illustration of the product structure, see Exhibit 2-11.

Strategic Business Unit Structure   A company might grow in size to the point where it becomes simply too unwieldy for the CEO to effectively oversee the operations of the company's numerous divisions. In this case, it may be necessary to modify the firm's structure from product to strategic business unit (SBU).

An SBU structure refers to the process of grouping (or recombining) different divisions into distinct groups or sectors. The grouping is based on some common strategic elements. The elements may include "an overlapping set of competitors, a closely related strategic mission, a common need to compete globally, ..., and technologically related growth opportunities."[12]

As can be seen in Exhibit 2-12, each group of businesses or SBU is headed by a vice president (sometimes called president) who reports directly to the CEO.

Exhibit 2-11   **Product Structure**

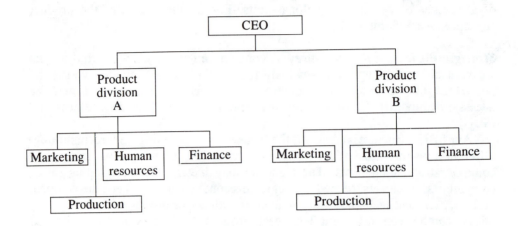

Advantages	Disadvantages

Advantages

1. It enhances the competitive position of each product as a result of specialization.

2. It makes it easier to assess the market performance of each product.

3. It enables each division to operate as a profit center.

4. It allows divisional managers to respond quickly to changes in their market.

5. It leads to the development of general managers.

Disadvantages

1. It can make it difficult for the CEO to exercise adequate control.

2. It can be costly as it results in the duplication of the same functions in several divisions.

3. It makes communication between headquarters and the various divisions difficult.

4. It may cause divisional managers to emphasize short-term profit at the expense of the long-term welfare of the firm.

Exhibit 2-12   **SBU Structure**

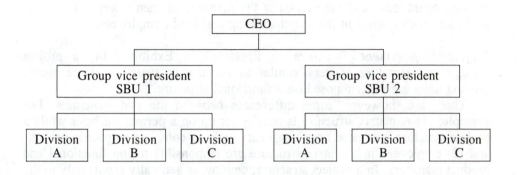

Advantages

1. It facilitates the allocation of corporate resources among SBUs.

2. It narrows the CEO's span of control.

3. It fosters better coordination among the SBU's division.

4. It helps in eliminating overlapping functions.

5. It helps in achieving synergy among the SBU's divisions.

Disadvantages

1. It makes communication between the CEO and divisional heads difficult.

2. It might create unhealthy competition among SBU heads for corporate resources.

3. It might lead to the abuse of SBU's autonomy by group heads.

Matrix Structure   Illustrated in Exhibit 2-13, the matrix structure is essentially a combination of the functional and product structures, with the latter superimposed on the former. As can be seen in the exhibit, functional departments are arrayed horizontally, while product departments are arrayed vertically.

The principal characteristic of the matrix structure is that each employee reports to two superiors simultaneously. For example, and as shown in Exhibit 2-13, employees in store operations have two bosses. The first is the manager of store operations, and the second is the manager of men's wear. The same holds true with respect to the merchandising and credit employees.

Project Management Structure   Presented in Exhibit 2-14, a project management structure is very similar to the matrix structure. Here again, product units are superimposed on a functional structure.

There are, however, some differences between the two structures. For example: (1) A matrix structure is usually set up on a permanent basis while a project structure is created on a temporary basis to complete a specific project, and (2) employees in a matrix structure are responsible to the functional and product managers. In a project structure, employees generally report only to the project manager. When the project is completed, employees are returned to their base departments.

Exhibit 2-13 **Matrix Structure**

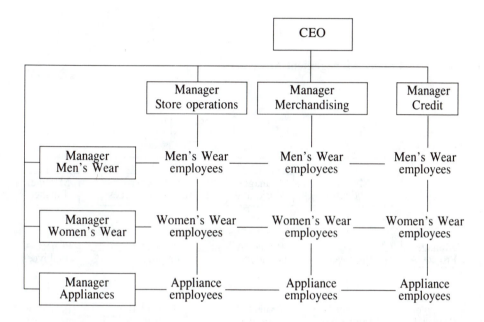

Source: Adapted from G.D. Smith, D.R.Arnold, and B.G. Bizzell, *Business Policy and Strategy* (Boston, Mass.: Houghton Mifflin Company, 1985), p. 172.

Advantages	**Disadvantages**
1. It utilizes the specialized expertise of both functional and product managers.	1. It subjects employees to two bosses.
2. It allows managers to respond more quickly to changes in the external environment.	2. It may cause power struggle between functional and product managers.
3. It makes for the economical use of human resources.	3. It may cause managers to spend too much time on conflict resolution.

Exhibit 2-14   **Project Management Structure**

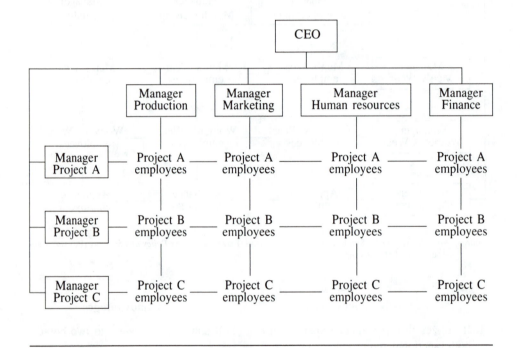

Structure Follows Strategy   While one structure might be suitable for implementing one strategy, it might not be as effective in the execution of another strategy.

For example, a company that pursues a strategy of concentration on a single product in a single market would be better off with a functional structure. However, a company whose strategy emphasizes product diversification would be more effective using a product instead of a functional structure. Similarly, when a company's strategy is based on the expeditious development of new products, its existing R&D function might not be the best tool for implementing the strategy. In this case, a project management structure would be more appropriate.

Centralization and Decentralization   The degree to which authority is delegated determines whether an organization is centralized or decentralized. Centralization, then, reflects the tendency of superiors to retain the decision-making authority in their own hands. Conversely, decentralization represents the tendency of superiors to share their decision-making power with their subordinates. Generally, decentralization tends to be more effective than centralization, as its advantages far outweigh those normally ascribed to the centralized system.

Appendix I
POLICIES

A policy is a general guide for action. It is a directive "designed to guide the thinking, decisions, and actions of managers and their subordinates in implementing an organization strategy."[13]

In contrast to strategy which typically deals with nonrecurring conditions, a policy is designed to assist managers throughout the organization in dealing with recurring or routine issues.

Purposes of Policy   Policies are devised to serve a variety of purposes. Among them are the following:

1. Policies free top management from dealing with routine or recurring issues that can be easily handled by subordinates.

2. Policies foster consistency and uniformity of action in dealing with similar issues that arise in different organizational units.

3. Policies delineate the boundaries of what constitutes an acceptable strategy. If a company's policy, for example, is to sell only high-quality products, managers in the affected departments will not develop, manufacture, or market any product unless it meets the company's standards.

Appendix J
LEADERSHIP STYLE

Leadership refers to "the expressed ability to influence the behavior of one's peers and the actions of one's subordinates toward accomplishing the organization's goals and objectives."[14] Leadership style is the degree of emphasis a manager places on production (getting the job done efficiently) or on people (satisfying employees' needs), or both. That is, whether the manager is basically task oriented or employee oriented.

The Leadership Grid ®   In the course of their studies of leadership, Blake and McCanse devised a leadership grid as a tool for classifying leadership styles. Displayed in Exhibit 2-15, the grid uses two dimensions: concern for production and concern for people. On the basis of these dimensions, and as shown in the exhibit, Blake and McCanse identified the following five leadership styles:

1. *Authority-compliance management or 9,1 style*. This is an autocratic style characterized by a high concern for efficient operations and a low concern for people.

2. *Impoverished management or 1,1 style*. Managers are not interested in their job and show little concern for either production or people. They do the minimum just to get by.

3. *Country-club management or 1,9 style*. Managers show little or no concern for production but a high concern for people. It is presumed that if people are well taken care of, production efficiency will take care of itself.

4. *Team management or 9,9 style*. Managers are able to reconcile effectively the requirements of efficient operations with the needs of their employees. Known as democratic leaders, these managers show the highest possible concern for both production and people.

5. *Middle-of-the-road management or 5,5 style*. Managers show average concern for production and people. In this situation, production level and employee satisfaction tend to be adequate.

Exhibit 2-15 **The Leadership Grid ® Figure**

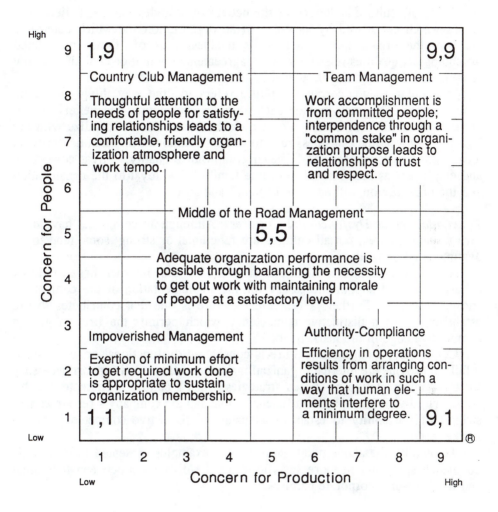

The Leadership Grid₍®₎Figure

Source: The Leadership Grid₍®₎ Figure from **Leadership Dilemmas—Grid Solutions,** by Robert R. Blake and Anne Adams McCanse. Houston: Gulf Publishing Company, p. 29. Copyright © 1991, by Scientific Methods, Inc. Reproduced by permission of the owners.

Appendix K
CORPORATE CULTURE

Corporate culture is defined as the pattern of attitudes, norms, beliefs, and values which are shared by members of an organization and which determine the way the organization conducts its business. All of "these interrelated psychological qualities reveal a group's agreement, implicit or explicit, on how to approach decisions and problems."[15]

In popular usage, corporate culture refers to "the way things are done around here." This may include such attitudes, behaviors, and beliefs as "do not disagree with your boss," "don't rock the boat," "don't socialize with the boss," "only wear dark business suits to work,"[16] "innovate or get out," "provide unsurpassed customer service," "never compromise quality," "treat coworkers and employees as members of the same family," "be loyal to the organization and the organization will be loyal to you," and so on.

Functional versus Dysfunctional Cultures   Although all companies have their own unique cultures, not all cultures are functional or strong; some tend to be dysfunctional or weak.

A functional culture is one that provides the internal organizational cohesiveness and support necessary for the implementation of the company's chosen strategies. Further, a functional culture is one that contributes to the establishment of a distinctive competency which permits the firm to gain a competitive edge in the marketplace.

Conversely, a corporate culture is considered dysfunctional or weak when it fails to provide the internal organizational cohesiveness and support necessary for the implementation of chosen strategies. Such a culture is characterized by confusion, divisiveness, and inefficiencies that sap the company's resources and strip it of the ability to establish a sustained distinctive competency in the marketplace.

To amplify the above point, consider the examples presented in Exhibit 2-16, which spells out in more specific terms the distinction between functional and dysfunctional corporate cultures.[17]

Appendix L
TARGET MARKETING

Target marketing is of three types. The first is called undifferentiated marketing. This describes a situation where a firm goes after the largest part of the market with one product, trying to attract as many customers as possible. The second is called concentrated marketing. Here, the company offers one product to a narrow market segment. The third is called differentiated marketing, and it occurs when a company offers several products, each designed for a specific market segment.

Exhibit 2-16 **Features of Functional and Dysfunctional Cultures**

A Functional Culture	**A Dysfunctional Culture**
1. Places a high premium on customer service.	1. Does not take the necessary measures to ensure customer service.
2. Adheres to high-quality standards.	2. Tolerates low-quality standards.
3. Respects employees and treats them as a valuable asset.	3. Takes employees' efforts and contributions for granted.
4. Emphasizes team work and family feeling.	4. Pays only lip service to group spirit.
5. Encourages creativity and innovation.	5. Stifles creativity and innovation.
6. Believes in the value of employee input to decision making.	6. Relies on downward communication and does not invite employee input.
7. Provides substantial material and psychological rewards to achievers.	7. Provides nominal material rewards to high achievers.

Appendix M
ADVERTISING BUDGET

Three methods are generally used in determining an advertising budget: percentage of sales, competitive matching, and affordability.

In the first method, a company sets its advertising expenditures at a specified percentage of current or anticipated sales, or at a percentage of the sale price. In the competitive matching method, the budget is set at a level that matches that of the company's major competitors. In the affordability method, also called the arbitrary method, executives determine their advertising budget on the basis of what they think the company can afford during a particular period of time.

Appendix N
QUALITY CONTROL TECHNIQUES

Quality control typically refers to the maintenance of appropriate levels of product or service reliability. Generally, companies use one or a combination of two techniques in ensuring the appropriate quality level: acceptance sampling and in-process sampling.

Acceptance sampling involves sampling finished goods to ensure that quality standards have been met. The key to acceptance sampling is determining what percentage of the products (i.e., 2, 5, or 25 out of 100) should be tested. The in-process-sampling technique assesses product quality during the manufacturing process so that the needed changes can be made before the product reaches the finished-product stage.

Appendix O
RESEARCH AND DEVELOPMENT

Focus   The word "focus" is used here to denote the time horizon (i.e., near term or long term) that characterizes the R&D activities. In this respect, R&D may be classified into two types: basic and applied. Basic research is characterized by its long-term focus. It represents an effort by scientists to seek knowledge for knowledge sake without having any specific commercial application in mind. From basic research often come totally unexpected but valuable findings that expand the frontiers of technology and translate into significant practical applications.

In contrast to basic research, applied research is characterized by its short-term focus. It is oriented toward enlarging knowledge that has a particular commercial application. The greater majority of companies tend to have an applied research focus. This is due to the fact that applied research is less costly and far less risky than basic research.

Posture   Posture refers to the stance a company seeks to assume in its industry with respect to product leadership. Generally, a firm's R&D posture may be described as innovative, protective, catch-up, or a combination of the three.[18]

An innovative strategy is an offensive strategy. It is primarily aimed at developing new products or production techniques, rather than emphasizing short-term profitability. This strategy takes a long-term view of the company, and its dividends may not be felt for many years.

A protective strategy is directed at improving the company's present products. It is a defensive strategy emphasizing maintenance of the firm's current market position. A catch-up strategy is another defensive strategy. A firm following this posture basically copies features of a competitor's product and incorporates them in its own product.

Appendix P
SUCCESSION PLANNING

Succession planning is the process of grooming managers to step into executive positions as they become vacant. A well-thought-out succession plan covers all managerial positions, including that of the chief executive officer.

Strategic human resource planning begins with the preparation of an inventory of the managers available within the organization. The inventory is compiled for each organizational unit. And it normally contains information on such things as the number of managers, their ages, skills, length of service, and promotability. The inventory also presents an estimate of future job vacancies typically created by ill health, retirement, deaths, dismissals, or voluntary terminations.

The primary purpose of such an inventory is to identify managers with the potential for promotion to a higher position. Once identified, these managers are then provided with the necessary training and coaching that will prepare them to assume the responsibilities associated with the higher position.

The formulation of a succession plan is valuable for three reasons. First, it formalizes the process of searching for executives with the qualifications that permit them to move up to higher positions when the need arises. Second, it serves to ensure the smooth and orderly transition of power. And third, it increases the chances that the new executive will enjoy the support and cooperation of his or her employees.

Appendix Q
PUBLIC AFFAIRS

Ethics   Ethics is defined as the rules of behavior that form the general conception of what is right and wrong for individuals, communities, and institutions.[19] In this context, an ethical conduct refers to any action that conforms to the behavioral standards generally sanctioned by society.

Social Responsibility   Social responsibility refers to those actions, taken voluntarily by an individual or an organization, which are geared toward the betterment of society. It involves such corporate actions as granting leaves of absence to employees to serve as volunteers in social welfare organizations or providing financial rewards to those employees who perform such service on their own time.

Thus, the principal difference between ethics and social responsibility is that while ethics represents a mandated behavior, social responsibility is voluntary.

Crisis Management   One of the primary functions of a public-affairs department involves the effective management of corporate crises. Corporate crisis is any disaster or emergency precipitated by an act of God, people, organizational structures, or technology that bring about damage to human life, natural and social environments, or corporate image.[20]

A sampling of such crises includes product tampering, accidents, terrorism, community protests, lawsuits, product defects, rumors, unethical conduct by company executives, executive kidnapping, labor strikes, boycotts, counterfeiting, hostile takeovers, system breakdowns, fire, sabotage, and so on.

Appendix R
THE MEANING AND COMPUTATION OF RATIOS

1. Liquidity Ratios

Current   The current ratio reflects the relationship between a firm's current assets and its current liabilities. It shows the extent to which the firm's assets can be converted to cash to cover the claims of short-term creditors.

$$\text{Current ratio} = \frac{\text{Current assets}}{\text{Current liabilities}}$$

Quick   Also called the acid test, the quick ratio measures the ability of a firm to meet its current obligations without having to sell its inventories.

$$\text{Quick ratio} = \frac{\text{Current assets-Inventories}}{\text{Current libilities}}$$

2. Activity Ratios

Inventory Turnover   The inventory-turnover ratio reflects the number of times inventories are replaced within a specific period of time. It demonstrates whether a firm keeps excessive, sufficient, or insufficient levels of inventory.

$$\text{Inventory turnover} = \frac{\text{Sales}}{\text{Inventory}}$$

Average Collection Period   The average-collection-period ratio is a measure of the average number of days needed for the collection of accounts receivable. This ratio is designed to answer the question: How long does the firm have to wait before it receives cash on sales that have been made?

Two steps are usually involved in the calculation of this ratio. First, the annual sales are divided by 360 to obtain the average sales per day. (The annual sales rather than the credit sales are used, since information on the latter is normally unavailable.) Second, the accounts receivable are then divided by daily sales.

$$1. \text{ Average daily sales} = \frac{\text{Sales}}{360}$$

$$2. \text{ Average collection period} = \frac{\text{Accounts receivable}}{\text{Average daily sales}}$$

Total Assets Turnover   A firm's total assets consist of current assets such as cash, inventory, and marketable securities as well as fixed (or long-term) assets such as plant, equipment, tools, fixtures, etc.   The total-assets-turnover-ratio indicates how well a firm manages these assets. It shows how many dollars of sales are supported by one dollar of total assets.

$$\text{Total assets turnover} = \frac{\text{Sales}}{\text{Total assets}}$$

3. Leverage Ratios

Total Debt to Total Assets   Also called the debt ratio, the total-debt-to-total-assets ratio measures the percentage of a firm's total assets that is borrowed to finance the firm's operations.

$$\text{Debt ratio} = \frac{\text{Total debt}}{\text{Total assets}}$$

Times Interest Earned   The times-interest-earned ratio reflects the extent to which a firm is able to pay its interest charges. It indicates the number of times interest payments are covered by available funds from earnings.

$$\text{Times interest earned} = \frac{\text{Net operating income}}{\text{Interest expenses}}$$

4. Profitability Ratios

Profit Margin   The profit-margin ratio gives the percentage of profit realized on each dollar of sales.

$$\text{Profit margin} = \frac{\text{Net income}}{\text{Net sales}}$$

Return on Equity   The return-on-equity ratio shows the percentage of earnings realized on the stockholders' investment.

$$\text{Return on equity} = \frac{\text{Net income}}{\text{Net worth}}$$

Appendix S
SOURCES OF INFORMATION ON INDUSTRY RATIOS

Ratios by themselves are not very meaningful. They take on particular significance only when compared against a bench mark. Such a comparison makes the firm's ratios much more informative by revealing whether the ratios are poor, satisfactory, or good.

One of the most popular approaches to determining the efficiency of a firm is to compare its key ratios against the industry standards or, more specifically, against those of comparable firms in the same industry. The cornerstone assumption of this approach is that members of the same industry are generally presented with similar problems and similar opportunities. Hence, a comparison with the industry norm can serve as a fairly accurate yardstick of judging whether the firm's performance is worse or better than that of competing firms.

There are several excellent sources that provide industry-wide averages. Here is a list of some of the major sources.
1. *Key Business Ratios* (N.Y.: Dun and Bradstreet, Inc.). Annual.
2. *Dun's Review* (N.Y.: Dun and Bradstreet, Inc.). September, October, and November issues of each year.
3. *Annual Statement Studies* (Philadelphia: Robert Morris Associates). Annual.
4. *Standard and Poor's Industry Surveys* (N.Y.: Standard and Poor's). Quarterly.
5. *Moody's Manuals* (N.Y.: Moody's Investors Service). Annual with semi-weekly supplements.
6. Leo Troy, *Almanac of Business and Financial Ratios* (Englewood Cliffs, New Jersey: Prentice-Hall, Inc.). Annual.
7. *Barometer of Small Business* (San Diego, California: The Accounting Corporation of America). Semiannual.
8. *Financial Studies of Small Business* (Arlington, Virginia: Financial Research Associates). Annual.

Observations on the Use of Industry Ratios

1. Use only industry ratios published at the time the case is written. If the case is written in 1990 (as indicated by the balance sheet), use ratios published in that year.

2. If the case involves a firm that engages in several industries, it is advisable to focus on the ratios of what you consider to be the firm's major or core business.

3. In presenting a firm's ratios and the industry averages, you may wish to use a format similar to the one displayed in Exhibit 2-17. The exhibit presents a summary of the ratios of ABC Manufacturing Co., a fictional firm, and industry averages.

Exhibit 2-17   **Summary of the Ratios of ABC Manufacturing Co.
as Compared with the Industry Average**

RATIO	FORMULA FOR CALCULATION	ABC RATIO	INDUSTRY AVERAGE
Liquidity:			
Current	$\dfrac{\text{Current assets}}{\text{Current liabilities}}$	1.5 times	1.9 times
Quick or acid test	$\dfrac{\text{Current assets-Inv.}}{\text{Current liabilities}}$	0.9 times	0.9 times
Activity:			
Inventory turnover	$\dfrac{\text{Sales}}{\text{Inventory}}$	7.9 times	7.2 times
Collection period	$\dfrac{\text{Accounts receivable}}{\text{Average sales/day}}$	39 days	41 days
Total assets turnover	$\dfrac{\text{Sales}}{\text{Total assets}}$	1.3 times	2.7 times
Leverage:			
Debt to total assets	$\dfrac{\text{Total debt}}{\text{Total assets}}$	64 percent	56 percent
Times interest earned	$\dfrac{\text{Net operating income}}{\text{Interest expenses}}$	3.5 times	3.7 times
Profitability:			
Profit margin	$\dfrac{\text{Net income}}{\text{Net sales}}$	2.0 percent	3.5 percent
Return on equity	$\dfrac{\text{Net income}}{\text{Net worth}}$	7.0 percent	12.6 percent

REVIEW QUESTIONS

1.   What is meant by *factoring* and why is it a useful analytical tool?

2.   Outline the process involved in profiling an organization's environment.

3.   Why are the corporate level and the business level combined for case-analysis purposes?

4.   Identify the steps of profiling the major components of the corporate/business level.

5.   You have been asked by your employer to analyze the company's strategy-implementation process. What subcomponents would you start examining?

6.   What are the steps that comprise the process of profiling the major components of the functional level?

7.   You are a consultant, and you have been retained to analyze the human-resource function of a large company. What aspects (or subcomponents) of the human-resource area would you investigate?

References

1.   W.H. Newman and J.P. Logan, *Strategy, Policy, and Central Management,* 8th ed., (Cincinnati, Ohio: South-Western Publishing Co., 1981), p. 8.

2.   D.J. McCarthy, R.J. Minichiello, and J.R. Curran, *Business Policy and Strategy: Concepts and Readings,* 3rd ed., (Homewood, IL.: Irwin, Inc., 1983), p. 227.

3.   C.W. Hofer and D. Schendel, *Strategy Formulation: Analytical Concepts,* (St. Paul, Minnesota: West Publishing Co., 1978), p. 20.

4.   Charles W. Hofer, "Toward a Contingency Theory of Business Strategy," *The Academy of Management Journal,* December, 1975, pp. 784-810.

5.   Laurence R. Jauch and William Glueck, *Business Policy and Strategic Management,* 5th ed., (N.Y.: McGraw-Hill Book Company, 1988), p. 55.

6.   Bruce L. Ellig, "Compensating the Board of Directors," *Compensation Review,* Vol. 15, No. 3, p. 16.

7.   Thomas Wheelen and David J. Hunger, *Strategic Management and Business Policy* (Readings, Mass.: Addison-Wesley Publishing Co., 1983), p. 49.

8.   Henry Mintzberg, "Strategy Making in Three Modes," *California Management Review,* Winter 1973, pp. 44-53.

9.   Robert Hershey, "Commercial Intelligence on a Shoestring," *Harvard Business Review,* Vol. 58, No. 5, September-October 1980, p. 22.

10.   D. Tsiantar, J. Schwartz, B. Cohn, and L. Wright, "George Smiley Joins the Firm," *Newsweek,* May 2, 1988, p. 46.

11.   Michael E. Porter, *Competitive Strategies: Techniques for Analyzing Industries and Competitors* (N.Y.: The Free Press, 1980), pp. 45-46.

12.   Arthur A. Thompson and A.J. Strickland II, *Strategic Management: Concepts and Cases,* 3rd ed., (Plano, Texas: Business Publications, Inc., 1986), p. 319.

13.   John A. Pearce and Richard B. Robinson, Jr., *Strategic Management: Strategy Formulation and Implementation,,* 3rd ed., (Homewood, IL.: Richard D. Irwin, 1988), p. 348.

14.   R.T. Justis, R.D. Judd, and D.B. Stephens, *Strategic Management and Policy: Concepts and Cases* (Englewood Cliffs, New Jersey: Prentice-Hall, Inc., 1985), p. 133.

15.   R.A. Kilman, M.J. Saxton, and R. Serpa, "Issues in Understanding and Changing Culture,"*California Management Review*, Vol. 28, No. 2, Winter 1986, p. 89.

16.   W. Jack Duncan, "Organizational Culture: Getting a Fix on an Elusive Concept," *The Academy of Management Review*, Vol. 28, No. 2, Winter 1986, p. 89.

17.   "Tom Watson Looks at the Past and Future," *The Wall Street Journal*, April 7, 1986, p. 229.

18.   Lloyd L. Byars, *Strategic Management: Planning and Implementation* (N.Y.: Harper and Row, Publishers, 1987), pp. 152-154.

19.   Chris Lee, "Ethics Training: Facing the Tough Questions," *Training*, Vol. 23, No. 3, March 1986, p. 33.

20.   I.I. Mitrof, P. Shrivastava, and F.E. Udwaidia, "Effective Crisis Management," *The Academy of Management Executive*, Vol. 1, No. 3, November 1987, p. 283.

Chapter 3

THE DESCRIPTIVE PHASE:
PROFILING THE EXTERNAL ENVIRONMENT

In the previous chapter, we set out to delineate the process involved in providing a profile of an organization's environmental conditions. It was indicated then that the first step toward this end is to separate the organization's conditions into two principal targets of investigation. They are an internal environment and an external environment. The preceding chapter also described the steps in gaining a picture of the internal environment. In this chapter, our focus will center on the process of providing a profile of the organization's external environment. This step corresponds to Part B of the strategic decision-making framework, illustrated in Exhibit 3-1.

STEPS OF PROFILING THE EXTERNAL ENVIRONMENT

To be able to obtain a comprehensive picture of an organization's external conditions, we need to follow three basic steps:

1. Break the external environmental conditions into major components. As shown in Exhibit 3-2, the external environment can be separated into two major components. These are a task environment and a general environment.

2. Subdivide each major component into its constituent parts or subcomponents. As portrayed in Exhibit 3-3, the task environment is disassembled into the subcomponents of industry, competitors, suppliers, customers, labor unions, and government regulators. On the other hand, the general environment is broken down into the subcomponents of demographics, culture, economy, politics, technology, and pressure groups.

3. Compile checklists geared toward gathering information on the subcomponents of the task environment and the general environment. Answers to the checklists furnish us with small pictures of these subcomponents. The compilation of these pictures should give us a larger picture of the external environment.

PART B.1: PROFILING THE TASK ENVIRONMENT: CHECKLISTS

The task environment refers to external forces that can affect, and are affected by, the organization. Hence, the influence between these forces and the organization is reciporcal. In the following pages, we will offer a sample of some of the questions that serve as tools for generating information on the subcomponents of the task environment.

Exhibit 3-1 A FRAMEWORK FOR STRATEGIC DECISION MAKING AND PROBLEM SOLVING

THE DESCRIPTIVE PHASE

A. Provide a profile of the organization's internal environment

1. Profile the corporate/business level in terms of:
   a. strategic managers
   b. environmental analysis
   c. strategy formulation
   d. strategy implementation
   e. strategy control

2. Profile the functional level in terms of:
   a. marketing
   b. production
   c. research and development
   d. human resources
   e. public affairs
   f. finance/accounting

B. Provide a profile of the organization's external environment

1. Profile the task environment in terms of:
   a. industry
   b. competitors
   c. suppliers
   d. customers
   e. government regulators
   f. labor unions

2. Profile the general environment in terms of:
   a. demographics
   b. culture
   c. economy
   d. politics
   e. technology
   f. pressure groups

THE DIAGNOSTIC PHASE

C. Diagnose the strengths:
   1. Identify the strengths of the corporate/business level
   2. Identify the strengths of the functional level
   3. Identify the organization's distinctive competency

D. Diagnose the weaknesses:
   1. Identify the weaknesses of the corporate/business level
   2. Identify the weaknesses of the functional level
   3. Determine the key weakness

E. Diagnose the opportunities:
   1. Identify the opportunities in the task environment
   2. Identify the opportunities in the general environment
   3. Determine the key opportunity

F. Diagnose the threats:
   1. Identify the threats in the task environment
   2. Identify the threats in the general environment
   3. Determine the key threat

G. Diagnose the major and subordinate problems with their symptoms and probable causes

H. Determine the organization's strategic match

I. Determine the organization's primary strategic match position

J. Diagnose the distinctive competency and the major weakness of the key competitors

THE PRESCRIPTIVE PHASE

K. Formulate a strategic plan:
   1. Write a new mission statement for the organization
   2. Set corporate objectives
   3. Make the strategic choice by selecting the most effective grand strategy
   4. Select a competitive strategy
   5. Formulate functional objectives and strategies

L. Establish the conditions necessary to implement the strategic plan

Exhibit 3-2   **Dividing the External Environment into Two Major Components: A Task Environment and a General Environment**

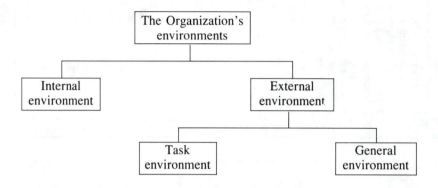

Exhibit 3-3 **The Major Components and Subcomponents of the External Environment**

Major Components	*Subcomponents*
Task environment:	Industry
	Competitors
	Suppliers
	Customers
	Labor unions
	Government regulators
General environment:	Demographics
	Culture
	Economy
	Politics
	Technology
	Pressure groups

Industry

1. What is the current growth rate of the industry in which the firm operates, and what is it expected to be over the next five years?
2. Is the size of the industry large or small? What is the geographic scope of the industry? Is it local, regional, national, or international?
3. Is the industry cyclical? That is, are the industry's profitability and sales characterized by regular peaks and valleys every few years? Are they closely tied to the economic cycles?
4. Is the industry seasonal? That is, are profitability and sales characterized by regular peaks and valleys every few months?
5. Is entry into the industry easy or difficult? What barriers do potential competitors face in entering the industry? Is the company constantly vulnerable to new rivals?
   [For an explanation of entry and exit barriers,]
   [see Appendix A.]
6. Generally, what is the future outlook of the industry?
   [For sources of information on industry,]
   [see Appendix B.]

Competitors

1. Who competes with the firm for the same market? Are the competitors local, regional, national, or multinational corporations?
2. Provide a picture of each key competitor in terms of: (a) market share, (b) breadth of product line, (c) price competitiveness, (d) advertising effectiveness, (e) product quality, (f) product innovation, (g) caliber of top management, (h) corporate culture, (i) experience curve, and (j) financial performance.
   [For the meaning of experience curve,]
   [see Appendix C.]
   [For outside sources of information on competitors,]
   [see Appendix D.]

Suppliers: Raw Materials

1. Does the firm depend on one supplier or multiple suppliers in satisfying its needs for raw materials?
2. Are the prices of the firm's suppliers and the quality of their input competitive?

Suppliers: Capital

1. Are creditors (suppliers of capital) available and willing to provide the firm with the necessary capital to implement its strategies?
2. Will the firm have any difficulty securing its capital needs in the future?

Suppliers: Labor

1. What is the future outlook of the labor supplies?
2. Will the firm face any difficulty in satisfying its requirement for personnel in the future?
        [For sources of information on labor availability,]
                [see Appendix E.]

Customers

1. Who are the firm's customers? Are they individual consumers, governmental, institutional, or industrial organizations?
2. If the customers consist of individual consumers, what are their characteristics in terms of age, income, education, occupation, sex, marital status, family size, geographic location, lifestyles, value system, and so on?
3. Is the size of the firm's market likely to shrink, remain the same, or expand over the next five years?
4. What are the customers' needs and wants? What aspects of the products and services do the customers value most: price, quality, dependable service, prestige, convenience?

Labor Unions

1. If the firm's employees are unionized, does the labor union's leadership exhibit an attitude of hostility or cooperation toward management?
2. When will the labor agreement expire? Is there a likelihood of a strike?
3. Is the union getting stronger or weaker? Is it losing or gaining membership?
4. If a labor union does not exist, is the firm faced with an external drive by a national labor organization to unionize its work force?

Government Regulators

1. Is the industry in which the firm operates heavily regulated?
2. Are government regulations expected to increase or decrease within the next five years?
        [For sources of information on government regulators,]
                [see Appendix F.]

PART B.2: PROFILING THE GENERAL ENVIRONMENT: CHECKLISTS

The general environment is composed of forces that can exert considerable influence on the organization. The organization, however, has little or no impact on such forces. The influence, therefore, tends to be largely one sided. Having offered checklists designed to generate profiles on the subcomponents of the task environment, we will now present similar checklists seeking to obtain pictures of the subcomponents of the general environment. These subcomponents include demographics, culture, economy, politics, technology, and pressure groups.

Demographics

1. What demographic trends are expected to emerge over the next five to ten years? Profile the demographic trends that can have a bearing on the firm's operations. The trends may pertain to such conditions as birth rates, death rates, life expectancy, age distribution, marriages, divorces, geographic distribution of population, population mobility, percentage of women in the work force, enrollments at colleges and universities, size of minority groups, immigration, and so on.
2. Will the firm's operations be affected by changes in the demographics of foreign markets? Provide a profile of such future changes.
                    [For sources of information on demographics,]
                         [see Appendix G.]

Culture

1. What changes are expected to occur in the society's culture (i.e., values or lifestyles) within the next five to ten years?
2. Does the firm operate in foreign markets? If so, what future cultural trends are likely to take shape in the firm's host countries?
                    [For sources of information on culture,]
                         [see Appendix H.]

Economy

1. What is the future state of the economy in terms of such forces as the growth rate of the gross national product (GNP), inflation rate, interest rate, disposable income, consumer spending, business spending, government spending, money supply, unemployment rate, corporate and individual tax rates, federal budget deficit, and balance of trade?
2. What changes in the international economy are likely to occur in the future?
                    [For sources of information on the economy,]
                         [see Appendix I.]

Politics

1. What significant political changes are expected to take place at the state and national levels?
2. Is the firm sensitive to political changes at the international levels? Are any significant political shifts predicted in the future relationship between the East and the West?
3. Are any significant political shifts predicted in the host countries where the company operates? Will the regimes of such countries continue to be stable, or will they become shaky as a result of political, religious, or social strife?
    [For sources of information on politics,]
    [see Appendix J.]

Technology

1. What technological changes or breakthroughs are anticipated to emerge in the general environment within the next five to ten years and which might have a significant impact on the firm's industry?
    [For sources of information on technology,]
    [see Appendix K.]

Pressure Groups

1. What pressure, or public interest, groups operate in the firm's general environment? Are they likely to be more active in the future?
2. Are there any indications of future social issues that might galvanize public interest groups into pressuring the firm to change the way it conducts its business?
    [For sources of information on pressure groups,]
    [see Appendix L.]

CHECKLISTS AND FACTORS

In this chapter and the preceding one, we have provided checklists on the subcomponents of the internal and external environments of the organization under examination. These checklists are geared toward generating profiles of the various subcomponents. Each profile is made up of critical pieces of information which we shall refer to in this section as factors. In this sense, the purpose of the checklists may be seen as providing factors on the subcomponents of the internal and external environmental conditions. Because of the importance of factor as a convenient descriptive tool, it is worthwhile to take a closer look at this concept.

The Meaning of Factor

A factor is any significant variable in the internal or external environment which can positively or negatively affect an organization's performance. By significant variable, we mean any decision, action, behavior, attitude, feeling, event, phenomenon, or trend that serves to contribute to the enhancement or impairment of the organization's operations. In simplistic terms, a factor is an answer obtained in response to a question aimed at eliciting information on the subcomponents of the internal and external environments.

To illustrate the concept of factor, let us assume that our principal interest is concerned with generating a profile of the organization's top management. To do this, we begin by compiling a checklist aimed at collecting information on members of the top-management team. The checklist might include such questions as:

1. How old are the top key executives?
2. Are they innovative and dynamic?
3. Do they possess a clear sense of direction?
4. Are they willing to make decisions involving some measure of risk?
5. Do they reach their decisions subjectively or through a rational, analytical process?
6. How do they view the presence of labor unions in their organization?

The responses obtained to these questions constitute factors which might be articulated in the following manner:

1. The top management team consists of executives ranging in age from 37 to 55 years, with the chief executive being 55, the president 45, and the three vice presidents 42, 40, and 37 respectively.
2. Based on the case information, the strategists appear to be highly innovative and dynamic.
3. They also seem to have a clear vision of where they want their organization to be five or ten years into the future.
4. Based on their past track record, the strategists are not averse to making decisions involving some measure of risk.
5. The decision-making process used by the strategizing team is subjective. It is solely based on their personal feelings and hunches rather than on a rational, analytical approach.
6. The top executives exhibit a great deal of distrust in, and animosity towards, organized labor. They view the labor union as a force chiefly oriented toward undercutting their authority and undermining the efficiency and competitive position of the firm.

Favorable and Unfavorable Factors

Earlier, we viewed a factor as any significant variable that can contribute to the enhancement or impairment of the organization's performance. A factor, then, may be favorable or unfavorable. If its present or expected influence serves to enhance the organization's operations, the factor is considered favorable. When the favorable factor exists in the organization's internal environment, it constitutes a strength. But, when it is located in the external environment, it constitutes an opportunity.

Conversely, if the present or expected impact of a factor can undermine the organization's strategic position, it is regarded as an unfavorable factor. When the unfavorable factor is observed in the organization's internal environment, it represents a weakness. However, when it is intrinsic to the external environment, it is viewed as a threat.

To amplify further the concepts of positive and negative factors, let us look at the six "internal organizational" factors listed earlier in our illustration involving the development of a profile of top management. A quick examination of that list would readily reveal that the first four factors (the top managers' relatively young age, their innovativeness and dynamism, their clear sense of direction, and their disposition to assume a measure of risk in decision making) qualify as positive factors. They are, in other words, indicative of the company's strengths. They can contribute to the enhancement of the company's performance.

It is important to note that a factor such as the one pertaining to the executives' relatively young age does not invariably symbolize an organizational strength. In a general sense, it might hold true. It cannot be treated, however, as an undisputed organizational asset in every situation irrespective of the individuals' other attributes. Before rushing to label a factor of this sort as a strength, we should take care to place it within a broader framework of information. That is essential for providing the supportive evidence to substantiate the observation.

Returning to the list of six factors, we can see that the last two (the executives' subjectivity in decision making and their animosity toward organized labor) tend to be negative in nature. Hence, they are indicative of organizational weaknesses, since they can actually or potentially impair the smooth functioning of the enterprise.

OBSERVATIONS ON THE DESCRIPTIVE PHASE

Before concluding our discussion of the descriptive phase, it is necessary to make the following useful observations:

1. The descriptive phase constitutes the most critical phase of the analysis framework.

The efficacy of the subsequent two phases, the diagnostic and the prescriptive, is wholly predicated on the accuracy and thoroughness of the organization's profile generated in the descriptive phase. For instance, if a certain factor is not reported in the descriptive phase, this factor might prove to be a symptom of a critical problem or a cause of the problem. When a symptom or a cause is not diagnosed and thus remains unknown to an analyst, it cannot be attacked and eliminated in the prescriptive phase.

In its significance, the descriptive phase is analogous to the process pursued by a physician giving a patient a comprehensive physical examination.

Before rendering a diagnosis of the patient's health and before prescribing any remedy, the physician first seeks to collect data about the patient's state of health. He (or she) sets out to gather information about the patient's family history. He also seeks to collect data about the patient's vital signs. He monitors the patient's heart rate, blood pressure, and temperature. He orders X-rays, biopsies, an electrocardiogram, blood tests, and the like. In so doing, the physician aims at one thing: the development of a general profile of the patient's physical conditions.

In analyzing an organization, our initial concern should be geared toward the same purpose. We should seek to formulate a comprehensive picture of the organization's environmental conditions to be used later for diagnostic and prescriptive purposes.

In the above context, the descriptive phase represents a repository of all the gathered factors or significant observations. From this repository, we should be able to extract the information necessary for making a diagnosis of the organization's strengths, weaknesses, opportunities, and threats. Put another way, all the factors that will eventually be utilized for diagnostic purposes should already have been embodied in the descriptive phase.

2. Not every case you analyze contains all the information needed for conducting a thorough examination of an organization's environmental conditions. The lack of information on the external environment can usually be remedied through library research. The same, however, cannot be said about missing information on the internal environment. If, for instance, no information is provided on the organization's strategy control or organizational structure, outside research might not be practical or helpful. In a situation such as this, you are better advised to apply only those aspects of the descriptive phase on which information on the internal conditions is provided.

3. The checklists presented in this chapter and the preceding one are not exhaustive. As the occasion demands, you may have to develop additional questions or subcomponents. This will be necessary if the checklists provided in the last two chapters prove to be either insufficient or inapplicable.

4. Not every response you obtain to every question on your checklists constitutes a factor in the context in which we used the term. Some of the information you gather may be neutral in nature.

For example, knowing that L.B. Johnson is the president, R.J. Smith the executive vice-president, and M.C. Roberts the vice-president of manufacturing serves to complete the picture we seek to formulate of an organization. But such information cannot be treated as a factor. It should, therefore, be observed that neutral information ought to be kept to an absolute minimum, since it cannot be profitably utilized for diagnostic purposes.

Appendix A
ENTRY AND EXIT BARRIERS

The state of competition prevailing in an industry is influenced by a variety of factors. Two of these are entry and exit barriers.

ENTRY BARRIERS   There generally exist seven major types of barriers to entry into an industry:
1. *Economies of scale*. Economies of scale refers to the notion that as a plant gets larger and its output increases, the average cost per unit decreases. Economies of scale deter entry by forcing the entrant to either come in at a large scale and risk strong reaction from the incumbents or come in at a small scale and accept a cost disadvantage. Both of these options are not desirable.
2. *Product differentiation*. Product differentiation means that established firms have brand identification and customer loyalty. New entrants must spend heavily if they are to overcome this barrier and develop their own differentiation.
3. *Capital requirements*. The need to invest large financial resources to compete effectively creates a strong barrier to entry.
4. *Access to distribution channels*. The extent to which distribution channels have already been served by established firms makes entry difficult.
5. *Cost advantages independent of size*. Established firms may have cost advantages not replicable by potential entrants regardless of their size. These include proprietary technology, favorable access to raw materials, government subsidies, and experience in the industry.
6. *Government policy*. This can be an entry barrier in the sense that government can limit entry into certain industries with such controls as licensing requirements and imposing limits on access to raw materials like coal lands.

7. *Reaction of incumbent companies*. Entry into the industry also hinges on the reaction of existing firms to the new entrant. Typically, a firm is likely to be hesitant about entering an industry:

 a) If incumbent companies have a history of retaliating aggressively against new firms.

 b) When established firms possess substantial financial resources to fight back.

 c) When the industry is characterized by slow growth which limits the ability of the industry to absorb a new player without depressing the sales of established companies.

EXIT BARRIERS   One of the key factors contributing to intense rivalry among competitors is the existence of barriers that prevent a competitor from exiting the industry. On occasions, exit barriers can be sufficiently high to force a company to stay in the industry. This may occur even if it is earning low or negative returns on its investment. Below are the major sources of exit barriers:

1. *Specialized assets*. Assets that are highly specialized to a particular business have low liquidation value.
2. *Fixed costs of exit*. These include labor agreements, resettlement costs, and maintaining capabilities for spare parts.
3. *Strategic interrelationships*. Interrelationships between the business unit and others in the company in terms of image, marketing ability, access to financial markets, and shared facilities can serve as an exit barrier.
4. *Emotional barrier*. This includes management's identification with the particular business, loyalty to employees, fear for one's own career, pride, and other reasons.
5. *Government and social restrictions*. These involve government discouragement of exit out of concern for job loss or economic effect. This type of exit barrier is common outside the United States.

Appendix B
SOURCES OF INFORMATION ON INDUSTRY

The sources in this appendix as well as in the subsequent ones are intentionally kept to a minimum so as not to overwhelm you with a long litany of publications. The short lists are also designed to encourage you to consult all of them. It is well to keep in mind that the quality of your report depends on the quality of its information. The quality of information is determined to a great measure by the diversity of sources you use in compiling it. Not only are you encouraged to consult all the sources provided in the appendixes, you are also urged to dig up additional ones on your own.

1. *Business Periodicals Index.*
2. *U.S. Industrial Outlook* (Washington, D.C.: Department of Commerce).
3. *Predicasts' Forecasts* (Cleveland, Ohio: Predicasts, Inc.).
4. *Standard and Poor's Industry Surveys* (N.Y.: Standard and Poor's Corp.).
5. *Standard and Poor's Stock Survey* (N.Y.: Standard and Poor's Corp.).
6. *Fairchild Fact File Publications* (N.Y.: Fairchild Publications, Inc.).
7. *The Value Line Investment Survey: Ratings and Reports* (N.Y.: Arnold Bernhard and Co., Inc.).

Appendix C
THE EXPERIENCE CURVE

The experience curve is a derivative of the learning curve. It is based on the observation that the number of labor hours it takes to produce one unit of a particular product declines predictably as the number of units produced increases. Typically, the production costs of a unit decrease by 25 to 30 percent each time the total output doubles. Put differently, the more experienced a firm is in manufacturing a product, the lower its production costs tend to be.

The experience curve is closely tied to market share and profitability. If the production costs of a unit drop by 25 to 30 percent each time the output doubles, then the company that makes the most units stands to have the lowest marginal costs. The firm with the lowest marginal costs is likely to capture the largest share of the market. Such a firm is also apt to enjoy a high return on investment.

Appendix D
SOURCES OF INFORMATION ON COMPETITORS

1. Annual reports of competitors.
2. Forms 10-K of competitors.
3. *Business Periodicals Index.*
4. *Advertising Age* (Chicago, IL.: Crain Communications, Inc.).
5. *Standard and Poor's Stock Survey* (N.Y.: Standard and Poor's Corp.).
6. *Moody's Stock Survey* (N.Y.: Moody's Investors Service).
7. *Moody's Manuals* (N.Y.: Moody's Investors Service).
8. *The Value Line Investment Survey: Ratings and Reports* (N.Y.: Arnold Bernhard and Co., Inc.).
9. *Standard and Poor's Register of Corporations, Directors, and Executives* (N.Y.: Standard and Poor's Corp.).
10. *Dun and Bradstreet's Reference Book of Corporate Management* (N.Y.: Dun and Bradstreet).

11. *Dun's Business Rankings*, (N.J.: Dun's Marketing Services).
12. *Who Is Who in Finance and Industry* (Chicago, IL.: Marquis Who's Who, Inc.).
13. *International Marketing Handbook* (Detroit, Michigan: Gale Research Co.).
14. *World Directory of Multinational Enterprises* (Detroit, Michigan: Gale Research Co.).
15. *Who Owns Whom: North America* (N.Y.: Dun and Bradstreet).
16. *Directory of Corporate Affiliations* (Skokie, IL.: National Register Publishing Co., Inc.).
17. *Moody's International Manual* (N.Y.: Moody's Investors Service).

Appendix E
SOURCES OF INFORMATION ON LABOR AVAILABILITY

1. *Business Periodicals Index.*
2. *The Wall Street Journal Index.*
3. *Social Sciences Index.*
4. *Statistical Abstracts of the U.S.* (Washington, D.C.: Department of Commerce, Bureau of the Census).
5. *Census of Population* (Washington, D.C.: Department of Commerce, Bureau of the Census).
6. *Market Profile Analysis* (Chicago, IL.: Donnelly Marketing Information Services).
7. *Predicasts Basebook* (Cleveland, Ohio: Predicasts, Inc.).

Appendix F
SOURCES OF INFORMATION ON GOVERNMENT REGULATORS

1. *Business Periodicals Index.*
2. *The Wall Street Journal Index.*
3. *The New York Times Index.*
4. *Consumer Legislative Monthly Report* (Washington, D.C.: Department of Health and Human Services, Office of Consumer Affairs).
5. *Federal Register* (Washington, D.C.: Department of Commerce).
6. *Monitor: Environmental Marketing Handbook* (Detroit, Michigan: Gale Research Co.).
7. *International Marketing Handbook* (Detroit, Michigan: Gale Research Co.).
8. *Overseas Business Reports* (Washington, D.C.: Bureau of International Commerce).

Appendix G
SOURCES OF INFORMATION ON DEMOGRAPHICS

1. *Business Periodicals Index.*
2. *Social Sciences Index.*
3. *Statistical Abstracts of the U.S.* (Washington, D.C.: Department of Commerce, Bureau of the Census).
4. *Census of Population* (Washington, D.C.: Department of Commerce, Bureau of the Census).
5. *Market Profile Analysis* (Chicago, IL.: Donnelly Marketing Information Services).
6. *Predicasts Basebook* (Cleveland, Ohio: Predicasts, Inc.).
7. *Survey of Buying Power Forecaster's Handbook* (N.Y.: Sales and Marketing Management Magazine).
8. *Editor and Publisher Market Guide* (N.Y.: Editor and Publisher).
9. *Survey of Business Power Data Service* (N.Y.: Sales and Marketing Management Magazine).
10. *Marketing Economics Guide* (N.Y.: Marketing Economics Institute).
11. *European Marketing Data and Statistics* (London: Euromonitor Publications, Ltd.).

Appendix H
SOURCES OF INFORMATION ON CULTURE

1. *Business Periodicals Index.*
2. *Social Sciences Index.*
3. *Reader's Guide to Periodical Literature.*
4. *The Wall Street Journal Index.*
5. *The New York Times Index.*
6. *European Marketing Data and Statistics* (London: Euromonitor Publications, Ltd.).

Appendix I
SOURCES OF INFORMATION ON THE ECONOMY

1. *Business Periodicals Index.*
2. *The Wall Street Journal Index.*
3. *Business Conditions Digest* (Washington, D.C.: Department of Commerce, Bureau of Economic Analysis).

4. *Economic Report to the President* (Washington, D.C.: Government Printing Office).
5. *Survey of Current Business* (Washington, D.C.: Department of Commerce, Bureau of Economic Analysis).
6. *The Kiplinger Washington Letter* (Washington, D.C.: Kiplinger Washington Agency).
7. *Statistical Abstracts of the U.S.* (Washington, D.C.: Department of Commerce, Bureau of the Census).
8. *Foreign Economic Trends and Their Implications for the U.S.* (Washington D.C.: Bureau of International Economic Policy and Research).
9. *International Economic Indicators and Competitive Trends* (Washington, D.C.: Bureau of International Economic Policy and Research).
10. *Overseas Business Reports* (Washington, D.C.: Department of Commerce, Bureau of International Commerce).
11. *International Marketing Handbook* (Detroit, Michigan: Gale Research Co.).
12. *Handbook of Nations* (Detroit, Michigan: Gale Research Co.).

Appendix J
SOURCES OF INFORMATION ON POLITICS

1. *Business Periodicals Index.*
2. *Social Science Index.*
3. *Reader's Guide to Periodical Literature.*
4. *The Wall Street Journal Index.*
5. *The New York Times Index.*
6. *Overseas Business Reports* (Washington, D.C.: Department of Commerce, Bureau of International Commerce).
7. *Handbook of Nations* (Detroit, Michigan: Gale Research Co.).

Appendix K
SOURCES OF INFORMATION ON TECHNOLOGY

1. *Business Periodicals Index.*
2. *Social Science Index.*
3. *Reader's Guide to Periodical Literature.*
4. *The Wall Street Journal Index.*
5. *The New York Times Index.*
6. *Applied Science and Technology Index.*

Appendix L
SOURCES OF INFORMATION ON PRESSURE GROUPS

1. *Business Periodicals Index.*
2. *Social Sciences Index.*
3. *Reader's Guide to Periodical Literature.*
4. *The Wall Street Journal Index.*
5. *The New York Times Index.*

REVIEW QUESTIONS

1. If you were to analyze the task environment, what subcomponents would you focus on?

2. If you were to analyze the general environment, what subcomponents would you focus on?

3. Why is competition considered a subcomponent of the task environment while demographics is considered a subcomponent of the general environment?

4. What is meant by *factor*, and in what four ways can it affect a business concern?

5. Is the following statement true or false: "The descriptive phase constitutes the most critical phase of the analysis framework." Explain your answer.

Chapter 4

THE DIAGNOSTIC PHASE 1

The second phase of the strategic decision-making framework is the diagnostic phase. In Chapter 1, diagnosis was defined as the process of examining a particular piece of information or factor and passing judgment on its meaning. Diagnosis represents the conclusion we arrive at concerning the possible impact certain factors can have on the organization.

THE LINK BETWEEN DIAGNOSIS AND THE DESCRIPTIVE PHASE

Diagnosis does not take place in a vacuum. Rather, it is wholly dependent on the availability of information. With no information, diagnosis becomes impossible. Without accurate information, reliable diagnosis cannot be made.

You recall from our discussion in the preceding two chapters, the collection of adequate and accurate information about an organization falls within the province of the descriptive phase. It is in this phase that we seek to gather all the factors requisite for developing a thorough understanding of the organization's internal and external environmental conditions. If such factors prove insufficient or deficient, our diagnosis of the issues will most likely be flimsy and erroneous.

OBJECTIVE OF THE DIAGNOSTIC PHASE

As noted above, in the diagnostic phase we endeavor to determine the implications the gathered factors have for the organization. In a strategic management context, we typically articulate these implications in terms of four major labels. As displayed in Exhibit 4-1, the labels include strengths, weaknesses, opportunities, and threats.

Although the descriptive and diagnostic phases complement each other, they differ in their objectives. In the descriptive phase, the aim involves the collection of all key factors about the organization's internal and external environments. On the other hand, the objective of the diagnostic phase is to attach the labels strengths, weaknesses, opportunities, and threats to the gathered factors. It is important to point out that all the other dimensions of the diagnostic phase derive, to a greater or lesser degree, from these four principal labels.

Exhibit 4-1   **Objectives of the Descriptive Phase**
              and the Diagnostic Phase

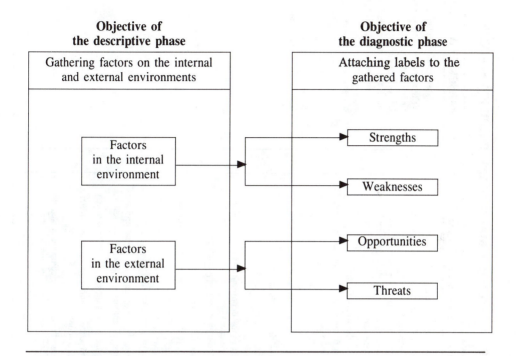

STEPS OF THE DIAGNOSTIC PROCESS

The diagnostic phase covers eight parts of the strategic decision-making framework. As can be seen in Exhibit 4-2, these are: (C) diagnose the strengths, (D) diagnose the weaknesses, (E) diagnose the opportunities, (F) diagnose the threats, (G) diagnose the major and subordinate problems, (H) determine the organization's strategic match, (I) determine the organization's primary strategic match position, and (J) diagnose the distinctive competency and the major weakness of key competitors. Each one of these parts represents an important step in the diagnostic process.

PART C: DIAGNOSING THE STRENGTHS

The first step in the diagnostic phase involves the identification of factors that constitute strengths. A strength is defined as any favorable factor in the organization's internal environment. It is a variable or condition that can either enhance the efficiency of the organization's internal operations or provide it with a competitive edge in the marketplace.

Exhibit 4-2   A FRAMEWORK FOR STRATEGIC DECISION MAKING AND PROBLEM SOLVING

THE DESCRIPTIVE PHASE

A. Provide a profile of the organization's internal environment

1. Profile the corporate/business level in terms of:
   a. strategic managers
   b. environmental analysis
   c. strategy formulation
   d. strategy implementation
   e. strategy control

2. Profile the functional level in terms of:
   a. marketing
   b. production
   c. research and development
   d. human resources
   e. public affairs
   f. finance/accounting

B. Provide a profile of the organization's external environment

1. Profile the task environment in terms of:
   a. industry
   b. competitors
   c. suppliers
   d. customers
   e. government regulators
   f. labor unions

2. Profile the general environment in terms of:
   a. demographics
   b. culture
   c. economy
   d. politics
   e. technology
   f. pressure groups

THE DIAGNOSTIC PHASE

C. Diagnose the strengths:
   1. Identify the strengths of the corporate/business level
   2. Identify the strengths of the functional level
   3. Identify the organization's distinctive competency

D. Diagnose the weaknessess:
   1. Identify the weaknesses of the corporate/business level
   2. Identify the weaknesses of the functional level
   3. Determine the key weakness

E. Diagnose the opportunities:
   1. Identify the opportunities in the task environment
   2. Identify the opportunities in the general environment
   3. Determine the key opportunity

F. Diagnose the threats:
   1. Identify the threats in the task environment
   2. Identify the threats in the general environment
   3. Determine the key threat

G. Diagnose the major and subordinate problems with their symptoms and probable causes

H. Determine the organization's strategic match

I. Determine the organization's primary strategic match position

J. Diagnose the distinctive competency and the major weakness of the key competitors

THE PRESCRIPTIVE PHASE

K. Formulate a strategic plan:
   1. Write a new mission statement for the organization
   2. Set corporate objectives
   3. Make the strategic choice by selecting the most effective grand strategy
   4. Select a competitive strategy
   5. Formulate functional objectives and strategies

L. Establish the conditions necessary to implement the strategic plan

Examples of a strength include a good balance of insiders and outsiders on the board of directors, a dynamic and resourceful chief executive, clearly stated objectives, a history of prudent choices of grand strategies, an organizational structure that meshes well with the firm's grand strategies, highly competent middle managers, competitive wages and salaries, efficient control system, large market share, full line of complementary products, high quality products, efficient customer service, innovative advertising, extensive distribution system, modern production facilities, large R&D budget, high rate of product innovation, low employee turnover, a good credit line, sustained profit performance, and so on.

Part C.1: Strengths of the Corporate/Business Level

To ensure that no significant strengths escape our attention and in order to impose some type of order on the process of diagnosing strengths, it is necessary to segment this process into three stages. We should: (1) identify the strengths of the corporate/business level, (2) identify the strengths of the functional level, and (3) determine the organization's distinctive competency.

We will first consider diagnosing the strengths of the corporate/business level. A highly effective way of identifying the strengths of this level involves the use of the outline shown in Exhibit 4-3. The exhibit displays the major components and subcomponents of the corporate/business level. As you recall, this outline was used in Chapter 2 as a tool for reporting factors. Now, we can utilize the same outline for presenting the strengths. Later, we will make good use of it when we endeavor to diagnose the weaknesses.

It is important to emphasize that, as is the case in reporting factors, strengths of the corporate/business level must be identified by the subcomponents rather than the major components. Thus, in diagnosing the strengths of the strategic managers, we should look for strengths in both the board of directors and top management instead of lumping all the strengths under one major component. In this way, we are more likely to accord equal attention to both of these critical subcomponents.

As shown in Exhibit 4-4, each subcomponent should be established as a separate heading followed by its own strengths.

N/A and N/I

If no strengths are observed in a particular subcomponent, the absence is indicated by the use of the letters N/A, meaning "not available." When you use N/A while looking for strengths, the abbreviation implies that the available information contains weaknesses but no strengths.

Exhibit 4-3 An Outline for Identifying Strengths of the Subcomponents of the Corporate/Business Level

---

Major Components	*Subcomponents*
Strategic managers:	Board of directors
	Top management
Environmental analysis:	Internal analysis
	External analysis
Strategy formulation:	Mission
	Corporate objectives
	Grand strategies
	Competitive strategies
Strategy implementation:	Organizational structure
	Policies
	Budgetary allocations
	Leadership
	Corporate culture
	Communication
	Motivation
Strategy control:	Establishment of standards
	Evaluation of performance
	Correction of deviations

When no information is given in the case on the subcomponent you are analyzing, use N/I. For example, if you are attempting to answer the questions in the checklist on the board of directors but are unable to because "no information" is given in the case on this subcomponent, indicate the lack of information with N/I. The abbreviation, N/I, then means no strengths or weaknesses can be found. For example:

Board of Directors: N/A
Top Management: N/I

The use of both N/A and N/I helps in generating a greater amount of class discussion, since the abbreviations call other students' attention to any missing strengths. They are also reflective of the thoroughness and accuracy of the analysis. The same benefits accrue in reports dealing with weaknesses, opportunities, and threats.

Chapter 8 contains an illustrative case analysis showing how to present the various dimensions of the diagnostic and prescriptive phases. Consult the chapter before conducting your own analysis.

Exhibit 4-4 An Illustration of the Format for Reporting Strengths of Strategic Managers

STRENGTHS OF THE STRATEGIC MANAGERS

The Board of Directors

1. Most members of the firm's board of directors are independent directors. This is a strength, because such members can critique the CEO's strategic decisions without fear of reprisal.

2. The board of directors is a forceful board, playing a catalyst, rather than a rubber stamp, role in running the firm. This is a strength, because the board can improve the quality of the strategy-making process.

3. Most of the directors possess extensive experience in the firm's industry.

Top Management

1. The CEO, the president, and the three vice presidents have a combined experience of 85 years in the industry.

2. The CEO's managerial mode is entrepreneurial. This is a strength, because it enables the organization to quickly capitalize on external opportunities.

3. The CEO's decision-making style is generally participative. He does not, however, hesitate to make unilateral decisions as the occasion demands.

Part C.2: Strengths of the Functional Level

The second stage in the strength-diagnosis process (Part C.2 of the analysis framework) consists of identifying the favorable conditions within the subcomponents of the functional level. Exhibit 4-5 provides an outline that serves as a useful tool for diagnosing the strengths of the subcomponents of marketing, production, R&D, human resources, public affairs, and finance/accounting.

Thus, in reporting the strengths of marketing it is well to set each of the subcomponents of products, marketing research, target market, sales volume, market share, pricing, distribution, and advertising and promotion as separate headings. Then relevant strengths are listed under each subcomponent. Once again, if no strengths can be found within a subcomponent or no information is given on the checklist of that subcomponent, indicate this fact with N/A for "not available." and N/I for "no information."

Part C.3: The Organization's Distinctive Competency

The effort to diagnose the organization's positive features at the corporate/business level and the functional level typically produces a long catalogue of strengths. This is particularly true in complex and comprehensive cases involving a large corporation.

Not all of these strengths, however, are equal in terms of their impact on the organization's performance. Most of them may be described as stabilizers. By stabilizer we mean any favorable internal condition that serves to maintain a state of steadiness or equilibrium within the organization. Stabilizers represent the minimal requirements that must be present before an organization can operate at an acceptable level of efficiency.

Other strengths, usually a few, represent distinctive competencies. A distinctive competency is a competitive strength. It is a key strength or a unique positive characteristic that sets the company apart from other firms in the same industry and provides it with a competitive edge. So, after identifying all the strengths of the corporate/business level and the functional level, we are required to isolate what we consider to be the organization's distinctive competency.

PART D: DIAGNOSING THE WEAKNESSES

A weakness refers to any negative or unfavorable factor in the organization's internal environment. It is a condition that can either strip the firm of the ability to achieve internal stability or imperil its very existence.

Exhibit 4-5 An Outline for Identifying Strengths of the Subcomponents of the Functional Level

Major Components	*Subcomponents*
Marketing:	Marketing research
	Target market
	Sales volume
	Market share
	Pricing
	Distribution
	Advertising and promotion
Production:	Location, newness, and layout of facilities
	Quality control
	Production capacity
	Inventory
Research and development:	Focus
	Posture
	Budget
Human resources:	Succession planning
	Recruitment and selection
	Training and development
	Performance appraisal
	Compensation
Public affairs:	Ethics
	Social responsibility
	Crisis management
Finance/accounting:	Management of cash
	Management of inventories
	Management of accounts receivable
	Management of total assets
	Management of debt
	Capital budgeting
	General profit picture

Examples of a weakness include a rubber-stamp board of directors, lethargic top management, lack of long and short-term objectives, an organizational structure that is out of sync with the company's grand strategies, poor communication between upper and lower-level managers, noncompetitive wages and salaries, declining market share, poor customer service, low quality products, inadequate advertising budget, ineffective R&D program, high employee turnover rate, and low return on investment.

The process of diagnosing weaknesses is similar to that of diagnosing strengths. That is, we need to: (1) identify the weaknesses of the corporate/business level, (2) identify the weaknesses of the functional level, and (3) determine the key weakness.

Part D.1: Weaknesses of the Corporate/Business Level

In diagnosing the weaknesses of the corporate/business level, we can utilize the outline presented previously in Exhibit 4-3. The outline lists the five major components of this level, namely, strategic managers, environmental analysis, strategy formulation, strategy implementation, and strategy control. Each one of these major components is broken down into subcomponents. Earlier, we used this outline in reporting strengths. Now, we can use the same outline to report the weaknesses of each of the subcomponents (see Exhibit 4-6).

Part D.2: Weaknesses of the Functional Level

After diagnosing the weaknesses of the corporate/business level, our next task involves the determination of the weaknesses of the functional level. To do that, we follow the same outline presented in Exhibit 4-5 which was used earlier in reporting strengths of the functional level. Each subcomponent should be established as a separate heading followed by its own weaknesses, if any (see Exhibit 4-7).

Part D.3: The Organization's Key Weakness

Having identified the weaknesses of both the corporate/business level and the functional level, we need now to determine the key weakness. The key weakness is a critical weakness. It is is an unfavorable internal condition which could place the firm at a competitive disadvantage, perhaps imperiling its very survival. From all the weaknesses that we have gathered about the firm, we are required to identify what we consider to be the most worrisome weakness. If no single weakness is truly critical, then we need to select the most serious of the identified weaknesses.

Exhibit 4-6   **An Outline for Identifying Weaknesses of the
Subcomponents of the Corporate/Business Level**

Major Components	*Subcomponents*
Strategic managers:	Board of directors Top management
Environmental analysis:	Internal analysis External analysis
Strategy formulation:	Mission Corporate objectives Grand strategies Competitive strategies
Strategy implementation:	Organizational structure Policies Budgetary allocations Leadership Corporate culture Communication Motivation
Strategy control:	Establishment of standards Evaluation of performance Correction of deviations

PART E: DIAGNOSING THE OPPORTUNITIES

In the descriptive phase, our library research as well as the textbook case itself have provided us with a substantial amount of information on the organization's external environment. In the diagnostic phase, we are required to carefully examine the gathered information with an eye toward diagnosing the organization's current and future opportunities and threats.

First, the opportunities. An opportunity is defined as any favorable factor in the external environment, which the organization can profitably exploit. Examples of an opportunity include a healthy industry growth rate, pending

Exhibit 4-7 An Outline for Identifying Weaknesses of the Subcomponents of the Functional Level

---

Major Components	*Subcomponents*
Marketing:	Marketing research
	Target market
	Sales volume
	Market share
	Pricing
	Distribution
	Advertising and promotion
Production:	Location, newness, and layout of facilities
	Quality control
	Production capacity
	Inventory
Research and development:	Focus
	Posture
	Budget
Human resources:	Succession planning
	Recruitment and selection
	Training and development
	Performance appraisal
	Compensation
Public affairs:	Ethics
	Social responsibility
	Crisis management
Finance/accounting:	Management of cash
	Management of inventories
	Management of accounts receivable
	Management of total assets
	Management of debt
	Capital budgeting
	General profit picture

shake-out that could drive smaller competitors out of the market, price war among the firm's suppliers, an increase in the size of the firm's customer base, relaxation in government regulations, lower inflation rates, declining interest rates, increase in consumer spending, improved political relations between the U.S. and a foreign country with a large market.

In diagnosing opportunities, we need to (1) identify the opportunities in the task environment, (2) identify the opportunities in the general environment, and (3) determine the key opportunity.

Parts E.1 and E.2: Opportunities in the Task and General Environments

The task and general environments refer to the forces that operate outside the organization. The task environment consists of such forces (or subcomponents) as industry, competitors, suppliers, customers, labor unions, and government regulators. Such conditions affect and are affected by the corporation. Thus, the influence between the organization and the task environmental forces tends to be reciprocal.

On the other hand, the general environment is composed of the following forces (or subcomponents): demographics, culture, economy, politics, technology, and pressure groups. Although the corporation is influenced by these forces, it tends to have little or no control on them. In this sense, the influence between the corporation and the general environmental forces largely flows in one direction.

A useful outline for diagnosing opportunities in the task and general environments is provided in Exhibit 4-8. The exhibit shows the two major components of the external environment, namely, the task and the general environments. Each one of these major components is divided into subcomponents.

In reporting opportunities of the task environment, we should list them under the subcomponents (i.e. industry, competitors, etc.,) rather than the major component. Similarly, opportunities of the general environment can be listed under each of the subcomponents (i.e., demographics, culture, etc.,). If no opportunities are found within a subcomponent or no information can be gathered on it, N/A (not available) and N/I (no information) should be used.

Part E.3: The Organization's Key Opportunity

Having compiled a list of the current and future opportunities in both the task and the general environments, we then attempt to determine the key opportunity. By key opportunity, we mean the most favorable external condition which the enterprise can exploit either through the use of its current strengths or by developing the requisite strengths.

Exhibit 4-8 **An Outline for Identifying Opportunities of the
Subcomponents of the Task and General Environments**

Major Components   *Subcomponents*

Task Environment: Industry
                                      Competitors
                                      Suppliers
                                      Customers
                                      Labor unions
                                      Government regulators

General Environment: Demographics
                                      Culture
                                      Economy
                                      Politics
                                      Technology
                                      Pressure groups

It is important to bear in mind that the earlier such an opportunity is spotted the greater the lead time the company will have in preparing itself to put the opportunity to full advantage. Companies that wait until an anticipated opportunity becomes an actual reality often find themselves at a competitive disadvantage. For one thing, they are unable to marshall their resources fast enough to make the most of the favorable condition. For another, by the time they make their move the market usually becomes too crowded with competitors, all clamoring for a larger piece of the pie. So, the old adage, "the early bird gets the worm," aptly describes a firm that spots an opportunity early enough to establish a comfortable lead in an uncrowded market.

PART F: DIAGNOSING THREATS

A threat is an unfavorable factor in the external environment, which can have a detrimental effect on the organization's strategic posture.

Examples of a threat include stagnant industry growth, the entry of a powerful competitor in the market, a decline in the number of suppliers, shrinkage in the size of the firm's target market, increased government regulations, high inflation rates, high interest rates, drop in consumer spending, unstable political climate, unfavorable cultural trends, technological breakthroughs that could make obsolete the company's products, and so on.

The process of diagnosing threats is identical to that involved in diagnosing opportunities. We need to (1) identify threats in the task environment, (2) identify threats in the general environment, and (3) determine the key threat.

Parts F.1 and F.2: Threats in the Task and General Environments

The outline presented earlier in Exhibit 4-8 serves as a useful tool for reporting threats in both the task and general environments. The observed threats in the task environment can be listed under each of the subcomponents of industry, competitors, suppliers, customers, and government regulators. Likewise, the observed threats in the general environment can be reported under the subcomponents of demographics, culture, economy, politics, technology, and pressure groups (see Exhibit 4-9).

Exhibit 4-9 **An Outline for Identifying Threats of the Subcomponents of the Task and General Environments**

Major Components	*Subcomponents*
Task Environment:	Industry
	Competitors
	Suppliers
	Customers
	Labor unions
	Government regulators
General Environment:	Demographics
	Culture
	Economy
	Politics
	Technology
	Pressure groups

Part F.3: The Organization's Key Threat

A key threat refers to any unfavorable factor in the external environment that can actually or potentially inflict the most damage on the organization. In this context, a key threat may also be viewed as a "sinker" in that it could conceivably cause the corporate ship to sink.

It is important to observe that when analyzing a case involving a successful corporation, we might not be able to spot any threat that constitutes a sinker or that can pose a mortal danger to the organization. In this situation, our task is to examine all the diagnosed threats and select the one we consider to be the most serious. Such a threat, even though it is not truly critical, would be our key threat.

Observations on Strengths, Weaknesses, Opportunities and Threats

Before concluding this segment of our discussion, it is worth emphasizing that two factors ought to be considered in determining if a particular environmental condition is a strength, weakness, opportunity, or threat. As displayed in Exhibit 4-10, the first is the favorableness of the observed condition, and the second is the type of environment where the condition lies.

Exhibit 4-10 **Factors that Determine Whether an Environmental Condition is Classified as a Strength, Weakness, Opportunity, or Threat**

Favorableness of Condition	Type of Environment	
	Internal Environment	External Environment
Favorable condition	Strength	Opportunity
Unfavorable condition	Weakness	Threat

If an observed condition is judged to be favorable to the organization, it can be either a strength or an opportunity. If it is located within the internal environment, it is a strength. But if it lies in the external environment, it is an opportunity. On the other hand, if an observed condition is judged to be unfavorable to the organization, it can be either a weakness or a threat. If the condition is internal, it is a weakness; if it is external, it is a threat.

PART G: DIAGNOSING THE MAJOR AND SUBORDINATE PROBLEMS WITH THEIR SYMPTOMS AND PROBABLE CAUSES

Part G of the diagnostic phase involves the determination of the organization's major and subordinate problems with their symptoms and probable causes. This section deals exclusively with the problem-solving process. As might be inferred from this part, the problem-solving process consists of three major elements. These are symptom, cause, and problem. This means that once a symptom is spotted, the strategist's task involves a vigorous search for the cause or causes. And once a logical linkage is established between the symptom and its causes, an identification of the problem or problems becomes possible.

Before we delve into the problem-solving process, let us first endeavor to shed some light on the meaning of its three elements - symptom, cause, and problem.

The Meaning of Symptom

In many organizational settings, the problem-solving process is initiated as a result of the emergence of a symptom. And this is the type of situation with which our discussion will be solely concerned.

A symptom is an indicator of the presence of a gap between the desired and actual conditions. It is a sign of the existence of a problem. A symptom may be viewed as a red flag or a warning light signalling that not all is well with the organization. It is the smoke that announces the existence of fire. Examples of a symptom include power struggle among top management, high production costs, low inventory turnover ratio, large accounts receivable, high rate of returned merchandise, backlog of unfilled orders, shrinking market share, declining sales volume, high employee turnover rate, high frequency of equipment breakdowns, low current ratio, coughing and sneezing, chest pain, dizziness, and headache.

The Meaning of Cause

Once a symptom is spotted, the strategist embarks on an effort to identify its underlying cause or causes.

A cause refers to the condition or force that lies at the root of the observed gap between the expected and the prevailing conditions. It is the trigger that gives rise to the symptom. A cause is the fire that produces the smoke. In Exhibit 4-11, you see an illustration of some symptoms with their probable causes.

The Differences Between Symptoms and Causes

In a strategic management context, symptoms and causes may be distinguished in three major ways:

1. From an organization's standpoint, a symptom is an internal weakness. It is an internal negative factor. A cause, however, may be either a weakness (an internal negative factor) or a threat (an external negative factor). For example, a low profit-margin ratio constitutes a symptom or an internal weakness. This symptom may be caused by poor-quality products (an internal weakness) or by aggressive competition (an external threat) or by both.

2. In general, a symptom is readily observable. Except in certain medical situations, a symptom usually makes itself known to us. We do not have to search for it. It can either be seen, heard, felt, smelled, or tasted. A cause, however, is typically hidden from view. It lurks below the surface and must, therefore, be dug up; hence the expression "the root cause" of a problem.

To illustrate, we do not need to search for evidence that we suffer from a general feeling of fatigue. If we have it, we know it. However, determining the exact cause of the fatigue is an entirely different matter. It might require the specialized skills and tools of an expert physician before the precise cause is unmasked. Similarly, in a business setting we need not carry out an extensive investigation to determine if profits are down or if employee turnover is high. These conditions can be readily and easily observed. But their causes might require considerable time, effort, and expense before they are pinpointed.

The fact that symptoms are usually easily determined but causes are not, explains why, in the preceding discussion, we often prefaced the word "causes" with the adjective "probable." During the diagnostic process, we are not absolutely confident that the causes we have identified are the actual root causes of the symptom. Such causes represent only our best judgement that they are the most likely triggers of the observed weakness. We can only be sure that they are the actual causes when the symptom vanishes after we have effectively attacked its perceived causes.

3. A symptom is a dependent variable or an effect. A cause, on the other hand, is an independent variable. In its existence, a symptom depends on the occurrence of another event or on a cause which acts as a trigger. In this context, a symptom receives its nourishment and support from the cause. By contrast, a cause is independent of the symptom. In its existence, it is not

conditioned by the presence of a symptom. Consequently, any remedial action that focuses on the symptom but ignores its cause represents a wholly futile effort as the symptom will resurface.

Exhibit 4-11 **An Illustration of Symptoms and Their Probable Causes**

Symptoms	*Probable Causes*
Power struggle among top executives	Differences in the decision-making style of the executives
Costly mistakes by lower-level managers	Poor recruitment and selection practices
Declining market share	Inadequate advertising budget
High frequency of equipment break-downs	Outmoded production facilities
Large accounts receivable	Lax collection policy
Chest pain	Blocked arteries
Itchy and watery eyes and nose	Exposure to pollen

Intermediate Factor

The effort to diagnose symptoms and causes does not always lead to a simple linkage between a symptom and a cause. On the contrary, there could be many levels of causes that spawn a particular symptom. So what appears at first glance as a cause might, after careful scrutiny, turn out to be a symptom of another cause which in turn might be symptomatic of still a deeper cause.

This type of situation involves what may be called an intermediate factor. Hence, an intermediate factor can be defined as any unfavorable factor that acts as a symptom and a cause at the same time.

Intermediate Factors and the Cause-Tracking Question

Let us illustrate the concept of an intermediate factor with an example. Assume that one of the symptoms we have observed while reading a case or analyzing an actual business organization is that the production manager (PM) is overburdened with work. Common sense and our educational background tell us that such a condition is unhealthy. It is a negative internal factor or a weakness that is symptomatic of another negative factor. Since a symptom is a signal of something else and is dependent for its existence on another factor, we set out to unearth the cause.

Let us assume that after reading the case further or after questioning the production manager, we conclude that the symptom is caused by the "PM's failure to delegate authority." Such a cause, as Exhibit 4-12 portrays, may be considered an intermediate factor. It is a cause of the "PM's work overload," but it must also be a symptom of some underlying cause. For one might legitimately ask: Why doesn't the PM delegate authority?

Thus, if the cause we have identified is merely an intermediate factor, we are then better advised to continue the investigation until we can unveil the root cause. To do that, we need to ask a vitally critical cause-tracking question which is: *What caused the cause?*

Exhibit 4-12 **A One-Level Intermediate Factor**

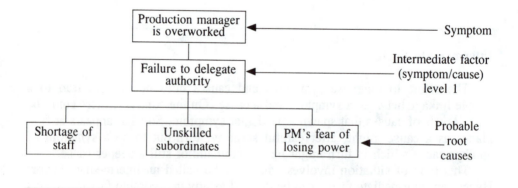

A One-Level Intermediate Factor

Let us apply the cause-tracking question to the previous example and ask: What caused the cause? That is, what caused the production manager's failure to delegate? By simply raising this question, we are forced to look for the specific reasons underlying the PM's inability to delegate. These reasons may include (1) shortage of staff, (2) unskilled subordinates, and (3) the PM's fear of losing power.

Consequently, and as displayed in Exhibit 4-12, our initial cause, the PM's failure to delegate, is not the bottom cause. Rather, it is a symptom of one, or a combination, of three probable underlying causes. That makes it an intermediate factor. It is both a symptom and a cause. It is a symptom of one of the three suspected causes, and it is a cause of the PM's heavy work load.

A Two-Level Intermediate Factor

You might have already suspected that each of the three probable causes of the PM's failure to delegate may themselves be viewed as intermediate factors. By asking the cause-tracking question, what caused the cause?, we might be able to nail down the specific reasons behind the shortage of staff, the unskilled subordinates, and the PM's fear of losing power.

The shortage of staff, for instance, may be attributed to a small staff budget, the unskilled subordinates to a lack of training, and the PM's fear of losing power to a sense of insecurity. In such a case, the causes that we considered earlier as probable root causes now become intermediate factors. If we stop our diagnosis at this point, and as shown in Exhibit 4-13, we will end up with two levels of intermediate factors separating the symptom from the probable root causes.

Limits of the Cause-Tracking Question

To what extent should we keep asking: what caused the cause? That is, how far down should we go in our effort to trace the probable root cause? As far as we are satisfied that:

1. The cause of the symptom is narrow and specific enough to permit the formulation of concrete and well-focused recommendations.

2. Any further search for another cause may be impractical or fruitless.

To illustrate the second point, consider the probable root cause of the production manager's fear of losing power which is insecurity. It certainly would be an interesting exercise in psychoanalysis to strive to ferret out the causes of the PM's insecurity. It is doubtless, however, that such an exercise will significantly improve our chances of devising the most practical solution, especially if the root cause lies deep in the manager's early childhood. In a case such as this, it would be prudent to halt the diagnostic effort and simply aim at tackling insecurity as the lowest or narrowest probable root cause.

Exhibit 4-13 **A Two-Level Intermediate Factor**

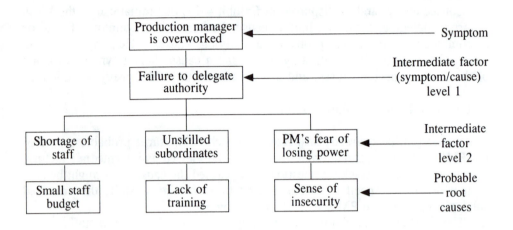

The Root Cause and the Prescriptive Phase

Our ability to trace a symptom to its most likely root cause is critical to the effectiveness of the next phase of the analysis framework, namely, the prescriptive phase. If we fail to get at the most probable root cause, our recommendations will miss their mark and will most likely be fruitless.

Take our earlier example involving the production manager who is overburdened with work. If we halt our diagnostic efforts with "failure to delegate" as the root cause, our solution will be off base and unrealistic. It is akin to taking a shot in the dark. That is because we have not bothered to find out why the PM does not delegate. We simply made an assumption that he (or she) does not like to delegate, an assumption that could be totally false. In which case, our recommendation to force the PM to delegate or provide him with the incentive to do so will seem utterly ridiculous to the PM who might not have enough staff to whom to delegate.

As we saw earlier, by asking the cause-tracking question, what caused the cause?, we can trace the symptom back to the narrowest possible cause. In our illustration shown in Exhibit 4-13, the symptom, "the PM is overworked," can be attributed to one, or a combination, of three probable causes: (1) small staff budget, (2) lack of subordinates' training, and (3) the PM's sense of insecurity. Notice how narrow these causes are when compared with our initial cause "failure to delegate authority." This type of specificity and narrowness can greatly enhance the quality and soundness of our recommendations.

In Exhibit 4-14, you see how our recommendations can vary with different types of causes. In one instance, we might recommend increasing the staff budget. In a second instance, we might suggest providing training to the subordinates to equip them with the skills that enable them to handle increased responsibilities. And in a third instance, we might suggest providing training to the manager himself to educate him in the benefits he can reap by sharing his authority with the subordinates.

In short, our recommendations can only be as good as our ability to nail down the narrowest and most specific cause.

Exhibit 4-14 **The Narrower the Causes Are, the More Focused the Recommendations Can Be**

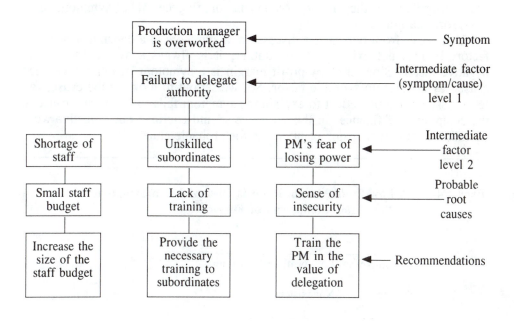

The Percolation Effect

Every organization is a system. That is, it is a dynamic organism consisting of interdependent parts each of which affects and is affected by the other parts. In this sense, a change in one organizational unit may set off a chain reaction of events that could ripple through the other units of the organization.

This phenomenon can be termed the percolation effect. It means that the continued existence of a weakness in one organizational unit can, if left unchecked, percolate and eventually seep into other units. Put differently, when a negative factor goes unnoticed and uncorrected in one component, its effects can bubble up to spill over into other components at the same level or at a higher or lower level in the organization.

The Percolation Effect and Intermediate Factors

The percolation effect described above is closely tied to the concept of intermediate factor. The linkage between the two can best be illustrated by offering the following sequence of observations:

1. A symptom is observed: low-profit margin
Consider the example given in Exhibit 4-15. You notice that a symptom has been identified in the major component of finance. The symptom is a low-profit-margin ratio.

You recall from our earlier discussion, a symptom is a dependent negative factor. It does not exist by itself. Rather, it is always spawned by another negative factor. Since the low-profit margin is a symptom, it must have been caused by another unfavorable factor. So, we set out to look for the cause. But let us assume that our effort to explain the symptom fails to locate any cause in the component of finance. In this case, we should continue our detective work by looking into other major components for probable clues.

Exhibit 4-15   **A Low-Profit-Margin Ratio Is Observed as a Symptom in the Major Component of Finance**

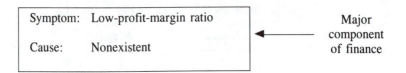

---

2. *A probable cause of the low-profit margin is identified: declining market share*

Assume that our search for the probable cause of the low-profit margin, and as shown in Exhibit 4-16, leads us to another unfavorable factor, namely, declining market share which belongs to the major component of marketing.

We are now in a position to establish a probable causal relationship between the two negative factors or weaknesses. That is, the low-profit margin (in the area of finance) is a symptom brought on by declining market share (in the area of marketing). If such a linkage appears reasonable to us, then all we have to do to eliminate the symptom is to successfully attack its cause.

You recall from our earlier discussion, however, that a cause such as declining market share is simply too broad to be tackled effectively. We need to narrow it down. We must expose the specific reason behind the decline in market share so as to formulate a more focused strategic plan. To do that, we should invoke our cause-tracking question, namely, what caused the cause? Or, what caused the decline in market share?

Let us assume once again that our investigative efforts fail to turn up any cause within the major component of marketing. In which case, we need to relaunch our diagnostic search in the hope of pinpointing the exact cause of the drop in market share which now appears to us more like a symptom than a cause.

Exhibit 4-16   **Declining Market Share Is a Probable Cause of the Low-Profit-Margin Ratio**

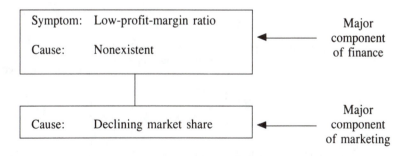

3. A probable cause for the market-share decline is identified: a high rate of returned merchandise

Our search for the root cause of the decline in market share might uncover another weakness that acts as a trigger to the symptom. The weakness could be a high rate of returned merchandise. As depicted in Exhibit 4-17, this weakness falls within the major component of production.

Once again, we could see a probable causal relationship between the three weaknesses we have been able to observe thus far. A low-profit-margin ratio (finance) is caused by declining market share (marketing) which is caused by a high rate of returned merchandise (production). This type of diagnostic reasoning makes the market-share decline an intermediate factor. It is both a cause and a symptom. It is a cause of the low-profit-margin ratio and a symptom of the high rate of returned merchandise.

But what caused the high rate of returned merchandise? If we are to be able to devise a sound strategic plan to reverse this trend, we need to determine why our customers are returning their merchandise. This prompts us to resume the diagnostic search for the root cause.

Exhibit 4-17   **A High Rate of Returned Merchandise Is a Cause of the Market-Share Decline**

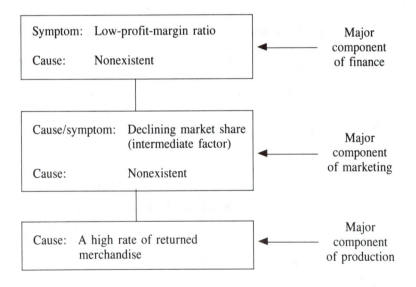

*4. A probable cause for the high rate of returned merchandise is identified:
    poor quality control standards*

Let us assume that by continuing our investigative work, we succeed in identifying poor quality control standards as the cause of the high rate of returned merchandise. This cause, as you can see in Exhibit 4-18, also falls within the major component of production. In which case, the high return of merchandise becomes another intermediate factor. It is a symptom of poor quality standards and a cause of the decline in market share.

Exhibit 4-18   **Poor Quality Control Standards Is a Probable Root
Cause of the Low-Profit-Margin Ratio**

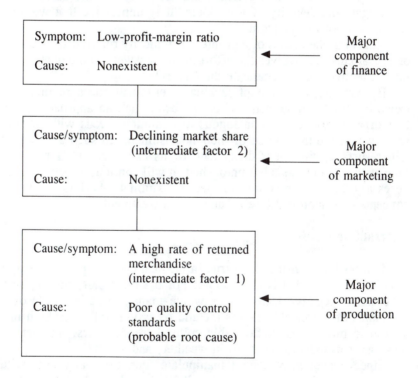

Poor Quality Control Standards and the Percolation Effect

It is clear from the above diagnostic chain that although our first observed symptom, low-profit margin, appeared in the major component of finance, its root cause was traced back to the area of production.

Since the root cause, poor quality control standards, was not tackled early enough, it began to percolate, giving rise to another weakness, namely, a high rate of returned merchandise. Because this weakness was not nipped in the bud, it, in turn, bubbled up, spawning a drop in the firm's market share. Due to management's failure to take a prompt action, the decline in market share eventually led to a low-profit margin ratio.

Put differently, the finance problem was caused by a marketing problem which, in turn, was caused by a production problem. In order to alleviate the finance problem, we must remove the marketing problem. To do that, we must focus our strategic plan on the causes which lie within the production area. These causes acted as a trigger to the higher-level symptoms.

Causal Treatment and Symptomatic Relief

It should be abundantly clear from the preceding discussion that to remove or mitigate the severity of a problem, it is imperative that we attack its root causes and not its symptoms.

Attacking the causes of a problem is typically referred to as causal treatment or causal cure. It involves the effort to find answers to the question: What is the most effective way to eradicate the causes?

By contrast, any attempt seeking to eliminate the symptom instead of the cause is called symptomatic relief. At best, such an approach provides only a temporary reprieve. It is analogous to trimming weeds without pulling up the roots which are the source of their nourishment. In such a case, the symptom will resurface, since it is dependent for its existence on its root cause. So, as long the root cause is left untouched, it will continue to provide the conditions necessary for the symptom to reemerge. Exhibit 4-19 offers an illustration of the concepts of symptomatic relief and causal treatment.

Untreatable Causes

In a business setting, as is true in medical cases, a problem may at times be traced to a cause that is untreatable. For the most part, such causes are apt to be external negative factors over which management has little or no control. Examples of untreatable causes include recession, inflation, high interest rates, a drop in birth rates, unfavorable cultural trends, wars, international political tensions, earthquakes, changes in weather, and so on.

Since management cannot manipulate such external causes with the same ease it can the internal causes, it will have to do its best to adapt to them. It must adjust its operations in such a way so as to be able to cope with the unfavorable changes in the most effective fashion.

The Meaning of Problem

Thus far in our discussion of the problem-solving process, we have explored the meaning of only two elements of the process, namely, symptom and cause.

Exhibit 4-19   **An Illustration of the Concepts of Symptomatic Relief and Causal Treatment**

Symptom	Cause	Symptomatic relief	Causal treatment
Low sales volume	Poor product design	Lower the prices	Beef up R&D budget and personnel
Conflict between two subordinates	Lack of clear lines of authority and responsibility	Transfer one subordinate to another area and replace him with a new subordinate	Draw up a clear list of job descriptions
Domestic firms are getting hurt by imported products	High quality of imports	Impose quotas on imports	Improve quality of domestic products
High employee turnover	Poor supervisory treatment	Provide employees with a wage increase	Provide leadership to supervisors
Federal budget deficit	Large government spending	Borrow money to cover expenses	Trim government spending, raise taxes
Declining market share	Unmotivated sales force	Hire more sales people	Set up an effective compensation policy
Depression	Loss of job	Use tranquilizers	Vigorously search for a new job
Being overweight	Overeating	Undergo a liposuction operation	Diet and exercise
Coughing and sneezing	Cold virus	Take antihistamine drugs	Rest and drink a lot of fluids

Now, we will attempt to clarify the meaning of the third element - problem.

The Random House College Dictionary defines a problem as "any question or matter involving doubt, uncertainty, or difficulty." In the minds of many people, a problem is a difficulty or a question for which there is, at the moment, no solution or no answer.

For our purposes, we will define a problem as a gap between the actual conditions and the desired conditions. It is a discrepancy between what exists and should exist. When a discrepancy is perceived between what is desired and what is attained, the strategist's task entails an effort to narrow the gap or eliminate it altogether.

The Difference Between Major and Subordinate Problems

A major problem is the most critical gap. It is the most worrisome of all the observed discrepancies between the desired and actual conditions and the one that demands the analyst's immediate attention. If the analyst diagnoses five gaps in an organization, the major problem represents the gap which causes him (or her) the most concern as it is likely to inflict the most harm on the organization.

A subordinate problem, on the other hand, represents a minor gap. It is less critical than the major problem in terms of its negative impact on the organization. Although a subordinate problem may not require the analyst's immediate attention, it should not be ignored. On the contrary, a watchful eye must be kept on the subordinate problem, for if it is not addressed at the appropriate time it could very well evolve into a major problem. Bear in mind that what is seen as a major problem at the moment was, at a certain point in the past, nothing more than a minor discrepancy that either went undetected or untackled.

Major vs. Subordinate Problems: An Illustration

To understand the difference between a major problem and a subordinate problem, consider the following example. Assume that you suddenly begin to experience a toothache. So you decide to see a dentist after several years of procrastination.

The dentist takes an X-ray of your teeth and discovers four cavities which he (or she) ascribes to tooth decay. Since the dentist, for obvious reasons, cannot treat all the four cavities (problems) in the same visit, he prioritizes them in terms of their severity. Then, he decides to tackle one problem at a time, starting with the major problem which to him is the tooth that is causing you the pain.

The other cavities are considered subordinate problems. Although treatment of the subordinate cavities may be postponed for a while, it cannot be neglected indefinitely. For if the minor cavities are not dealt with in time, they are certain to develop into major problems. And the longer you wait in taking the necessary action, the more expensive and the more painful the treatment will be.

Statement of the Problem

In a strategic management setting, it is useful to state a problem in terms of the major components of the internal environment. As you recall from our previous discussion, the major components of the internal environment are:

Strategic managers	*Production*
Environmental analysis	*Research and development*
Strategy formulation	*Human resources*
Strategy implementation	*Public affairs*
Strategy control	*Finance/accounting*
Marketing	

Thus, a problem can be stated as follows:

The problem is:	The strategic managers
The problem is:	Strategy formulation
Or the problem is:	Marketing

When we say that the problem is the strategic managers, strategy formulation, or marketing we are in effect saying that the conditions which exist within each of these major components are not what we desire them to be. There is a gap between what should exist and what actually exists. So, in order to eliminate the problem or bridge the gap, we might have to (1) alter the conditions in such a way so that the actual conditions are transformed into desired conditions, or (2) take the actions necessary to minimize or deflect the damaging impact of the unalterable conditions.

Benefits of Stating Problems in Terms of Major Components

There are two principal benefits for articulating a problem in terms of the major components of the internal environment.

1. The approach helps in setting a clear distinction between a problem, a symptom, and a cause.

To illustrate, let us assume that two of the factors observed in the organization under analysis are: (1) the firm's market share has declined by eight percent within the past two years, and (2) the firm's advertising budget is inadequate. Now, is the declining market share a problem or a symptom of a problem? If it is a problem, what is its symptom? If it is a symptom and the inadequate advertising budget is the problem, what caused the problem? If the inadequate advertising budget is a cause and the declining market share is the symptom, then what is the problem?

As you can see, things can get pretty confusing. By expressing the problem in terms of a major component and using the negative factors as symptoms and causes only, we should be able to minimize the confusion. In our illustration, the problem with its symptom and cause can be stated as follows:

The problem: Marketing
Symptom: Declining market share
Cause: Inadequate advertising

Additional examples of how a problem with its symptom and cause is stated can be found in Exhibit 4-20.

2. The second benefit to be derived from stating a problem in terms of the major component is that the approach serves as an effective means of pinpointing the organizational area where a remedial action should be undertaken. Thus, stating that the problem is marketing tells us which individuals might have contributed to the problem and which individuals ought to be in charge of tackling it.

Exhibit 4-20   **An Illustration of Stating a Problem with Its Symptom and Cause**

Problem	Symptom	Probable Cause
1. Strategic Managers	Power struggle among top executives	Differences in the decision-making style of executives
2. Human resources	Costly mistakes by lower-level managers	Poor recruitment and selection practices
3. Marketing	Declining market share	Inadequate advertising budget
4. Production	High frequency of equipment breakdowns	Outmoded production facilities
5. Finance	Large accounts receivable	Lax collection policy
6. Heart disease	Chest pain	Blocked arteries
7. Hay fever	Itchy and watery eyes and nose	Exposure to pollen

The Process of Diagnosing Major and Subordinate Problems

The process of diagnosing major and subordinate problems is comprised of six steps. We will first present the steps and then illustrate each with an example. The steps are:
1. List the unfavorable factors (weaknesses and threats) by the   major components of the internal and external environments.
2. Identify the symptoms.
3. Specify the major symptom and the minor symptoms.
4. Determine the probable causes of each symptom.
5. Diagnose the major problem with its symptom and probable causes.
6. Diagnose the subordinate (minor) problems with their symptoms and probable causes.

Listing Unfavorable Factors

The first step in diagnosing the major and subordinate problems involves taking a look at the information collected in the descriptive phase. From this information, we compile a list of all the unfavorable factors in the case. The negative factors could be internal weaknesses or external threats. These factors should then be classified by the major components (i.e., strategic managers, strategy formulation, production, task environment, etc.) to which they belong.

Let us assume that after carefully examining the factors reported in the descriptive phase, we are able to compile the list of weaknesses and threats displayed in Exhibit 4-21.

Identifying the Symptoms

Having prepared an inventory of the unfavorable factors by major components, we move to the next step which involves identifying those negative factors that constitute symptoms. A symptom, as was noted earlier, is an internal weakness. It is a dependent factor or an effect brought on by another unfavorable factor.

By examining the list of negative factors shown in Exhibit 4-21, we are able to spot the following symptoms:
1. The firm's failure to exploit external opportunities.
2. Directionless top management.
3. Top management is not fully aware of the performance of branch offices.
4. Middle and lower-level managers are not informed of the firm's strategies.
5. A 4% decline in the firm's return on equity.
6. A high collection period ratio.

Exhibit 4-21   The First Step in Diagnosing the Major and Subordinate Problems Is to Compile a List of the Unfavorable Factors by Major Components

---

Strategic Managers
1   Directionless top management.
2. Top management is not fully aware of the performance of branch offices.

Environmental Analysis
1. The firm's failure to exploit external opportunities.
2. Lack of efficient external scanning mechanism.

Strategy Formulation
1. Lack of a coherent mission statement.
2. Lack of specific objectives.

Strategy Implementation
1. Middle and lower-level managers are not informed of the firm's strategies.
2. Lack of adequate downward communication.

Strategy Control
1. Branch managers do not provide top management with regular performance reports.
2. Lack of specific performance standards for branch offices.

Marketing
1. A 10% cut in the advertising budget.

Finance
1. A 4% decline in the firm's return on equity.
2. A high collection period ratio.
3. Inefficient collection practices.

Task environment
1. Entry into the market of an aggressive competitor.

General Environment
1. A 7% drop in consumer spending.

Specifying the Major Symptom and Minor Symptoms

After identifying the symptoms in the case, we need to determine which symptom is major and which symptoms are minor.

A major symptom represents the most worrisome dependent weakness. It is the negative internal effect that demands immediate attention. By contrast, a minor symptom is less troubling. Its treatment may be put off for a little while but cannot be indefinitely neglected. As was observed in our discussion of the major and subordinate problems, a minor symptom today may, if left untreated, develop into a critical symptom tomorrow.

In our illustration, an examination of the six symptoms listed earlier reveals the following major symptom and minor symptoms, with the minor symptoms arrayed in terms of their relative seriousness:

Major symptom: A 4% decline in the firm's return on equity.
Minor symptom 1: Directionless top management.
Minor symptom 2: Top management is not fully aware of the performance of branch offices.
Minor symptom 3: The firm's failure to exploit external opportunities.
Minor symptom 4: Middle and lower-level managers are not informed of the firm's strategies.
Minor symptom 5: A high collection period ratio.

It is worth noting that the determination of major and minor symptoms is not always easy. Analysts, due to their divergent value systems and priorities, often disagree on what constitutes a critical symptom or the most troubling weakness. So do not be surprised if what you view as a major symptom is perceived only as a subordinate weakness by another analyst. Be prepared, however, to use logical reasoning and cogent arguments to back up your position.

Determining the Probable Causes

The third step in diagnosing the major and subordinate problems involves the determination of the probable causes of each symptom. In Exhibit 4-22, you see a list of the causes that might have been responsible for each of the observed symptoms. These causes are extracted from the unfavorable factors presented earlier in Exhibit 4-21.

Exhibit 4-22 **Probable Causes of the Observed Symptoms**

Major symptom: A 4% decline in the firm's return on equity (finance/accounting)
Causes: (1) A 10% cut in the advertising budget (marketing)
                  (2) Entry into the market of an aggressive competitor (task environment)
                  (3) A 7% drop in consumer spending (general environment)

Minor symptom 1: Directionless top management (strategic managers)
Causes: (1) Lack of a coherent mission statement (strategy formulation)
                  (2) Lack of specific objectives (strategy formulation)

Minor symptom 2: Top management is not fully aware of the performance of branch offices (strategic managers)
Causes: (1) Branch managers do not provide top management with regular performance reports (strategy control)
                  (2) Lack of specific performance standards for branch offices (strategy control)

Minor symptom 3: The firm's failure to exploit external opportunities (environmental analysis)
Cause: (1) Lack of efficient external scanning mechanism (environmental analysis)

Minor symptom 4: Middle and lower-level managers are not informed of the firm's strategies (strategy implementation)
Cause: (1) Lack of adequate downward communication (strategy implementation)

Minor symptom 5: A high collection period ratio (finance/accounting)
Cause: (1) Inefficient collection practices (finance/accounting)

Diagnosing the Major Problem

A major problem refers to the component where the major, or the most critical, symptom lies.

In our illustration, the major symptom is diagnosed as "A 4% decline in the firm's return on equity." Since this symptom falls within the component of "finance/accounting," then "finance/accounting" is viewed as the major problem.

There are three probable causes for this problem. One, "A 10% cut in the advertising budget," lies in the area of marketing. The second, "Entry into the market of an aggressive competitor," is located in the task environment. And the third, "A 7% drop in consumer spending," is traceable to the general environment.

As a result, our diagnosis of the major problem can be presented as follows:

Major Problem: Finance/accounting
Symptom: A 4% decline in the firm's return on equity (finance/accounting)
Causes: (1) A 10% cut in the advertising budget (marketing)
                  (2) Entry into the market of an aggressive competitor (task environment)
                  (3) A 7% drop in consumer spending (general environment)

Diagnosing Subordinate Problems

A subordinate problem refers to the component where a minor symptom exists.

In our illustration, five minor symptoms are identified. These are: "Directionless top management," "Top management is not fully aware of the performance of branch offices," "The firm's failure to exploit external opportunities," "Middle and lower-level managers are not informed of the firm's strategies," and "A high collection period ratio."

The components where these minor symptoms lie are considered subordinate problems. For example, the first minor symptom, "Directionless top management," is observed in the component of "strategic managers." Hence, "strategic managers" is treated as a subordinate problem. The same approach can be used in stating the other subordinate problems.

In Exhibit 4-23, you see a format for presenting the results of the process of diagnosing the major and subordinate problems.

Exhibit 4-23   **A Format for Presenting the Results of the Process of Diagnosing the Major and Subordinate Problems**

A Diagnosis of the Major and Subordinate Problems

Major Problem: *Finance/accounting*
Symptom: A 4% decline in the firm's return on equity (finance/accounting)
Causes: (1) A 10% cut in the advertising budget (marketing)
(2) Entry into the market of an aggressive competitor (task environment)
(3) A 7% drop in consumer spending (general environment)

Subordinate Problem 1:   *Strategic managers*
Symptom: Directionless top management (strategic managers)
Causes: (1) Lack of a coherent mission statement (strategy formulation)
(2) Lack of specific objectives (strategy formulation)

Subordinate Problem 2:   *Strategic managers*
Symptom: Top management is not fully aware of the performance of branch offices (strategic managers)
Causes: (1) Branch managers do not provide top management with regular performance reports (strategy control)
(2) Lack of specific performance standards for branch offices (strategy control)

Subordinate Problem 3:   *Environmental analysis*
Symptom: The firm's failure to exploit external opportunities (environmental analysis)
Cause: (1) Lack of efficient external scanning mechanism (environmental analysis)

Subordinate Problem 4:   *Strategy implementation*
Symptom: Middle and lower-level managers are not informed of the firm's strategies   (strategy implementation)
Cause: (1) Lack of adequate downward communication (strategy implementation)

Subordinate Problem 5:   *Finance/accounting*
Symptom: A high collection period ratio (finance/accounting)
Cause: (1) Inefficient collection practices (finance/ accounting)

REVIEW QUESTIONS

1. How does the objective of the diagnostic phase differ from the objective of the descriptive phase?

2. List the steps (or parts) that make up the diagnostic process.

3. If you were to analyze the strategy-formulation process of a firm, what subcomponents would you examine?

4. If you were to analyze the strategy-implementation process of a firm, what subcomponents would you focus on?

5. What is the difference between a stabilizer and a distinctive competency?

6. Define the following terms: strength, weakness, opportunity, and threat.

7. Explain whether each of the following two factors is a strength or an opportunity: (1) The firm enjoys a strong credit rating, and (2) the firm has the largest share of the market.

8. Define the following: problem, symptom, and cause. Illustrate your answer with an example.

9. In a strategic management context, symptoms and causes may be distinguished in three ways. What are they?

10. What is an intermediate factor? How can you determine whether a cause is actually the root cause or whether it is merely a symptom of another cause?

11. What is meant by the *percolation effect*?

12. Explain the difference between causal treatment and symptomatic relief. Illustrate with an example.

13. If the symptom is *declining market share* and the cause is *poor product design*, how would you state the problem?

Chapter 5

THE DIAGNOSTIC PHASE 2

The previous chapter was concerned with the first five parts of the diagnostic phase. These are diagnosing the strengths (Part C), diagnosing the weaknesses (Part D), diagnosing the opportunities (Part E), diagnosing the threats (Part F), and diagnosing the major and subordinate problems with their symptoms and causes (Part G). In this chapter, we will explore the last three parts of the diagnostic phase. As displayed in Exhibit 5-1, the parts include determining the organization's strategic match (Part H), identifying the organization's primary strategic match position (Part I), and diagnosing the distinctive competency and the major weakness of the key competitors (Part J).

PART H: DETERMINING THE STRATEGIC MATCH

The strategic match refers to the process of relating the internal strengths and weaknesses to the external opportunities and threats. This process is vitally important. For unless management is thoroughly aware of how the company's strengths and weaknesses relate to the external opportunities and threats, it will be unable to formulate strategies aimed at exploiting the opportunities and staving off the threats. In this context, the strategic match dictates the direction which the firm ought to pursue in the future.

DIMENSIONS OF THE STRATEGIC MATCH

The process of matching the results of the internal and external environmental analyses may produce four strategic dimensions. As can be seen in Exhibit 5-2, the dimensions are: constraint, leverage, maintenance, and vulnerability.[1]

Constraint

The first dimension of the strategic match is constraint. This dimension exists when the firm's ability to seize an external opportunity is hamstrung, or constrained, by an internal weakness. Constraint, then, is a match between an internal weakness and an external opportunity.

An illustration of the constraint position comes from the U.S. Postal Service. The popularity of fast-mail delivery (an opportunity) has prompted many companies to enter, and capitalize on, the new market. Among these are Airborne, Emery Air Freight, Purolator Courier, and Federal Express. Being in the mail business, the U.S. Postal Service decided to avail itself of the

Exhibit 5-1   A FRAMEWORK FOR STRATEGIC DECISION MAKING AND PROBLEM SOLVING

THE DESCRIPTIVE PHASE

A. Provide a profile of the organization's internal environment

1. Profile the corporate/business level in terms of:
   a. strategic managers
   b. environmental analysis
   c. strategy formulation
   d. strategy implementation
   e. strategy control

2. Profile the functional level in terms of:
   a. marketing
   b. production
   c. research and development
   d. human resources
   e. public affairs
   f. finance/accounting

B. Provide a profile of the organization's external environment

1. Profile the task environment in terms of:
   a. industry
   b. competitors
   c. suppliers
   d. customers
   e. government regulators
   f. labor unions

2. Profile the general environment in terms of:
   a. demographics
   b. culture
   c. economy
   d. politics
   e. technology
   f. pressure groups

THE DIAGNOSTIC PHASE

C. Diagnose the strengths:

1. Identify the strengths of the corporate/business level
2. Identify the strengths of the functional level
3. Identify the organization's distinctive competency

D. Diagnose the weaknessess:

1. Identify the weaknesses of the corporate/business level
2. Identify the weaknesses of the functional level
3. Determine the key weakness

E. Diagnose the opportunities:

1. Identify the opportunities in the task environment
2. Identify the opportunities in the general environment
3. Determine the key opportunity

F. Diagnose the threats:

1. Identify the threats in the task environment
2. Identify the threats in the general environment
3. Determine the key threat

G. Diagnose the major and subordinate problems with their symptoms and probable causes

H. Determine the organization's strategic match

I. Determine the organization's primary strategic match position

J. Diagnose the distinctive competency and the major weakness of the key competitors

THE PRESCRIPTIVE PHASE

K. Formulate a strategic plan:

1. Write a new mission statement for the organization
2. Set corporate objectives
3. Make the strategic choice by selecting the most effective grand strategy
4. Select a competitive strategy
5. Formulate functional objectives and strategies

L. Establish the conditions necessary to implement the strategic plan

Exhibit 5-2 **The Constraint, Leverage, Maintenance, and Vulnerability Dimensions of the Strategic Match**

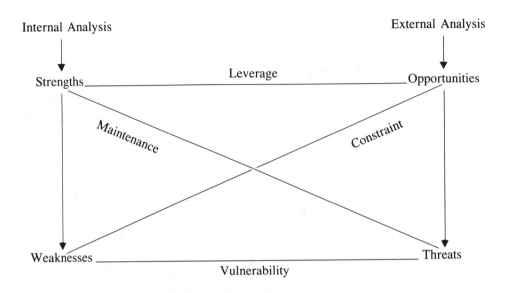

opportunity. So, it introduced its Express Mail which was advertised as an overnight mail service that "delivers excellence for less."

So far, however, the Postal Service's venture has not produced the desired dividend, showing how tough it is for a big government bureaucracy to compete with the private sector. The ability of the Postal Service to fully exploit the fast-mail opportunity has been severely hampered by four intractable weaknesses, namely, poor customer service, lack of follow-up on lost business, lack of its own air fleet, and fixed prices that the Postal Service cannot manipulate as private companies normally do if market dynamics warrant it.[2]

Another example of constraint is provided by the Xerox Corporation. Although this company invented the personal computer in the 1970s, it was never able to capitalize on the growth of the computer market. Xerox dropped out of the mainframe computer business in 1975 and the personal computer business in the mid-1980s. The major weakness that prevented Xerox from becoming a major player in the computer business was the constant strife between the Xerox groups that make work stations on the one hand and those that make copiers and printers on the other.

The company has launched an effort to enter the market and has hired a CEO to implement the new strategy. One of the first tasks of the CEO is to eliminate the internal weakness by bridging the gap between the various warring groups.[3]

Leverage

The leverage dimension represents a situation where the firm possesses the strengths necessary to exploit an external opportunity. Leverage, then, is a match between an internal strength and an external opportunity.

Of the four strategic match dimensions, leverage is the most advantageous. Here, the company is faced with an attractive external condition and has, or can develop, the capabilities to capitalize on it. This explains why this dimension is termed "leverage." It means that the firm can use its internal resources as a "lever" to maximize its profit-making capabilities.

Recently, aerospace companies found themselves in a potentially lucrative leverage position resulting from President George Bush's 30-year commitment to build a moon base and explore Mars. The program is expected to cost hundreds of billions of dollars. One of the firms possessing the strengths needed to exploit such an opportunity is Martin Marietta Corp. which had previously built two Viking Explorers to Mars.[4]

Leverage and Strategic Windows

One aspect of leverage that has been popularized by Derek F. Abell of Harvard University is the strategic window.[5] The basic notion underlying this concept is that certain future opportunities last for only a limited period of time. If an organization has the necessary capabilities to exploit them, then a strategic window opens. If it fails to make its move during this period, the window is closed and the opportunity lost.

Successful exploitation of a strategic window is predicated on two imperatives. First, as was described above, the company must possess, or be able to develop, the required strengths. Second, it must prepare a well-thought-out strategy and be prepared to put it into effect just when the strategic window opens. If the first requirement is present but the company fails to time its move to coincide with the opening of the strategic window, the window will be shut before the firm fully implements its strategy.

Here are a couple of examples of a strategic window:

1. The decline of the U.S. dollar in the late 1980s opened a window of opportunity for California vintners to export their product to Japan. The cheaper dollar made California wine much less expensive than European competitors. Sensing this long-awaited window of opportunity, the California vintners leaped through, capturing 15.6 percent of the Japanese market.[6] This window of opportunity, however, is not going to last forever. It will be closed as soon as the dollar begins to regain its strength.

It is worthwhile to note that this same window of opportunity was not properly exploited by the U.S. auto industry. The weak dollar made Japanese cars expensive in the U.S., thus providing the three big auto makers with a valuable opportunity to regain their market share. However, instead of seeking long-term gains in market share, the U.S. auto companies opted to boost short-term profits by raising prices instead of seeking long-term gains in market share.[7]

2. The Reagan years were kind to intra-industry consolidation. Under previous administrations, this would have been barred by tough enforcement of antitrust laws. In 1988, the last year of the Reagan administration, companies embarked on a massive wave of mergers and acquisitions. They viewed the 1988 year as a window of opportunity that might be closed with the election of a new president. According to one market analyst, "1988 is a political opportunity that won't last forever."[8]

Maintenance

In a maintenance situation, one of the firm's key strengths becomes imperiled by an external threat. Thus, maintenance is a match between an internal strength and an external threat. Companies falling in this position generally strive to maintain or protect their market position.

Visa, a leader in the credit-card business, found itself in a maintenance position when American Express launched a new credit card called Optima. With about two million card holders, Optima presented Visa with a serious challenge. To maintain its market share, Visa began to fight back with ads that point out that it is more widely accepted by merchants than American Express.[9]

Vulnerability

The vulnerability dimension is the most disadvantageous situation for a firm to be in. It occurs when an external threat is poised to strike one of the firm's key weaknesses. So, vulnerability is a match between an internal weakness and an external threat.

The more severe the threat is and the more critical the weakness that is targeted by the threat, the greater the damage the company is likely to incur. Every year, thousands of business concerns fold primarily because their internal structure is so fragile that it cannot withstand the onslaught of hostile external forces.

Consider, for example, Osborne Computer Corporation. In 1981, Adam Osborne founded his company to produce the first portable computer at a low price. The company's first machine, Osborne I proved to be a wild success, propelling the company's annual sales from zero to nearly $100 million in only 18 months. In 1983, however, the company filed for court protection under Chapter 11 of the Bankruptcy Act.

The failure of Osborne Computer Corporation stemmed from a deadly combination of hostile external forces and crippling internal weaknesses. The external forces consisted of mounting competitive pressures, led by IBM's Personal Computer which became a kind of standard almost overnight.

Osborne's efforts to prevent competitors from encroaching on his market were hampered by a host of weaknesses. Chief among these were Osborne's autocratic style, serious engineering and communication difficulties, poor financial controls, and poor inventory controls. The fatal blow came when word leaked out that the company was about to introduce a new product. Consequently, the sales of the Osborne I collapsed as customers waited for the improved model and dealers canceled orders.[10]

VALUE OF THE STRATEGIC MATCH DIMENSIONS

The principal value of identifying the strategic match dimensions, and as Exhibit 5-3 shows, is that they link the internal strengths and weaknesses to the external opportunities and threats. From this linkage, management can tell (1) which of the company's strengths can be used to exploit an external opportunity, (2) which strength is exposed to an external threat, (3) which weakness blocks the company's ability to exploit an opportunity, and (4) which weakness is a likely target for a threat.

PART I: DETERMINING THE PRIMARY STRATEGIC MATCH POSITION

Because a firm is likely to have both strengths and weaknesses and because it might be faced with both opportunities and threats, it might be falling in two or more strategic match positions at the same time. For strategy-formulation purposes, however, it is necessary to determine the firm's primary or major position in the strategic match. Such a determination will dictate the main direction the enterprise should follow.

There are two ways of accomplishing this task. The first consists of carefully examining the environmental conditions grouped under the four dimensions and then decide on the company's primary position. Since it relies totally on personal opinion, this method tends to be highly subjective and somewhat unreliable.

The second approach to determining the primary strategic match position of an enterprise involves the use of one of the portfolio planning techniques.

PORTFOLIO PLANNING TECHNIQUES

The term "portfolio" is used in reference to the collection of strategic business units (SBUs) owned by a firm. Hence, portfolio planning can generally be defined as an evaluative tool designed to assess the relative performance of each of the businesses that makes up the parent company. In terms of our

Exhibit 5-3 **An Illustration of the Four Dimensions of the Strategic Match**

Constraint

Weaknesses

Lack of international marketing experience

Inefficient distribution system

Opportunities

Rapid expansion of overseas market

The domestic industry's growth rate will be 15% in the coming decade

Leverage

Strengths

Firm has the largest market share of the 35-45 age group

Firm specializes in high-quality products only

Firm's management is growth-oriented

Opportunities

The 35-45 age group is expected to have the largest growth rate of any segment of the population in the next 10 years

The disposable income of this group will rise by 10% in 5 years

Consumers are becoming more quality-conscious

The prime interest rate is declining and is likely to remain low for the next five years

Maintenance

Strengths

Large market share

Quality products

Threats

A powerful foreign competitor is planning to enter the firm's market

The foreign competitor has a strong reputation for quality products

An expected rise in the cost of raw materials

Vulnerability

Weaknesses

High-priced products

Labor intensive

Difficulty in maintaining skilled workers

Threats

Prices of the foreign competitor are considerably lower

Rising labor costs

Anticipated shortage of skilled workers

---

discussion in this chapter, portfolio planning is viewed as a technique of determining the strategic match position of an SBU in light of its internal and external environmental conditions.

Several portfolio-planning techniques have been developed for purposes of examining an SBU. The most popular of these are the Boston Consulting Group (BCG) growth/share matrix and the General Electric planning grid.

THE BCG GROWTH/SHARE MATRIX

Developed by the Boston Consulting Group (BCG), the growth/share matrix is the simplest and most popular portfolio-planning technique. It also "represents perhaps the most significant contribution to strategic planning over the last two decades."[11]

Presented in Exhibit 5-4, the BCG matrix is built upon two criteria. The first is the relative market share which is an internal condition; and the second is the rate of market (or industry) growth which is an external condition. Thus, of all the various internal environmental conditions, the BCG chooses to use relative market share as a critical measure of an SBU's health. And of all the possible external environmental conditions, it singles out market growth as the sole gauge of external attractiveness.

In terms of the BCG matrix, then, the strategic match represents an effort to determine the position of a firm on a matrix by matching a single internal variable, relative market share, with a single external variable, market growth.

Relative market share is defined as the market share of the SBU as compared to the market share of the SBU's largest competitor. The cut-off point between high and low market share is 1.0. Anything above 1.0 reflects a high market share; anything below it shows a low market share. Thus, if Company X has a sales volume of $100 million and its largest competitor has a sales volume of $50 million, then Company X's relative market share is 2.0. If the converse is true, the relative market share of Company X would be 0.5. The rate of market growth, the second criterion in the BCG matrix, refers to the anticipated rate of sales increase and is typically derived from past market performance. In a broad sense, the line of demarcation between high growth and low growth is 10 percent. An industry whose annual growth rate exceeds 10 percent is generally considered to be healthy or attractive. By contrast, an industry whose growth rate falls below the 10 percent mark is generally regarded as a maturing industry.

It should be remembered, however, that this figure is highly fluid and can be significantly lower or higher depending on whether it is reflective of real or inflation-driven growth. In years of double-digit inflation, for instance, an industry will show more than 10 percent revenue increases without actually growing.

Once the relative-market share and the market-growth rate of each SBU are determined, the various SBUs can be plotted as circles in the matrix. The size of each circle reflects the sales volume of the SBU which it represents. In Exhibit 5-4, and for illustrative purposes, we plotted ten SBUs in the four cells. Two of the SBUs are question marks, three are stars, three are cash cows, and two are dogs.

Exhibit 5-4   **BCG Growth/Share Matrix**

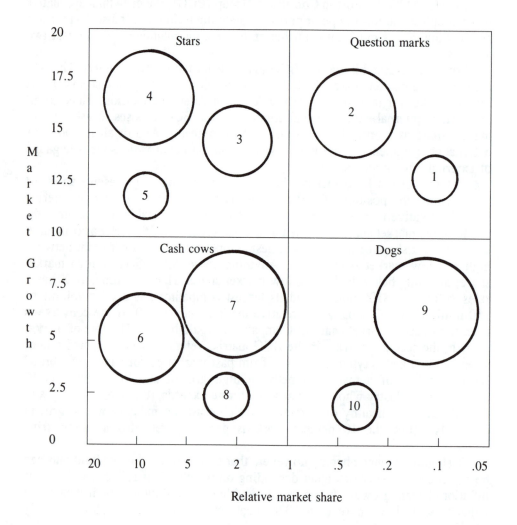

Source: Barry Hedly, ''Strategy and the Business Portfolio,'' *Long-Range Planning,* February 1977, p. 10.

Question Marks

Question marks are businesses or products that have a low share of a high-growth market. Question marks are so called because they are new ventures and, as such, their survival is uncertain. They are also known as problem children, since they demand a great deal of attention, care, and patience.

Due to their low market share, question marks generate little cash. In many cases, they tend to have a negative funds-flow position and must be supported by funds generated by the company's other SBUs, principally the cash cows. In this context, a question mark is a "cash guzzler," requiring the infusion of substantial investments as a means of expanding its market share.

In terms of the previously described strategic match dimensions, a question mark is in some ways similar to a constraint position. An example of a question mark is Premier, a smokeless cigarette introduced by RJR Nabisco in 1989. Although it took a decade to research and develop, and although the company planned to spend $1 billion to market it, Premier was pulled off the shelves of the stores after only five months. Consumer response to the product was disastrous. Many smokers who tried Premier didn't like the taste. They also complained about the price, which ran 25 to 30 percent higher than real cigarettes. They also rejected the high-tech feel of the partly aluminum inhaler.[12]

Stars

When a question mark survives its turbulent formative years and then manages to capture a large share of its market, it is transformed into a star. Thus, a star is an SBU that enjoys a high share of a rapidly growing market. A star may also be viewed as an SBU falling into a leverage position. Strategically, this is the most advantageous position for a business to be in.

An example of a star is the NutraSweet unit of G.D. Searle. The discovery of this natural low-calorie sweetener produced a wave of profits for the once-troubled parent company. By 1987, NutraSweet had 90 percent share of the $1.5 billion artificial sweetener market.[13]

Cash Cows

A cash cow is a former star whose market growth rate has slowed down. Put differently, a cash cow is an SBU that has a dominant market share in a mature or a low-growth industry. In terms of the four strategic match positions, a cash cow is in some respects similar to a maintenance position.

Unlike the question mark and the star, a cash cow generates more funds than it needs for maintaining its market-leadership position. Due to the low growth of the industry, little or no investment is made for expansion purposes. The excess funds which the cash cow produces are typically harnessed to support the corporation's cash-consuming SBUs. Clearly, cash cows represent an exceedingly valuable financial resource.

An example of a cash cow is the tobacco business unit of Philip Morris Cos. Despite the steady decline of cigarette smoking in the U.S. in recent years, this unit continues to produce 53 percent of Philip Morris's sales of $27.7 billion. Due to the bleak outlook of the tobacco industry, the company has used its cash cows' funds to diversify into other industries, notably the food and beer markets.[14]

Dogs

A dog is an SBU that is characterized by low market share in a declining market. It is similar to a vulnerability position in the strategic match. An SBU may become a dog in one of two ways. First, a question mark might never get off the ground. Thus, instead of moving toward a star position, it falls into the dog house. Second, a cash cow might begin to lose its competitive edge in a market where growth has taken a turn for the worse.

On the whole, a dog represents an undesirable unit. As a result, management strives to harvest it. This is done by withholding any type of investment in the business and by embarking on drastic cost-cutting measures. Once the business is milked, management may proceed to liquidate it.

MARKET SHARE IN THE BCG MATRIX

The BCG matrix attaches a special significance to market share. As we saw earlier in Exhibit 5-4, the best performers in this matrix are the stars and the cash cows. Both of these SBUs, if you recall, enjoy a strong share of their respective markets. Conversely, the poor performers in the matrix are the question marks and the dogs, each of which is characterized by a weak market share. In view of this, the BCG suggests that the road to profitability begins with the endeavor to establish, and hold on to, a larger share of the market.

THE GE PLANNING GRID

A second portfolio planning technique that can be used in determining the strategic match of an SBU firm is the GE planning grid. It was developed jointly by General Electric Company and McKinsey and Co.

Depicted in Exhibit 5-5, the nine-cell grid is designed to compensate for the limitations of the BCG matrix in two ways. First, instead of the high/low classifications used in the BCG matrix, the GE grid uses the three classifications of high, average, and low. In this way, the grid allows for SBUs to fall in the middle. Second, the GE grid does not use the BCG's two criteria of market share and market growth in evaluating SBUs. Rather, and as described below, it utilizes business strength (or competitive position) and industry attractiveness as evaluative dimensions.

In terms of the GE planning grid, a strategic match represents a relationship between a company's internal business strength and the external environment attractiveness.

Exhibit 5-5   **General Electric Planning Grid**

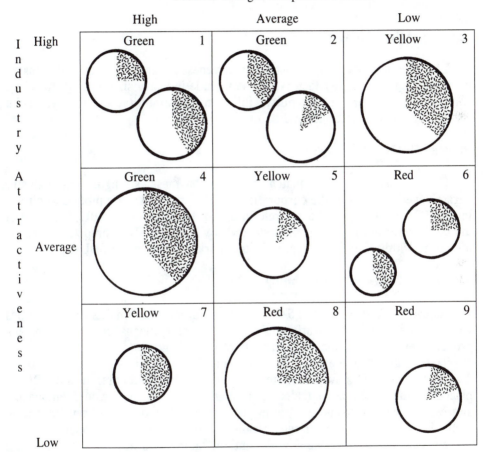

Green Zone   = Go (i.e., grow or invest).
Yellow Zone = Proceed with caution (i.e., selectively grow, harvest, divest, or liquidate).
Red Zone   = Don't go (i.e., harvest, divest, or liquidate).

Business Strength

Business strength refers to the SBU's internal capabilities which permit it to compete effectively in its market. Because business strength reflects the SBU's competitive resources, the two terms "business strength" and "competitive position" are often used interchangeably.

Business strength is a composite dimension, encompassing an assortment of factors. Included in these are market share, breadth of product line, sales distribution effectiveness, price competitiveness, advertising effectiveness, location and newness of production facilities, product quality, caliber of top management, customer service, and so on.[15]

Industry Attractiveness

Like business strength, industry attractiveness is also a composite dimension incorporating several key factors. These include industry size, growth, pricing, competitive structure, profitability, inflation vulnerability, cyclicality, social issues, legal considerations, and so on.[16]

Plotting SBUs

On the basis of the match between business strength and industry attractiveness of each of the corporation's SBUs, the SBUs are plotted as circles in the GE planning grid. Each circle in the grid stands for an SBU. The size of the circle reflects the size of the industry in which the SBU competes. And the pie slices within the circles represent the market share of the SBUs.

The Three Zones of the Planning Grid

As can be seen in Exhibit 5-5, the GE planning grid consists of three zones whose colors symbolize traffic lights. Thus, green means go, yellow means proceed with caution, and red means stop or don't go.

This means that the zone in which an SBU is positioned will eventually determine the SBU's future strategic direction. For example, if the SBU is placed in the green zone (cells 2, 1, and 4), its strategy would emphasize aggressive investment and long-term growth. If it is plotted in the yellow zone (cells 3, 5, and 7), the strategy would be selective or situational. That is, management needs to proceed with caution, taking into account the prevailing conditions at the time. And if the SBU falls in the red zone (cells 6, 9, and 8), its strategy would eschew capital investment, emphasizing instead short-term profitability.

ADOPTING THE GE PLANNING GRID AS A STRATEGIC MATCH MATRIX

Of the two planning portfolio matrixes described previously, we will use, with some modifications, the GE planning grid in determining a firm's primary strategic match position. Aside from sharing the simplicity of the BCG growth/share matrix, the GE planning grid, by virtue of its nine cells, allows SBUs to fall not only in high or low positions but also in average positions.

You recall that the GE planning grid consists of three zones (green, yellow, and red). For purposes of our discussion, however, we will view it as having four dimensions. As explained earlier, these dimensions represent four possible linkages between the internal and external conditions. And instead of using the terms "green," "yellow," and "red," we will use "constraint" (which is similar to question mark in the BCG matrix), "leverage" (star), "maintenance" (cash cow), and "vulnerability" (dog).

Thus, constraint stands for a match between internal weaknesses and external opportunities, leverage for strengths and opportunities, maintenance for strengths and threats, and vulnerability for weaknesses and threats. As a result, and as will be discussed in the next chapter, there can be four possible clusters of strategies, each corresponding to one strategic match position. Hence, we can talk of constraint strategies, leverage strategies, maintenance strategies, and vulnerability strategies.

POSITIONING A FIRM ON THE MATRIX

The process of determining the primary strategic match position of a firm, through the use of the GE planning grid, involves three steps:
1. Identify the firm's business strength or competitive position.
2. Determine industry attractiveness.
3. Position the firm in the relevant cell of the matrix.

DETERMINING BUSINESS STRENGTH

Positioning a company on the strategic match matrix begins with the determination of the firm's business strength.

Business strength is used here in the general sense to denote the firm's capabilities or what it can and cannot do in the marketplace. Viewed in this way, business strength reflects the firm's competitive position. So, a company that has a high business-strength rating tends to be competitively strong. Conversely, a company with a low business-strength rating tends to be competitively weak.

As shown in Exhibit 5-6 which involves ABC Manufacturing Company (a hypothetical firm), assessment of the firm's business strength or competitive

Exhibit 5-6   Determining the Business Strength/Competitive Position of the ABC Manufacturing Company

Success factors	Weight	Against Competitor A		Against Competitor B	
		Rating**	Weighted score	Rating**	Weighted score
1. Market share	.30	1	.30	1	.30
2. Breadth of product line	.06	3	.18	2	.12
3. Sales distribution effectiveness	X*	-	-	-	-
4. Price competitiveness	.04	4	.16	3	.12
5. Advertising effectiveness	.07	2	.14	1	.07
6. Facilities location and newness	.02	4	.08	3	.06
7. Production capacity	.04	3	.12	2	.08
8. Relative product quality	.10	3	.30	1	.10
9. R & D position	X*	-	-	-	-
10. Caliber of top management	.11	2	.22	1	.11
11. Customer service	.08	3	.24	2	.16
12. Experience curve	.02	4	.08	3	.06
13. Corporate culture	.07	3	.21	2	.14
14. Profitability ratios	.09	2	.18	1	.09
Total	1.00		2.21		1.41

*X means that the criterion is not applicable
**1 means that the firm's competitive position is very weak
    5 means that the firm's competitive position is very strong

position is comprised of four components: success factors, weight, rating, and weighted score.

Success Factors

The first step in assessing a firm's business strength requires the selection of a set of evaluation criteria. As displayed in Exhibit 5-6, we have chosen 14 criteria for use as a general basis for evaluating the firm's competitive position. These criteria are typically called success factors. That is because a company that does well on them tends to be successful in the industry, and a company that does poorly on the criteria tends to do poorly in the market.

Below is a list of the criteria with the questions that need to be asked as a means of generating information about the firm under analysis:[17]

1. Market share: What is the company's current market share?
2. Breadth of product line: Does the firm offer a limited or full line of products?
3. Sales distribution effectiveness: Does the firm have effective channels of distribution? Does it have a large sales force?
4. Price competitiveness: Are the firm's prices high or low in comparison with key competitors?
5. Advertising effectiveness: How many dollars of sales does the company receive on every dollar it spends on advertising?
6. Facilities location and newness: Are the firm's facilities well-located and are they new?
7. Production capacity: Does the firm have adequate production capacity to meet customer demand on time?
8. Relative product quality: How does the quality of the firm's products compare with that of the competitors?
9. R & D position: Is the company a leader or a follower in terms of the rate of product innovations?
10. Caliber of top management: How good are members of the top management team? Are they effective leaders? Do they make sound decisions? Have they been able to run the company successfully?
11. Customer service: Is the company known for good customer service?
12. Experience curve: How long has the firm been in the industry? Does the firm employ the latest technological innovations to enhance the quality of its production process?
13. Corporate culture: What type of culture characterizes the company? Is it conducive to efficient operations?
14. Profitability ratios: What are the company's profit-margin and return-on-equity ratios? How do they compare with the industry averages?

Weight

The success factors presented above do not carry the same impact. Some of them play a more critical role than others in influencing the firm's degree of success in the industry.

The second column, weight, is designed to allow for the varying degrees of influence the different success factors might have. Thus, when we assign a weight of .30 to market share and a weight of .06 to breadth of product line, we are in effect saying that the size of market share is substantially more significant in determining the firm's competitive success than the diversity of its products. This is another way of stating that market share is a more accurate gauge of the firm's business strength than the breadth of product line.

Observations on the Weighting Process

It would be instructive at this point to make a few observations relative to the weighting process.
1. The weights assigned to success factors should always add up to 1.00.
2. Weights assigned to success factors in one industry, say the soft-drink industry, do not necessarily apply to other industries such as the fast-food and auto industries.
3. When a particular success factor does not apply to an industry, it is marked with an X.
4. The weighting process is inherently subjective, since the weights are invariably influenced by the analyst's own personal opinion and predispositions. However, the subjectivity can be considerably mitigated by involving several individuals in the weighting process. The individuals can assign their weights first separately and then join together to debate their rationale until a consensus is reached.

Rating

In the third column of Exhibit 5-6, we attempt to rate our firm, the ABC Manufacturing Company, against its first leading competitor, Competitor A. To do that, we will use a scale of 1-5, with 1 reflecting a weak competitive position and 5 a strong competitive position.

Weighted Score

A weighted score for each success factor is obtained by multiplying the weight by the rating. To obtain an average score, we simply add up all the weighted scores. The obtained average score serves as an index of the firm's business strength or its competitive position. If the index is high, it is indicative of a strong competitive position. If it is low, it reflects a weak competitive position.

The same procedure can be repeated in assessing the company's standing with respect to other key competitors. It is important to observe, however, that when the assessment involves several competitors, only one business-strength index is used. This can be accomplished simply by adding and averaging the company's various indexes against all the leading competitors in the industry.

As can be seen in Exhibit 5-6, the business-strength index of ABC Manufacturing Company against Competitor A is 2.21 and against Competitor B is 1.41. This gives ABC an average business-strength index of 1.81 out of possible 5, reflecting a weak competitive position.

DETERMINING INDUSTRY ATTRACTIVENESS

Industry attractiveness refers to all the favorable and unfavorable conditions in the firm's external environment. In other words, it denotes the collection of opportunities and threats that exist now or are expected to emerge in the future.

As can be seen in Exhibit 5-7 involving ABC Manufacturing Company, the assessment of industry attractiveness consists of four components: evaluation criteria, weight, ranking, and weighted score.

Evaluation Criteria

The evaluation criteria are measures designed to determine the degree of favorableness of the firm's external environment. Although the specific criteria might vary from industry to industry, a general list of evaluation bench marks can be generated. Exhibit 5-7 displays 17 such criteria.

Below is a set of questions intended to help you gather information about each criterion:

1. Industry growth: Is the industry growing, stagnating, or receding? What is the industry's projected growth rate over the next five years?
2. Size: Is the size of the industry large or small? Is it local, national, or international in scope? Is the size shrinking or expanding?
3. Profitability: Is the industry profitable? Is it expected to continue to be profitable in the future?
4. Cyclicality: Does the industry profitability fluctuate on a rather regular basis every few years? That is, is profitability tied to economic cycles?
5. Seasonality: Is the industry seasonal? Does its profitability go up, for instance, in the summer or during the Christmas holidays but go down during the rest of the year?
6. Entry/exit barriers: Is it difficult for new companies to enter the industry? Is it difficult for existing companies to exit the industry?
7. Customers: Will there be significant changes in the size, composition, and

Exhibit 5-7   **Determining Industry Attractiveness of ABC Manufacturing Company**

Evaluation criteria	Weight	Ranking**	Weighted score
1. Industry growth	.30	5	1.50
2. Size	.05	4	.20
3. Profitability	.09	5	.45
4. Cyclicality	.03	4	.12
5. Seasonality	.06	3	.18
6. Entry/exit barriers	.05	5	.25
7. Customers	.06	3	.18
8. Competitors	.06	4	.24
9. Suppliers	.04	4	.16
10. Government regulations	.04	3	.12
11. Labor unions	.02	3	.06
12. Demographics	.05	5	.25
13. Culture	.04	5	.20
14. Economy	.06	5	.30
15. Politics	.03	3	.09
16. Technology	.02	4	.08
17. Pressure groups	X*	-	-
Total	1.00		4.38

*X means that the evaluation criterion does not apply to this particular industry
** 1 means that the evaluation criterion (or the industry condition) is very unattractive
   5 means that the evaluation criterion is very attractive

needs of the firm's customers?

8. Competitors: Is the industry highly competitive? Is competition likely to ease or get worse in the future? Are prices in the industry fairly stable or is the industry characterized by discounting?
9. Suppliers: Are the supplies of raw material, capital, and labor plentiful and reliable? Are future supply trends favorable?
10. Government regulations: Is the industry heavily regulated? Will there be a change in the number of regulations in the future?
11. Labor unions: Is the industry highly unionized? Are the unions militant or cooperative?
12. Demographics: What future demographic trends are anticipated? How would they affect the industry?
13. Culture: What new cultural trends are likely to emerge in the future? Would they have a positive or a negative impact on the industry?
14. Economy: Is the future outlook of the economy bright or dim? Base your conclusion on forecasts of the inflation, interest, and unemployment rates.
15. Politics: Is the political climate in the area where the company operates stable? Is the political climate stable in foreign countries where the industry has substantial investment? Is it likely to continue that way?
16. Technology: What future technological changes are likely to take place in the industry? Would they represent opportunities or threats to the firm?
17. Pressure groups: Will there be any new social issues that might expose the industry to strong pressure by public interest groups?

Weight

Not all industry-attractiveness criteria are equal in their significance. Some tend to play a greater role in determining industry attractiveness than others. The varying degrees of significance are reflected in the second column of Exhibit 5-7 where different weights are assigned to different criteria. Thus, when we assign a weight of .30 to growth and .05 to size, we are indicating that industry growth is a great deal more important than industry size in influencing our perception of industry attractiveness.

We should point out that some criteria might not be significant at all, or they might not be applicable to the industry in question. In that case, the criteria are marked with an X. It is also well to remember that the weights assigned to all criteria should add up to 1.00.

Ranking

After assigning weights to the evaluation criteria, we then attempt to rank the criteria in terms of their attractiveness, using a scale of 1 to 5. A ranking of 1 indicates that the criterion is an unattractive condition. On the other hand, a ranking of 5 shows that the criterion is reflective of an attractive condition.

Weighted Score

In the last column, a weighted score is obtained by multiplying the ranking and the weight figures. The weighted scores are then added up to produce an average score which serves as an index, reflecting the firm's industry attractiveness. When the index is high, it shows that the industry, or more accurately the external environment, is attractive or is characterized by opportunities. When the index is low, it shows that the industry, or the external environment, is unattractive or is characterized by threats. In the illustration provided earlier in Exhibit 5-7, the industry attractiveness of ABC Manufacturing Company is 4.38, reflecting a highly attractive industry.

POSITIONING THE FIRM ON THE STRATEGIC MATCH MATRIX

The third and final step in determining the firm's primary strategic match dimension is to position the firm on the strategic match matrix. As displayed in Exhibit 5-8, the horizontal axis of the matrix represents business strength/competitive position, while the vertical axis represents industry attractiveness.

In our hypothetical case, involving ABC Manufacturing Company, the business strength/competitive position index is 1.81, while the industry attractiveness index is 4.38. With these two indexes, the firm's strategic position, as Exhibit 5-8 depicts, is close to the constraint dimension. This means that the company suffers from some weaknesses which block its ability to exploit the available external opportunities and move into the leverage position.

In such a case, management is called upon to identify and eliminate the weaknesses. The identification of such weaknesses should be relatively easy at this point since they have already been diagnosed earlier in the analysis (see Exhibit 5-3). As you recall, a match between the internal and external conditions was previously made in terms of four dimensions: constraint (or a match between weaknesses and opportunities), leverage (strengths and opportunities), maintenance (strengths and threats), and vulnerability (weaknesses and threats).

So, after the firm's primary strategic match position has been determined, management can go back to the conditions listed under the four dimensions to identify the specific strengths, weaknesses, opportunities, and threats inherent in the firm's position. From this perspective, the matching of conditions under the four dimensions can now be seen as a convenient and useful way of spelling out the company's internal and external conditions.

It is necessary to indicate that if an SBU falls in the middle cell of the strategic match matrix, it should be moved to the nearest neighboring cell.

THE STRATEGIC MATCH MATRIX AND MULTI-BUSINESS FIRMS

Our discussion of the strategic match matrix has been limited to a single-business firm. It should be remembered, though, that the same procedure can be applied to a multi-business firm. In the latter case, where the company might consist of several strategic business units (SBUs), a separate assessment must be made of each SBU's strategic match position. Then all the SBUs are plotted as circles on the matrix.

Exhibit 5-8 **Positioning ABC Manufacturing Company on the Strategic Match Matrix**

Business Strength/Competitive Position

		High	Average	Low
I n d u s t r y	**High**	Leverage 3	ABC 2	Constraint 1
A t t r a c t i v e n e s s	**Average**	4	5	6
	Low	Maintenance 7	8	Vulnerability 9

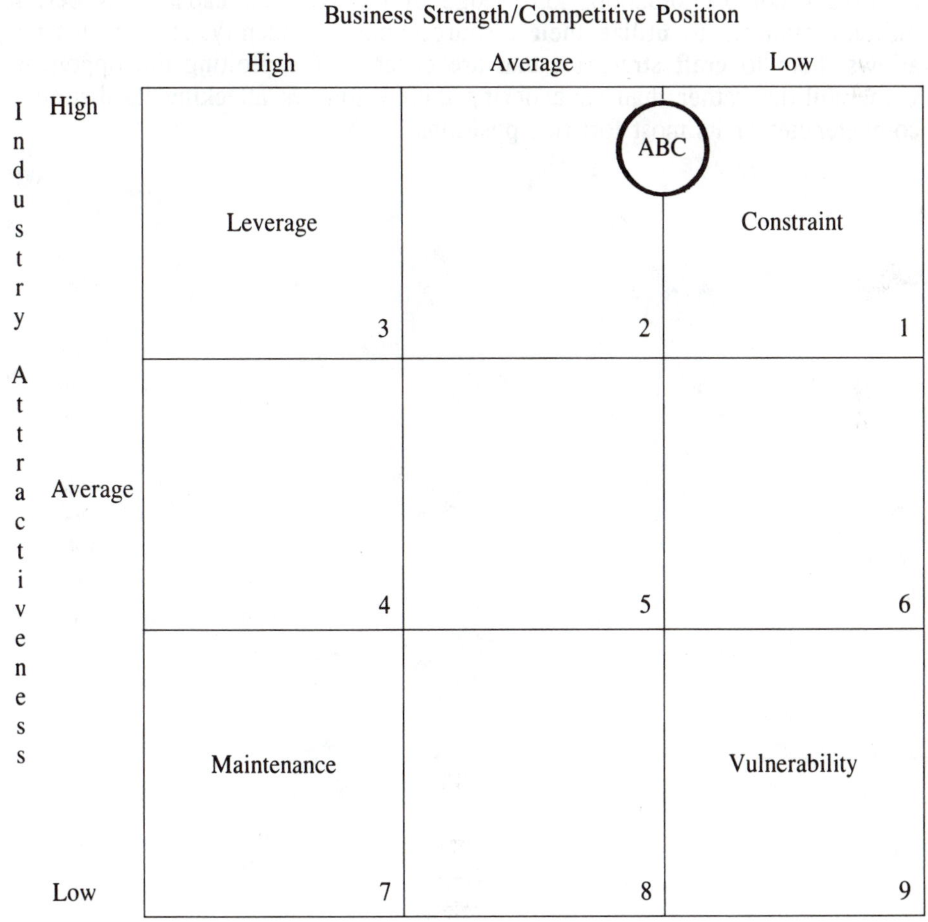

PART J: DIAGNOSING THE DISTINCTIVE COMPETENCY AND THE MAJOR WEAKNESS OF THE COMPETITORS

The last step in the diagnostic phase is the identification of the distinctive competency and the major weakness of each key competitor (Part J). Information for this step can be easily and readily gleaned from the analysis of the organization's business strength/competitive position which has already been conducted in the previous step. Such analysis, as you recall, involves a thorough examination of the strengths and weaknesses of each of the company's main rivals. From the strengths of each competitor, we select the distinctive competency. And from the weaknesses, we specify the major or critical weakness.

Knowledge of the key competitors' distinctive competencies and major weaknesses is of critical importance to formulating a sound strategic plan. As in a military combat situation, knowledge of the enemy's capabilities permits military planners to utilize their resources more prudently. It, for instance, allows them to craft strategies that are capable of exploiting the opponent's vulnerabilities rather than squandering their resources attacking its distinctive competencies or its most fortified positions.

REVIEW QUESTIONS

1. What is the strategic match, and what is its principal objective?

2. Identify and briefly explain the four dimensions of the strategic match.

3. How are leverage and strategic windows related?

4. What concept does the collapse of the Osborne Computer Corporation illustrate? Elaborate.

5. List one internal condition and one external condition that illustrate the dimensions of constraint, leverage, maintenance, and vulnerability.

6. What is meant by portfolio planning and what is its purpose?

7. What criteria are used in the Boston Consulting Group (BCG) matrix and the General Electric Planning Grid as a basis for determining a firm's primary strategic match dimension?

8. What do the following concepts mean: question mark, star, cash cow, and dog?

9. According to the experience curve concept, the more a company produces the lower its costs tend to be. Discuss the factors that account for the reduction in costs.

References

1. The terms of the strategic match dimensions are adapted from Andrew D. Szilagyi, *Management and Performance*, 2nd ed., (Glenview, IL.: Scott, Foresman and Company, 1984), pp. 159-161.

2. "The U.S. Postal Dis-Service," *The Wall Street Journal*, March 1, 1988, p. 1; and Leonard M. Apcar, "For Post Office, Overnight Mail Service Is Absolutely, Positively, Not So Easy," *The Wall Street Journal*, June 2, 1985, p. 31.

3. John Markoff, "Company Re-enters Computer Business," *The New York Times*, June 10, 1989, p. 23.

4. Roy J. Harris Jr., "Firms Rejoice over Reborn U.S. Space Program," *The Wall Street Journal*, July 24, 1989, p. B2.

5. Derek F. Abell, "Strategic Windows," *Journal of Marketing*, July, 1987, Vol. 4, pp. 21-26.

6. Ted Holden and Joan C. Hamilton, "Japanese Wine Lovers Are Drinking to California's Health," *Business Week*, August 15, 1988, p. 57.

7. Joseph B. White, "After a Brief Pause, Japanese Auto Makers Gain on Detroit Again," *The Wall Street Journal*, March 23, 1989, p. A1.

8. "A New Strain of Merger," *Business Week*, March 21, 1988, p. 122; and Pat Widder, "Merger Flurry a Blizzard to Be," *The Chicago Tribune*, March 2, 1988, Section 3, p. 1.

9. Jeff Bailey, "Optima Jumps into Ranks of Top Credit Cards," *The Wall Street Journal*, October 4, 1988, p. B1.

10. Erik Larson, "Osborne Takes Little of the Blame for Fall of His Computer Company," *The Wall Street Journal*, October 31, 1983, p. 35; Erik Larson and Ken Wells, "Shaken Osborne Computer Seeking a Suitor in the Face of Possible Failure," *The Wall Street Journal*, September 12, 1983, pp. 27 and 38; and "Osborne Goes into Chapter 11," *Business Week*, September 26, 1983, p. 50.

11. Peter Lorange, *Corporate Planning: An Executive Viewpoint* (Englewood Cliffs, N.J.: Prentice-Hall, 1980), p. 6.

12. Peter Waldman and Betsy Morris, "RJR Nabisco Abandons Smokeless Cigarette," *The Wall Street Journal*, March 1, 1989, p. B1.

13. Wendy L. Wall, "Marketing NutraSweet in Leaner Time," *The Wall Street Journal*, May 7, 1987, p. 32.

14. A. Duncan, M. Oneal, and K. Kelly, "Beyond Marlboro Country," *Business Week*, August 8, 1988, pp. 54-56.

15. Charles W. Hofer and Dan Schendel, *Strategy Formulation: Analytical Concepts* (St. Paul, Minnesota: West Publishing Co., 1978), p. 4.

16. *Ibid*.

17. Adapted from Hofer and Schendel, 1978. *Ibid*, p. 76.

Chapter 6

THE PRESCRIPTIVE PHASE

The third phase of the analysis framework, as Exhibit 6-1 shows, is the prescriptive phase.

To prescribe is to advise or recommend the adoption of a set of future actions and behaviors and the avoidance of others. The prescriptive phase, then, is concerned with delineating the strategies needed to make an ailing organization healthy and to ensure that a healthy organization remains healthy or becomes healthier.

FUNCTIONS OF THE PRESCRIPTIVE PHASE

The prescriptive phase seeks to perform any or all of the following functions:

1. To map out a strategic plan designed to utilize the organization's internal capabilities to exploit the external opportunities and to minimize the damaging effects of the external threats.

2. To remove, or lessen the severity of, whatever problems are currently plaguing the organization, thereby bridging the gap between the existing conditions and the desired conditions.

3. To create new conditions so as to prevent the same or similar problems from cropping up in the future.

Clearly, when we are engaged in analysis of a firm that is mired in a host of difficulties, all three functions apply. Conversely, when the analysis involves a successful firm, only the first function is relevant.

PART K: FORMULATING A STRATEGIC PLAN

As depicted in Exhibit 6-1, the prescriptive phase is composed of two parts. These are: formulating a strategic plan (K) and establishing the conditions necessary to implement the strategic plan (L). We will first address Part K.

In formulating a strategic plan, and as shown in Exhibit 6-1, you need to:
1. Write a new mission statement for the organization.
2. Set corporate objectives.
3. Make the strategic choice by selecting the most effective grand strategy.
4. Select a competitive strategy.
5. Formulate functional objectives and strategies.

154

Exhibit 6-1 A FRAMEWORK FOR STRATEGIC DECISION MAKING AND PROBLEM SOLVING

THE DESCRIPTIVE PHASE

A. Provide a profile of the organization's internal environment
1. Profile the corporate/business level in terms of:
   a. strategic managers
   b. environmental analysis
   c. strategy formulation
   d. strategy implementation
   e. strategy control
2. Profile the functional level in terms of:
   a. marketing
   b. production
   c. research and development
   d. human resources
   e. public affairs
   f. finance/accounting

B. Provide a profile of the organization's external environment
1. Profile the task environment in terms of:
   a. industry
   b. competitors
   c. suppliers
   d. customers
   e. government regulators
   f. labor unions
2. Profile the general environment in terms of:
   a. demographics
   b. culture
   c. economy
   d. politics
   e. technology
   f. pressure groups

THE DIAGNOSTIC PHASE

C. Diagnose the strengths:
1. Identify the strengths of the corporate/business level
2. Identify the strengths of the functional level
3. Identify the organization's distinctive competency

D. Diagnose the weaknesses:
1. Identify the weaknesses of the corporate/business level
2. Identify the weaknesses of the functional level
3. Determine the key weakness

E. Diagnose the opportunities:
1. Identify the opportunities in the task environment
2. Identify the opportunities in the general environment
3. Determine the key opportunity

F. Diagnose the threats:
1. Identify the threats in the task environment
2. Identify the threats in the general environment
3. Determine the key threat

G. Diagnose the major and subordinate problems with their symptoms and probable causes

H. Determine the organization's strategic match

I. Determine the organization's primary strategic match position

J. Diagnose the distinctive competency and the major weakness of the key competitors

THE PRESCRIPTIVE PHASE

K. Formulate a strategic plan:
1. Write a new mission statement for the organization
2. Set corporate objectives
3. Make the strategic choice by selecting the most effective grand strategy
4. Select a competitive strategy
5. Formulate functional objectives and strategies

L. Establish the conditions necessary to implement the strategic plan

PART K.1: WRITING A NEW MISSION STATEMENT

The first step in constructing a strategic plan is to write a new mission statement for the organization under analysis. The mission statement, as well as the other four components of the strategic plan, are all discussed in Appendixes D, E, F, and G of Chapter 2. Be sure to read these appendixes carefully before attempting to develop your strategic plan. Also, see Chapter 8 containing an illustrative case analysis.

As a reminder, though, when writing a mission statement make certain to incorporate the following elements or concepts into it:
1. Business domain
2. Products or services
3. Distribution channels
4. Customers
5. Management's beliefs and values

PART K.2: SETTING CORPORATE OBJECTIVES

Corporate objectives refer to the results sought by the organization as a total entity. In formulating corporate objectives, you need to:
1. Set the organization's long-term, or five-year, objectives.
2. Set the organization's short-term, or one-year, objectives.

To avoid any overlap between corporate objectives and functional objectives, which will be discussed shortly, you are better advised to state corporate objectives in terms of profitability. Included in this are such measures as earnings per share, return on equity, profit-margin ratio, net income, stock price, dividend rates, and so on.

Be sure to state your objectives in measurable terms within a time frame.

[For an explanation of corporate objectives,]
[see Chapter 2, Appendix E.]

PART K.3: MAKING THE STRATEGIC CHOICE

The strategic choice is a decision involving the selection of a grand strategy (or strategies) which you consider to be the most effective means of accomplishing the firm's corporate objectives. The strategic choice process consists of four steps: (1) Determine the organization's primary strategic match position, (2) generate alternative grand strategies appropriate for the primary strategic match position, (3) evaluate the comparable benefits of the alternative grand strategies, and (4) select the most effective strategy or strategies.

1. Determine the organization's primary strategic match position.

The first step involves identifying the particular strategic match dimension that most closely fits the firm. You have already done that in Part I of the diagnostic phase. So, you already know if the company is in a constraint, leverage, maintenance, or vulnerability dimension.

**[For a discussion of the primary strategic
match position, see Chapter 5.]**

2. Generate alternative grand strategies for the firm's strategic match position.

After determining whether the firm is in a constraint, leverage, maintenance, or vulnerability position, you need to develop the alternative grand strategies suitable for that position.

In Appendix F of Chapter 2, 13 grand strategies were explored. Some of these strategies are more appropriate for certain dimensions than for others. Exhibit 6-2 offers a suggested scheme as to which grand strategies may be used with a particular position on the strategic match. We may, therefore, speak of constraint strategies, leverage strategies, maintenance strategies, and vulnerability strategies. Rather than considering all the grand strategies as viable options, the evaluation is confined only to those strategies most applicable to the firm's primary strategic match position.

It is important to recognize that the strategies comprising the four clusters are not mutually exclusive. Rather, one strategy might be suitable for use in more than one dimension. For example, although joint venture is shown in Exhibit 6-2 as suitable for the maintenance dimension, it can just as effectively be used with a constraint position.

Constraint Strategies

As Exhibit 6-2 shows, a company falling in a constraint, or question mark, dimension (weak competitive position and high industry attractiveness) may select from six alternative grand strategies: (1) concentration, (2) vertical integration, (3) horizontal diversification, (4) harvest, (5) divestiture, or (6) liquidation.

These strategies represent a blend of growth and decline strategies. Inclusion of growth strategies (the first three) in this cluster suggests that management would be well advised to start by thoroughly analyzing why the firm has not been able to capitalize on its high-growth market before giving up hope and turning to decline strategies.

Leverage Strategies

A company in a leverage, or star dimension, (strong competitive position and high industry growth) may choose from among six possible grand strategies: (1) concentration, (2) market development, (3) product development, (4) product innovation, (5) vertical integration, or (6) concentric diversification. All of these are growth strategies oriented toward firmly cementing the company's market leadership and minimizing its risks by diversifying into other product lines.

Exhibit 6-2   **Grand Strategy Clusters That May Be Used with the Constraint, Leverage, Maintenance, and Vulnerability Dimensions of the Strategic Match**

Business Strength/Competitive Position

Strong   Weak

High	Leverage Strategies	Constraint Strategies
I n d u s t r y	1. Concentration 2. Market development 3. Product development 4. Product innovation 5. Vertical integration 6. Concentric diversification	1. Concentration 2. Vertical integration 3. Horizontal diversification 4. Harvest 5. Divestiture 6. Liquidation
A t t r a c t i v e n e s s	**Maintenance Strategies** 1. Concentric diversification 2. Conglomerate diversification 3. Joint venture 4. Product development	**Vulnerability Strategies** 1. Retrenchment/turnaround 2. Harvest 3. Divestiture 4. Liquidation

Low

Thrust of the Strategic Clusters

1. Constraint: Dominate industry, delay growth, or harvest
2. Leverage: Invest/grow strongly
3. Maintenance: Protect position or earn
4. Vulnerability: Harvest or divest

Maintenance Strategies

A company in a maintenance, or cash cow, dimension (strong competitive position and low industry growth) also uses growth strategies. But it does so for defensive rather than offensive purposes. That is, management is primarily concerned with maintaining or protecting the firm's strong position in the face of unfavorable external conditions, principally a maturing market. The four strategies of concentric diversification, conglomerate diversification, joint venture, or product development permit the firm to utilize its excess funds to diversify into related and unrelated businesses.

Vulnerability Strategies

Finally, a company falling into a vulnerability, or dog, dimension (weak competitive position and stagnant market growth) may choose from among four stability and decline strategies: (1) retrenchment/turnaround, (2) harvest, (3) divestiture, or (4) liquidation.

3.   Evaluating alternative grand strategies.

Having specified the company's strategic match position and having isolated the strategy cluster appropriate for that dimension, the strategist's next task entails the evaluation of the alternative strategies within the cluster. Such a task is not easy. There is not one single evaluative approach that can lead to the selection of a strategy that guarantees success. Different companies, and for that matter different strategists, use different approaches. Most of these approaches, however, may be placed into three categories: unstructured, semi-structured, and structured approaches.

The Unstructured Approach

This approach is highly informal and does not follow a specific step-by-step procedure. Rather, and at best, it involves a general discussion of the comparative benefits of the available strategic options. Strategists who use the unstructured approach tend to rely heavily on intuition in appraising the superiority of a particular strategic option. Hence, the unstructured method may aptly be described as an intuitive approach.

Intuition refers to "innate or instinctive knowledge, a quick or ready apprehension, without obvious recourse to inference or reasoning."[1] Managers with intuitive ability tend to have a vision, a gut feeling, of what is coming and know how to move their organization in response to that vision.[2] When the data does not provide a clear answer to a problem, the intuitive executives "have the uncanny ability to sense what should be done."[3]

We should add, however, that intuitive decisions do not occur in a vacuum. On the contrary, they represent "the result of digestion of masses of information blended with experience, insight, and an intellectual capability to sift through the irrelevant and focus quickly on the critical."[4] But the strategists' perception of what is "irrelevant" or "critical" may sometimes cause them to dismiss too hastily some highly viable options. Thus, a strategic choice might be made "before any of the alternatives were elaborated to any extent that would enable a formal evaluation of their comparative benefits."[5]

The Semi-Structured Approach

Unlike the unstructured approach which primarily relies on "gut feeling", the semi-structured approach is relatively more formal and involves the use of rather a specific procedure. In this approach, a particular set of evaluative criteria are first agreed upon by the strategizing team. It is then followed by group discussions aimed at determining how each strategic option fares with respect to its potential to satisfy each criterion.

A whole range of criteria may be used for assessing the desirability of a given alternative. Below is a sample of such criteria along with the questions that can be utilized as a basis for group discussions.

1. Management familiarity: Has management used this strategy before? Does the new strategy represent a radical departure from the company's past strategies? Research has shown that managers are generally more apt to continue the use of a past strategy due to their familiarity with the strategy. But if a change is deemed vitally important to the firm, managers will change their strategy but only incrementally or in small steps. On the whole, managers tend to give preference to a strategy that represents only a minor departure from the old strategy.[6]

2. Corporate culture: Is the strategy consistent with the firm's corporate culture? Will the adoption of the strategy necessitate a change in the culture? Is the strategy worth undertaking such a measure?

3. Distinctive competency: Does the strategy enable the firm to use its distinctive competency to exploit external opportunities?

4. Risk: Does the strategy involve a high or low level of risk? Is the strategy consistent with the CEO's attitude toward risk?

5. Timing: Will the adoption of the strategy give the company a head start over competitors? How long will the strategy take to produce the expected dividends?

6. Competitors' reaction: Will the strategy provoke a powerful competitor into taking a retaliatory action? Does the firm possess the resources that enable it to engage in a protracted war with a powerful rival?

7. Capital: Does the strategy require large capital outlays? Does the company possess the needed capital?

8. Human resource: Does the company have the personnel with the necessary skills to implement the strategy?

9. Regulations: Will the strategy subject the firm to heavy legal constraints? Will it be viewed as a violation of the antitrust laws?

10. Labor unions: Will the strategy antagonize the labor union?
11. Demographics: Are demographic trends favorable? Will the strategy capitalize on the trends?
12. Culture: Will the strategy enable the firm to take advantage of favorable cultural trends?
13. Economy: Are economic trends relative to such things as interest rate, inflation rate, GNP growth rate, and so on, favorable for the strategy?
14. Politics: Is the political climate at the local, national, or international levels stable enough for the adoption of the strategy?
15. Technology: Can the company use its existing technology in implementing the strategy, or will the strategy require the adoption of new technology?
16. Pressure groups: Is the strategy likely to arouse the ire of any pressure groups? Will it, for instance, be viewed by environmental activists as harmful?

The Structured Approach

The structured approach involves a specific step-by-step procedure designed to enhance the objectivity of the strategic choice process. In this approach, an effort is made to quantify the discussions, thus forcing strategists to scrutinize more closely the viability of each strategy.

The structured approach may take many forms. One of its versions, shown in Exhibit 6-3, is applied to the constraint grand-strategy cluster. For illustrative purposes, only two alternative grand strategies are used: concentration and vertical integration.

Use of the structured approach involves four steps: (a) establish evaluation criteria, (b) assign weights to the criteria, (c) rate each alternative strategy against the criteria, and (d) obtain a composite weighted score.

a. Establish Evaluation Criteria

This step is identical to the one used in the semi-structured approach. In Exhibit 6-3, 16 criteria are suggested. The list, it should be emphasized, is by no means exhaustive. New criteria may be added as the occasion demands. On the other hand, some criteria may be deleted if they are seen as impertinent to the strategies under consideration.

b. Assign Weights

The criteria used in evaluating alternative strategies do not hold the same value to the organization. Clearly, some are much more critical than others. To reflect the varying significance of the criteria, different weights are assigned to different criteria, with all the weights adding up to 1.00.

Exhibit 6-3　**An Illustration of the Use of the Structured Approach in Evaluating Two Alternative Constraint Strategies**

Evaluation criteria	Concentration			Vertical Integration	
	Weight	Rating*	Weighted score	Rating*	Weighted score
1. Management familiarity	.09	5	.45	3	.27
2. Corporate culture	.08	5	.40	4	.32
3. Distinctive competency	.08	4.5	.36	5	.40
4. Risk	.09	5	.45	2	.18
5. Timing	.06	4	.24	4	.24
6. Competitors' reaction	.07	3	.21	2	.14
7. Capital	.09	4	.36	3	.27
8. Human resources	.06	5	.30	3	.18
9. Regulations	.04	5	.20	2	.08
10. Labor unions	.03	5	.15	5	.15
11. Demographics	.06	4	.24	3	.18
12. Culture	.06	4	.24	2	.18
13. Economy	.08	3	.24	4	.32
14. Politics	.02	5	.10	5	.10
15. Technology	.08	5	.40	4	.40
16. Pressure groups	.01	5	.05	2	.02
Total	1.00		4.4		3.4

* 1 means that the strategy is not very desirable in terms of the evaluation criterion
5 means that the strategy is very desirable in terms of the evaluation criterion

Subjectivity of the Weighting Process. As might be inferred, the weighting process lends itself to considerable subjectivity. Each weight simply represents the perception of the evaluator. The evaluator's perception naturally reflects the convergence of largely personal influences, including his or her own attitudes, needs, aspirations, loyalties, and so on. The intruding subjectivity, however, may be lessened by asking several individuals to perform the weighting process separately. After thus determining the weights, the individuals can then get together to compare, and provide the rationale for, their decisions. In this manner, reasonably objective weights may be agreed upon.

c. Rate Each Strategic Option

The third step in the evaluation process involves rating each strategic option in terms of its ability to satisfy the criterion. A rating scale of 1 to 5 may be used for this purpose, with 1 indicating a highly undesirable strategy and 5 a highly desirable strategy.

The primary questions that need to be answered in this step are: Is the strategy desirable in terms of the evaluation criterion, or does the strategy conflict with the criterion? If it conflicts with the criterion, the strategy is judged to be undesirable and is given a rating of 1. If it does not, it is viewed as desirable and is given a rating of 5.

As is the case in the previous step, subjectivity is bound to creep into the rating process. But once again, the group approach may help to keep personal influences to a minimum.

d. Obtain a Composite Weighted Score

The last step in the evaluation process is obtaining a weighted score. This is simply produced by multiplying the rating score by the weight. By adding up all the weighted scores of a strategy, a composite score is obtained for that strategy. When the same procedure is applied to all the alternative grand strategies, it produces as many composite scores as there are strategic options.

4. Selecting a Strategy

Whether using the unstructured, semi-structured, or structured approach in evaluating available strategic options, the process usually culminates in the selection of a particular grand strategy. This strategy represents the most likely means of achieving the organization's objectives. When using the structured approach, the strategic choice involves the grand strategy with the highest composite score.

Observations on the Strategy-Evaluation Approaches

None of the three previously discussed approaches to strategy evaluation can be described as the best. A successful strategy selection is often a blend of facts, feelings, and even some measure of luck. The strategic choice is an extremely complex and difficult process. No one has yet been able to come up with a sure-fire formula that ensures a risk-free strategy.

The structured approach to strategy selection, presented earlier, is not intended to be the formula that guarantees the right strategy. Its most valuable benefit is that it provides a useful framework for the systematic discussion of issues. As a strategic planner at General Electric Co. put it: "You eventually have to make a subjective decision, but you put into it all the hard information you can."[7] In commenting on the value of the structured approach, Steiner and Miner observe: "There is no best way for all companies to make decisions... Even so, to the degree a formal, rational, structured approach can be used, the company will likely benefit."[8]

Because it is more likely to generate maximal class discussion and because it serves as a tool of reviewing important strategic management concepts, it is recommended that you use the structured approach in your analysis.

Combination Strategy

The strategic choice does not have to be a single strategy. It may involve a combination of strategies. A company, for instance, may follow a concentration strategy and a backward-integration strategy. It may choose to go with a combination of horizontal and concentric-diversification strategies. Or it may combine a market-development strategy with product development, and so on.

Contingency Strategies

Contingency strategies refer to plans formulated to deal with future conditions with low probability of occurrence. Such strategies are drawn up in response to the question: What if? Or what if unexpected future events do actually come about?

Strategic managers are keenly aware that in charting a long-term course for their organization, they are treading on treacherous waters. Many of the external environmental dynamics that must enter into their calculations cannot be predicted with a maximal degree of certainty. As a result, strategists endeavor to develop various scenarios, with each scenario representing a different set of assumptions about the future and each serving as a basis for a distinct strategy.

In general, three scenarios are developed: the most likely, the optimistic, and the pessimistic scenarios. The most likely scenario is a projection of the desirable and undesirable events that have a high probability of occurrence in the future. It is this scenario that is used as a basis for making the strategic choice. Hence, such a strategy is viewed as a primary rather than a contingency strategy.

The optimistic scenario involves assumptions about highly desirable future conditions that have a low probability of occurrence. Conversely, the pessimistic scenario embodies assumptions about highly undesirable future conditions whose probability of occurrence is also low. Both of these scenarios serve as a basis for developing contingency strategies. A contingency strategy based on the optimistic scenario serves to capitalize on the most favorable events if they occur. Conversely, a contingency strategy based on the pessimistic scenario aims at staving off the damaging impact of the unfavorable conditions should they materialize.

In the above context, contingency strategies enable organizations to "pre-plan better ways of coping with unfavorable and favorable events before they occur."[9]

PART K.4: SELECTING A COMPETITIVE STRATEGY

Competitive strategies are of three types: (1) Overall cost leadership, (2) product differentiation, and (3) focus.

Your task in this step involves the selection of one of these strategies for the organization. Use your knowledge of the organization's internal and external environmental conditions in making the competitive strategic choice.

After making the competitive strategic choice, it is essential that you provide the rationale behind your decision. Explain why you chose this particular competitive strategy. Further, provide your reasoning for rejecting each of the other two strategies.

[For an explanation of the three competitive strategies,]
[see Appendix G of Chapter 2.]

PART K.5: FORMULATING FUNCTIONAL OBJECTIVES
AND STRATEGIES

The next step in the process of formulating a strategic plan entails the determination of objectives and strategies for the various functional areas. In a business concern, typical functional areas include marketing, production, R&D, human resources, public affairs, and finance/accounting.

Formulating Functional Objectives

Functional objectives are the results sought by each of the firm's various functional areas or departments. For each of the relevant functional areas, you need to:
1. Set a long-term, or five-year, objective.
2. Set a short-term, or one-year, objective.

Formulating Functional Strategies

After setting long and short-term objectives for the relevant functional areas, appropriate strategies should be drawn up to achieve the objectives.

In the interest of brevity, you need only to formulate a short-term or an annual strategy. Such a strategy is oriented toward the accomplishment of the short-term objective. Once you develop a solid grasp of the skills and concepts inherent in an annual strategy, you should be able to apply the same knowledge to the subsequent annual strategies. After all, a five-year strategy is in essence nothing more than a set of five annual strategies.

Guidelines for Formulating Functional Strategies

In formulating a functional strategy, it is well to adhere to five fundamental guidelines: (1) Organize your recommendations by the subcomponents of each functional area, (2) make your recommendations as concrete as possible, (3) estimate the amount of time (i.e., a time table) needed to implement each recommendation, (4) give an estimate of the budget or cost required to implement the recommendations, and (5) make an estimate of the savings (i.e., benefits) that may be realized from the implementation of your recommendations.

1. Organize the recommendations by subcomponents

Whenever possible, organize your recommendations by the subcomponents of the functional area where a strategy is being developed. For example, if you are developing a marketing strategy, all or some of the subcomponents of products, marketing research, target market, sales volume, market share, pricing, distribution, and advertising and promotion may be established as separate headings. And below each heading, you can present whatever recommendations you deem necessary to improve that particular subarea.

In the above context, if you would like to see an improvement in the company's advertising program, avoid saying: "Improve advertising." Instead, and as depicted in Exhibit 6-4, set advertising as a subheading, and below it state specifically the steps that should be undertaken to improve advertising. The same holds true regarding other functional areas. For instance, instead of saying: "Improve recruitment and selection," use this subcomponent of human resources as a heading, followed by your concrete recommendations as to how to improve recruitment and selection.

For an illustration of the structure of functional strategies, see Exhibit 6-4. Also, consult Chapter 8 for an illustrative case analysis.

2. Make concrete recommendations

A functional strategy as a whole is as good as the recommendations it incorporates. If the recommendations are general, vague, or abstract, the functional strategy loses its usefulness. And the converse is true. The more specific, the clearer, and the more concrete the recommendations are, the more valuable and the more implementable the functional strategy tends to be.

Notice how general and, therefore, difficult to implement the recommendation "Improve advertising" is when compared with "Reduce network TV advertising by 20 percent." Likewise, the recommendation "Improve recruitment and selection" is certainly highly abstract in nature. It should be made more specific through such recommendations as "Hire three new recruiters" or "Increase regional campus visits from two to four visits a year."

Exhibit 6-4   **An Illustration of the Structure of a Short-Term (Annual) Functional Strategy**

Marketing

Long-Term Objective: Increase market share from 10% to 20% in 5 years
Short-Term Objective: Increase market share from 10% to 11% in 1 year

Short-Term Strategy

	Time S*	Table C*	Budget	Savings
Marketing Research				
1. Conduct a survey to determine the satisfaction of current customers with the content and packaging of the product. The survey should focus on those aspects of the product that the customers like the most and the least.	1/1	3/1	$25,000	
2. A concomitant survey should be conducted on the nonusers. The purpose of this survey is to reveal the reasons why such customers prefer the competitors' products to the company's offerings.	1/1	4/1	25,000	
Target Market				
1. At the present, management does not appear to have a clear idea of what its specific target market is. The results of marketing research should be helpful in delineating the company's target market. Preliminary data, however, strongly suggest that the target should consist of customers in the 25 to 40 age group.	4/1	5/1		

*S = Starting date
 C = Completion date

Sales

1. Strengthen the sales force by hiring two sales people with at least five years of experience in the industry.	1/1	4/1	80,000	
2. Modify the compensation plan of the sales force. Upgrade the base salary from $20,000 to $25,000 a year and increase the commission from 5% to 6.5% of sales.	1/1	4/1	460,000	

Pricing

1. Establish an aggressive pricing policy. The company's prices should always be 2% lower than the direct competitors.	1/1	3/1		

Distribution

1. Consolidate the ten warehouses into six strategically located distribution centers.	1/1	6/1		300,000
2. Strengthen the truck fleet by purchasing four new trucks.	1/1	6/1	120,000	

Advertising and Promotion

1. Reduce network TV advertising by 20% and increase print media advertising by 30%.	1/1	2/1	200,000	200,000
2. Utilize product reliability and value as the principal themes of the ad campaign.	4/1	7/1		
3. Run an attractive weekly supplement in local newspapers, offering coupons and special discounts.	4/1	12/1	50,000	
4. Continue to offer rebates since they have proved their effectiveness in generating more sales.	4/1	12/31	250,000	
5. Back up the advertising compaign with good customer service anchored in the "customer always right" motto. Provide all concerned employees with the necessary skills to handle customers' needs and complaints courteously and efficiently.	1/1	12/31	20,000	
Total	12 months		$1,230,000	$500,000

Ask *How?*. Since the concreteness of recommendations represents a critical determinant of the worth of a functional strategy, it merits further elaboration.

There are two interrelated methods of fostering the specificity of recommendations. The first involves organizing recommendations by the subcomponents of a functional area. We have already described this approach. The other method, which is tightly linked to the first, involves asking the question: How? Or, how can the recommendation be carried out?

For optimal benefit, the question: How? should be posed immediately after the short-term objective of a functional area has been established. In this sense, the objective itself can be conceived of as a recommendation.

Let us assume that the short-term objective of the functional area of marketing is "To increase market share from 10% to 12% in one year." By asking How? Or how can this objective (i.e., recommendation) be accomplished? we can narrow the general avenues of actions available to us. One such avenue, or an answer to the question, might be to "Improve advertising." Since this recommendation is too broad to be of practical value, we should again pose the question: How? Or, how can we improve advertising? The answer or answers to the question should greatly smooth the generation of highly specific and implementable suggestions.

3. Setting a time table

Every strategy should have a time table, indicating the starting date (S) and the completion date (C) of each recommendation.

In a business setting, the time table must, of course, be as precise as possible. That is because a time table serves as a critical control mechanism. It tells the subordinates when they are to start a project and when they are expected to complete it. Without a time table, a strategy becomes open-ended and its completion date is left entirely to the discretion of the subordinates.

Consider the importance of a time table to a home builder. Can you imagine the builder operating without a time schedule? Can he let the foundation excavators, carpenters, plumbers, electricians, heating contractors, and decorators begin their work at any time they choose and finish it whenever they please? Of course not. In fact, building contractors make a concerted effort to ensure that every phase of the project is started and completed on specific dates. For if one phase (say the foundation work) is not finished on time, the house frame cannot be erected. If the frame is not completed on schedule, other phases of the project such as plumbing, electrical wiring, or heating will have to wait. In which case, the entire project could be thrown off schedule, causing the contractor to incur additional unwarranted costs.

It is necessary to stress that in a classroom setting, an approximate, rather than precise, time table would be sufficient. The purpose of this dimension of functional strategy development is to underscore the significance of the concept rather than the figures. Once the concept is solidly implanted in your mind, you can strive for precision in actual work situations, taking into consideration the particular job conditions prevailing at the time.

4. Determining a budget

With a few exceptions, all strategies cost money to implement. Just as your plan to go to college, buy a car, or take a trip cost money, so do functional strategies. It is the responsibility of the functional strategists to specify the budget required to put their strategies into force.

Determining the budget is a crucial dimension of a functional strategy. In fact, it can go a long way in either enhancing the acceptability of the strategy to higher management or dooming it to an early death. Bear in mind that capital is the lifeline of all organizations, and management is typically disinclined to part with it unless there are compelling reasons to do so. Consequently, functional strategists must not only be able to provide as precise a budget as possible but must also be armed with the facts and figures necessary to defend it convincingly.

Just as we did in our discussion of the time table, it is worth observing that in a classroom setting, your budgetary figures need not be precise. The idea here is to make you develop a full appreciation of the importance of budget and to view it as an integral part of any strategic plan.

5. Determining the Savings

Good strategists think not only in terms of time table and cost. They also consider the savings that may be realized as a result of implementing their strategic plan. There are two advantages to the inclusion of estimated savings in a strategy. The first is that it makes the strategy complete, since it incorporates all the essential ingredients of a well-thought-out plan of action. The second is that it enhances the salability of the strategy. Because it strives for cost efficiency, a strategy that reflects the anticipated savings can have a great appeal to senior management. Therefore, its chances of adoption tend to be much greater than strategies that merely add to the company's operational costs.

Consequences of Omitting the Time Table, Budget, and Savings

It is important to point out that omitting the time table, budget, and savings constitutes a serious structural defect in a functional strategy. More to the point, the omission can produce two negative results.

First, the omission can cast serious doubts on the competency of the strategist and his (or her) grasp of what constitutes a realistic and implementable strategy. Second, it can cause the reader, usually a superior, to conclude that if the strategy is deficient in terms of the time table, budget, or savings, the rest of the strategy is likely to be equally deficient and cannot be taken seriously. Both of these negative effects are apt to cast a long shadow on the strategist's prospects for advancement in the organization.

PART L: ESTABLISHING THE CONDITIONS
NECESSARY TO IMPLEMENT THE STRATEGIC PLAN

The second part (L) of the prescriptive phase of the analysis framework involves the establishment of the conditions that facilitate the implementation of the strategic plan. The creation of such conditions is crucial to strategic success. Unless the proper conditions are installed, the best-conceived strategies could falter. In this sense, it may be stated that whereas good strategies cannot salvage poor implementation, good implementation may salvage poor strategies.

In our earlier discussion, we touched upon three of the conditions that could facilitate implementation. They are time table, budget, and savings. Other facilitators of implementation include organizational structure, policies, leadership, corporate culture, communication, and motivation.

Exhibit 6-5 provides a checklist designed to assist you in creating the internal conditions necessary for the successful execution of your strategic plan.

Exhibit 6-5   **A Checklist for Establishing the Conditions Necessary to Implement the Strategic Plan**

Organizational Structure

1. Which of the following organizational structures would be most suitable for the chosen grand strategy: entrepreneurial, functional, geographic, product, strategic business unit, matrix, or project structure?
2. Explain your choice.
3. Who should be in charge of implementing the strategic plan?
4. Who should be in charge of evaluating the progress of implementing the strategic plan?

[For an explanation of organizational structures,]
[see Appendix H of Chapter 2.]

Policies

1. Establish two policies at the corporate/business level.
2. Establish one policy for each of the functional areas of marketing, production, research and development, human resources, public affairs, and finance.
3. From the above corporate/business policies and functional policies, select *one* policy. Then, write procedures and a rule for that one policy.

[For the meaning of corporate/business policies]
[and functional policies, see Appendix A.]

[Also, see the illustrative case analysis,]
[in Chapter 8.]

Leadership

1. Which of the following leadership styles would you recommend for the organization: authority-compliance management, country-club management, team management, or middle-of-the road management?
2. Justify your choice.

[For a discussion of leadership styles,]
[see Appendix J of Chapter 2.]

Corporate Culture

1. Would the current corporate culture facilitate the implementation of the strategic plan, or is there a need for a new culture?
2. If a need exists for a new corporate culture, what type of culture should be created?
3. Explain your decision.

[For an explanation of corporate culture,]
[see Appendix K of Chapter 2.]

Communication

1. What aspects of your strategic plan ought to be communicated to members of the organization?
2. What media or methods would you recommend that top management use in communicating the strategic plan to members of the organization?

Motivation

1. Which of the following approaches would you emphasize as a means of motivating employees and securing their commitment to the strategic plan: participative management, financial rewards, nonfinancial rewards, sanctions?
2. Explain your view.

A CONCLUDING OBSERVATION:
THE COMMUNICATION DIMENSIONS OF THE CASE METHOD

A course that relies as heavily on the case method as the strategic management course typically does, tends to involve a great deal of communication among students.

Whenever you present a report containing your analysis of a case, the report is invariably followed by group discussion. Other members of the class, in effect, subject your analysis to their own analysis. They might seek clarification of certain issues, they might disagree with your conclusions, they might challenge your logic, and they might see the need for strategies different from the ones that you propose for the organization under study.

In this context, the case method serves as a communication forum or a marketplace for the free exchange of ideas. As such, it affords students a valuable opportunity to practice, and even acquire, effective communication skills.

The appendixes at the end of this chapter are intended to provide you with useful tips on how to play your communication role effectively. The communication skills with which the appendixes deal are handling criticism (Appendix B), expressing criticism (Appendix C), overcoming nonparticipation (Appendix D), avoiding overparticipation (Appendix E), preparing a written report (Appendix F), and presenting an oral report (Appendix G).

Appendix A
POLICIES

An essential condition of successful strategy implementation is the institution of appropriate policies. A policy is a general guide for action. It is a directive designed to guide managers and their subordinates relative to the type of decisions they can or cannot make. The establishment of sound policies serves to create a stable internal environment, thus permitting the enterprise to focus its resources on effectively executing its strategy without internal distractions.

In contrast to strategy which typically deals with nonrecurring conditions, a policy is designed to assist managers throughout the organization in dealing with recurring, repetitive, or routine issues. In this sense, a policy may be viewed as a shortcut to thinking and acting.

Corporate/Business Policy

Corporate/business policies address issues of concern to the organization as a whole rather than to a specific functional area. They are intended to preserve the integrity of the company's mission and protect its basic tenets. The establishment of such policies makes it clear to all members of the organization which strategies, actions, or behaviors will or will not receive the commitment and support of the company.

Here are some examples illustrating corporate/business policies:

1. Only companies with related products or services may be acquired.
2. All critical parts used in assembling our products must be purchased in-house.
3. All new products must earn 20% pre-tax profit.
4. No individual can serve on the board of directors if he or she serves on the board of a competitor.
5. Sales figures are a trade secret and cannot be divulged to the public.
6. This bank's policy forbids financing hostile takeovers.
7. We market our computers through the company's own retail outlets and not through independent dealers.
8. To the extent possible, all overseas positions should be filled with local managers.
9. No SBU will be kept in the portfolio unless its products rank No. 1 or No. 2 in market share or have a good chance of achieving that level.
10. Technology and advertising know-how developed in one division must be shared with other divisions.

Functional Policy

Functional policies are guidelines that help in defining the actions and decisions of the members of each functional area.

Below are examples of policies in the functional areas of marketing, production, R&D, human resources, public affairs, and finance/ accounting.

Marketing
1. Only one distributor is allowed to market our products in a sales territory of 20,000 people or less.
2. All advertising messages must be consistent with the society's standards of ethics.
3. Our policy is not to accept unsolicited suggestions for advertising.

Production
1. Full maintenance of production facilities is done on a weekly basis.
2. Ten percent of finished goods must be tested for quality.
3. The highest quality raw materials must be used in manufacturing the product.

Research and development
1. Only research with the promise of commercial application may be pursued.
2. All projects must first be approved by the R&D Review Committee before they are submitted to the group head.
3. Thirty percent of sales must come from products developed in the past five years.

Human Resources
1. All new managers at the entry level must undergo a two-year, job-rotation program.
2. Job candidates are interviewed by both human resource officers and concerned line managers.
3. All employees will receive written performance evaluations twice a year with merit bonuses awarded in December of each year based on work performance.

Public Affairs
1. Sabbatical leaves up to six months may be granted to employees who wish to serve as volunteers in social welfare organizations.
2. Financial contributions are made to worthy organizations in the Chicago area only.
3. When a crisis occurs, full and factual information must be provided to the public as soon as possible.

Finance/Accounting
1. Debt should not exceed 60 percent of the company's total assets.

2. Credit may be extended only to customers with at least $50 million in annual sales.
3. All outstanding bills must be collected within a period not to exceed 30 days after the due date.

Changing a Policy

Although they constitute relatively enduring decisions, policies are subject to change. Over time, and due to alterations in the organization's internal or external environments, some policies might become obsolete or dysfunctional. In this case, they will have to be modified or dropped altogether.

Procedures

Policies are ordinarily translated into procedures. Procedures are simply a series of steps or actions, often performed sequentially, to implement a given policy. All types of business activities may be covered by procedures. These range from methods of adjusting a customer's claim to the ways of maintaining adequate inventory control.

Rules

A rule is an explicit directive that specifies the action that can or cannot be taken. A rule may or may not be related to a procedure or policy. When a rule is not derived from either a procedure or a policy, it serves as a standing order. An example of a standing order that is not derived from a procedure is "No Smoking."

Frequently, however, a rule flows from both a procedure and a policy. Consider the following example which illustrates a rule that is derived from a procedure which, in turn, is derived from a policy:

Policy: An Educational Assistance Program is offered to all employees as a means of providing them with the educational background and skills needed to offer efficient and professional service to our customers.

Procedures: Employees interested in applying for the Educational Assistance Program are required to adhere to the following procedures:

1. The employee is to complete an Educational Assistance request form.

2. The request form is to be forwarded to and approved by the employee's manager.

3. The following points are to be detailed on the request:

   a. Anticipated plan of study
   b. Career objectives

c. Relevance of the degree or educational program to current job and career objectives.
d. The manager's explanations as to how the degree program will enhance current job and career objectives.

4. A separate form is to be completed and approved for each course at least three weeks prior to the course starting date.

Rule: The company will not approve more than two courses per academic term.

Appendix B
HOW TO HANDLE CRITICISM

1. Anticipate and tolerate criticism

Differences of opinion in group discussions are normal. They arise in any group engaged in analyzing and solving problems. It is the presence rather than the absence of conflict that is the norm in group deliberations.

Differences of opinion are primarily spawned by the group members' divergent perceptions of the same issue and divergent needs. Different individuals, therefore, have their own rose-colored glasses through which they see and judge events in their environment. So when other people criticize your analysis and disagree with your opinions and conclusions, they might be spurred by purely honest differences in perception and needs.

Whatever the reason behind it, criticism will occur. So, anticipate it whenever you make any type of presentation. Once you learn to anticipate criticism as a natural product of group discussions, you will begin to tolerate it. Hence, do not operate on the premise that your analysis is beyond reproach. On the contrary, your operating assumption should be that no matter how thorough your analysis is, it will still be subject to challenge by others. This is most particularly true when students' performance in the course is determined by their participation in class discussions.

2. Maintain your composure

The mere expression of criticism by others does not necessarily imply that your views are inherently unsound. It could very well be that the critic's position is ungrounded.

But however unfair or unfounded the criticism might sound to you, make sure to respond to it in a rational, logical, and objective manner. Avoid emotionalism. Do not accuse the critics of asking foolish or stupid questions, and do not belittle them for raising a point that has already been discussed.

Being "cool under fire" can be a valuable asset for getting ahead in the business world.

3. Accede to reasonable criticism

When you sense that your argument cannot stand up against counterviews, be flexible enough to modify or abandon your position altogether. Never assume a recalcitrant attitude when you realize full well that your argument is too tenuous to be defended successfully. Other people will respect you more for exhibiting readiness to accede to a counterpoint than for stubbornly sticking to an indefensible position.

Appendix C
HOW TO EXPRESS CRITICISM

1. Soften your criticism with a positive note

Whenever feasible, try to give some credit for the other speaker's viewpoint by finding some area of agreement. Look for a point in the speaker's presentation that deserves your praise and compliment him or her for it. Do not begin your comments with a negative statement such as: "I disagree with you totally," or "You are entirely wrong."

To be sure, forthright statements of disagreement such as the above can occasionally bring life to an otherwise listless discussion. They render the exchange of views more vibrant and make the participants more alert and more involved. But before you resort to this approach, make certain that the other person possesses the personality attributes necessary to handle your criticism without leaving a bitter taste in his or her mouth. Reserve your forceful criticism to that time when you have developed adequate knowledge of the temperament of the various members of the group. Only then can you express your criticism in a manner that is keyed to the unique disposition of each member.

2. Take issue with the point, not the speaker

In making your criticism, confine your statements to the content of the speech without attacking the speaker. A statement such as: "You show total ignorance of strategic management," merely attacks the speaker and is likely to do more damage to your image than to the speaker's.

3. Restate the speaker's view if necessary

Do not be vague regarding what you are refuting. Do not overstate or exaggerate what the other person has said, and do not willfully put words in his or her mouth. If you are in doubt about the speaker's position, restate his view as clearly and accurately as you can.

4. Be forceful

Tact is an essential quality of constructive criticism. It implies smoothness and adroitness in expressing counterviews. But tact should not be taken to mean sacrificing the forcefulness or assertiveness with which you make your point. You can be forceful without being offensive.

When asking a question, some students seem to be readily content with the speaker's response, even if they consider the response to be unsatisfactory. They let the speaker off the hook too easily for fear of embarrassing him.

Depending on your assessment of the situation and the speaker's characteristics, you might have to press your point if the speaker's response is not direct and to the point. You might have to ask one or more follow-up questions as a means of getting the speaker to fully clarify his position. Bear in mind that such a practice can be quite beneficial to the student targeted by the questions. It serves to put his persuasive and logical skills to the test.

Appendix D
HOW TO OVERCOME NONPARTICIPATION

1. Maintain a positive attitude

Positive attitude is greatly facilitated through good preparation. Do your homework well by reading the case thoroughly and familiarizing yourself with all the key issues. Then approach the discussions from the perspective that your analysis of the issues is as sound as anybody else's.

Never minimize the worth of your views. The habitually quiet individuals are typically their own harshest critics. Let other members of the group judge the value of your contributions, and you'll find it is highly likely that your ideas are as good as, if not superior to, those of the outspoken members of the class.

2. Crack the fear barrier

The most formidable barrier facing you, if you are a bashful individual, is making your first contribution. Once you pass this hurdle, you will realize that participation is much less painful than you initially thought. You will also discover that speaking up can indeed be a rewarding experience, as it is apt to provide you with the sense of success needed to bolster your self-confidence.

It is important to remember that you need not emulate the more forceful and highly assertive members of the class by taking a controversial stand or asking tough questions. Your first effort might involve a neutral or nonprovocative question where you ask the speaker to clarify a point or explain a concept. Such a question serves to provide you with a feel for what it is like to speak in a group situation.

Keep in mind that the key to overcoming the fear of participation in group discussions is to practice participation. For as the saying goes: "The only way to learn to ride a horse is to ride a horse."

3. Be an early participant

Do not wait too long before you make your first contribution. Be sure to get involved in the discussions as early as possible.

When you speak early, you are more likely to continue to participate, as success breeds confidence and confidence leads to more frequent participation. On the other hand, if you prolong the period of time before you start your comments, you are likely to be more hesitant and more fearful.

4. Be alert

Effective participation demands constant alertness to the discussions. Follow the deliberations closely and come in with your comments immediately after the speaker has made his or her remarks.

Appendix E
HOW TO AVOID OVERPARTICIPATION

1. Be courteous

A group discussion is an interactive process, involving the exchange of information. It is not a one-way communication where one individual does all the talking.

Always be conscious of the amount of time it takes you to make a point. Express your views as concisely as possible, and then give the others a chance to express their own views.

2. Tackle one topic at a time

When it's your turn to speak, avoid tackling several topics simultaneously. Limit yourself to one idea per contribution. Do not fall into the trap of becoming a "chain" talker. Instead of trying to ask two or more questions at the same time, ask one question at a time, thereby giving other students a chance to ask their questions.

Appendix F
HOW TO PREPARE A WRITTEN REPORT

To improve the quality of your written report, you need to pay particular attention not only to the content but also to the structure of the report. The structure of a complete business report is made up of several parts. Included in these are the title page, letter of transmittal, preface, table of contents, list of illustrations, summary, text, appendixes, footnotes.

For purposes of preparing a written case analysis, your report should include the following basic parts:
1. Title page
2. Table of contents
3. List of illustrations
4. Text
5. Appendix
6. Footnotes

Title Page

The title page presents the following pieces of information: (1) the title of the report, (2) the name of the person or persons to whom the report is submitted (for example, Prepared for: Professor R.J. Smith), (3) the name of the person preparing the report (for example, Prepared by: John Adam), and (4) the date the report is submitted. These four elements of the title page should be evenly and neatly spaced out over the entire page.

Table of Contents

The table of contents represents an outline of the report and is prepared when the entire report has been completed. The table of contents includes a list of the main headings of the report text and the page number on which each heading begins in the text.

List of Illustrations

If the report contains a number of charts and exhibits, a separate list of illustrations may be set up for them. The list of illustrations immediately follows the table of contents and gives the title of each exhibit and the page number where it appears.

Text

The text is that part of the report where the subject matter of the report is discussed. In a general sense, the text is usually divided into three elements: introduction, body, and conclusion. However, in a case analysis course, the text of the report should reflect the particular structure of the analysis framework used by the instructor. For example, when utilizing the analysis framework presented in this book, the report text could be organized along the various parts of the framework.

Appendix

Placed at the end of the text, the appendix (or appendixes) is used to present additional material that might be helpful to the reader. Such material is either too lengthy to be included in the text or does not contribute significantly to the thorough treatment of the subject matter. For instance, certain financial data or a journal article might be too long to include in the text as it may obstruct the smooth flow of an idea. However, if such additional information is thought to be of interest to some readers, it might be placed at the end of the report in the form of an appendix.

Footnotes
Whenever you use material from another source, you should acknowledge the source in the form of a footnote. The borrowed material is typically assigned a number in the text and then a footnote corresponding to that number is used, giving a full citation of the source of the material.

The footnote may be placed at the end of the report or at the bottom of the page where the quoted material appears. When the footnote is placed at the end of the report, its number is typed even with the footnote line and it is not indented. When the footnote is placed at the bottom of the page, its number is raised half a space and is usually indented five spaces.

There is not one standard style of constructing footnotes. Your guiding principle, however, should be to provide sufficient information about your source to enable the reader to locate that source without any difficulty. Below is one method of footnoting books, magazines and journals, and government publications.

1. For a book
Provide the following information: Name of the author or editor, title of the book, edition if applicable, place of publication, name of publisher, date of publication, and page number. For example:

[1] Charles W. Hofer and Dan Schendel, <u>Strategy Formulation: Analytical Concepts</u> (St. Paul: Minnesota, 1978), pp. 69-71.
[Used when footnotes are placed at the bottom of the page]

1. Charles W. Hofer and Dan Schendel, <u>Strategy Formulation: Analytical Concepts</u> (St. Paul: Minnesota, 1978), pp. 69-71.
[Used when footnotes are placed at the end of the report]

2. For an edited book
Provide the same information as above with the addition of ed. after the author's name. For example:

[2] A.A. Thompson, Jr., A.J. Strickland III, and W.E. Fulmer, ed., <u>Readings in Strategic Management</u>, 2nd ed., (Plano, Texas: Business Publications, Inc., 1984), pp. 149-163.

3. For a magazine or journal article

Provide the name of the author, title of the article, title of the magazine or journal, volume number, issue number, date of publication, and page number of the article. For example:

³Gregory H. Dobbins and Stephanie J. Platz, "Sex Differences in Leadership: How Real Are They?" The Academy of Management Journal, Vol. 11, No. 1, January, 1986, pp. 118-127.

4. For a government publication

Provide the name of the government agency authoring the publication, title of the publication, place of publication, publisher, date of publication, and page number. For example:

⁴Bureau of the Census, Census of Population (Washington, D.C.: U.S. Department of Commerce, 1980), p. 30.

5. For a source cited two or more times in a row

When you cite the same source two or more times in a row, use Ibid which means in the same place. If the page number is different, Ibid is followed by the page number. For example:

⁵Ibid.

⁶Ibid., p. 55.

6. For a source cited earlier in the footnotes

If you cite one source and then two or more footnotes later you wish to cite the same source again, provide the last name of the author, followed by the page number. For example:

⁷Dobbins and Platz, p. 125.
Or:
7. See Reference No. 2 (Dobbins and Platz, 1986), p. 125.

7. For an author with more than one publication

If you have cited more than one publication by the same author, provide the last name of the author and the first few words of the title. For example:

⁸Dobbins and Platz, Sex Differences, p. 126.

Appendix G
HOW TO PRESENT AN ORAL REPORT

1. Avoid the manuscript speech

A manuscript speech refers to a public-speaking situation where you read your entire presentation word for word. Since reading from a manuscript is characteristic of a novice speaker, it should be avoided. With your eyes riveted to the pages of the text, you are unlikely to sustain the listeners' interest in your topic for a considerable length of time.

To ensure that the delivery of your speech is as effective as the speech content, strive to use the extemporaneous style. To speak extemporaneously is to rely only partially on the manuscript. And to be able to do that, you need to follow three steps:

First, make an outline of the major points and subpoints that make up the entire speech.

Second, acquaint yourself thoroughly with the concepts or ideas underlying each major point and subpoint. Go over the concepts as many times as is necessary until they become firmly entrenched in your mind.

Third, practice your speech, using only the outline of the major points and subpoints as a guide.

2. Establish eye contact

A critical ingredient that makes for a successful presentation involves the establishment of eye contact with members of the audience. When engaged in a conversation with another person, you typically look the person in the eye. The same habit ought to be applied in delivering a speech.

To be a good speaker, avoid looking at one particular person or at one side of the audience all the time. Strive to change your target, shifting your eye contact from one side of the room to the other or from one person to another as you typically would in conversing with a group of friends.

3. Use facial expressions and gestures

Just as eye contact can be a valuable communication tool, so are such other nonverbal cues as facial expressions and gestures. The face and the hands are capable of depicting a staggering number of significant meanings. Sophisticated speakers are keenly aware of that, and they constantly seek to optimize the use of these tools to support or complement their spoken words.

It is important to remember that practicing your speech beforehand is a crucial key to the use of nonverbal cues. You cannot possibly make spontaneous facial expressions and gestures when you are inextricably tied to the manuscript. An intimate knowledge of the speech content resulting from a careful rehearsal of the speech can free you from the shackles of the text. In this way, you are able to concentrate not only on what to say but on how to say it.

4. Change your speaking rate

A poor speaker is either too fast or too slow for his or her audience. In either case, it is highly doubtful that he will succeed in gaining an attentive audience. When his speaking rate is fast, the speaker is apt to lose his listeners due to their inability to keep up with and grasp his ideas. Conversely, when his speaking rate is slow, he is also likely to lose his audience, this time due to sheer boredom.

Effective oral presentation calls for varying the rate of speaking. Two of the essential imperatives that should go into determining the most appropriate speaking rate are (1) the size of the audience and (2) the relative importance of the ideas to be communicated.

When you address a large group, your delivery rate should be slower than the rate you would typically use in addressing a small group. If you seek to emphasize a critical point, let your voice linger, thereby making the important point stand out prominently. In contrast, if you judge a point to be of relatively lesser importance, you need to communicate it at a faster rate.

5. Change your voice pitch and volume

Talking too rapidly or too slowly is not the only characteristic of a poor public speaker. He or she also has a tendency to talk either too loudly or too softly. In the former case, he is likely to irritate his listeners; and in the latter, he makes it difficult for them to hear his message.

As is the case in normal conversational speech, the pitch of your voice should fluctuate. By skillfully balancing pitch variations, you can avoid boring your listeners with a monotonous, flat, or dull pitch.

REVIEW QUESTIONS

1. What functions does the prescriptive phase perform?

2. What are the steps involved in formulating a strategic plan?

3. What is the difference between the unstructured, semi-structured, and structured approaches to evaluating alternative strategies?

4. In formulating a functional strategy, it is necessary to adhere to certain fundamental guidelines. What are they?

5. Discuss the concept of scenario.

6. Briefly, explain the two methods that may be used in ensuring the concreteness of recommendations.

7. What negative effects does the omission of a time table, budget, and savings from a functional strategy have on the strategy formulator?

References

1. G.A. Steiner, J.B. Miner, and E. Gray, *Management Policy and Strategy: Text, Readings, and Cases*, 3d ed., (N.Y.: Macmillan Publishing Co., 1986), p. 130.

2. Weston H. Agor, "How Top Executives Use Their Intuition to Make Important Decisions," *Business Horizons*, January/February, 1986, p. 50.

3. Stephen C. Harper, "Intuition: What Separates Executives from Managers," *Business Horizons*, September/October, 1988, p. 14.

4. See Reference No. 1 (Steiner, Miner, and Gray, 1986), p. 130.

5. E.R. Alexander, "The Design of Alternatives in Organizational Contexts," *Administrative Science Quarterly*, Vol. 24, 1979, p. 382.

6. Charles E. Lindblom, "The Science of Muddling Through," *Public Administration Review*, Vol. 19, 1959, p. 81.

7. John K. Ryans, Jr., and William L. Shanklin *Strategic Planning: Concepts and Implementation* (N.Y.: Random House, 1985), p. 201.

8. G.A. Steiner, J.B. Miner, and E. Gray, *Management Policy and Strategy: Text, Readings, and Cases,* 2d ed., (N.Y.: Macmillan Publishing Co., 1982), p. 297.

9. Dale D. McConkey, "Planning for Uncertainty," *Business Horizons*, Vol. 30, No. 1, January/February, 1987, p. 40.

Chapter 7

An Illustrative Case A

The Descriptive Phase (Parts A and B) of the Analysis Framework was used in generating a profile of the United States Gypsum Corporation.

188

A PROFILE OF UNITED STATES GYPSUM CORPORATION, 1990

Submitted to:
A.J. Almaney, Ph.D.
510: Strategic Management
DePaul University
Chicago, IL 60604

Submitted by:
Group 5
Jacquelyn Jenkins
Keith Landauer
Richard Pekosh
David Schact

November 29, 1990

TABLE OF CONTENTS

Part   **Page**

Descriptive Phase

Overview   192

History of Gypsum   193

History of USG Corporation   194

Internal Analysis of USG Corporation   196
A.1 Profile of the Corporate Business Level   196
A.2 Profile of the Functional Level   201

External Analysis of USG Corporation   204
B.1 Profile of the Task Environment   204
B.2 Profile of the General Environment   215

Endnotes   219

LIST OF EXHIBITS

Exhibit   **Page**

1. Members of the Board of Directors   198

2. Market Share in the Gypsum Industry, 1989   202

3. Consolidated Balance Sheet   205

4. Consolidated Statement of Earnings   206

5. Operating Performance   207

6. Cash Sources and Cash Uses   208

7. Financial Ratios   209

UNITED STATES GYPSUM CORPORATION

OVERVIEW

United States Gypsum Corporation is a Fortune 200 company that manufactures building materials and other products for use in the repair and construction industries in the United States and Canada. The corporation is composed of five subsidiaries: United States Gypsum Company, USG Interiors Company, L&W Supply Company, DAP Inc., and CGC Inc.

Producing gypsum and gypsum related products is the major function of the United States Gypsum, L&W and CGC subsidiaries. In this arena, the major competitors in North America are National Gypsum Company, Domtar, Inc., Georgia Pacific Corporation and the Celotex Corporation. In 1989, United States Gypsum Company had a U.S. market share of 34%, and was labeled the leading gypsum producer in the world, supported by L&W Supply and Canada-based CGC.[1] Gypsum accounted for 57% of USG's 1989 sales and 75% of its profits.[2]

USG Corporation's subsidiary, USG Interiors, and a portion of CGC, Inc. are responsible for producing building interiors. CGC is the leading gypsum board producer in Eastern Canada. In 1989, USG Interiors was most cited for the success of its ceiling tile sales to Europe, a market which is expected to grow 20% over the next few years. DAP's primary responsibility is the manufacture of materials for remodelling and repair purposes. DAP boasts several leading competitive brands. For the interiors market, the major competitors are Celotex Corporation, National Rolling Mills, Armstrong World Industries, and the Chicago Metallic Corporation. These non-gypsum producing entities are responsible for approximately 40% of USG's total sales and are expected to grow by approximately 10% in 1990, due to USG's presence in Europe and the Far East.[3]

The primary products generated by the gypsum producing entities, the company's primary product, include: wallboard, sheathing, baseboard, mobile home board, lay-in panels, soffit board, lawn and garden gypsum, agricultural gypsum, plaster, industrial gypsum cements and fillers, spray textured finish, textured panels, cement board and joint compound.[4]

The distribution channels used by USG include mass merchandising, building material dealers, contractors, distributors and industrial and agricultural users. It is important to note that USG's sales of gypsum products for new construction vary according to the time of year, however, the market for repairs and remodelling remains relatively stable year round. USG has its facilities (plants, mines, ships) located in areas of North America, Europe, Australia, New Zealand and Malaysia.[5]

The past few years have been relatively hectic for USG Corporation. It has faced numerous lawsuits for asbestos related illnesses, and property damages, and additional suits for price-fixing, and for violation of employee rights. In the middle 1980s, USG's stock price began to fall and one of USG's stockholders, Desert Partners Ltd., threatened to take over the company. USG was opposed to Desert Partners unsolicited bid and decided to fight the attempted take-over.

Recent news indicates that USG experienced an $11 million loss in the third and fourth quarters of 1990.[6] Was USG's decision to recapitalize a reasonable step? New home and building construction has been down for the past four years, and is expected to remain that way for the next decade, particularly in large cities.[7] In the meantime, USG's inventories are accumulating, forcing its plants to operate only six days a week rather than its usual seven. What will USG do in response? It is the purpose of the following case analysis to determine the best answers to these questions.

HISTORY OF GYPSUM

Gypsum, known as "the mineral with memory" can be melted down and processed into any form. It is found in mines and quarries around the world. Legend has it that a Chinese shepherd built his campfire on white rock (which was gypsum). The fire removed the water from the gypsum (gypsum is 28% water by weight) and left a white powder. The next morning the shepherd dumped water on the embers of the campfire. The water mixed with the white powder into a fluid and that later hardened into rock (gypsum). At the time, the shepherd thought that he witnessed a miracle; however, it is essentially the process used today to change gypsum into plaster. Historical evidence indicates that gypsum was used 5,000 years ago in pyramids in Egypt. Artists such as Leonardo da Vinci, created works on gypsum plaster in palaces. In the late 1700s, Lavoisier, a French chemist, worked with gypsum (also referred to as plaster of paris) to determine its secrets.[8]

Benjamin Franklin introduced gypsum to the U.S. for agricultural use. Until gypsum was discovered in New York, it was imported from Nova Scotia. The first very large scale use of gypsum in buildings was in the 1893 World's Columbian Exposition, in which several model buildings were completely structured with gypsum. In the early 1900s, gypsum board was used for partitions in New York City's buildings.[9] Gypsum's near fire-proof quality made it a prime candidate for building construction.

HISTORY OF UNITED STATES GYPSUM CORPORATION

United States Gypsum company was founded in 1902, and was comprised of a group of small gypsum suppliers. It was incorporated in Illinois in 1920, and reincorporated in Delaware in 1966 and again, in 1985. USG's original mission at the time of its founding in 1902, was to "develop and produce gypsum products of such consistent quality and performance that they would become the industry standard of excellence".[10]

In 1906, USG's president, Sewell Avery, was largely responsible for recruiting a competent staff and implementing modern manufacturing and marketing policies needed to develop USG. USG hired geologists to search for gypsum deposits, skilled engineers to mine the mineral, and researchers to experiment to find its best uses. In the early years, USG prided itself for the efficiency with which it produced products and for its preoccupation for employee safety, the latter of which was uncommon in the early 1900s.[11]

The year 1915 marked the beginning of USG's product line expansion. It began producing lime and sheetrock gypsum wallboard. Sheetrock paved the way for development of gypsum sheathing, drywall and panels. Two of gypsum's biggest assets are the ease and speed with which it permits one to construct, and its near fireproof quality. These features lead the U.S. government to contract with USG during both world wars. In World War II, USG supplied over one billion square feet of wallboard for military facilities.[12]

Through the years, USG continued to expand its product lines through innovation and diversification. The company began producing acoustical wood fiber, metal insulation, roofing and water resistant gypsum core. Today, gypsum wallboard has replaced plaster in almost all new office buildings and homes.[13] In its diversification efforts, USG has acquired a myriad of companies and resold several of them, including: BPB Industries, Ltd., London England; United Cement Company of Alabama; Warren Paint and Color Company in Nashville; Kinkhead Aluminum Industries; Float-Away Door Company; Chicago Mastic Company and Hollytex Carpet Mills of California.[14]

USG's impressive history however, is marred with a few problems. In 1975, USG, which held 34% of the gypsum market, National Gypsum (25% of the market) and Georgia Pacific (13% of the market) were accused by the U.S. Justice Department of price-fixing. The charges were dropped in 1980 in exchange for a $2.9 million tax settlement that USG paid to the IRS.[15] Beginning in the late 1970s, USG was attacked by the public for using asbestos related products in buildings, and by its own employees claiming illnesses relative to exposure to asbestos.[16]

In October of 1987, one of USG's common shareholders, Desert Partners, Ltd., indicated that it had purchased 9.8% of USG common shares and proposed a leveraged buy-out which USG refused. In February 1988, Desert Partners offered to purchase 21.5 million shares of common stock at $42 per share. The tender offer was later amended to increase the amount of common stock subject to purchase to 39 million shares. The USG board refused the offer and searched for other alternatives, its objectives being to "treat all shareholders equally, provide short-term investors quick returns, provide long-term investors security and keep the corporation public."[17] To accomplish this, USG developed a recapitalization plan in May of 1988 which offered each shareholder $37.00 per share in cash, $5.00 pay-in-kind securities and one new share of common stock in the new company for each old share. Although the deal was valued at $49.00 per share compared to $42.00 per share from Desert Partners, this promise to shareholders caused USG to take on $2.5 billion in debt.[18]

USG sought to finance this debt by acquiring $1.6 billion from foreign and domestic banks, by selling off some of its assets, and by strictly managing its cash flow. The company received $400 million for Masonite Corporation and $58 million for Marlite Division. The company sold its corporate headquarters to Manufacturers Life Insurance Co. of Toronto for $60 million. It also received $6.4 million for sale of its corporate jet.[19]

Further cutbacks included:
- DAP's closing of two of its plants in California and Georgia
- United States Gypsum Company's starting of a plant, productivity incentive program
- L&W Supply's closing or consolidation of 18 distribution centers and its new policy of leasing rather than buying cars and trucks for transport
- CGC's consolidating of ceiling and acoustical tile into one division called CGC Interiors.[20]

As a result of this restructuring, USG owes only $840 million of its original bank loan but has a total debt of $2.4 billion.

Certain financial analysts question USG's recapitalization decision. First, the company based its decision on expectations for steady housing starts, growth from remodeling and increased non-residential construction. USG's 10 year forecast failed to include a contingency plan which addressed the possibility of a recession. Second, the company expected to receive more money from the sale of its three business than it actually did. Analysts do believe that one positive aspect of the recapitalization is that employees now own a much larger share of the company which may protect USG from another hostile takeover threat.[21]

As of October 30, 1990, USG's common stock was selling for less than $2.00 per share, which is largely due to the company's current financial condition. USG's bond prices have also dropped as a result of National Gypsum's and Celotex's recent filings for Chapter 11. Additionally, USG is paying high interest expense for the loans it used to recapitalize. And, recent articles report that USG suffered an $11 million net loss during the current quarter and will be forced to further restructure its organization and implement even tighter cash flow solutions.[22]

PART A   PROFILE OF THE INTERNAL ENVIRONMENT

Part A.1   **Profile of the Corporate/Business Level**

Top Management

The Board of Directors for USG could be characterized as an oversight board, their major role being to govern the operation of the company. The board is composed of six USG management directors, and eight independent directors. The board also has a representative from BPB Industries, a London-based construction company (see Exhibit 7-1). The board carries out its functions through six committees: executive committee, compensation committee, audit committee, public affairs committee, finance committee, and committee on directors.

The newly appointed CEO, Eugene B. Connolly, has been with the company for 32 years. Prior to this position, he was Executive Vice President and Director of USG, Director of USG International, Ltd., and Director of USG Export Corporation.[23] His decision-making style can be characterized as that of strategic management. The state of affairs at USG and its sheer size would not permit one man to dictate all of the decisions. He needs the support of the board members, the stockholders and his managers in order to succeed with the recapitalization plans. Also, especially with the current financial strain due to the recapitalization, more than one man will have to be involved in the strategy-making process. Connolly's managerial mode appears to be the strategic planning mode. It is a combination of the entrepreneurial and adaptive modes, and involves examining USG's internal environment as well as its external environment.

The executive officers at USG are all between the ages of 45 and 65 with some possessing legal in addition to business backgrounds. They have all held senior positions in various areas of the corporation for five or more years. Additionally, some serve on the boards of other corporations.

Management, according to the annual report, is aware of the firm's strengths and weaknesses in its internal environment. Periodic reports and observations are used to reveal their findings. Management's decision to divest certain subsidiaries, harvest others and reduce overall costs in certain areas is an indication that they are in tune with the company's strong and weak points. Not only is management itself aware, but it strives to keep its employees aware by circulating newsletters and providing them with a 1-800 telephone number to dial every few days for USG updates.

Environmental Analysis

USG is very heavily influenced by its external environment. The company forecasts its sales/profitability on a yearly basis, using data obtained from housing starts, the repair and remodel markets, and the level of interest rates. Further, the company's levels of gypsum sales vary according to the time of year. USG experiences its highest sales from mid-Spring to mid-Autumn.

Strategy Formulation

The corporation has a very comprehensive, well-defined mission statement, or operating philosophy. Taken directly from the annual report, its statement is to:
- Maintain honest, reliable, and superior customer service and technical support.
- Achieve an outstanding safety record. USG's safety record at its gypsum plant is far superior to most U.S. manufacturers.
- Provide employees with pay and benefits that are competitive with the industry.
- Improve profitability and reduce debt to enhance shareholder value.
- Conduct improved product development and highly focused research.
- Be the most efficient and lowest cost producer in our business.[24]

USG's long-term corporate objective is to remain a leader in its core business (manufacturing building materials). In the short-run, its objective is to

Exhibit 7-1 **Composition of USG's Board of Directors**

W.H. Clark, Chairman and Chief Executive Officer, Nalco Chemical Company

Eugene B. Connolly, President and Chief Executive Officer

James C. Cotton, Chairman, President and Chief Executive Officer, Navistar International Corporation

James C. Cozad, Chairman and Chief Executive Officer, Whitman Corporation

Robert J. Day, Chairman of the Board

Anthony J. Falvo, Jr., Executive Vice President and Chief Operating Officer

David W. Fox, President and Chief Executive Officer, The Northern Trust Company

Philip C. Jackson, Jr., Formerly Vice Chairman, Central Bank of the South

Ralph C. Joynes, Vice Chairman

Eugene Miller, Vice Chairman and Chief Financial Officer

John B. Schwemm, Formerly Chairman and Chief Executive Officer, R.R. Donnelly and Sons Company

Jack D. Sparks, Formerly Chairman of the Board, Whirlpool Corporation

Alan J. Turner, Chairman and Chief Executive, BPB Industries

W.L. Weiss, Chairman and Chief Executive Officer, Ameritech

concentrate on reducing its long-term debt by focusing on expense control and cash flow management.

For its grand strategy, USG relies on product development and innovation. The company considers itself to be a technological leader in its field. According to the 1989 annual report, each subsidiary of USG had new products planned for introduction in 1990.

The company has two competitive strategies. The first one, technological leadership, is also one of its grand strategies. Because the firm holds 34% of the market share, USG also relies heavily on its reputation, which is excellent amongst its customers due to outstanding service. Even though market share may increase, due to National Gypsum's and Celotex's recent filings for Chapter 11, USG's investors tend to be leery because they realize that USG's success depends heavily on the fluctuation of interest rates, and are aware that the company is in debt.

Strategy Implementation

USG's corporate structure can be characterized as a strategic business unit (SBU) structure. USG's major SBU's are United States Gypsum, USG Interiors, L&W Supply Corp., DAP Inc. and CGC. Inc. The SBUs are all comprised of groups of divisions that share strategic elements of customer, competitors, and technology.

Due to its size, USG could not exist without well-defined policies; however, events have occurred over the years which indicate that certain of USG's policies have been questionable. For example, USG Corporation's Acoustical Products unit ordered its employees to stop smoking on the job and at home, or they would lose their jobs. This declaration was sparked by the fact that USG was named in numerous asbestos related lawsuits. The company chose this route as one of the measures of protecting itself against future lawsuits from workers who developed lung cancer. The policy was based on information obtained from the World Health Organization which indicated that smokers who worked in an asbestos environment were more likely than non-smokers to get lung cancer. Because the affected workers did not have a union, they could be forced to accept the policy at work, which was stated to them formally, in writing and in person. However, many employees and activist groups felt that trying to enforce non-smoking at home would not only be impossible, but would infringe on people's rights so USG backed down on that policy.[25]

Regarding communication, USG was attacked by employees during the restructuring phase for not keeping its employees abreast of happenings.

Employees were forced to find out through rumors and the press where cuts were being made, and whose jobs were being affected. This coupled with the new Employment Retirement Income Security Act of 1973 which states that employees have the right to know about their benefits, also lead to the new "open policy".[26] The company developed five ways to keep its employees informed, including: USG Bulletin, a daily printing of urgent messages; Looking Ahead, a bi-monthly publication that deals with company's debt; USG Today, a 1-800 telephone number for updated information on USG; USG Employee Communications Guide, a tool which USG officers and managers use to make presentations to employees; and Video News, a financial reference for USG.

A history provided by USG company indicates that even as early as the 1920s, when most companies used a task management managerial style, USG used the team management style. The company appeared to be equally concerned with employees and their safety as it was with the actual production of the products.

Given the high value USG appears to have for its customers, products, quality and employees, one can only assess that USG has a very functional culture. The company emphasizes innovation and open communication in its corporate culture. The fact that USG's employees now own a larger portion of stock than they did before the take-over bid, and are interested in having daily information on the company indicates that USG's employees are motivated.

Management appears to handle USG's budgetary allocations as best as possible given that resources are largely dependent on external sources. The only question posed is whether or not USG should have chosen to recapitalize and assume the debt when it did.

Strategy Control

USG's strategic managers are heavily involved in strategy control, establishment of standards of evaluation and performance, and correcting deviations. Its comprehensive annual report reveals that the company is constantly evaluating the performance of each of its divisions, and adjusting for corrections. Any deviations from strategy control to date, may be due to the fact that USG did not plan for such a serious recession, which has undoubtedly effected their long-term strategies.

Part A.2   **Profile of the Functional Level**

Marketing

In the area of marketing, USG maintains a long-standing tradition of producing high quality products along with a total commitment to excellence in providing consistently reliable customer service before and after the sale. USG's major products are gypsum wallboard, caulks and sealants, plaster, joint compound, cement board, ceiling and acoustical tile and industrial gypsum products. These products are typically used in new residential, commercial and industrial building construction and in areas associated with building restoration and renovation. USG is the worlds leading gypsum producer and is the largest supplier of gypsum products in the United States with approximately 34% of the market share (see Exhibit 7-2). Gypsum board product distribution is considered another corporate strength. L&W Supply Corporation is USG's distribution subsidiary which operates 132 distributorships strategically located throughout the U.S.

Gypsum product pricing has been declining steadily since 1987. This price decline has been due in part to both greater industry-wide production and recent depressed construction activity levels. Sales volume has been relatively flat at USG for several years. The flat sales volume, along with the price decline, has yielded flat annual total revenues for USG. For 1989, the breakdown of USG sales were as follows; USG Corporation $1,032 million (47% of sales); USG Interiors Inc. $549 million (25% of sales); L&W Supply Corp. $485 million (22% of sales) and other products $125 million (6% of sales).

USG owns and maintains 22 domestic gypsum board plants that are evenly distributed throughout the U.S. USG also has production facilities located in Canada, Mexico and Europe. They own thirteen gypsum mines and quarries located in the U.S. and Canada. Although total corporate capital spending was down 7% from $84 million in 1988 to $78 million in 1989, expenditures were up $46 million for 1989 in the area of plant modernization and upgrading.

Production

Quality control is an integral part of USG's production philosophy which in turn results in USG's reputation for providing high quality products. USG's plants typically run at or near capacity, this allows USG to consistently remain a low cost producer. In recent months, production has been reduced to six days per week due to weak demand. Inventory levels have risen in recent months, which indicates further evidence of the weakening demand for gypsum products.

Exhibit 7-2 **Market Share in the Gypsum Industry**

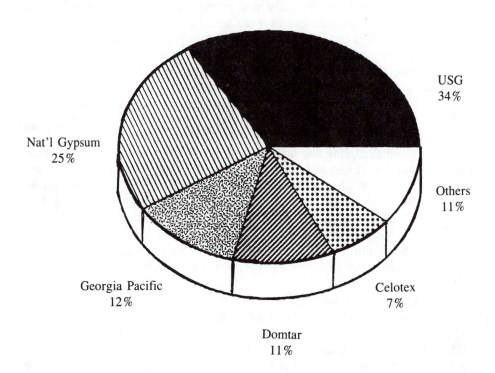

**Market Share
Gypsum Industry - 1989**

USG
34%

Nat'l Gypsum
25%

Others
11%

Georgia Pacific
12%

Celotex
7%

Domtar
11%

Rearch & Development

USG's research and development strategy is generally applied research. USG's major research goal is to continually upgrade its products in order to maintain its high standards. Due to USG's recapitalization and the recent weakened gypsum market, research expenditures have fallen from $24 million in 1987 to $19 million in 1989. USG owns three research facilities, one in Libertyville, Illinois, which focuses on product development, one in Avon, Ohio, which focuses on interior products, and one in Dayton, Ohio, which concentrates on sealant products.

Human Resources

USG incorporates a long-term plan for orderly succession of management personnel. Executives typically have many years of experience with the corporation and have managed key units of the business operation. Employees take an active role in supporting their company which is evidenced by their 26.5% ownership of USG's outstanding common stock. USG has a commitment to its employees to continually keep them informed as to the current status of the company. A system of bimonthly newsletters sent to all employees is one of many programs aimed at keeping employees up to date in regard to company programs. Additionally, USG offers an annual incentive program based on corporate profits for upper management employees. This program will assure that management decisions are in line with the goal of corporate profit maximization.

Public Affairs

A quote from USG's 1989 annual report states "USG has always prided itself on its high ethical standards."[27] These standards apply at all levels of USG operations. USG maintains a fundamental prerequisite of producing products of only the highest quality and top level customer service. Such a policy indicates USG's utmost commitment to social responsibility in the marketplace.

Finance/Accounting

Of all USG's internal aspects, their weakest area is currently finance and accounting. This is largely due to the decision to offset the corporate takeover threat in July of 1988. The resulting financial affect of USG's decision to recapitalize was the addition of a $2.5 billion debt obligation on top of USG's existing $200 million debt at that time. In 1989, USG's debt was reduced from $2.6 billion to $2.4 billion. The company paid out $297 million in interest for 1989. Without USG's heavy debt obligation, net operating profit for the year would have been $304 million instead of their reported net earnings of $28 million. These facts indicate that the internal operation of USG remains strong and that the debt obligation incurred in 1988 is the root cause of USG's weak financial position. For financial data, see Exhibit 7-3 (consolidated balance sheet), Exhibit 7-4 (consolidated statement of earnings), Exhibit 7-5 (operating performance), Exhibit 7-6 (cash sources and cash uses), and Exhibit 7-7 (ratios).

PART B   **PROFILE OF THE EXTERNAL ENVIRONMENT**

Part B.1   **Profile of the Task Environment**

Industry

Gypsum is grouped into the building materials industry and is dependent on new residential and nonresidential markets as well as the repair and remodel market. These markets are tied to the economy, interest rates, inflation, and availability of credit. Thus, the building materials industry is cyclical, being a poor market when the economy is poor and a strong market when the economy is healthy. Also, "sales of gypsum products are seasonal to the extent that sales are generally greater from middle of spring through the middle of autumn than during the remaining part of the year."[28]

The outlook for the building materials industry looks bleak. *Value Line Investment Survey* states:

> Improvements in the building materials industry doesn't look to be at hand. Weak demand in the new housing market coupled with economic weakness in many parts of the country and stricter lending standards, is likely to prevent any gains in the residential and commercial construction sectors of the economy.[29]

Value line goes on to state that even though unemployment "has been fairly stable and at relatively low level for some time now, we sense a certain uneasiness among potential home buyers about the course of the economy. This skittishness will likely keep the new residential construction market in a slump into 1991".[30]

Exhibit 7-3   **Consolidated Balance Sheet, as of December 31**

(All dollar amounts in millions)	1989	1988
Assets		
Current Assets:		
Cash and cash equivalents (primarily time deposits)	$ 66	$ 250
Receivables (net of reserves, 1989—$12; 1988—$11)	303	278
Inventories	125	125
Net assets of discontinued operations	—	21
Total current assets	494	674
Property, plant and equipment, net	883	906
Purchased goodwill, net	143	146
Other assets	82	95
Total assets	1,602	1,821
Liabilities and Stockholders' Equity		
Current Liabilities:		
Accounts payable	127	125
Accrued expenses		
Interest	70	73
Payrolls	23	26
Taxes other than taxes on income	14	16
Recapitalization and restructuring	12	30
Other	124	112
Notes payable	1	1
Long-term debt maturing within one year	168	260
Taxes on income	7	23
Dividends payable	5	16
Total current liabilities	551	682
Long-term debt	2,261	2,384
Deferred income taxes	214	206
Minority interest in CGC Inc.	14	20
Stockholders' Equity/(Deficit):		
Preferred Stock—$1 par value; authorized 36,000,000 shares—		
$1.80 Convertible Preferred Stock (initial series)—outstanding at		
December 31, 1989 and 1988—none	—	—
Common Stock—$0.10 par value; authorized 300,000,000 shares;		
outstanding at December 31, 1989—54,155,686 shares and		
December 31, 1988—53,967,275 shares (after deducting 102,467		
shares and 11,810 shares, respectively, held in treasury)	5	5
Capital received in excess of par value	15	12
Deferred currency translation	(3)	(6)
Reinvested earnings/(deficit)	(1,455)	(1,482)
Total stockholders' equity/(deficit)	(1,438)	(1,471)
Total liabilities and stockholders' equity	1,602	1,821

Exhibit 7-4 **Consolidated Statement of Earnings, Years Ended December 31**

(All dollar amounts in millions except per-share figures)	1989	1988	1987
Net sales	$2,192	$2,248	$2,255
Cost of products sold	1,645	1,672	1,599
Gross profit	546	576	656
Selling and administrative expenses	242	254	269
Recapitalization and restructuring expenses	—	20	53
Operating profit	304	302	334
Interest expense	297	178	69
Interest income	(10)	(13)	(5)
Other expense, net	15	16	16
Nonrecurring gains	(33)	—	(50)
Earnings from continuing operations before taxes on income	35	121	304
Taxes on income	9	48	131
Earnings from continuing operations	26	73	173
Discontinued Operations:			
Operating earnings, net of taxes	—	9	31
Gain on divestitures, net of taxes	2	43	—
Net earnings	28	125	204
Earnings per Common Share:			
Continuing operations	.48	1.38	3.36
Discontinued operations	.03	1.00	.60
Net earnings per common share	.51	2.38	3.96

Exhibit 7-5   **Operating Performance**

Net Sales
($ in millions)

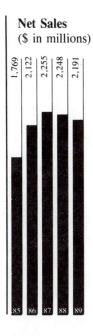

Gross Profit
($ in millions)

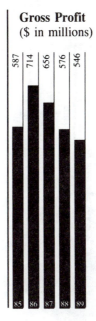

Operating Profit
($ in millions)

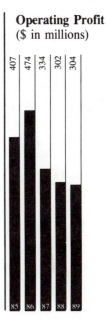

DEBT OBLIGATION

**Scheduled Total
Debt Level**
As of December 31
($ in millions)

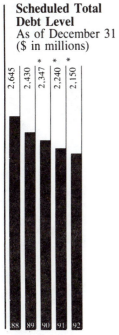

*USG estimates

**Term Loan Repayment
Schedule By Year**
($ in millions)

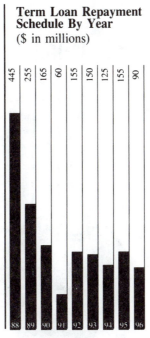

Exhibit 7-6 **Cash Sources and Cash Uses**

1989 Cash Sources

1989 Cash Uses

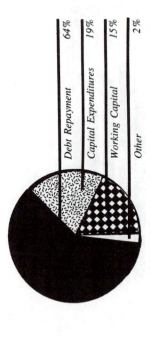

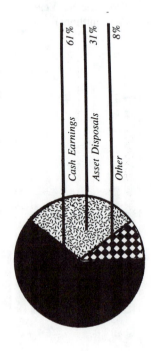

Debt Repayment 64%

Capital Expenditures 19%

Working Capital 15%

Other 2%

Cash Earnings 61%

Asset Disposals 31%

Other 8%

Exhibit 7-7 **Financial Ratios**

Ratio	Formula for Calculation	USG Ratio	Industry Average
Liquidity Ratios			
Current Ratio	$\dfrac{\text{Current Assets}}{\text{Current Liabilities}}$	.90 times	*
Quick or Acid Test	$\dfrac{\text{Current Assets — Invent}}{\text{Current Liabilities}}$	.67 times	*
Activity Ratios			
Inventory Turnover	$\dfrac{\text{Sales}}{\text{Inventory}}$	17.5 times	*
Collection Period	$\dfrac{\text{Accounts Receivable}}{\text{Sales per Day}}$	50 days	*
Total Asset Turnover	$\dfrac{\text{Sales}}{\text{Total Assets}}$	1.37 times	*
Leverage Ratios			
Debt to Total Assets	$\dfrac{\text{Total Debt}}{\text{Total Assets}}$	141%	*
Times Interest Earned	$\dfrac{\text{Net Operating Income}}{\text{Interest Expenses}}$	1.02 times	*
Profitability Ratios			
Profit Margin	$\dfrac{\text{Net Income}}{\text{Net Sales}}$	1.28%	*
Return on Equity	$\dfrac{\text{Net Income}}{\text{Net Worth}}$	—1.9%**	*

Source: 1989 corporate annual report for USG Corporation

* Competitors are either privately held or have other primary industries, such as forestry. Therefore, meaningful industry ratios are unavailable.

** The negative value for Net Worth produces a Return on Equity ratio that is also negative. While this is not a comparable ratio to the industry, it is representative of USG's current financial position. The negative Net Worth occurred as a result of USG's recapitalization.

The above forecast was written on July 27, 1990, before the Iraqi invasion of Kuwait. The invasion has caused the price of crude oil to more than double in just two and a half months. This event will certainly create even more uneasiness among potential home buyers about the future of the economy. In fact, new home construction "slumped for an eighth straight month in September" creating "the longest slide since statistics were first kept in 1959, and activity has slowed nationally to a recession-era pace."[31]

Another event that has hurt the building material industry has been the Savings and Loan crisis. "The home building industry, which drives the building materials segment, relies on massive amounts of credit to buy land and purchase materials for building houses. The S&L crisis, however, has spawned new regulations that prevent S&L's from lending large amounts to any one creditor in the real estate industry."[32]

Overall, the industry in which USG competes is headed for hard times in the future. The Iraqi invasion, the S&L crisis, and predictions of an economic recession may all have the effect of reducing the size of the market in which USG operates.

Competitors:

National Gypsum

National Gypsum is an integrated, diversified manufacturer and supplier of products and services for the building, construction and shelter markets.[33] The company has three continuing business segments. The first is the Gold Bond Building Products Division which produces gypsum wallboard and related products. Second, the Austin Company provides design, engineering and construction services. The third segment encompasses specialty items including a lime stone quarry and plant, two vinyl manufacturing plants, and a metal products plant. The company estimates to have approximately 25% of the US gypsum products market. National Gypsum feels that export sales are immaterial to the company as a whole.[34]

The company has gypsum manufacturing plants in Arizona, California, Georgia, Illinois, Indiana, Iowa, Louisiana, Maryland, Michigan, New Hampshire, New Jersey, New York, North Carolina, Ohio and Texas. National Gypsum owns several mines in the U.S., one in Mexico and one in Nova Scotia. It has enough estimated recoverable gypsum to last approximately 67 years based on 1988 production. It also owns three mills that manufacture paper used in the production of wallboard. The company estimates on average a 96% annual utilization of its optimum productive capacities.[35]

On April 29, 1986, the company effected a leveraged buy-out transaction in the form of a merger whereby Aancor Acquiring Corporation merged with and into the company. All of the outstanding capital stock of Aancor is held by the company's senior management and certain other investors. There is no public market for the common stock of the company.

The company's Form 10-K gives the impression that environmental issues are not one of its higher priorities. In discussing capital expenditures for pollution control, the 10-K stated:

> The estimated capital expenditures referred to above will impact the Company's earnings to some degree since funds expended for these purposes generally provide minimal, if any, monetary return on the investment, and may divert capital from income producing activities. However, the Company does not believe that its capital expenditures for pollution control during the past year or its presently anticipated capital expenditures for this purpose have had or will have a material impact on its earning or competitive position.[36]

The company's expenditure for pollution control was $.6 million dollars in 1988 or .05 of 1% of net sales. The company was planning to increase this expenditure.

The table below lists statistics for the gypsum and related products segments of National Gypsum. Sales represent consolidated net sales for the entire company, volume represents board feet of gypsum.

Year	Sales (mil)	Sales Volume (billion bd. ft.)	Operating Profit Margin
1988	$570.8	5.3	20.4%
1987	623.5	5.2	26.8%
1986	682.8	5.1	33.7%

Georgia-Pacific

Georgia-Pacific is an integrated manufacturer and distributor of a wide range of building products and pulp and paper products. It sells these products through its 144 distribution centers located in the U.S. Its gypsum products are sold by the corporations' distribution centers to building supply retailers ranging from traditional lumber yards to consumer-oriented home centers. These distribution centers enable Georgia-Pacific's manufacturing plants to operate at efficient rates of output by providing outlets for the plant's full production.[37]

Georgia-Pacific ranks third in the manufacture of gypsum products in the U.S., accounting for approximately 12% of the total domestic production. The company owns gypsum mines, quarries and deposits in Iowa, Kansas, Michigan, Nevada, Texas, Utah, Wyoming and Nova Scotia. It owns ten gypsum board plants located adjacent to these deposits or on ports served from the Nova Scotia quarry ocean vessels. The gypsum plants are running at approximately 78% of capacity. It estimates their current reserves are sufficient for a 45 year supply. Gypsum research is based in Decatur, Georgia. Laboratories at universities and other institutions are also utilized in the development of new products.[38]

The company employs approximately 44,000 people. The majority of the hourly workers are members of unions. The company considers its relationship with its employees to be good.[39]

Georgia-Pacific has had a long-standing concern for the quality of the environment in which it operates. The company's operations are subject to extensive regulation by federal, state and local agencies concerning environmental compliance. In the past, Georgia-Pacific has made significant capital expenditures to comply with regulation and expects to make significant expenditures in the future to maintain such compliance. Capital expenditures for pollution control facilities was approximately $39 million in 1989 (.4 of 1% of net sales) and budgeted $66 million in 1990.[40]

The table below lists statistics for the building products segment of Georgia-Pacific which includes gypsum as well as plywood, wood panels, lumber, and roofing materials. The sales volume numbers are for gypsum board only.[41]

Year	Sales (mil)	Sales Volume (billion bd. ft)
1989	$6,088	2.4
1988	6,029	2.4
1987	5,755	2.6

Domtar

Domtar Inc. is a Canadian based company that manufactures and markets a wide range of products through four operating groups; Pulp & Paper Products, Packaging, Chemicals and Construction Materials. It has 16,000 employees and runs 61 facilities in Canada and 14 in the U.S. Its operations are supported by a network of warehouses and sales offices across Canada and in certain areas of the U.S. as well as representatives abroad. Twenty-nine percent of its consolidated sales comes from the Construction Materials Group, with gypsum products as the largest component.[42]

The company holds approximately 11% of the U.S. gypsum market and 35% of the Canadian market. It produces gypsum board at five plants in Canada and eight plants in the U.S. Eight of the plants are integrated with their own rock supply. Domtar estimates that its current reserves of gypsum are ample for 25 years at current and anticipated production levels.[43]

Listed below are statistics for Domtar. Sales represent consolidated net sales for the entire company, volume represents board feet of gypsum.

Year	Sales (mil)	Sales Volume (billion bd. ft)
1988	$2,266	3.2
1987	1,975	3.4
1986	1,689	2.3

Celotex

The Celotex Corporation is a subsidiary of Jim Walter Corporation which in turn is owned by Hillsborough Holdings Corporation. Jim Walter Corporation is a diversified company that started in the business of selling, constructing, and financing shell-type and partially-finished homes. It has expanded into the manufacturing and distributing of a wide range of building materials for residential, commercial and renovation/remodeling uses, products for industrial uses, products for water and waste transmission and the development of natural resources including coal, marble, granite, limestone, oil, gas and gypsum. The company's other businesses include production of coke and industrial chemicals, distribution of a full line of fine printing papers, retail and wholesale credit jewelry operations, and insurance services.[44]

The Celotex Building Products Division manufactures foam insulation, gypsum board, mineral ceiling tiles, lay-in panels and fiberboard sheathing. It markets its products primarily to building materials dealers and wholesalers, distributors and specialized applicators. The company employs 16,750 people.

Celotex's policy is to own its plants and facilities and mineral deposits. Its gypsum reserves are located at three gypsum plants and are estimated to be sufficient for more than 50 years at present and projected annual rates of consumption.[45]

Suppliers

The issue of suppliers is not a major concern in the gypsum wallboard market. All the major competitors own their own mines and quarries of gypsum rock and in most cases have proven reserves to supply themselves for the next thirty or more years. The other major component of drywall is paper for outer coating and this is produced from waste paper which is in abundant supply. This waste paper and other raw materials used in this industry are purchased from numerous local and national firms. USG states that there should be no problems as to the availability of raw materials in the foreseeable future.

USG's gypsum and other plants are substantial users of thermal energy. The company uses primarily six major fuel types in the following order: natural gas 74%, electricity 10%, coal 6%, oil 5%, coke 4%, and steam 1%. These fuels come from various suppliers and USG feels that there will be sufficient supplies for the foreseeable future.[46]

Customers

The customers for the industry vary from large to small. The product is distributed through different channels to mass merchandisers, building material dealers, contractors, distributors and industrial and agricultural users. For USG, export sales to foreign unaffiliated customers represented less than 10% of consolidated net sales. Also, no single customer accounted for more than 4% of consolidated net sales.[47]

Government Regulators

National Gypsum which produces similar products to USG's, is involved with the government as a generator of hazardous substances found in disposal sites at which environmental problems are alleged to exist. Owners of the sites as well as certain other classes of persons are subject to claims brought by state and federal regulatory agencies pursuant to statutory authority. Since 1981, the EPA has sought compensation and remedial action from waste generators, site owners and operators and others under the Comprehensive Environmental Response, Compensation, and Liability Act of 1980 ("CERCLA" or "Superfund") which authorizes such action by the EPA regardless of fault or the legality of the original disposal.[48] Since USG and National Gypsum produce similar products, it is likely that USG is also regulated by the EPA and CERCLA with regard to its disposal practices.

Three companies produce approximately 75% of the wallboard market. In 1975, the Justice Department won a price-fixing conviction against the top four manufacturers, USG, National Gypsum, Georgia-Pacific, and Jim Walter (Celotex). The case was later appealed and all charges were dropped in 1980 in exchange for a tax settlement. Again in 1984, the Justice Department started a preliminary investigation into price fixing in the industry. Since the industry is dominated by three major players, the Justice Department represents an important government regulator in the gypsum market.

Part B.2   **Profile of the General Environment**

Demographics

Based on the U.S. Census Bureau statistics, housing's role in the economy and therefore the gypsum market, is expected to decline in the 1990s because fewer young people will be demanding homes. Americans from 25 to 34 years old make up the age group that is most likely to be first time home buyers. The population of their age group is expected to decline from 43.3 million Americans in 1987 to 36.2 million in the year 2000.[49]

The housing industry contributed nearly $220 billion to the Gross National Product (GNP) of the U.S. in 1988. However, a decrease of 100,000 housing starts will result in a drop of $12.5 billion in the GNP. The number of new housing units started dropped from 1.8 million in 1986 to 1.4 million in 1989. That 400,000 drop in new housing starts, from 1986 to 1989, reflects about a $50 billion drop in the GNP in the last four years. Economists expect that trend to continue with an estimated 1.2 million housing starts in 1990 and 1.0 million in 1991.[50]

Other factors that decrease the housing demand include: Americans are marrying at a later age, divorcing less frequently, and staying in their parents' homes longer. Also, the Bureau of Labor Statistics calculates that inflation-adjusted investment in residential construction will increase just 0.4% annually during the 1990s compared to 3.9% in the 1970s and 1.2% in the 1980s.[51] Canadian sales volumes of gypsum board products have been hurt by a drop in housing starts that has been more severe than in the U.S.[52]

Culture: N/I

Economy

The gypsum industry is suffering from weak prices which stem from soft demand for gypsum products. Sales of gypsum products tend to be seasonal and are generally greater from the middle of spring through the middle of autumn than during the rest of the year. The business is also affected by the cyclical behavior in the new residential and non-residential construction markets. The lackluster new residential construction market is the main reason for the reduced demand. One major producer reported price realizations of $87.36 per thousand square feet in the second quarter of 1989 which was down from $89.93 in 1988. The price peaked at $127.50 per thousand square feet in the fourth quarter of 1985 and hit the previous cyclical bottom of $74.73 in 1982. The 1989 prices are below the 1982 price level when adjusted for inflation.[53]

Another contributing factor of the soft demand of gypsum is the weak office building market, evidenced by a 17% vacancy rate nationwide. Cities such as Chicago, Cleveland, Washington, D.C., and New York are particularly over-built. The demand for gypsum products in the repair and remodeling market, which tends not to be cyclical, has been strong, but not strong enough to make up for the weakness in the residential and non-residential/commercial markets. The repair and remodeling market continues to grow and command a larger share of the total demand annually.[54]

Technology

New sources of gypsum have arisen from measures to control acid rain. Efforts to reduce the amount of sulphur emissions from coal burning power stations have resulted in a new supply of gypsum. One desirable by-product from the process of scrubbing sulphur that is sent up the power station chimneys is gypsum. The desulphurization process removes at least 90% of the sulphur dioxide while it produces gypsum that is 95% pure which makes it suitable for commercial use.[55]

Northern Indiana Public Service Company (NIPSCO), prompted by impending federal acid-rain legislation and U.S. Energy Department monetary contributions, is installing what could become the prototype scrubber for other urban-area electric generators in the 1990s. The NIPSCO scrubber is scheduled to open in mid-1992 and will produce 150,000 tons of gypsum annually - enough gypsum to make 150 million square feet of wallboard which is enough for 18,750 single family homes. USG is negotiating with NIPSCO to purchase the gypsum that they plan to produce for a USG plant in Northern Indiana. Using NIPSCO generated gypsum will save USG the 900 mile rail transportation costs from their nearest gypsum mine, in addition to mining costs.[56]

The scrubber may have a limited application. First, gypsum is abundant in most parts of the U.S. which is reflected in the dirt-cheap price of $2.00 a ton. Second, gypsum is a heavy mineral and transportation is the most expensive component of the cost in the gypsum wallboard industry. (Transportation costs make overseas export of gypsum products economically unfeasible. Also, wallboard cannot withstand the humidity encountered during transit). Potential power plants that could economically use scrubbers need to be near large metropolitan areas that use large quantities of wallboard. Currently, only three of five electric generators that produce gypsum can sell their output. The other two either produce inferior quality gypsum or cannot find buyers. The U.S. Environmental Protection Agency has identified 115 power plants that will fail to comply with recent federal acid rain legislation. Some utilities will likely switch to low-sulphur coal and others will shut down. Experts predict that an average of 10 new scrubbers will open a year either on existing plants or incorporated into new plants in the 1990s.[57]

European efforts to curtail acid rain are ahead of the measures in the U.S. The Central Electricity Generating Board (CEGB) in Britain has one desulphurization plant that produces 1.1 million tons of gypsum annually. BPB Industries controls 96% of the British gypsum market and mines 3 million tons of gypsum a year. If the CEGB includes similar plants at other power stations it will have the capacity to produce as much gypsum as BPB mines annually. This new source of gypsum has encouraged two new entrants in the British gypsum market. The power stations in West Germany produce so much gypsum that they pay plaster board manufacturers to take the gypsum off their hands.[58]

Louisiana-Pacific has developed a new wallboard product called fiber gypsum board. Fiber gypsum board will not need the two sheets of paper liner used on typical gypsum board which represent about 30% of the cost of making wallboard. Instead it will use wood fiber within the board which should give the board greater strength, better soundproofing and fire-retardant properties than typical wallboard. Also, the new technology has enabled Louisiana-Pacific to reduce energy costs, another significant cost factor, per unit of production. Those cost reductions may give them an important cost advantage.[59]

During our class presentation which was attended by USG's Brad James, Vice President - Strategic Management, we learned that USG also has a paper-less gypsum wallboard product. This new product, based on fiber gypsum board costs, should give USG a significant cost advantage, especially over its next largest competitor, National Gypsum.

Pressure Groups

USG, a former asbestos products manufacturer, is now one of many defendants involved in numerous lawsuits that seek compensatory and punitive damages for costs associated with the maintenance, removal and replacement of asbestos products. USG stopped manufacturing asbestos products more than a decade ago. A variety of defendants have engaged in those lawsuits including: school districts; state and local governments; colleges and universities; hospitals and private property owners. USG has denied the substantive allegations of each of the property damage lawsuits and intends to defend them vigorously except when advantageous settlements are possible. As of December 31, 1989, USG in cases lost, has paid out $1.5 million in punitive damages and $2.7 million in compensatory damages; however, USG plans to appeal those awards. USG has had to institute insolvency proceedings against certain former USG insurance carriers who provided them with excess insurance coverage during the 1970s and early 1980s. It is possible that USG will have to pay costs that would otherwise have been covered by those insurers. It is not possible to predict the number of additional lawsuits alleging asbestos-related claims that may be filed against USG. USG management, based on experience in the cases filed to date and anticipated insurance coverage, maintains that the asbestos-related litigation will not have a material adverse effect on USG's consolidated financial position.[60]

Endnotes

1. United States Gypsum Corporation, *1989 Annual Report* (Chicago, IL: United States Gypsum Corporation), p. 10.

2. Stuart J. Benway, "Building Materials," *Value Line Survey*, (New York, N.Y., 1990), Vol. 45, Part 3, p. 877.

3. *Ibid.*

4. United States Gypsum Corporation, *10-K Report* (Washington, DC.: Securities and Exchange Commission, 1989), p. 5.

5. *Ibid.*, p. 9.

6. "11 Million Net Loss Prompts USG Layoffs," *Chicago Tribune*, October 24, 1990, Section 3, p. 1.

7. "Chicago's Office Glut Could Outlast Decade," *Crain's Chicago Business*, October 26, 1990, p. 56.

8. "Products and Processes," *USG Corporation Training Manual*, (Chicago, IL.: USG Corporation, 1990), pp. 5-9.

9. *Ibid.*, p. 8.

10. *Ibid.*, p. 5.

11. *Ibid.*

12. *Ibid.*, p. 7.

13. "Wall to Wall," *Forbes*, July 2, 1984, p. 45.

14. *Moody's Industrial Manual*, 1990, pp. 6400-6401.

15. *Forbes, op. cit.*, p. 45.

16. *10-K 1989 Report, op. cit.*, p. 12.

17. *USG Annual Report, 1989, op. cit.*, p. 4.

18. *Chicago Tribune*, October 24, 1990, *op. cit.*, p. 4.

19. *USG Annual Report, 1989, op. cit.*, p. 4.

20. *Ibid.*, p. 8.

21. "A Vote for Readers," *Financial World*, December 27, 1988, pp. 10-11.

22. "National Gypsum and Parent Seek Chapter 11 Status," *The Wall Street Journal*, October 30, 1990, p. B8.

23. *Standard and Poors Register of Corporate Directors* (New York: Standard and Poors, 1990), p. 286.

24. *USG Annual Report, 1989, op. cit.*, p. 3.

25. "Hup 2-3-4! No Smoking," *Industry Week*, February 9, 1987, pp. 24-25.

26. "Lending an Ear to Employee Relations," *Chicago Tribune*, June 29, 1989, Section 3, p. 4.

27. *USG Annual Report, 1989, op. cit.*, p. 3.

28. *USG 10-K Report, 1989, op. cit.*, p. 5.

29. Stuart J. Benway, *op. cit.*, p. 851

30. *Ibid.*

31. "Midwest Bucks Housing Slide," *Chicago Tribune*, October 18, 1990, Section 3, pp. 1 and 5.

32. Stuart J. Benway, *op. cit.*, p. 851.

33. *Moody's Industrial Manual, 1990*, p. 314.

34. USG, *10-K Report, 1988*, pp. 2-5.

35. *Ibid.*

36. *Ibid.*, p. 3.

37. *Moody's Industrial Manual, 1990, op., cit.*, p. 314.

38. *USG 10-K Report, 1988*, p. 4.

39. *Ibid.*, p. 6.

40. *Moody's Industrial Manual, 1990, op. cit.*, p. 315.

41. *Ibid.*, pp. 315-317.

42. *Domtar 10-K Report, 1989*, p. 4.

43. *Ibid.*, p. 16.

44. *Jim Walter Corporation 10-K Report, 1987*, p. 2.

45. *Ibid.*, p. 7.

46. *USG 10-K Report 1989, op. cit.*, pp. 5 and 8.

47. *USG Annual Report, 1989*, p. 30.

48. *USG 10-K Report, 1988*, p. 30.

49. "What's Pulling the Rug Out from Under Housing," *Business Week*, January 23, 1989, p. 104-105.

50. *Construction Review*, July/August 1990, p. 9.

51. *Business Week*, January 23, 1989, *op. cit.*, pp. 104-105.

52. Stuart J. Benway, *op. cit.*, p. 877.

53. "Gypsum also in the Doldrums," *Industry Surveys-Building and Forest Products*, December 14, 1989, p. B87.

54. *Ibid.*

55. "Utility to Generate Walls as Well as Watts," *Chicago Tribune*, April 22, 1990, Section 7, pp. 1-2.

56. *Ibid.*

57. *Ibid.*

58. "Gypsum: Acid Cloud, Silver Lining," *Economist*, October 15, 1988, pp. 73-74.

59. *Industry Surveys-Building and Forest Products, op. cit.*, p. B87.

60. *USG 10-K Report, 1989*, pp. 11-13.

Chapter 8

An Illustrative Case B

The Diagnostic and Prescriptive Phases (Parts C through L) of the Analysis Framework were used in preparing the following analysis of United States Gypsum Corporation.

ANALYSIS OF UNITED STATES GYPSUM CORPORATION, 1990

Submitted to:
A.J. Almaney, Ph.D.
GSB 510: Strategic Management
DePaul University
Chicago, IL 60604

Submitted by:
Group 5
Jacquelyn Jenkins
Keith Landauer
Richard Pekosh
David Schacht

November 29, 1990

TABLE OF CONTENTS

Part   **Page**

Diagnostic Phase

C.1   Strengths of the Corporate/Business Level 227
C.2   Strengths of the Functional Level 230
C.3   Distinctive Competency 232
D.1   Weaknesses of the Corporate/Business Level 234
D.2   Weaknesses of the Functional Level 235
D.3   Critical Weakness 238
E.1   Opportunities in the Task Environment 238
E.2   Opportunities in the General Environment 238
E.3   Key Opportunity 239
F.1   Threats in the Task Environment 239
F.2   Threats in the General Environment 240
F.3   Key Threat 240
G.1   Unfavorable Factors by Major Component 240
G.2   Major & Minor Symptoms & Probable Causes 241
G.3   Listing of Major & Subordinate Problems 243
H   USG's Strategic Match 245
I   USG's Primary Strategic Match 246
J   Competitors' Distinctive Competency/Weakness 247

Prescriptive Phase

K.1   Mission Statement 250
K.2   Corporate Objectives 252
K.3   The Strategic Choice 252
K.4   Competitive Strategy 252
K.5   Functional Objectives & Strategies 254
L.1   Implementation - Organizational Structure 260
L.2   Implementation - Policies 260
L.3   Implementation - Procedures & Rules 261
L.4   Implementation - Leadership 261
L.5   Implementation - Corporate Culture 262
L.6   Implementation - Communication 262
L.7   Implementation - Motivation 262

LIST OF EXHIBITS

Exhibit   **Page**

1.   Ratio Summary 233

2.   Ratio Summary 237

3.   Determining The Business Strength/Competitive Position of USG   248

4.   Determining Industry Attractiveness 249

5.   Positioning of USG on the Strategic Match Matrix 250

6.   Evaluating Alternative Grand Strategies 253

Part C.1   **Strengths of the Corporate/Business Level**

Strategic Managers

Board of Directors
1.   USG's Board of Directors is composed of only six USG management directors, and eight independent directors. This mix is a strength for USG. Having a larger number of board members that are not affiliated directly with the company will help bring fresh ideas and insight to decision-making sessions.
2.   USG also is privileged to have a member of London-based BPB on its board. Recent studies indicate that it is becoming increasingly important to have international representation on boards.

Top Management
1.   Eugene B. Connolly, the company's CEO has a 32 year tenure with USG in different areas of the corporation. He is familiar with the company's past crises and triumphs and will therefore be able to make reasonable future decisions based on his past experiences. As mentioned in the profile, his exposure to other areas of USG will aid him as well.
2.   Connolly's decision-making mode can be characterized as being participative. Given USG's current position, an autocratic decision-making mode would be unwise and most likely, unacceptable by directors and board members.
3.   Connolly's managerial mode is strategic planning mode. The strategic planning mode is a combination of the adaptive and entrepreneurial modes. This dual planning mode is a strength for USG because it requires the CEO to consider the internal environment of the organization in conjunction with its external environment.
4.   Top managers at USG have all held senior positions for various areas of the corporation for 5 or more years, a definite strength.

Environmental Analysis
1.   Management's decision to divest certain subsidiaries, harvest others and reduce overall costs through vigorous cash flow management is an indication that the company analyzes its internal environment and makes decisions based on their findings. The company also seeks to make much of the findings available to its employees daily by way of several techniques, including an 800 number.

Strategy Formulation

Mission Statement
1.   USG's mission statement is very well-defined in its annual report. The statement covers the major elements required in a good mission statement, including technology. The mission statement is a definite strength for the company, given the tentative position it was placed in by Desert Partners. The statement reflects USG's concern for its employees and shareholders.

Corporate Objective
1.   As stated in USG's annual reports, the company's long-term objective is to remain a leader in its core business (manufacturing building materials). The objective is straight-forward and contains the necessary elements for a good objective, namely, that it is a result that the entire organization must continue to achieve for the rest of the organization's existence.
2.   USG's short-term objective of reducing its debt by focusing on cash flow management and selling assets is a strength as well. In order to pay back the loan it took from the banks for its stockholders in 1988, this objective is required.

Grand Strategies
1.   USG's mission statement emphasizes new product development and focuses on R&D. This means that several of USG's divisions have new products planned for the year 1990, including new improvements on products and manufacturing techniques. This is an indication that USG stresses innovation as one of its grand strategies.
2.   Evidence in USG's history, 10K reports and annual reports reveals that the company relies heavily on concentric diversification. This is the acquisition of firms with related products. Examples of these are USG's acquisition of various cement, paint, metal and carpeting companies, all of which help to provide more products to USG's consumers.
3.   It can only be speculated, given USG's size that it uses either a semi-structured or structured approach in evaluating grand strategies. It is highly unlikely that the company's managers would rely on intuition alone to make major decisions.

Competitive Strategies
1.   USG prides itself as being a technological leader in its industry. This means it uses the competitive strategy of product differentiation. The focus USG places on R&D and innovation is verification of this position.

Strategy Implementation

Organizational Structure
1.   USG is composed of several SBU's. The SBU structure is an asset to
      USG because it allows for easier allocation of resources, removes some
      of the pressure from the CEO and eliminates overlapping of functions in
      the organization. The structure allows each SBU to increase its level of
      focus on the products for which it is responsible.

Leadership
1.   A definite asset to USG is its concern for its employees, particularly
      given the heavy-duty manufacturing in which the company engages. In
      such industries, the task management style is typically used. However,
      USG uses team management, which involves equal concern for employees
      and production.

Culture
1.   USG's culture can be characterized as being very functional. As stressed
      in its annual report, USG places a high value on its customers, employees
      and product quality. This is a strength for the company because everyone
      knows instinctively on what to focus.

Communication
1.   Communication has become one of USG's most valuable assets in its
      difficult time. Once criticized for inefficient communication, the company
      has developed a 1-800 number to keep its employees up-to-date, an
      employee communications guide, a bi-monthly newsletter and videotape
      which informs employees of occurrences in the financial arena.

Motivation
1.   The fact that USG's largest number of shareholders are its employees is
      an indication that the employees are motivated to help the company
      succeed. This is a strength, because without the backing of its employees,
      USG would have a great deal of difficulty succeeding, particularly since
      it stresses customer relations. No information was provided relative to
      employee turnover or incentives.

Establishment of Standards
1.   USG's preoccupation with technological leadership and customer service
      are both indications that these 2 items are standards for the company.
      Anything less than the standard would not be acceptable.

Correction of Deviation
1.   USG's recent quick reaction to further restructure its company after it was announced that the company had incurred a net loss in the 3rd quarter of 11 million dollars is a strength for the company. This loss, largely due to external factors, may not have been planned for a few years back. Therefore, drastic measures were needed.

Part C.2   **Strengths of the Functional Level**

Marketing

Products
1.   USG maintains a longstanding tradition of developing and producing only the highest quality gypsum board and its related products.
2.   USG's major concentration is in the building products and restoration field. They produce wallboard, caulks and sealants, plaster, joint compounds, cement board, ceiling and acoustical tile, and industrial gypsum products.

Market Share
1.   USG's main internal strength is their position as the worlds leading gypsum producer and number one supplier of gypsum products in the U.S., with 34% of the total market share.

Target Market
1.   Gypsum products are typically used in residential, commercial and industrial building construction. With this broad end use mix, the impact of up and down cycles in the various areas of the construction industry can be minimized.
2.   No single customer of USG accounts for more than 4% of their company's total sales. This is a strength in that with such a wide customer base, USG does not overly rely on a few preferred customers.

Distribution
1.   L&W Supply Corporation is USG's main product distribution subsidiary. L&W owns 132 distributorships strategically located throughout the U.S., which affords product delivery at a minimal cost.

Production

Facilities
1.   USG owns and operates 22 domestic gypsum board plants that are evenly distributed throughout the U.S. This distribution is an advantage in that

regional swings in the construction industry will not severely impact USG's overall production.

2. USG owns and operates 13 gypsum mines and quarries in the U.S. and Canada. By having the source of raw materials relatively close to USG's production facilities, raw material transit expenses can be minimized.

Capital Expenditures
1. USG is committed to maintaining and modernizing its existing production facilities. Although total corporate capital expenditures were down 7% from $84 million in 1988 to $78 million in 1989, expenditures for modernizing, replacing and expanding existing production facilities were up $6 million from the 1988 level.

Quality Control
1. Quality control is strongly emphasized in all production areas. This results in USG's reputation for providing high quality products.

Production Capacity
1. USG plants typically run at or near capacity. This allows USG to consistently remain a low cost producer in relation to its competitors.

Research & Development

1. Research and development at USG is generally directed toward applied research. USG's research goal is to continually upgrade their products so that their tradition of high quality standards is maintained.

Human Resources

Succession Planning
1. A strength for USG is the company's longstanding plan for orderly succession of management personnel. Managers typically have many years of service with the corporation and have held many important managerial positions. This policy acts as a stabilizing influence at all levels of the company.

Employee Relations
1. Employees take an active role in supporting USG. 26% of all USG stock is employee owned.
2. USG is committed to keeping its employees informed as to the current status of the company. Several new programs have been initiated with the purpose of providing corporate information to all employees.

Compensation
1. An annual incentive program based upon company profits has been established for upper management employees. This program should assure that all management decisions are based on the goal of profit maximization.

Public Affairs

Ethics & Social Responsibility
1. USG is particularly proud of its consistently high ethical standards. These standards apply to all levels of USG operations. USG maintains a fundamental pre-requisite of producing products of only the highest quality. Such a policy indicates USG's utmost commitment to social responsibility in the marketplace.

Finance & Accounting

Management of Debt
1. Total debt due to recapitalization was reduced from $2.6 billion in 1988 to $2.4 billion in 1989. Although the debt reduction is relatively small, it is an indicator that financially, USG is moving in the right direction. (For financial ratios, see Exhibit 8-1.)

Management of Costs
1. Cost of products sold and selling and administrative costs were down 1.6% and 4.7% respectively from 1988 to 1989. This indicates that management efforts toward cost reduction are paying off.

Part C.3   **Distinctive Competency**

The distinctive competency of USG is the company's overall marketing philosophy to develop and produce only the highest quality gypsum products. USG is the world's leading gypsum producer with 34% of the market in the U.S. The company's products must meet very high quality standards that are established throughout all phases of production. Efficient production then ties in with USG's distribution centers that are strategically located throughout the U.S. and Canada. Customer service is a very high priority at USG. USG believes strongly in its product line and is committed to providing the utmost in customer satisfaction.

Exhibit 8-1 **Ratio Summary**

Ratio	Formula for Calculation	USG Ratio	Industry Average
Liquidity Ratios			
Current Ratio	$\dfrac{\text{Current Assets}}{\text{Current Liabilities}}$	.90 times	*
Quick or Acid Test	$\dfrac{\text{Current Assets — Invent}}{\text{Current Liabilities}}$	.67 times	*
Activity Ratios			
Inventory Turnover	$\dfrac{\text{Sales}}{\text{Inventory}}$	17.5 times	*
Collection Period	$\dfrac{\text{Accounts Receivable}}{\text{Sales per Day}}$	50 days	*
Total Asset Turnover	$\dfrac{\text{Sales}}{\text{Total Assets}}$	1.37 times	*
Leverage Ratios			
Debt to Total Assets	$\dfrac{\text{Total Debt}}{\text{Total Assets}}$	141%	*
Times Interest Earned	$\dfrac{\text{Net Operating Income}}{\text{Interest Expenses}}$	1.02 times	*
Profitability Ratios			
Profit Margin	$\dfrac{\text{Net Income}}{\text{Net Sales}}$	1.28%	*
Return on Equity	$\dfrac{\text{Net Income}}{\text{Net Worth}}$	−1.9%**	*

Source: 1989 corporate annual report for USG Corporation

* Competitors are either privately held or have other primary industries, such as forestry. Therefore, meaningful industry ratios are unavailable.

** The negative value for Net Worth produces a Return on Equity ratio that is also negative. While this is not a comparable ratio to the industry, it is representative of USG's current financial position. The negative Net Worth occurred as a result of USG's recapitalization.

PART D   DIAGNOSING THE ORGANIZATION'S WEAKNESSES

Part D.1   **Weaknesses of the Corporate Business Level**

Strategic Managers

Top Management
1.   One weakness for USG is that its executive officers (with the exception of one, are all 45 and older. The youngest is 43. One reason for this may be USG's emphasis of succession planning. Despite the cliche "the older the wiser," USG might benefit from more "younger blood" in high positions.

Environmental Analysis

External Analysis
1.   USG's failure to plan for a recession in its long-range planning after assuming the debt marks a serious weakness for the company, particularly since the sale of the company's primary product relies so heavily on the economy.
2.   The fact that the building and construction market had been in a slump for the past two years when USG made its decision to assume the debt means that the company did not use its external scanning mechanisms effectively. The mechanisms it relies on are fluctuations in the economy, repair and remodel market forecasts, and weather predictions for the construction season.

Strategy Formulation

Corporate Objectives
1.   A more well-defined time frame for the corporate objective than "remain an industry leader" could be used, although this is a minor weakness.

Grand Strategies
1.   USG has divested a large number of SBU's. This is a weakness because it lessens the amount of product offerings USG has for its customers.

Strategy Implementation

Policies
1.   USG's policy of not hiring smokers and its attempt at making its employees stop smoking at home, was an infringement on people's rights. This weakness, however, has been overcome.

Budgetary Allocations
1.   USG's strategic plan to recapitalize has put the company in a very bad position financially. Two years later, the company faces additional restructuring and another possible recapitalization.

Part D.2   **Weaknesses of the Functional Level**

Marketing

Sales Volume
1.   Sales volume for gypsum products has been relatively flat since the mid 1980s. This is due in large part to the recent decline in construction activity, especially residential construction.

Pricing
1.   Since 1987, gypsum product pricing has been on a steady decline. Pricing declines have been 13% in 1987, 14% in 1988 and 4% in 1989. This trend is due in part to both greater industry-wide production and the recent depressed construction activity levels. All have had a negative impact on USG pricing.

Production

Production Capacity
1.   Due to recent declines in demand for gypsum products, several plants have reduced output by cutting production to six days per week.

Inventories
1.   Inventories have recently been increasing due to the lack of demand. This is a negative indicator in the production area.

Research & Development

Budget
1.   Due to USG's recapitalization and weak gypsum market, research and development expenditures have declined from $24 million in 1987 to $19 million in 1989.

Public Affairs

Crisis Management
1.   USG is currently involved along with several other corporations in litigation for several class action suits against them pertaining to asbestos in their products. Many of these cases have already been settled although this is a negative factor. The remaining open cases should not have a material adverse affect on the company's financial condition.

Finance & Accounting

Management of Cash
1.   Recent developments in the gypsum industry have left USG in a weaker cash position than management would like. Cash reserves have fallen from $250 million at the end of 1988 to $66 million at the end of 1989. (For financial ratios, see Exhibit 8-2.)

Management of Inventories
1.   Due to weak demand for gypsum products, USG's inventories have risen in the past few months.

Management of Debt
1.   Although USG's debt obligation was reduced from $2.6 billion in 1988 to $2.4 billion in 1989, they remain in an extremely weak financial position due to their 1988 recapitalization. Interest payments in 1989 totaled $297 million on an operating margin of only $304 million. This statistic clearly indicates management of debt as the major corporate weakness at this time.

Capital Budgeting
1.   Overall capital expenditures have fallen 7% from $84 million in 1988 to $78 million in 1989. This indicates a weakness in an area where USG typically prefers to remain strong.

General Profit Picture
1.   Based on the 3 year trend of declining profits for USG, the near term profit picture looks bleak (1987 earnings $204 million, 1988 earnings $125 million and 1989 earnings $32 million). USG's debt obligation will continue to negatively impact corporate profits for several years to come. The construction industry shows little if any promise of a turnaround in the near future.

Exhibit 8-2   **Ratio Summary**

Ratio	Formula for Calculation	USG Ratio	Industry Average
Liquidity Ratios			
Current Ratio	Current Assets / Current Liabilities	.90 times	*
Quick or Acid Test	Current Assets — Invent / Current Liabilities	.67 times	*
Activity Ratios			
Inventory Turnover	Sales / Inventory	17.5 times	*
Collection Period	Accounts Receivable / Sales per Day	50 days	*
Total Asset Turnover	Sales / Total Assets	1.37 times	*
Leverage Ratios			
Debt to Total Assets	Total Debt / Total Assets	141%	*
Times Interest Earned	Net Operating Income / Interest Expenses	1.02 times	*
Profitability Ratios			
Profit Margin	Net Income / Net Sales	1.28%	*
Return on Equity	Net Income / Net Worth	−1.9%**	*

Source: 1989 corporate annual report for USG Corporation

* Competitors are either privately held or have other primary industries, such as forestry. Therefore, meaningful industry ratios are unavailable.

** The negative value for Net Worth produces a Return on Equity ratio that is also negative. While this is not a comparable ratio to the industry, it is representative of USG's current financial position. The negative Net Worth occurred as a result of USG's recapitalization.

Part D.3   **Critical Weakness**

The key weakness of USG can be found in the financial condition of the company. The $2.6 billion debt obligation incurred in July of 1988 in response to the hostile takeover bid by Desert Partners Inc. has placed USG in a very vulnerable financial position. In 1989, $297 million were paid out in interest on USG's total debt. Most of the interest expense was due to the recapitalization. With USG's net operating margin of only $304 million for 1989, one can clearly see the reason behind their paltry earnings of $32 million on revenues of $2.2 billion. The recapitalization debt will undoubtedly adversely affect many areas of USG's operations. Research and development expenditures have already been reduced. Although capital expenditures for maintenance and modernization were slightly up for 1989, it is doubtful that such expenditure increases can continue. This will ultimately affect USG product quality.

PART E   DIAGNOSING THE ORGANIZATION'S OPPORTUNITIES

Part E.1   **Opportunities in the Task Environment**

Competitors
1.   Both National Gypsum, the second largest gypsum product maker in the U.S., and Celotex, the fifth largest producer, filed for Chapter 11 in the last six weeks. While these two companies are mired in deep financial difficulties and attempt to reorganize, USG has the window of opportunity to increase its gypsum product market share by attracting these companies' customers.

Part E.2   **Opportunities in the General Environment**

Technology
1.   Technological breakthroughs are emerging whereby paperless wallboard products can be manufactured. Paper represents 30% of the cost of making a typical wallboard. Also, a paperless wallboard requires less energy to dry than typical wallboard. A paperless wallboard would give USG a significant cost advantage over its larger competitors.

Part E.3   **Key Opportunity**

USG's key opportunity lies in the large market from which National Gypsum and Celotex may exit. These two competitors have recently filed for Chapter 11 protection. National Gypsum and Celotex, combined, hold 36% of the gypsum product market. USG could use their new paper-less wallboard product, with its potentially significant cost advantages, to capture parts of those two companies' respective market shares.

PART F   **DIAGNOSING THE ORGANIZATION'S THREATS**

Part F.1   **Threats in the Task Environment**

Industry
1.   Sale of gypsum products is seasonal, which, coupled with a bad economy, could make the market for the products even worse.

Government Regulators
1.   The Comprehensive Environmental Response, Compensation, and Liability Act (CERCLA) authorizes the EPA to seek compensation and remedial actions for clean up of waste disposal sight regardless of fault or legality of original disposal.

Customers
1.   Litigations are continuing regarding maintenance or removal and replacement of products containing asbestos.

Competitors
1.   If National Gypsum goes out of business, then the remaining companies are faced with picking up bigger shares of the asbestos litigation payout.

Investors
1.   USG's bond prices have dropped as a result of National Gypsum's and Celotex's filings for Chapter 11. This will force USG's interest rates on their bonds to rise if they need to borrow money in the future.

Part F.2   **Threats in the General Environment**

Economy
1.   Gypsum market is tied to the economy, interest rates, inflation, and availability of credit, all of which are predicted to be poor in the future.
2.   Iraq's invasion of Kuwait and its direct impact on fuel costs is another definite threat. Increased fuel costs will have a direct adverse impact on an already weakened economy.

Part F.3   **Key Threat**

USG's key threat is the economy. Housing starts have dropped significantly over the last four years. Experts expect for the trend to continue through this year and next. There is an overabundance of office buildings, many of which are empty, throughout the nation. Economists believe that the impending recession will worsen before it gets better. The Iraqi conflict with its imminent threat to world peace and the cost of oil could bring on even worse economic conditions overnight.

PART G   **DIAGNOSING THE ORGANIZATION'S MAJOR AND MINOR PROBLEMS**

Part G.1   **Listing the Unfavorable Factors By Major Component**

Environmental Analysis
1.   Erroneous forecasts predicting a ten year increase in the housing starts, repair and remodelling market, and non-residential construction

Strategy Formulation
1.   Decision to prevent hostile takeover by recapitalizing the company and assuming a large debt

Strategy Implementation
1.   Sold off assets
2.   Cost reduction
3.   Debt repayment

Marketing
1.   Sales have slid 6% for the first 9 months of this year compared to last year and have slid 4% for the third quarter.

Finance
1.   Stock currently selling for less than $2 per share compared to a high of $55.90 per share in 1987
2. $11 million loss for the third quarter of 1990
3.   Company's poor leverage ratios: USG   Industry
     Total Debt/Total Sales   103%   23%
     Times Interest Earned   1.02   4.36
4.   High percentage of operating profit goes for interest payments (98% in 1989 versus 21% in 1987 before the recapitalization)

Human Resources
1.   Cut work force by 7,000 employees in last 2 years and are planning significant layoffs in the future

Production
1.   Inventory build-up had caused plants to cut back operations to only 6 days a week.

Task Environment
1.   Stockholders, under advisement of strategic managers, voted to approve the recapitalization.
2.   Low price for gypsum wallboard due to competition
3.   Cyclical nature of gypsum wallboard market

General Environment
1.   Decline in residential and non-residential markets
2.   Current poor economic conditions
3.   Savings and loan crisis
4.   Low price of gypsum due to poor economy

Part G.2   Listing of Major & Minor Symptoms with Probable Causes

Major
Symptom: High percentage of operating profit goes for interest payments on debt (98% of net operating income in 1989 as compared to 21% in 1987, before the recapitalization). (Finance/Accounting)

Probable
Causes: 1. Decision to prevent hostile takeover by recapitalizing the company and assuming a large debt (Strategy Formulation)
                 2. Stockholders, under advisement of strategic managers, voted to approve the recapitalization (Stockholders)

Symptom: $11 million loss for the third quarter of 1990 (Finance/Accounting)

**Intermediate
Factor**: Decline in residential and non-residential markets (General Environment)

**Probable
Causes**:
1. Current poor economic conditions (General Environment)
2. Savings and Loan crisis (General Environment)
3. Low price for gypsum wallboard due to competition (Task Environment)
4. Cyclical nature of gypsum wallboard market (Task Environment)

Symptom: Cut work force by 7,000 employees in last 2 years and are planning significant layoffs in the future (Human Resources)

**Probable
Causes**:
1. Sold off assets (Strategy Implementation)
2. Cost reduction (Strategy Implementation)
3. Debt repayment (Strategy Implementation)
4. Slump in economy (General Environment)

Symptom: Stock selling for less than $2 per share (Finance/Accounting)

**Probable
Causes**:
1. National Gypsum filing for Chapter 11 has made investors nervous about the building materials industry (Task Environment)
2. Flat residential and non-residential markets (General Environment)
3. Company's poor leverage ratios:

	USG	Industry
Total Debt/Total Sales	103%	23%
Times Interest Earned	1.02	4.36

(Finance/Accounting)

Symptom: Sales have slid 6% for the first 9 months of this year compared to last year and have slid 4% for the third quarter (Marketing)

**Intermediate
Factor**: Decline in residential and non-residential markets (General Environment)

Probable
Causes: 1. Current poor economic conditions (General Environment)
2. Savings and loan crisis (General Environment)
3. Low price for gypsum wallboard due to competition (Task Environment)
4. Cyclical nature of gypsum wallboard market (Task Environment)

Symptom: Inventory build-up had caused plants to cut back operations to only 6 days a week (Production)

Probable
Cause: 1. Erroneous forecasts predicting a 10 year increase in the housing market (Environmental Analysis)

Part G.3   **Listing of USG's Major & Subordinate Problems**

Major
Problem: Finance/Accounting

Symptom: High percentage of operating profit goes for interest payments for debt (98% of net operating income in 1989 versus 21% in 1987 before the recapitalization) (Finance/Accounting)

Causes: 1. Decision to prevent hostile takeover by recapitalizing the company and assuming a large debt (Strategy Formulation)
2. Stockholders, under advisement of strategic managers, voted to approve the recapitalization (Stockholders)

Subordinate
Problem 1:   Finance/Accounting

Symptom: $11 million loss for the third quarter of 1990 (Finance/Accounting)

Intermediate
Factor: Decline in residential and non-residential markets (General Environment)

Causes: 1. Current poor economic conditions (General Environment)
2. Savings and loan crisis (General Environment)
3. Low price for gypsum wallboard due to competition (Task Environment)
4. Cyclical nature of gypsum wallboard market (Task Environment)

Subordinate
Problem 2: Human Resources

Symptom: Cut work force by 7,000 employees in last 2 years and are planning significant layoffs in the future (Human Resources)

Causes:
1. Sold off assets (Strategy Implementation)
2. Cost reduction (Strategy Implementation)
3. Debt repayment (Strategy Implementation)
4. Slump in economy (General Environment)

Subordinate
Problem 3: Finance/Accounting

Symptom: Stock selling for less than $2 per share (Finance/Accounting)

Causes:
1. National Gypsum and Celotex's filings for Chapter 11 has made investors nervous about the building materials industry (Task Environment)
2. Flat residential and non-residential construction markets (General Environment)
3. Company's poor leverage ratios:

	USG	Industry
Total Debt/Total Sales	103%	23%
Times Interest Earned	1.02	4.36

(Finance/Accounting)

Subordinate
Problem 4: Marketing

Symptom: Sales have slid 6% for the first 9 months of this year compared to last year and have slid 4% for the third quarter (Marketing)

Intermediate
Factor: Decline in residential and non-residential markets (General Environment)

Causes:
1. Current poor economic conditions (General Environment)
2. Savings and loan crisis (General Environment)
3. Low price for gypsum wallboard due to competition (Task Environment)
4. Cyclical nature of gypsum wallboard market (Task Environment)

Subordinate
Problem 5:   Production

Symptom: Inventory build-up had caused plants to cut back operations to only 6 days a week (Production)

Probable
Cause: 1. Erroneous forecasts predicting a 10-year increase in the housing market (Environmental Analysis)

PART H   **DETERMINING USG'S STRATEGIC MATCH**

Constraint

Weaknesses
1. Company has large debt due to recapitalization

Opportunities
1. National Gypsum, the second largest, and Celotex, fifth largest competitor, both filed for Chapter 11

Maintenance

Strengths
1. USG holds the largest portion of gypsum wallboard market due to its innovative techniques and reputation

Threats
1. Gypsum wallboard sales are declining

1.2 Competitors are reducing their wallboard prices

2. Places a high value on its employees and maintains good communication with them

2. Economic conditions are forcing USG to reduce its work force

Vulnerability

Weaknesses
1. USG designed a poor strategic plan based on an overly optimistic forecast

Threats
1. The economy is not matching USG's forecast

PART I   **DETERMINING THE PRIMARY STRATEGIC**
                                                      MATCH POSITION

When determining the primary strategic match position of a company, a portfolio planning technique may be utilized. There are two methods or techniques available for determining a company's primary strategic match: the Boston Consulting Group matrix and the General Electric planning grid. We have chosen the GE planning grid to evaluate USG. The GE method involves (1) the evaluation of the company's business strengths/competitive position, and (2) the evaluation of industry attractiveness. The results of these two steps are then plotted on the GE planning grid.

Determining The Business Strength/Competitive Position

The first step used in determining USG's strategic match position involves an analysis of USG's current business strengths and competitive position in relation to its competitors. This process, as explained below, consists of selecting success factors, assigning weights to them, rating the factors, and obtaining a weighted score that is reflective of the company's performance in relation to its competitors.

Success Factors
The success factors are the items chosen to evaluate the firm in its industry. Companies that rate well on these items tend to be successful in their industry while those companies that rate low in the evaluation tend to be unsuccessful.

Weights
Different weights are assigned to different success factors to indicate the varying importance of the factors. These weights total 1.00, and are divided in different proportions among the factors depending on how the evaluator views their importance. When a success factor does not apply to the industry under review an "X" is placed in the appropriate column.

Rating
Rating for the success factors is made on a scale of one (1) to five (5). It is used to determine how the company under evaluation compares with its competitors for a particular success factor. A one is indicative of a weak competitive position and a five indicates a strong competitive position.

Weighted Score
The weighted score is calculated by multiplying the weight by the rating for each industry competitor under each success factor. The weighted scores for each company are summed, and these totals are then averaged together. This

average indicates the company's business strength/competitive position on the horizontal axis of the GE planning grid.

Analysis of USG's business strength/competitive position is illustrated in Exhibit 8-3. USG received a score of 4.6 against its key competitors, namely, National Gypsum, Georgia-Pacific, Domtar, and Celotex.

Determining Industry Attractiveness

Industry attractiveness is an evaluation of all the positive and negative conditions in the company's external environment. These can include competitors, government regulations, and demographics. These items contain the existing and possible opportunities and threats.

The process used in determining the industry attractiveness is similar to the one used in assessing the company's business strength/competitive position. That is, it involves selecting a set of evaluation criteria, assigning weights to them, rating the criteria, and obtaining a weighted score that is reflective of the attractiveness or favorableness of the external environment of the company.

When applied to USG, this process has produced an industry attractiveness score of 1.68 which indicates that the gypsum industry is not very attractive. In other words, the industry presents USG with more threats than opportunities. (See Exhibit 8-4.)

Positioning the Firm in the GE Matrix

With a score of 4.6 for business strength/competitive position and a score of 1.68 for industry attractiveness, USG can be placed in the maintenance position on the GE planning grid. (See Exhibit 8-5.)

PART J	COMPETITORS' DISTINCTIVE COMPETENCY AND MAJOR WEAKNESS

National Gypsum

Distinctive Competency: National holds the second largest share of gypsum products market in the United States

Major Weakness: The company filed for Chapter 11 recently

Georgia-Pacific

Distinctive Competency: It is more diversified than USG. The pulp and paper divisions, which are in a stable market and are a substantial part of total sales will help carry the building products division through bad economies.

Major Weakness: The company has a low gypsum facility usage (78% compared to USG's 96%)

Exhibit 8-3 **Determining the Business Strength/Competitive Position of the USG**

Success Factors	weight	National Gypsum		Georgia-Pacific		Domtar		Celotex	
		rating	score	rating	score	rating	score	rating	score
1. Market share	0.30	5	1.50	5	1.50	5	1.50	5	1.50
2. Breadth of product line	0.08	5	0.40	5	0.40	5	0.40	5	0.40
3. Distribution	0.08	3	0.24	3	0.24	5	0.40	5	0.40
4. Price competitiveness	0.06	4	0.24	4	0.24	4	0.24	5	0.30
5. Advertising effectiveness	xxxx								
6. Facilities location and newness	0.10	5	0.50	3	0.30	5	0.50	5	0.50
7. Production capacity	0.05	5	0.25	5	0.25	5	0.25	5	0.25
8. Relative product quality	0.05	5	0.25	4	0.20	5	0.25	5	0.25
9. R & D position	0.03	5	0.15	5	0.15	5	0.15	5	0.15
10. Customer service	0.08	5	0.40	5	0.40	5	0.40	5	0.40
11. Caliber of top management	xxxx								
12. Experience curve	0.05	5	0.25	5	0.25	5	0.25	5	0.25
13. Corporate culture	0.02	5	0.10	4	0.08	4	0.08	4	0.08
14. Profitability ratio	0.10	4	0.40	1	0.10	3	0.30	4	0.40
	1.00		4.68		4.11		4.72		4.88

USG's overall competitve position   4.60

xxxx - evalution criteria does not apply
1 - USG's competitve position is very weak
5 - USG's competitive position is very strong

Domtar

Distinctive Competency: It is a Canadian based company with the leading market share of Canadian wallboard market.

Major Weakness: Since it is a foreign company, if it wants to increase its share of the larger U.S. market, it must export to the United States.

Celotex

Distinctive Competency: Celotex is a subsidiary of Jim Walter Corporation which has construction firms as other subsidiaries which become direct clients for Celotex products.

Major Weakness: Jim Walter Corporation is owned by Hillsborough Holding Company which could decide to divest or liquidate Celotex if the economy becomes bad enough. Celotex recently filed for Chapter 11.

Exhibit 8-4 **Determining Industry Attractiveness of USG**

Evaluation Criteria

	weight	rating	score
1. Industry growth	0.30	1	0.30
2. Size	0.03	3	0.09
3. Profitability	0.02	1	0.02
4. Cylicality	0.06	1	0.06
5. Seasonality	0.05	1	0.05
6. Entry/exit barrier	0.05	1	0.05
7. Customers	0.06	3	0.18
8. Competitors	0.03	4	0.12
9. Suppliers	0.03	5	0.15
10. Government regulators	xxxx		0.00
11. Labor unions	xxxx		0.00
12. Demographics	0.07	2	0.14
13. Culture	0.03	3	0.09
14. Economy	0.20	1	0.20
15. Politics	0.02	4	0.08
16. Technology	0.03	3	0.09
17. Pressure groups	0.02	3	0.06
	1.00		1.68

xxxx - criteria does not apply
1 - evaluation criteria (or industry condition) is unattractive
5 - evaluation criteria (or industry condition) is attractive

Exhibit 8-5   **Positioning USG on the Strategic Match Matrix**

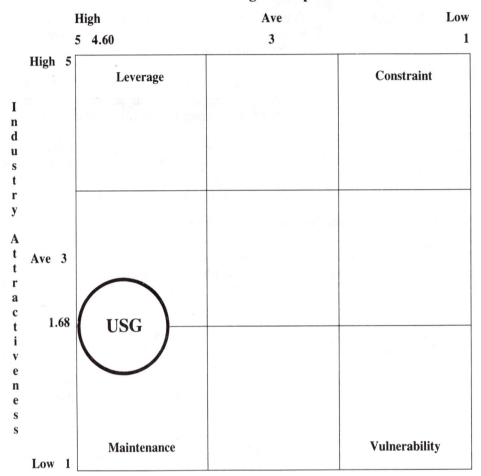

Business Strength/Competitive Position

PART K   FORMULATING A STRATEGIC PLAN

Part K.1   Mission Statement

Business Domain

USG is involved in the building material products industry. Our products are extensively used in the residential, commercial and industrial construction industries. As a minimum, it is our intention to maintain our current position as the world's leading gypsum and associated products producer and whenever possible, capitalize on any opportunity to further enhance our market share. Achieving these goals will require management's continued pursuit of excellence in all areas of research, production and marketing.

Products

USG produces gypsum wallboard, plaster, joint compound, cement board, ceiling tile, acoustical tile and industrial gypsum products for the building construction industry. We will continue our tradition of providing products of only the highest caliber of quality. Our goal is to always seek improvements in our products through research, production and marketing.

Distribution Channels

One of USG's major strengths is our ability to strategically locate our distributorship evenly throughout the U.S. and Canada. By strategically locating our distributorship, USG will be able to rapidly respond and adapt to regional economic swings in the construction industry.

Customers

USG's customers are wholesale and retail building supply companies. Customer service both before and after the sale will continue to be the highest priority at USG. We continually strive to improve on our receptiveness to our customers' needs and desires.

Management's Beliefs & Values

USG's absolute commitment to high product quality and customer service will continue. Our customers are the lifeblood of the corporation; therefore, we must satisfy all of their desires. No detail, large or small, will be overlooked in improving customer service. USG cannot afford to lose its position as the world's leader in the gypsum industry.

USG's strong reputation is due in large part to our employee's desire for excellence in the work place. USG recognizes the importance of a cooperative, professional work force, therefore it is management's responsibility to reward and reinforce such attitudes. At all USG plants, employee safety takes priority over all production concerns. Management holds a deeply ingrained concern for all its employee's well being.

USG has long held high its obligation to its shareholders and will continue to do so. Our recapitalization program initiated in 1988 was executed in the best interest of our shareholders, and we are confident that our debt reduction program will allow USG to emerge as a very financially sound and stable corporation.

USG has always prided itself on its high ethical standards and its social responsibility to the community and its surroundings. Government regulations and standards will continue to be met and most desirably exceeded. USG and its employees will continue to actively participate in community affairs and will remain open-minded in response to any criticism or complaint registered against the company.

Part K.2   Corporate Objectives

Long-Term Objectives

1. Increase profit margin ratio from 1.28% to 20% by January 1, 1996
2. Increase net income from $28 million to $250 million by January 1, 1996
3. Reduce total debt to total asset ratio from 1.41 to 0.80 by January 1, 1996

Short-Term Objectives

1. Increase profit margin ratio from 1.28% to 5% by January 1, 1992
2. Increase net income from $28 million to $60 million by January 1, 1992
3. Reduce total debt to total asset ratio from 1.41 to 1.20 by January 1, 1992

Part K.3   Making The Strategic Choice

Utilizing the structured approach in selecting grand strategy, and as shown in Exhibit 8-6, USG's best grand strategies would be product development and joint venture. As the company pays off its debt and the economy improves, the company can focus on the other grand strategies relative to its position, namely concentric diversification and conglomerate diversification.

Part K.4   The Competitive Strategies

The best competitive strategy for USG is to maintain its position as a cost leader in the gypsum board industry. There are so few competitors in this arena that this should not be difficult for USG to maintain. The company already possesses a very strong competitive position, and the outlook for its next largest competitor, National Gypsum with its recent filing for Chapter 11, is very grim at the present time.

Exhibit 8-6 **Evaluating Alternative Grand Strategies**

Evaluation Criteria	weight	Concentric Diversification		Conglomerate Diversification		Joint Venture		Product Development	
		rating	score	rating	score	rating	score	rating	score
1. management familiarity	0.05	4	0.20	1	0.05	2	0.10	4	0.20
2. corporate culture	0.03	3	0.09	1	0.03	2	0.06	3	0.09
3. distinctive competencies	0.20	2	0.40	1	0.20	3	0.60	4	0.80
4. risk	0.09	2	0.18	1	0.09	4	0.36	4	0.36
5. timing	0.02	1	0.02	1	0.02	3	0.06	4	0.08
6. competitors' reaction	0.11	3	0.33	1	0.11	3	0.33	2	0.22
7. capital	0.10	1	0.10	1	0.10	3	0.30	2	0.20
8. human resources	0.04	4	0.16	2	0.08	3	0.12	5	0.20
9. regulation	0.03	5	0.15	5	0.15	3	0.09	3	0.09
10. labor unions	xxxx		0.00		0.00		0.00		0.00
11. demographics	0.09	2	0.18	5	0.45	3	0.27	3	0.27
12. culture	xxxx		0.00		0.00		0.00		0.00
13. economy	0.20	1	0.20	4	0.80	2	0.40	2	0.40
14. politics	xxxx		0.00		0.00		0.00		0.00
15. technology	0.02	4	0.08	1	0.02	4	0.08	5	0.10
16. pressure groups	0.02	3	0.06	4	0.08	3	0.06	4	0.08
	1.00		2.15		2.18		2.83		3.09

xxxx - factor does not apply
1 - strategy is not desirable in terms of the evaluation criteria
5 - strategy is desirable in terms of the evalution criteria

Given that gypsum board is not a product on which much variation can be done, product differentiation would not be the best competitive strategy for any gypsum wall board manufacturer. Although USG can use the new technology for a paper-less wall board to lower its production costs, the new product will not offer any new uses to the customers.

A focus strategy would not be an appropriate competitive strategy for USG. Carving out a special niche with either a specific group of customers, a narrow geographic area, or a particular use of the product, would only cut USG off from its broadest base of potential customers.

Part K.5   **Functional Objectives & Strategies**

Marketing

Long-Term Objective: Increase USG's gypsum board market share from 34% to 49% by December 1996

Short-Term Objective: Increase USG's gypsum board market share from 34% to 40% by December 1991

Short-Term Strategy

Marketing Research	Start*	Compl	Budget	Savings
Survey National Gypsum's customers to determine why they prefer National Gypsum over USG	11/16	12/15	$ 50K	------
Promotion				
Implement special promotions in National Gypsum's target markets to entice new customers, once the results of the survey are reviewed	12/31	06/30	$ 250K	------

*Start = starting date, Compl = completion date, K = thousand, M = million

Sponsor neighborhood beautification programs to attract potential customers who are interested in home-improvement	2/15	10/31	$ 250K	------
Sales				
Motivate USG's sales and distribution outlets to attract National Gypsum's customers	11/16	06/30	$ 50K	------
Increase sales quotas by 10% for sales and distribution outlets located in National Gypsum's markets	11/16	06/30	$ 100K	------
Target Market				
Concentrate on repair and remodel markets for short-term dollars	01/01	12/15	------	------
Concentrate on home and building construction market as the economy improves	06/15	------	------	------
Total	12 months		$ 700K	------

Production

Long-Term Objective: Allow only 10% of total gypsum wallboard produced to accumulate in inventory at any given time, and return operating schedule to normal (7 days/week) by December 31, 1996.

Short-Term Objective: Decrease inventory build-up to one quarter of its current level by December 1991.

Short-Term Strategy

Production Capacity	Start	Compl	Budget	Savings
Production and operations managers will work in conjuction with sales forecasters to determine necessary output levels	01/01	12/31	$ 80K	$ 2M
Inventory				
Inventory control managers will keep marketing managers informed of wallboard inventory levels, thus permitting marketing managers to adjust the price of the material relevant to the amount of inventory in stock	01/01	12/31	$ 75K	------
Inventory control managers will allocate a certain percentage of excess wallboard for donation to organizations which provide for the needy	01/01	12/31	$ 25K	------
Total	12 months		$180K	$ 2M

Research & Development

Long-Term Objective: To acquire 5% of total gypsum used to produce wallboard from coal burning power plants that employ the desulphurization process (which is also environmentally sound).

Short-Term Objective: To market a competitive paper-less wallboard product by June 1991.

Short-Term Strategies

	Start	Compl	Budget	Savings
Posture				
Utilize a protective strategy in the short-term and allocate the R&D dollars saved in this effort to pay-off debt	01/01	06/31	------	$ 2M
Increase relationships with companies that produce large amounts of gypsum via desulphurization to save on mining and transportation costs	01/01	12/31	$ 10K	$ 750K
Market paper-less gypsum wallboard product by June 1991	01/01	06/30	$ 500K	------
Total	12 months		$ 510K	$ 2.75M

Human Resources

Long-Term Objective: Implement a training program by December 1995 which will train all employees in at least one other area to make them more valuable to USG and to give them some direction if laid off.

Short-Term Objective: Make necessary adjustments to staffing levels over the next year reflecting the decrease in production capacity, the selling of USG's assets and the combining of certain of USG's divisions.

Short-Term Strategies

	Start	Compl	Budget	Savings
Performance Appraisal				
Increase employee/manager interface during difficult times to maintain employee morale	11/16	12/31	------	------

Training & Development

Encourage employees to participate in the training programs during the next five years	11/16	12/31/95	$ 150K	------
Offer resume-writing and interview training classes for employees that are laid off	11/16	06/30	$ 55K	------
Increase dismissed employees awareness of free psychological counseling services	11/16	06/30	$ 5K	------

Recruitment & Selection

Implement a hiring freeze for the next twelve months	11/16	12/31	------	$ 600K

Succession Planning

Continue current highly acknowledged practice of succession planning for managers	11/16	------	$ 100K	------
Total	12 months		$ 310K	$ 600K

Public Affairs

Long-Term Objective: Enhance USG's image in the eyes of the public over the next 5 years

Short-Term Objective: Donate .5% of excess wallboard in inventory over the next year to various charity organizations, such as the Salvation Army

Short-Term Strategies

Social Concerns

	Start	Compl	Budget	Savings
Emphasize company's position relative to conserving the environment by emphasizing that USG obtains 5% of gypsum from desulphurization and uses recycled paper to produce gypsum wallboard	01/01	------	$ 50K	------
Begin relationships with charity organizations that could use the gypsum board for the poor in need of shelter	01/01	12/31	$ 200K	------
Total	12 months		$ 250K	------

Finance & Accounting

Long-Term Objective: Decrease debt obligation by $500 million over the next 5 years

Short-Term Objective: Decrease debt obligation by $100 million over the next year

Short-Term Strategy

Budgets

	Start	Compl	Budget	Savings
Target a certain portion of operating income toward paying off the debt - savings will result from reduced debt	01/01	12/31	$ 100M	$ 10M
Total	12 months		$ 100M	$ 10M

PART L   **ESTABLISHING THE CONDITIONS NECESSARY TO IMPLEMENT THE STRATEGIC PLAN**

Part L.1   **Organizational Structure**

USG's organizational structure is the SBU structure. This structure helps USG to better allocate its resources to avoid overlapping of functions. USG's financial position makes this structure an asset. Implementation should begin at the top and trickle down to all the SBU's, with each SBU head holding primary responsibility for ensuring the new programs are implemented. At the end of each quarter, the corporate strategic managers should evaluate the progress of their plan.

Part L.2   **Policies**

Corporate/Business Level
1. The corporate/business level managers will hold weekly meetings for the next year to discuss the economy's condition and its effects on USG and the company's other competitive positions. Sales forecasts will be made to reflect the findings.
2. The corporate business level managers will make themselves more "visible" to the employees by way of visiting departments and plants on a monthly basis and interfacing directly with employees about the company's future.

Marketing Department
Heads of the marketing department will meet with corporate managers every 6 months to make sure sales forecasts are achievable and match the objectives stressed by the strategic managers. If they do not, one or both will be changed.

Production
Production managers will ensure that inventory build-up does not reach excess and is maintained in accordance with demand for their product.

Research & Development
Research and Development will continue to be innovative in basic research once USG's financial conditions improve. Until such time, Research and Development will use the protective strategy.

Human Resources
Workers will be trained in more than one area so that they can be of more use to USG and more versatile in the general work environment should further lay-offs become necessary.

Public Affairs
Every effort will be made to shed a positive light on USG and downplay its association with asbestos poisoning.

Finance & Accounting
The finance and accounting departments will make quarterly reports to all staff on progress of debt reduction to assure that the progress is adequate and also increase the company's focus on debt reduction.

Part L.3   **Translating a Policy into Procedure & Rules**

Policy:
The strategic managers at USG and the heads of the marketing departments will hold a strategy meeting at least once every three months.

Procedures:
1. The meeting will be called by the chair who is to be elected by a majority vote of the SBUs' heads.
2. The secretary of the chair is responsible for taking minutes of the meetings.
3. At every meeting, the following topics should be part of the agenda:
   a) current and future trends in the gypsum market
   b) % of new housing starts expected
   c) level of interest rates
   d) % of remodeling expected
   e) current price of gypsum
   f) competitors' positions

Rule:
No decision can be adopted without the approval of two-thirds of the participants.

Part L.4   **Leadership**

USG should continue with its team management style. A task management style could be detrimental to employees, yet country-club might cause production of sub-standard products. Middle of the road management would be unacceptable because the company definitely needs an active, caring management system to keep it afloat.

Part L.5   Corporate Culture

Even through the recent difficult times USG's corporate culture has remained strong and functional. Employees still believe the company serves important markets and that it is well respected by its customers. Top management must continue to keep the culture of the company focused on safety, quality, market leadership and the environment.

Part L.6   Communication

Aspects of the strategic plan that directly affect human resources and finance should be communicated to USG employees by way of USG's hot-line and newsletters.

Part L.7   Motivation

Participative management and non-financial rewards might be the best incentives for USG employees at this point. The company is not in a financial position to offer substantial monetary rewards to all of its employees.

STRATEGIC MANAGEMENT CASES

Case 1

MARY KAY COSMETICS, INC.:
CORPORATE PLANNING IN AN ERA OF UNCERTAINTY

Mary Kay Cosmetics, Inc. of Dallas, Texas, is an international manufacturer and distributor of skin care products, makeup items, toiletry items, accessories and hair care products. Founded in 1963 by Mary Kay Ash, a highly motivated entrepreneur, the firm experienced spectacular sales growth in its early years. As a direct selling organization, much of its success was based on motivating and constantly replenishing its over 170,000 member sales force. Mary Kay had planned to become "the finest and largest skin care teaching organization in the world."

Senior management recognized in early 1989 that the firm was suffering from some of the same problems which were effecting the whole direct-sales industry. The company was suddenly having problems attracting new recruits who would become "Beauty Consultants" and "Sales Directors" as well as consumers of the strategy which had been developed by the firm's founder. The organization was repositioning itself for future growth. The question was now, "What do we need to do to get us where we want to go, to reach the kind of customer we want to reach, to recruit the kind of consultant we want to recruit?"

BACKGROUND INFORMATION

Mary Kay Cosmetics was founded on September 13, 1963 in Dallas, Texas, by Mary Kay (now Mary Kay Ash). The company had an initial working capital of $5,000, the right to use a skin care formula that had been created by a hide tanner, and nine saleswomen. The first headquarters was a five-hundred-square-foot storefront in Exchange Park, a large bank and office building complex in Dallas.

This case was prepared by James W. Camerius of Northern Michigan University and is intended to be used as a basis for class discussion rather than to illustrate either effective or ineffective handling of an administrative situation. Presented to the Midwest Society for Case Research Workshop, 1989. All rights reserved to the author and to the Midwest Society for Case Research. Copyright © 1989 by James W. Camerius.

The first basic line of cosmetics was manufactured to specification under the label of "Beauty by Mary Kay" by another firm. It included what was called the "Basic Skin Care Set." It consisted of a limited number of basic items which when used as the company suggested provided a balanced program of skin care. The firm also sold custom wigs. Wigs were styled at the headquarters location and at skin care shows and were originally used as a traffic generator. They were discontinued in 1965. Management believed that it could achieve corporate success in direct sales by establishing a "dream company" which would be based on the personal philosophies of the founder. The Mary Kay philosophy suggested that every person associated with the company, from the Chairman of the Board to the newest recruit, live by the golden rule, "Do unto others as you would have them do unto you," and the priorities of God first, family second and career third.

Initial corporate strategies included heavy emphasis on personal relationships, opportunities for women to fully utilize their skills and talents, no geographical restrictions on sales territories, and a sales presentation in the home for no more than five or six women. Merchandise was available for immediate delivery from stock. All products were sold on a cash basis. Every Mary Kay representative was considered an independent businessperson to be remunerated in the form of commission. Pink was selected as the corporate color.

By 1989, Mary Kay Cosmetics, Inc. had again become a private corporation after going public in 1968. It had sales in 1988 of $405,730,000, a sales staff of 170,000 Beauty Consultants and Sales Directors, a compensation structure to allow women to earn commensurate with their individual abilities and efforts, and total brand awareness of 90% of all women. Mary Kay was ranked by the *Wall Street Journal* as an industry leader in basic skin care research and in product development. The company had a new production facility, a new warehouse, and a new corporate headquarters in Dallas, all of which were internally financed. The product line was distributed throughout the United States and through wholly owned subsidiaries in Australia, Canada, Argentina, and West Germany. The average number of Beauty Consultants, their average productivity and net sales for the years 1984-1988 are shown in Figure 1.

THE MARY KAY MYSTIQUE

Much of the initial and continuing success of the firm was attributed to the entrepreneurial spirit of its founder and chairman emeritus, Mary Kay Ash. Mary Kay traced her strong-willed, competitive spirit to the constant, positive reinforcement her mother gave her while growing up in Texas. "I was taught to put my best effort into everything I did, and I can honestly say that I've always done that," Mary Kay said. "I competed with myself and strove to excel." Her "you can do it" philosophy guided the company through the challenges and setbacks of its early years.

FIGURE 1

Analysis of Mary Kay
Independent Beauty Consultants

1984-1988

Year	Average Number of Consultants	Average Productivity	Net Sales ($000)
1988	170,316	$2,382	$405,730
1987	148,080	$2,199	$325,647
1986	141,113	$1,807	$255,016
1985	145,493	$1,711	$248,970
1984	173,101	$1,603	$277,500

Mary Kay spent 13 years of her professional direct sales career with Stanley Home Products, Inc. She became one of the firm's leading sales persons and was promoted to management. She also worked for another 11 years in a similar position with a company in Houston called World Gift. After becoming its national training director for 43 states, she left the organization. Later upon deciding that retirement did not satisfy her, she developed a strategy and philosophy that was to become Mary Kay Cosmetics. She became its first president. A son, Richard Rogers, joined her upon the death of her second husband. Another son, Ben, and a daughter, Marilyn, eventually became part of the organization.

As president, Mary Kay became a walking showcase for the company's products. Her values and motivational incentives became the basis for the firm's marketing program. Her definitions of happiness brought women to the firm as beauty consultants, sales directors, and users of the product line. "Under her 'frills and lace' is a high-powered businesswoman who has built a skin care empire, and in a pioneering style," suggested *Marketing and Media Decisions*, a trade magazine. The color pink, her "favorite" color, was found in her attire, her office, her home and every facet of corporate life.

A unique and idealistic individual, Mary Kay Ash was called "one of the most influential and respected personalities in business and philanthropic circles" by

Executive Female, a respected magazine among entrepreneurs. She also received many of the most distinguished cosmetic, direct sales and professional awards, including "Cosmetic Career Women of the Year," "Direct Selling Hall of Fame," and the 1978 "Horatio Alger Award." She was the cover feature on several magazines, including the *Saturday Evening Post; Business Week* named her one of America's top corporate women, and *Time* cited her in its economy and business section. She also appeared on such television shows as "Sixty Minutes," "Phil Donahue," and "Good Morning America."

"Far from being an employer," indicated Nicole Woolsey Biggart in a recent book on direct selling organization leadership, "Mary Kay Ash...is mother, sister, guardian angel, and patron saint to the women who sell her products." In this context a national sales director maintained, "We don't adore Mary Kay, we admire her, and we would want to emulate her." In the belief that "adore" versus "admire" was a good distinction, management felt that Mary Kay had positioned the company for the day when "she no longer would be here." As president, Mary Kay had maintained, "Although Mary Kay Cosmetics was created as the dream of one woman, it has long since achieved independent existence. And because our company is grounded in a solid foundation of specific values and principles, its continuance no longer depends upon any single person."

A number of programs were in place to cushion the eventual departure of Mary Kay from active management. Initially, her philosophy was captured on film, in books, and in articles written about her. Also a national sales director program, made up of the firm's top saleswomen, was established to emphasize continuing the Mary Kay spirit in the company. Mary Kay was developed as an entity as opposed to an individual by perpetrating all of the ideas that she felt should be part of her "dream company." "This is important," indicated Richard C. Bartlett, the current president in an interview, "here we are talking about philosophical beliefs which traditionally, in business and religion and other organizations, do continue on if the organization is imbued with them."

On November 10, 1987, Mary Kay Ash was named chairman emeritus. Richard R. Rogers, her son, was named chairman. Richard C. Bartlett, whose initial experience in direct selling was with Tupperware and later as Vice President of Marketing at Mary Kay, was named president and chief operating officer. "I plan to remain active in the firm on a continuing basis, working with salespeople," indicated Mary Kay. "Our sales force now consists of tens of thousands of skilled sales professionals, and they are supported by an experienced management team."

THE CORPORATE CONCEPT

The original corporate strategy of the firm was based on the "Mary Kay Marketing Plan." In the plan, the sales force or "Beauty Consultants" sold the company's skin care products at home demonstration shows. They were supervised and motivated by "sales directors" who also were responsible for replenishing the sales force on a continuing basis with new recruits. The plan was a corporate strategy designed to include the best features and avoid the mistakes Mary Kay had previously encountered in her twenty years with direct selling companies.

As a part of the plan, the marketing program was intended to foster retail sales to ultimate consumers. Commissions were earned by Beauty Consultants on products sold at retail prices to ultimate consumers. All products were purchased directly from the company and were based on the same discount schedule. All Sales Directors were once Beauty Consultants, thus avoiding the multilevel practice of selling franchises or distributorships.

In the plan there were no territories to limit where Consultants could sell or recruit. The Consultant was required to purchase a "showcase" of basic products and carry an inventory. Consultants were encouraged to sell only Mary Kay products during their skin care classes to avoid creating trademark confusion and divided effort.

Consultants were considered to be self-employed. The marketing plan was intended to support the independent contractor status. At the corporate level, management was expected to manufacture quality cosmetics, plan product and market development, provide for discounts and commissions, advertise, plan for working capital for corporate growth, and offer incentive awards and prizes for Beauty Consultants who excelled in sales, recruiting, or leadership.

One of the most unique aspects of the marketing plan was the use of national and regional seminars, career conferences, and management conferences which individuals could attend on a voluntary basis for inspiration, training, and general professional upgrading. At the national level, this strategy manifested itself annually in what the company called "Seminar." Seminar was an elaborately produced series of four consecutive three-day sessions which attracted a total of 24,000 sales participants to the Dallas Convention Center.

The highly motivational event had a tradition of recognition, education, and entertainment. It included hours of classes on product knowledge, marketing and sales techniques, and other business management topics. It culminated in an awards night in which thousands of glamorous, elegantly dressed, bejeweled women received extravagant recognition as achievers in the organization. Mary Kay traditionally presided over the event. She appeared on stage, sometimes emerging at the top of a series of lighted stairs, sometimes arriving in a carriage drawn by white horses and surrounded by footmen.

Typically, participants would proceed to the stage to claim expensive prizes such as mink coats, gold and diamond jewelry, trips to places like Acapulco, and use of new pale-pink Cadillacs, Buicks, and Oldsmobiles. "So in our company, we eliminated practical gifts," indicated Mary Kay, "I would try to choose prizes that would excite and thrill the recipient. I thought that the best prizes were things a woman wanted but probably wouldn't buy for herself." The legendary pink Cadillac, for many, became a symbol of Mary Kay Cosmetics and its incentive programs.

THE CHANGING EXTERNAL ENVIRONMENT

All of the firm's products were sold on the principal bases of price and quality in highly competitive markets. On the basis of information available to it from industry sources, management believed there were some 13,000 companies (including both direct sales and manufacturing companies) that had products that competed with Mary Kay. The firm competed directly with direct sales companies in sales of cosmetics products and indirectly with firms which manufactured cosmetics and toiletry items which were sold in retail or department stores. It also competed in the recruiting of independent sales persons from other direct selling organizations whose product lines may or may not have competed with those of Mary Kay.

The direct selling industry consisted of a few well-established companies and many smaller firms which sold about every product imaginable including toys, animal food, plant care products, clothing, computer software, and financial services. Among the dominant companies were Avon (cosmetics), Amway Corp. (home cleaning products), Shaklee Corp. (vitamins and health foods), Encyclopedia Britannica, Tupperware (plastic dishes and food containers), Consolidated Foods' Electrolux (vacuum cleaners), and the Fuller Brush Co. (household products). Avon Products, Inc., was substantially larger than Mary Kay in terms of total independent sales people, sales volume and resources. Several other competitors such as Revlon, Inc., a firm that sold cosmetics primarily through retail stores, were larger than Mary Kay in terms of sales and had more resources.

By the late 1980's corporate management at Mary Kay considered the direct selling industry and the cosmetics industry to be at maturity. The spectacular sales growth characteristics of the 1960's and 1970's had given way to a pattern of stagnant revenue and profit growth. The industry was having difficulty attracting new sales people who generated much of its sales growth and provided a return to sales directors. Competition for the customer was great as there were not as many users coming into the market. Industry problems were blamed on a number of factors: the increasing number of working women, which cut into both the number of available recruits and sales targets; the improvement in the economy, which encouraged women to avoid involvement in part-time sales and to shop for more expensive beauty products; shorter product life cycles, which forced new products, new innovations and twists of existing products which were getting old; and the growing competition from firms selling similar products. There were also hostile takeovers, such as the 1989 bid of Amway Corporation for Avon Products, Inc., and leveraged buyouts, such as the December, 1985, LBO of Mary Kay by its founders. According to President Bartlett, senior management would have to "react by being much more flexible, by being able to come out with new products, by introducing new innovations, and by developing new strategies for existing products that were getting old."

Industry research had identified Avon, a direct competitor, as having products which were used by older people who wanted a less expensive product. Noxell, the manufacturer of Cover Girl products, was viewed as the creator of a moderately upscale product line that appealed to a younger market. Estee Lauder was a product line that was a more upscale and appealed to an older market segment. In product image, Estee Lauder had been historically in an envious position. The firm cultivated this in all of its literature, all of its packaging, and in all of its product formulas. Revlon, whose image varied by product line, was sold through department stores and mass merchandisers. It built a multi-billion dollar business by buying out old established lines like Max Factor, Charles of the Ritz, Germain Monte, Diane Von Furstenberg, and Almae.

Although maturity was sometimes looked on with disfavor, Mary Kay executives felt that this did not mean a lack of opportunity for increased profitability or lack of opportunity to increase sales. The changing nature of competition in the cosmetics market was identified as one of the strategic concerns in the design of the Mary Kay product line. Both the mass market and upscale segments of the skin care marketplace were perceived to be changing rapidly. In both cases a plethora of new entries emerged, some from well established American firms such as Estee Lauder, some from innovative American firms such as S.C. Johnson, and some from European or Japanese firms. One example was an entry from L'Oreal, a European firm. The skin care line, Plentitude, was sold through mass market outlets. An example of a Japanese firm was the Kao Safina line which was introduced through Kao's American acquisition, Jergens Skin Care.

The changing nature of science and technology was also identified as a strategic concern in an analysis of the external environment. Management felt that the period of the late 1980's and the early 1990's would see the debut of several new "cosmeceuticals;" products marketed as drugs and capable of making drug claims, but with wide impact on the pharmaceutical and cosmetics markets. Upjohn's Rogaine and Ortho Laboratories' Retin-A, treatments for Acne which doubled as anti-wrinkle creams, were predicted to become over-the-counter drugs within the next two to three years. New drug applications for six to eight other retinoids were known to be under way with anti-aging claims. At the same time, greater understanding of skin physiology enabled the development of more advanced traditional skin care products, including those which could legitimately make counterirritant claims and those which could protect users from environmental damage, such as from the sun.

The decade also saw a proliferation of regulatory activity affecting the cosmetics industry. In the United States such activity was seen from the Food and Drug Administration (FDA), the Federal Trade Commission (FTC), Congress and various state legislatures. At the same time, cosmetics regulations were changing in the European Economic Community (EEC) countries and in Argentina, Canada, and Australia. Prospects for expansion into Mexico and Thailand presented the challenge of learning to deal with regulations in markets that were new to Mary Kay. It was clear that a new wave of regulatory activity affecting the industry had commenced. Ingredients, claims, packaging, testing, advertising and other activities of the cosmetics industry were being closely scrutinized by regulators and legislators with a view toward regulatory control. A series of hearings held by Congressman Ron Wyden, D-OR, during 1988 were predicted to produce new cosmetics legislation in Congress.

Corporate research revealed that the Mary Kay customer was primarily identified by its beauty consultants. The company did very little direct customer prospecting. Beauty consultants found their customers one by one or in small groups through referrals, and through holding skin care classes where they might know one person but not the other members of the group. The typical Mary Kay customer was a female, in her late thirties, married, and caucasian. Geographically, she lived in all fifty states as well as in those countries where Mary Kay had operations. Most customers were rural and suburban as opposed to urban. The Mary Kay method of selling was perceived by management to be more disposed to the woman who might not have easy access to a store and also appeared to lend itself on the supply side to mobility by automobile. By occupation, customers were "white collar," and professional with moderate incomes and a high school education with some college. In practice, the upper and lower ends of a market segmented by social stratification variables tended to be neglected. Consultants were perceived to be slightly more upscale than their typical customer and customarily sold down to lower levels of social stratification.

The senior vice president of Mary Kay, Ms. Barbara Beasley, had hoped to expand the customer base through greater penetration in three key segments; blacks, hispanics, and mature women. In a corporate analysis of the changing consumer, she concluded that because of greater education and disposable income, many more women were becoming regular users of product lines used previously by only a few consumers. Increased consumer sophistication meant that high performance products would be required that had claims that were meaningful and would fit within the Mary Kay context of a teaching orientation. The market was identified as becoming increasingly segmented by usage as consumers gravitated toward brand positions such as those formulated for sensitive skin, for contact lens wearers, for mature skin, and for ethnic consumers.

MARKETING STRATEGIES

Several marketing strategies emerged as the result of an overall reexamination of existing corporate strategies. The area receiving initial attention was the product line. The lines, as reviewed in Figure 2, consisted of skin care products for women and for men, glamour items, toiletry items for women and for men, accessories and hair care products. Skin care products, in various formulas related to skin type, included cleaners, skin fresheners, facial masks, moisturizers and foundation makeup, and were sold in sets as a five-step beauty program. Glamour items or cosmetics included lip and eye colors, mascaras, blushers, eye liners, face powder and lip gloss. Toiletry items included hand and body lotions, bath products, and colognes. Hair care products consisted of shampoo, conditioners and hair spray. Accessories such as samples, makeup mirrors, cosmetics bags and travel kits were sold primarily as hostess gifts, business supplies or sales aids.

THE PRODUCT LINES

There had been no significant additions to the product line in the first thirteen years of the company. Mary Kay had purchased the rights to a line that she had been using personally for about ten years. Initially, the line consisted of only ten products, focused on skin care. Although management evaluated the product line on an ongoing basis, adjustments were kept to a minimum. Corporate policy had been to purposely limit the line to a minimum number of essential skin care and glamour items. Each company consultant was encouraged to carry a basic inventory. With a product line of no more than fifty items, inventory could be kept at a manageable level, products could be delivered immediately, and product information could be kept at a manageable level.

The Mary Kay product strategy was to offer "preeminent" products to customers. According to management definition, each product sold was "to be outstanding; to stand above others; to have paramount rank, dignity or importance." This was to mean products would be of excellent quality, be competitively priced, and be safe to use. As the product line was limited, compared to competition, each individual product had to appeal to a reasonable large segment of consumers. New product introductions were made in the cosmetics, skin care, fragrances, and toiletries markets. The five year product plan was to focus on three major areas: 1) update, enhance and improve current product lines, formulations, and packaging; 2) introduce significant new products in the treatment/skin care category; and 3) introduce a completely updated glamour line which would include a new system for recommending and using color, new product formulations, new packaging, and updated shades. The value-added provided by the Consultant would be enhanced by offering consumer-oriented videos, brochures, profiles, packaging inserts, and other educational material.

FIGURE 2

Product Line by Sales Percentage

Year Ended
December 31,

	1988	1987	1986	1985
Skin Care Products for Women .	38%	40%	46%	41%
Skin Care Products for Men . . .	1	2	1	1
Glamour Items	28	32	24	31
Nail Care Products	7	-	-	-
Toiletry Items for Women	13	13	15	13
Toiletry Items for Men	3	3	3	2
Hair Care Products	1	1	2	2
Accessories	9	9	9	10
Total	100%	100%	100%	100%

The Mary Kay Color Awareness program was introduced to update the glamour line. Its intent was to simplify the selection of glamour makeup shades by guiding women in their own color decisions and was based on three key principles: skin tone, personal preference and wardrobe. With the program, the sales force had the ability to help customers make color choices in these areas. A line of color-coordinated eye shadows, lip colors, and blushers was introduced to support the program.

A reformulated skin care line specifically designed for men was introduced in 1987 as part of the strategy to update the skin care line. It consisted of a cleansing bar, toner, facial conditioner and oil absorber, sunscreen, moisturizer and shave cream. It replaced a product the company called Mr. K skin care which was the women's products repackaged in brown tubes. Management made its appeal to women who bought the product for men by saying, "Don't you care about your husband's skin? Look what it did for you. Look what it can do for him." Management predicted that this would be a growth area as more and more men started to care about their skin.

A skin care program called "skin wellness" was introduced as an education program for consumers on awareness of the factors that would impact the skin, particularly what sunlight was going to do. It was considered a natural fit for Mary Kay because of the teaching orientation of the sales process. It educated the consumer on how to identify certain kinds of skin cancers in the early stages. It advised a monthly program of skin self-examination in which the consumer would literally look over her body from head to toes in a mirror. Irregularities would be checked again in a month to see if they had changed. There was no mention of Mary Kay products in the program. Although perceived as a consumer affairs, goodwill and trust building program, the consumer could buy products from Mary Kay which would help with protection from the sun.

PACKAGING

Pink was selected as the corporate color because Mary Kay thought that attractive pink packages would be left out on display in the white bathrooms in vogue in 1963. The entire product line, however, had recently been repackaged. Every item was changed to make graphics consistent, to be up to date, and to have individual identity but still look like it was part of the Mary Kay family of products. A new corporate logo, a mix of gold and hot yellow to symbolize the heat of the sun and its eclipse, was featured on the new packages. A new shade of pink, one which was more mauve and less yellow, was selected to compliment the logo. It was considered to be more subtle, more current, more upscale than the shade pink that had become the corporate color. It was part of the quality and value image that the company wanted to convey. The new pink would ultimately find its way onto company trucks, uniforms, promotional material and ultimately the Cadillacs.

ADVERTISING AND PROMOTION

In the early 1980's, when the company was growing at a very fast rate, management experimented with consumer advertising. The program was initiated in the sales division, not marketing. The advertising campaign involved magazines as well as television advertisements. Although no great change in consumer demand was documented, the reaction from the sales force was very positive. Management had concluded that if it were to use advertising in the future, it would want to impart a message to the consumer that would improve the corporate image and support the field sales force in the form of recognition and compensation.

Management justified its lack of interest in consumer advertising by claiming that it spent what its competitors spent on advertising in compensating the sales force. About thirty-three percent of total dollar income of the firm was estimated to go back to the field sales force in terms of commission and rewards. Promotional efforts were concentrated on rewarding the field sales force for their accomplishments. In Seminar, for example, thousands of consultants and sales directors were presented with more than $5 million in selected prizes for their outstanding performance.

The firm had an active public relations and publicity program which centered on Mary Kay Ash, launching new products in fashion magazines, and publicizing the activities and accomplishments of the field sales force. Press releases in the form of corporate publicity and financial information were a part of this program.

DIRECT SUPPORT

A direct support program was introduced as part of a program to "build a company of substance, to create a product line of high quality and to provide a service of value to the consumer." The program involved direct mail. Consultants sent the names of their customers to corporate headquarters. Management then did a mailing to the customer that appeared to come from the Beauty Consultant. An upscale, four-color brochure plus a personal letter was included that identified both the consultant and consumer by name. The beauty consultant would then follow up by telephone to the consumer to inquire if the information had been received. Initially, the program created some suspicion from the field sales force. Sales people thought that management was going to take these customer names and create a house account and service customers directly. "So we worked on that for a while," contended Ms. Barbara Beasley, Senior Vice President Marketing, "and I think we were able to prove to them that our objective was not to bypass the consultant in starting up this direct mail program, but rather to support the consultant, which is why it's called direct support." The direct support program was based on the consultant's contacts. If the consultant did not make the follow-up telephone call, if the consultant didn't deliver the products to the consumer, then no sale was ever made. All products always were sold through the sales force.

Beauty Consultants were offered products at wholesale discounts from suggested retail prices, for resale to retail customers. At retail, the Mary Kay product line was priced competitively, just below brands which were distributed through department stores and generally well above direct retail store/mass distributed brands. Company literature included suggested retail prices, but the ultimate retail price was determined by the consultant who could charge less then the suggested retail by running her own promotions. "She can ultimately set the retail," said Ms. Curran Croskeys, Vice President of Product Marketing at Mary Kay, "She buys it at a discount off retail, so it's up to her as to how much profit she wants to make."

PLANNING IN A MARKETING ORIENTATED FIRM

Philosophically, corporate planning at Mary Kay Cosmetics was based on the golden rule, "Do unto others as you would have them do unto you," and the priorities of God first, family second, and career third. Mary Kay maintained, "I've found when you just let go and place yourself in God's hands, everything in your life goes right. I believe we have success because God has led us all the way." In this context she identified her son, Richard Rogers, Chairman of the Board and Chief Executive Officer, as a "brilliant administrator and outstanding corporate planner [who] is recognized as one of today's bright, young financial geniuses." "Yet," she noted, "not even he can look at computer printouts or market surveys and truly predict the future."

On a more operational basis, the management team was led by Mr. Bartlett as President and Chief Operating Officer. The organization, in Mr. Bartlett's experience, was really focused on celebrating the achievements of the sales force. In a typical organization chart, he maintained, the board chairman, the president, vice presidents and managers were ordered down to the sales organization. At Mary Kay the situation was thought of in the reverse. The sales force was perceived to be at the top. The president's job was to support the executive team, who in turn supported other people, who in turn supported the sales force. "The program was based upon," as Mr. Bartlett suggested, "loyalty to the people involved, loyalty to the product, and loyalty to the plan." There was a loyalty to the people, such as the director who brought the consultant into the business. There was product brand loyalty built up because the company found that it's a rare woman who could effectively sell the company's products that didn't believe in them. And there was loyalty to the plan in the form of compensation, recognition, and incentive contests that recognized sales people as individuals for their achievements.

The mission statement of the firm, as illustrated in Figure 3, summarized the attitudes of management towards people in field sales as well as customers. It was considered an all exclusive statement of what the company wanted to be. As President Bartlett indicated, "We used to have financial goals as part of the mission statement, and we have gone away from that. That didn't work as well for us." Having a flexible, philosophically oriented statement yielded some clearly delineated objectives for the corporation. Division and department objectives supported the mission statement.

To emphasize the importance of the corporate mission statement, President Bartlett had it printed up on small tent cards. These were distributed to all of the employees to remind them of the fundamental social and economic purpose of the firm. On the other side of the tent card were three words: "listen, listen, listen."

Manufacturing was emphasized in the first statement of preeminence because management felt that consumer driven organizations needed to have competitive products and excellence in manufacturing to survive. As part of the changing focus at Mary Kay, the Senior Vice President of Research and Development/Quality Assurance reported directly to the president. Previously, the R & D and quality assurance programs had reported inside the manufacturing group. "I wanted, frankly," indicated President Bartlett, "to draw the manufacturing group into this mission so that they were not feeling separate from it; they are a part of it."

The use of the phrase personal care products in the mission statement was a revision of an older mission statement that included the phrase: "being the leading teaching oriented skin care cosmetic company." This was a narrow statement that tended to focus on skin care only. The personalized service phrase was a continuation of what the firm had done well at for twenty-five years. Management did not want this area to be neglected by other changes in the mission. Convenience was included because the strength of the firm was thought to be in the consultant. When the customer lost the consultant it became inconvenient to buy Mary Kay products. Included was the phrase, "through our independent sales force." The sales force was thought to "drive" the objectives of the company.

FIGURE 3

The Mary Kay Mission

To achieve preeminence in the manufacturing

and marketing of personal care

products by providing personalized service,

value and convenience to Mary Kay

customers through our independent sales force.

Richard C. Bartlett, President

There was no formal planning department at Mary Kay Cosmetics. The emphasis was placed on having a corporate mission that would be flexible and could be looked back on from time to time, as opposed to a strategy that said the firm was expected to reach certain goals in a specific year. Management felt that, as a basic strategy, a team of flexible, hard-hitting, and adaptable executives would be better able to handle the major changes that were occurring in the external environment. A recent appointment of Dr. Myra Barker as Senior Vice President of Research & Development/Quality Assurance and chief scientific officer reflected this strategy. "This reflects our concern for being in harmony with what might hit us scientifically in the cosmetic marketing world," indicated President Bartlett. "Good strategy is implementation strategy--where you don't get off with a planning group and say, 'This is where we'er going to arrive at an X time in the future.' ...but you're flexible enough, and you have the intellectual muscle to adapt to change."

"I fear a rigidly in place plan" and "I fear formal planning departments" were responses of President Bartlett when asked in his Dallas office if Mary Kay Cosmetics had a formal plan for looking ahead. Bartlett had concluded that "we have an over-riding mission which we can look back on, and I'd rather view the mission we have, as opposed to a locked in concrete strategy that says we will come out at such and such a place in the year 2000." "While I say that," he maintained, "there is no way that we can really anticipate all the major changes coming at us now, the geometric progression of information, governmental interference, regulation and all the myriad of factors that we have to face."

Although there was not a formal strategic planning department at Mary Kay Cosmetics, the product line was planned out five years. Each year key executives, such as the president, department heads, directors and all who might be involved in implementing the strategy, would meet to brainstorm sociological, consumer, industry and scientific trends. Out of this meeting would emerge a product plan. For three years out it was very detailed, showing what the firm was doing every month. President Bartlett felt that such planning was necessary to anticipate the changes that they knew were going to happen. "You gain flexibility by having this type of plan," suggested Ms. Curran Croskeys, Vice President of Product Marketing, "by having a track to follow you accomplish the plan in a routine way. You use brain power and other resources to change if you have to."

THE CONTEMPORARY CHALLENGE

One era ended and another began when Mary Kay Cosmetics experienced its first sales decline in 1984. The early era is a case study in entrepreneurship. The latter era is a study in the efforts of an established organization attempting to achieve its objectives in a changed business environment. Mary Kay's initial objective was, "to establish a company that would give unlimited opportunity to women." In the late 1980's there was an increase in full-time job opportunities for women elsewhere. Not only were they not available to sell the product, but they were not at home to buy it.

Mary Kay Cosmetics, Inc. had for over twenty-five years focused on celebrating the achievements of its sales force. Much of the forward momentum in that sales force had come from the entrepreneurial spirit of Mary Kay Ash, the founder of the company. Mary Kay had been elevated to the position of Chairman Emeritus. A new management team was in place. The firm had repositioned itself to meet the challenges of a new decade. The question was now, could the firm accomplish its corporate mission and objectives in this changing environment?

DISCUSSION QUESTIONS

1. Evaluate and justify the personal selling strategy of Mary Kay Cosmetics. What factors should a manufacturer consider before choosing to include personal selling as a form of promotion in the marketing mix?

2. What evidence is there to conclude that the marketing concept is understood and applied by Mary Kay management?

3. Evaluate the strategies that Mary Kay management has introduced as part of its positioning strategy. How much impact will these strategies have in the competitive environment as the firm seeks profitable growth in the marketplace?

4. How important is a mission statement in giving direction to strategy development in a marketing orientated organization?

5. How much importance is placed on the planning function at Mary Kay Cosmetics?

6. What conclusions can you draw from a review of the financial performance of Mary Kay Cosmetics, Inc. from the years 1978-1988?

7. Discuss the importance of changes in the external environment. How much impact do they have on strategic planning in organizations like Mary Kay Cosmetics?

8. How much impact is the "retirement" of Mary Kay Ash likely to have on the forward momentum of the organization? What decisions and actions should be undertaken to continue Mary Kay Ash's formula for success?

APPENDIX A
MARY KAY CORPORATION
CONSOLIDATED BALANCE SHEETS
December 31, 1988 and 1987
ASSETS

	1988	1987
Current assets:		
Cash and cash equivalents	$15,039,000	$11,500,000
Accounts receivable	5,345,000	3,330,000
Inventories:		
Raw materials	15,172,000	11,206,000
Finished goods	34,567,000	22,865,000
	49,739,000	34,071,000
Note receivable	-	17,267,000
Deferred income tax benefit	3,790,000	695,000
Other current assets	3,482,000	2,587,000
Total current assets	77,395,000	69,450,000
Property, plant and equipment, at cost: Land	4,932,000	2,950,000
Buildings and improvements	16,268,000	12,483,000
Furniture, fixtures and equip.	49,459,000	40,046,000
Construction in progress	3,385,000	605,000
	74,044,000	56,084,000
Less accumulated depreciation	28,296,000	16,878,000
	45,748,000	39,206,000
Assets held for sale	10,000,000	9,215,000
Identified intangible assets	103,820,000	108,558,000
Goodwill	31,205,000	32,624,000
Long-term investment at market	13,630,000	-
Other assets	7,245,000	2,515,000
	$289,043,000	$261,568,000

Source: Annual Report

APPENDIX A (continued)

CONSOLIDATED BALANCE SHEET
LIABILITIES AND CAPITAL DEFICIENCY

Current liabilities:		
Accounts payable	$ 15,513,000	$ 12,529,000
Accrued liabilities	45,097,000	34,876,000
Deferred sales	7,685,000	4,567,000
Current port. of long-tm debt	18,000,000	31,000,000
Total current lib.	86,295,000	82,972,000
Long-term debt	81,035,000	75,000,000
Debentures	124,258,000	106,765,000
Notes payable to related parties	73,231,000	73,231,000
Deferred income taxes	333,000	1,665,000
Other liabilities	24,648,000	12,259,000
Commitments		
Capital deficiency:		
$4.50 Class A noncumulative part con. pref. stock, $1.00 par value	530,000	530,000
730,000 shares authorized, 529,945 shares issued and outstanding Common stock, $1.00 par value;	366,000	366,000
1,100,000 shares authorized, 365,963 shares issued and outstanding		
Capital in excess of par value	5,335,000	
Accumulated deficit	(36,902,000)	(28,380,000)
Investment valuation allowance	(1,911,000)	–
Less amount not "pushed down" to equity of subsidiary	(68,175,000)	(68,175,000)
Total capital deficiency	(100,757,000)	(90,324,000)
	$289,043,000	$261,586,000

Source: Annual Report

APPENDIX A (continued)

CONSOLIDATED STATEMENTS OF OPERATIONS
Years Ended December 31, 1988 and 1987

	1988	1987
Net sales	$405,730,000	$325,647,000
Cost of sales	104,503,000	86,501,000
Selling, gen. & admin. exp.	206,797,000	207,359,000
Operating income	38,430,000	31,787,000
Insurance proceeds	-	-
Write down of assets	(11,000,000)	(4,696,000)
Interest and other income, net	3,137,000	3,884,000
Interest expense	(37,248,000)	(40,391,000)
Loss before income taxes and extraordinary items	(6,681,000)	(9,416,000)
Provision for income taxes	1,495,000	5,876,000
Loss before extraordinary items	(8,176,000)	(15,292,000)
Extraordinary expenses, net of related income tax benefit of $423,000 in 1988 and $5,327,000 1987	822,000	5,596,000
Net loss	$ (8,998,000)	$(20,888,000)

APPENDIX A (continued)

CONSOLIDATED STATEMENTS OF CASH FLOWS
Years Ended December 31, 1988, 1987

	1988	1987
Cash flows from operating activities:		
Net loss......................	$ (8,998,000)	$(20,888,000)
Adjustments to reconcile net loss to net cash provided by operating activities:		
Depreciation...................	8,288,000	9,180,000
Amortization...................	6,410,000	7,052,000
Defined benefit retirement program expense..............	3,598,000	-
Accretion expense..............	17,493,000	14,834,000
Deferred tax provision.........	(7,522,000)	(106,000)
Write down of assets...........	11,000,000	4,696,000
Loss on disposition of assets..	27,000	325,000
Extraordinary expenses.........	1,245,000	10,923,000
Changes in assets and liabilities:		
Decrease (increase) in:		
Accounts receivable.........	(1,806,000)	(125,000)
Inventories.................	(15,870,000)	(12,767,000)
Income tax receivable.......	-	6,206,000
Other current assets........	(895,000)	(464,000)
Goodwill....................	-	-
Other assets................	(392,000)	(195,000)
Increase (decrease) in:		
Accounts payable............	2,984,000	589,000
Accrued liabilities.........	11,283,000	8,817,000
Deferred sales..............	1,858,000	(1,996,000)
Other liabilities...........	(458,000)	(343,000)
Federal income tax refund....	3,986,000	10,164,000
Other, net..................	729,000	745,000
Net cash provided by operating act.	32,960,000	36,656,000
Cash flows from investing activities:		
Purchases of investment........	(15,541,000)	-
Capital expenditures...........	(6,025,000)	(2,576,000)
Proceeds from sales of assets..	383,000)	1,130,000
Net cash provided by (used in) investing activities:..........	(21,183,000)	(1,446,000)

APPENDIX A (continued)

CONSOLIDATED STATEMENTS OF CASH FLOWS
Years Ended December 31, 1988, 1987

	1988	1987
Cash flows from financing activities:		
Principal payment of long-term debt.........................	(90,000,000)	(125,733,000)
Increase in long-term debt.....	(82,535,000)	90,000,000
Cost of refinancing debt.......	(1,569,000)	(8,596,000)
Proceeds from loans from life insurance policies...........	796,000	
Net cash used in financing act...	(8,238,000)	(44,329,000)
Net increase (decrease in cash and cash equivalents)..........	3,539,000	(9,119,000)
Cash and cash equivalents at beginning of year..............	11,500,000	20,500,000
Cash and cash equivalents at end of year......................	$ 15,039,000	$ 11,500,000
Additional information:		
Cash payments (refunds) for:		
Interest (net of amounts capitalized)................	17,290,000	29,107,000
Income taxes................	4,755,000	(15,235,000)
Noncash financing activities:		
Restructuring an existing note receivable:		
Decrease in note receivable....	$ 17,267,000	-
Decrease in accounts receivable	1,000,000	-
Increase in note receivable....	(11,000,000)	-
Increase in assets held for sale........................	(10,000,000)	-
Increase in deferred taxes.....	2,733,000	-
Restructuring an existing note payable:		
Decrease in long-term debt.....	(16,000,000)	-
Decrease in accrued liabilities	(862,000)	-
Increase in long-term debt.....	16,500,000	-
Increase in deferred taxes.....	362,000	-

APPENDIX B
Mary Kay Cosmetics, Inc., Dallas, Texas
Financial Performance
1978-1988

Year	Net Sales (000)	Net Profit (000)	Total Assets (000)	Net Worth (000)
1988	$405,730	$ (8,998)	$289,043	$(100,757)
1987	325,647	(20,888)	261,568	(90,324)
1986	255,016	(55,502)	284,180	(69,351)
1985	13,547 (1)	(1,306)	328,922	(13,647)
	235,513 (2)	21,286	272,166	183,304
1984	277,500	33,781	217,554	163,746
1983	323,758	36,654	180,683	131,725
1982	304,275	35,372	152,457	95,316
1981	235,296	24,155	100,976	61,952
1980	166,938	15,135	74,431	38,633
1979	91,400	9,632	50,916	24,618
1978	53,746	4,873	36,305	25,947

Source: Company Annual Reports

(1) Period From December 5 to December 31, 1985

(2) Period Ended December 4, 1985

APPENDIX C
Avon Products Inc., New York
Financial Performance
1978-1986

Year	Net Sales (000)	Net Profit (000)	Total Assets (000)	Net Worth (000)
1986	$2,883.10	$158.70	$2,296.30	$ 681.30
1985	2,470.10	(59.90)	2,289.00	926.40
1984	2,605.30	181.70	2,287.50	1,157.10
1983	2,607.60	172.90	2,256.80	1,273.10
1982	2,710.10	186.60	2,227.60	1,245.10
1981	2,725.20	216.50	1,611.90	930.50
1980	2,569.10	242.10	1,583.10	928.30
1979	2,377.50	244.00	1,417.00	866.30
1978	2,086.30	233.60	1,282.40	770.70

Source: Company Annual Reports

APPENDIX D
Shaklee Corporation, San Francisco, CA
Financial Performance
1978-1986

Year	Net Sales (000)	Net Profit (000)	Total Assets (000)	Net Worth (000)
1986	$398,030	$59,123	$344,214	$233,904
1985	406,043	13,016	277,161	164,276
1984	459,115	13,207	260,660	154,451
1983	538,729	35,145	261,795	151,125
1982	471,876	24,008	222,074	120,758
1981	454,522	24,543	191,670	105,601
1980	411,331	12,071	173,191	86,979
1979	314,149	21,288	164,707	78,859
1978	275,369	19,294	112,991	61,691

Source: Company Annual Reports

APPENDIX E
Direct Selling Industry
1980-1988

Year	Retail Sales (000)	Salespeople
1988	$9,695,556	3,996,000
1987	8,789,415	3,614,000
1986	N/A	N/A
1985	8,360,000	5,129,994
1984	8,640,000	5,808,928
1983	8,575,000	5,114,276
1982	8,500,000	4,933,413
1981	N/A	N/A
1980	7,500,000	4,908,947

Source: Direct Selling Association - 1988

References

Ash, Mary Kay, *Mary Kay*, New York: Harper & Row, Revised Edition, 1986.

Ash, Mary Kay, *Mary Kay on People Management*, Warner Books, Inc., 1984.

Ballen, Kate, "Get Ready for Shopping at Work," *Fortune* (February 15, 1988) p. 95, 98.

Barker, Myra, (January 31, 1989), Interview with Senior Vice President of R&D/QA, Mary Kay Cosmetics, Inc., Dallas, Texas.

Barmash, Isadore, *More Than They Bargained For: The Rise and Fall of Korvettes*, New American Library, 1981.

Bartlett, Richard C., (January 31, 1989), Interview with President, Mary Kay Cosmetics, Inc., Dallas, Texas.

Beasley, Ms. Barbara, (January 31, 1989), Interview with Senior Vice President of Marketing, Mary Kay Cosmetics, Inc., Dallas, Texas.

Biggart, Nicole Woolsey, *Charismatic Capitalism: Direct Selling Organizations in America*, University of Chicago Press, 1989.

Chase, Marilyn, "At the Shaklee Corp., Selling Is Believing," *Wall Street Journal* (March 9, 1989) p. B8.

Chase, Marilyn, "Looking for Miracles, Young and Old Flock to Purchase Retin-A," *Wall Street Journal* (February 12, 1988) p. 1, 7.

Coughlin, Marilyn, "Making a Business of Belief: Sociologist Examines the Direct-Selling Industry in America," *The Chronicle of Higher Education* (July 19,1989) p. A5-A6.

Croskeys, Curran, (January 31, 1989), Interview with Vice President of Product Management, Mary Kay Cosmetics, Inc., Dallas, Texas.

"Direct Marketers Adapt to New Lifestyles," by the Associated Press, Chicago: *Marketing News* (June 19, 1989) p. 7.

Direct Selling Association, *A Statistical Study of the Direct Selling Industry in the United States: 1980-1985*, A Report Prepared by the Direct Selling Association, Washington, D.C.: Direct Selling Association, October, 1986.

Direct Selling Association, *The 1988 Direct Selling Industry Survey,* A Report prepared by the Direct Selling Association, Washington, D.C.: Direct Selling Association, July, 1989.

Dolan, Carrie, "Entrepreneurs Often Fail as Managers," *Wall Street Journal* (May 15, 1989) p. B1.

Dunkin, A. and Ducas, C., "How Cosmetics Makers Are Touching Up Their Strategies," *Business Week* (September 23, 1985) p. 66-68, 73.

Fannin, Rebecca, "The Beauty of Being Mary Kay," *Marketing & Media Decisions* (December, 1982) p. 58-61.

"Flight of the Bumblebee," *Forbes* (August 12, 1985) p. 12.

Hattwick, Richard E., "Mary Kay Ash," *The Journal of Business Leadership* (Spring, 1988) p. 21-40.

Hilder, David B. and Trachtenberg, Jeffrey A., "Avon Stock Sags on Withdrawal of Amway Bid," *Wall Street Journal* (May 19, 1989) p. A4.

Kingan, Adele, "Entrepreneur's Corner: Mary Kay Ash, Founder and Chairman of the Board, Mary Kay Cosmetics, Inc.," *Executive Female* (November-December, 1982) p. 12-14.

"Mary Kay Board Approves New Bid by Firm's Founder," *Wall Street Journal* (July 2, 1985) p. 16.

"Mary Kay Cosmetics, Inc. Business Brief," *Wall Street Journal* (February 11, 1985) p. 28.

"Mary Kay Cosmetics, Inc. Business Brief," *Wall Street Journal* (December 4, 1985) p. 59.

"Mary Kay Cosmetics Gets Buyout Offer From Managers, Valued at $280 Million," *Wall Street Journal* (May 31, 1985) p. 4.

"Mary Kay Cosmetics: Looking Beyond Direct Sales to Keep the Party Going," *Business Week* (March 28, 1983) p. 130.

"Mary Kay Cosmetics Picks Rogers as Its Chairman," *Wall Street Journal* (November 10, 1987) p. 42.

"More Than a Cosmetic Success, 1920," *Wall Street Journal* (March 28, 1989) p. B1.

Nissen, Beth, "Woman to Woman: Mary Kay Sales Agents Zero In On Prospects In Their Living Rooms," *Wall Street Journal* (September 28, 1978) p. 1, 24.

Olive, David, "All the Way with Mary Kay," *Canadian Business* (November, 1984) p. 77-81.

Rinefort, Foster, (July 31, 1989) Interview with management consultant, Eastern Illinois University, Charleston.

Rothbart, Dean and Cohen, Laurie P., "About Face: The Party at Mary Kay Isn't Quite So Lively, As Recruiting Falls Off," *Wall Street Journal* (October 28, 1983) p. 1, 12.

Rothman, Andrea, "For James Preston, It's Still Avon Calling," *Wall Street Journal,* (December 9, 1988) p. B13.

Schifrin, Matthew, "Peeking Inside LBO's" *Forbes* (June 13, 1988) p. 66, 68.

Sloan, Pat, "Mary Kay, Jafra Shows Dramatic Growth," *Advertising Age* (August 23, 1982) p. 22.

Sloan, Stanley H., "Avon Calling: Cosmetics Firm Makes A Strong Comeback From a Recession Dip," *Wall Street Journal* (April 6, 1977) p. 1, 17.

Trachtenberg, Jeffrey A., "Sallie Cook is One in a Million Reasons Amway Like Avon," *Wall Street Journal* (May 19, 1989) p. A1, A4.

Case 2

HARLEY-DAVIDSON, INC.: THE EAGLE SOARS ALONE

In May of 1987, Vaughn Beals, Chief Executive of Harley-Davidson, Inc. and Thomas Gelb, Vice-President of Operations, made a difficult decision. They had turned Harley-Davidson around on a dime and were now poised for continued success with a fine-tuned production process and an exciting new product line. However, in a continued effort to maintain low costs, Beals and Gelb were forced to give a contract for eight electronically controlled machining centers worth $1.5 million to Japanese-owned Toyoda Machine Works. Even though the Toyoda production site for the machining centers was in Illinois, Beals would have preferred to buy from an American Company. But he was constrained because of the Japanese company's ability to deliver both high quality and low price.

Beals was well aware of the implications of the decision. He had previously toured several Japanese motorcycle plants during Harley's turnaround and had been impressed with their efficiency and quality. Beals understood the pressure that foreign competition had put on his company, and on other manufacturing-intensive companies in the U.S. as well.

Nonetheless, the decision reflected Harley's commitment to quality and reliability, and also indicated the company's willingness to change with the competitive environment.

Beals and his small management team turned around a company that really symbolized America. Harley-Davidson motorcycles represented freedom and rugged individualism. Beals had put Harley back as the market leader in the super-heavyweight (more than 851cc) motorcycle market. Harley owned 33.3%

This case was prepared by Lieutenant Commander Stuart Hinrichs, Professor Charles B. Shrader of Iowa State University, and Professor Alan N. Hoffman of Bentley College. The authors would like to thank Linda Zorzi, assistant to V.L. Beals, CEO and Chairman of Harley-Davidson Motor Company, for information she provided in preparing this case. The authors would also like to thank Lieutenant Michael Melvin and Blaine Ballantine of Iowa State University for providing helpful information. Reprinted by permission.

of that market in 1986 compared to Honda's 30.1%. As of August of 1987, Harley had 38% of the large-cycle market and total company sales were expected to rise from under $300 million in 1986 to over $600 million in 1987[1] (see Exhibit 1).

Exhibit 1 Harley-Davidson

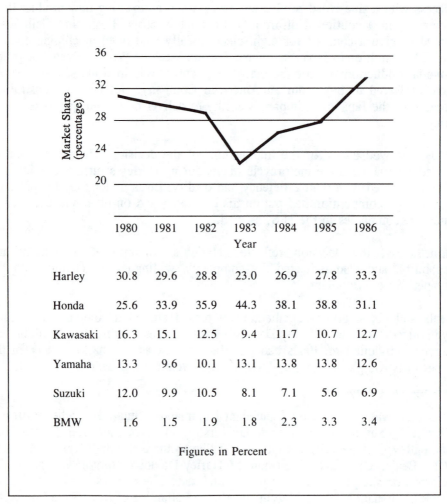

	1980	1981	1982	1983	1984	1985	1986
Harley	30.8	29.6	28.8	23.0	26.9	27.8	33.3
Honda	25.6	33.9	35.9	44.3	38.1	38.8	31.1
Kawasaki	16.3	15.1	12.5	9.4	11.7	10.7	12.7
Yamaha	13.3	9.6	10.1	13.1	13.8	13.8	12.6
Suzuki	12.0	9.9	10.5	8.1	7.1	5.6	6.9
BMW	1.6	1.5	1.9	1.8	2.3	3.3	3.4

Figures in Percent

Source: 1986 *Annual Report*

Yet Beals knew that to stabilize that performance, his company needed to diversify. The Milwaukee-based company manufactured motorcycles and motorcycle accessories, as well as bomb casings and other products for the military. In 1986, Harley acquired Holiday Rambler Corporation, a recreational vehicle company. Beals believed that it would fit perfectly with the other businesses, and it was in one industry that was free from Japanese competitors.

Beals knew that Harley had to continue to improve both its production and its human resource management techniques if it was to remain strong, competitively. And he also realized that his company's basic product, super-heavyweight ("hog") motorcycles, had the loyal customers and brand image upon which successful competitive and diversification strategies could be built. The company's nonmotorcycle businesses were performing well and the Holiday Rambler acquisition looked promising. Now the challenge Beals faced was how to keep the company moving down the road at high speed.

History[2]

The Harley-Davidson story began in 1903 when William Harley, aged 21, a draftsman at a Milwaukee manufacturing firm, designed and built a motorcycle with the help of three Davidson brothers: Arthur, a pattern maker employed by the same company as Harley; Walter, a railroad mechanic; and William, a tool maker. At first, they tinkered with ideas, motors, and old bicycle frames. Legend has it that their first carburetor was fashioned from a tin can. Still, they were able to make a three-horsepower, twenty-five-cubic-inch engine and successfully road test their first motorcycle.

Operating out of a shed in the Davidson family's backyard, the men built and sold three motorcycles. Production was expanded to eight in 1904 and in 1906 the company's first building was erected on the current Juneau Avenue site of the main Milwaukee offices. On September 17, 1907, Harley-Davidson Motor Company was incorporated.

Arthur Davidson set off to recruit dealers in New England and in the South. William Harley completed a degree in engineering, specializing in internal combustion engines, and quickly applied his expertise in the company: He developed the first V-twin engine in 1909. He followed this with a major breakthrough in 1912--the first commercially successful motorcycle clutch. This made possible the use of a roller chain to power the motorcycle. The first three-speed transmission was offered in 1915.

During the early 1900s the U.S. experienced rapid growth in the motorcycle industry, with firms such as Excelsior, Indian, Merkel, Thor, and Yale growing and competing. Most of the early U.S. motorcycle companies turned out shoddy, unreliable products. But this was not considered to be true for Harley-Davidson and Indian cycles. Early continued success in racing and endurance made Harleys favorites among motorcyclists. The company's V-twin engines became known for power and reliability.

During World War I, Harley-Davidson supplied the military with many motorcycles. By virtue of very strong military and domestic sales, Harley-Davidson became the largest motorcycle company in the world in 1918.[3] The company built a 300,000 square foot plant in Milwaukee, Wisconsin in 1922, making it one of the largest motorcycle factories in the world.[4]

In the late 1930s, Harley-Davidson dealt a strong competitive blow to the Indian motorcycle company: it introduced the first overhead-valve engine. The large, 61-cubic-inch engine became very popular and was thereafter referred to as the "Knucklehead." Indian could not make a motorcycle to compete with these Harleys.

Harley introduced major innovations in the suspension of its cycles in the 1940s. However, in 1949 Harley first met with international competition, from Great Britain. The British motorcycles, such as Nortons and Triumphs, were cheaper, lighter, better handling, and just as fast, even though they had smaller engines.

To counter the British threat, Harley-Davidson further improved the design of the engines, and thereby increased the horsepower of their heavier cycles. The result, in 1957, was what some consider to be the first of the modern superbikes: the Harley Sportster. It was also during the 1950s that Harley developed the styling that made it famous.

As the 1950s drew to a close, new contenders from Japan entered the lightweight (250cc and below) motorcycle market. Harley welcomed the little bikes because it believed that small-bike customers would quickly move to larger bikes as the riders became more experienced. The Japanese cycles proved to have some staying power, however, and Japanese products began to successfully penetrate the off-road and street cycle markets. In the 1960s Japan entered the middleweight (250-500cc) market.

As Harley entered the 1960s, it made an attempt to build smaller, lightweight bikes in the U.S. But the company found it difficult to build small machines and still be profitable. As a result, Harley acquired 50% of Aermacchi, an Italian cycle producer, and built small motorcycles for both street and off-road use. The first Aermacchi Harleys were sold in 1961.[5] The Italian venture endured until 1978, but was never highly successful. Few took Harley's small cycles seriously; some Harley dealers refused to handle them. In the meantime, Japanese cycles dominated the small and middleweight markets. Harley seemed trapped in the heavyweight segment.

In an attempt to expand its production capacity and raise capital, Harley went public in 1965. The company merged with the conglomerate AMF, Inc. in 1969. AMF, a company known for its leisure and industrial products, expanded Harley's production capacity from 15,000 units in 1969 to 40,000 units in 1974.[6] With the expanded capacity, AMF pursued a milking strategy, favoring short-term profits rather than investment in research and development, and retooling. The Japanese continued to improve while Harley began to turn out heavy, noisy, vibrating, laboriously handling, poorly finished machines.

In 1975, AMF failed to react to a serious Japanese threat. Honda Motor Company introduced the "Gold Wing," which quickly became the standard for large touring motorcycles, a segment that Harley had owned. At the time, Harley's top-of-the-line touring bike sold for almost $9,000 while the comparable Honda Gold Wing was approximately $7,000.[7] Not only were Japanese cycles priced lower than similar Harleys, but Japanese manufacturing techniques yielded operating costs that were 30% lower than Harley-Davidson's.

Motorcycle enthusiasts more than ever began to go with Japanese products because of their price and performance advantages. Even some loyal Harley owners and police department contracts were lost. The company was rapidly losing ground both in technological advances and in the market.

Starting in 1975 and continuing through the middle 1980s, the Japanese companies penetrated the big-bore, custom motorcycle market with Harley look-alikes with V-twin engines.[8] The Honda "Magna" and "Shadow," the Suzuki "Intruder," and the Yamaha "Virago" were representative of the Japanese imitations. In a short time the Japanese captured a significant share of the large cycle segment and controlled nearly 90% of the total motorcycle market.[9]

During AMF's ownership of Harley, its motorcycles were strong on sales but relatively weak on profits. AMF did put a great deal of money into Harley and production went as high as 75,000 units in 1975.[10] But motorcycles never seemed to be AMF's priority. For example, in 1978, motorcycles accounted for 17% of its revenues but for only 1% of profits. AMF was more inclined to emphasize its industrial products and services.

The Turnaround[11]

Vaughn Beals served as Harley's top manager during its last six years under AMF control. Beals was uncomfortable with AMF's short-term orientation and unwillingness to confront the problems caused by imports. Consequently, in June of 1981, a subgroup of Harley management, including Beals, completed a leveraged buyout of Harley-Davidson from AMF. To celebrate, Beals and the management team made a Pennsylvania-Wisconsin motorcycle ride, proclaiming, "The Eagle Soars Alone."

Beals knew that reversing the company's momentum would not be easy, especially without the help of the former parent. Indeed, things first began to get worse. Harley suffered its first operating loss in 1981. In 1982, many motorcycles were coming off the assembly line with defects, registrations for heavyweight motorcycles were falling, and the Japanese were continuing to penetrate Harley's market segments. Company losses for the year totalled over $25 million.[12] Several Japanese companies built up inventories in the face of a declining market and engaged in aggressive price discounting.

Beals petitioned the International Trade Commission (ITC) for temporary protection from Japanese "dumping" practices in 1982. He accused the Japanese of dumping large quantities of bikes in the U.S. and selling them for prices much below what they were in Japan. The U.S. Treasury had previously found the Japanese guilty of excess-inventory practices, but the nonpartisan ITC ruled that the practices had not adversely affected the sales of Harley-Davidson motorcycles. Therefore, no sanctions were placed on the Japanese companies. The Japanese continued price competition and many thought that Harley would soon buckle from the pressure.

However, in 1983, with the help of many public officials including Senator John Heinz of Pennsylvania, Harley was able to obtain protection from the excess-inventory practices of the Japanese. In April of 1983, President Reagan, on the recommendation of the ITC, imposed a declining five-year tariff on the wholesale prices of Japanese heavyweight (over 700cc) motorcycles. The tariff schedule was as follows:

1983	45%
1984	35%
1985	20%
1986	15%
1987	10%

The effects of the tariff were mixed. Much of the Japanese inventory was already in the U.S. when the tariff went into effect, and prices of those units were not affected. Also, dealers selling Japanese cycles sharply reduced prices on older models, and thus hurt the sale of new bikes.

On the other hand, the tariff signaled that Japanese over-production would not be tolerated, so that Harley would have some breathing room and management would have a chance to reposition the company. Beals and others inside the company felt that the dumping case and the tariff protection helped focus the company on developing its competitive strengths and on improving the production process. They also believed that the tariffs were the result of the government's recognition of Harley's overall revitalization effort. The process of whipping the once proud American company back into shape had begun several years before the tariff went into effect.

Improving Production[13]

In the early years Harley had been successfully run by engineers. Beals' background was in engineering as well, and he began to focus on the beleaguered production process. Until 1982, the company used a batch production system that produced only one model at a time. The final line work force would vary from 90-140 people depending on which model was being produced on a given day.

To make the production system more efficient, Beals, Thomas Gelb, and others on the management team, implemented what they called their productivity triad that included the following:

1. An inventory system that supplied materials as needed.
2. An employee involvement and development program.
3. A computer-aided design and manufacturing program.

The Materials As Needed (MAN) system stabilized the production schedule, and helped reduce excess inventory. Under this system, production worked with marketing to make more accurate demand forecasts for each model. Based on these forecasts, precise production schedules were established for a given month and were not allowed to vary by more than 10% in subsequent months. A production method was adopted whereby a different mix of models was produced every day. This was referred to as the "jelly bean" method.

Under the MAN system, Harley also required its suppliers to become more compliant to their quality requirements. Harley offered long-term contracts to suppliers who conformed to the quality requirements and who delivered only the exact quantity needed for a given period of time. Harley also integrated backward into transporting materials from suppliers: when the Harley-Davidson transportation company made scheduled pickups from suppliers, Harley had greater control over the shipments, and was thereby able to cut costs.

Before the 1983 tariff was imposed, Beals, Gelb, and others visited several Japanese motorcycle plants and learned the importance of employee development and employee involvement. As a result, rigorous training programs were developed. By 1986, over one-third of the employees were trained in statistical process control, or the ability to sample and analyze data while performing a job. Set-up times were reduced with the use of ideas gleaned from quality circles—problem-solving sessions between workers, managers, and engineers.

Further improvements in the production process were made by Walter Anderson, senior production engineer, with the help of Harley employees and management. Whereas components had formerly run down straight lines, Anderson organized workers into a series of "work cells." A work cell consisted of a few workers in a small area with all the machines and tools they needed to complete a job. The work cells were often arranged in U-shaped configurations that allowed for intensive work within a cell and reduced the total movement of components through the process. The use of cells also improved employee efficiency, because workers stayed at the same work station all day yet enjoyed variety in their tasks.

Harley also invested heavily in research and development. One payoff of this investment was a computer-aided design (CAD) system developed by the research and development group, that allowed management to make changes in the entire product line while maintaining elements of the traditional styling. The company's R&D group developed a more efficient engine in 1983 and a new suspension in 1984. Harley was soon recognized to be an industry leader in many aspects of production, including belt-drive technology, vibration isolation, and steering geometry. Since 1981, the company had allocated a major portion of its revenues to R&D each year.

Beals' emphasis on production brought big payoffs for the company. Harley's defect rate was reduced to nearly perfect, 1% in 1986. The company also lowered its breakeven point from 53,000 units in 1982, to 35,000 units in 1986.[14] Many companies visited Harley for seminars and advice on how to improve efficiency.

Perhaps one of the greatest indicators of Harley's production turnaround was evidenced through one of their oldest pieces of equipment—a huge, sheet-metal forming machine known simply as the "Tool." The Tool, originally built in Milwaukee but later moved to the York plant in Pennsylvania, was used to forge the "Fat Bob" gas tanks for all the FX and FXR series bikes. There was no operating manual nor maintenance book for the Tool, yet the company still used this old legendary machine to crank out modern, high-quality products.

In March of 1987, Vaughn Beals appeared before a Washington, D.C. news conference and offered to give up the tariff protection, which was intended to last until the middle of 1988. Congress praised the announcement and commended the company for its success. President Reagan even visited the York plant in celebration of the event.

Corporate Structure[15]

According to Beals, one of the most important contributions to the company's turnaround was the savings obtained by a drastic reduction in salaried staff, a result of Beals' exposure to the Japanese management systems. The number of managers at each plant was reduced, and each manager was given responsibility for everything at the plant: hiring, operations, productivity, etc.

The number of line employees was also reduced. Line employees were given individual responsibility to inspect products for defects, apply quality-control measures, determine quotas and goals, and make production decisions.

A majority of the company's employees participated actively in quality-circle programs. The quality circles were used not only to improve efficiency but also to address other issues. One such issue was job security. Both the reduction in staff and the increased productivity caused workers to worry about their jobs. However, the quality circles came up with the idea to move some sourcing and fabricating of parts in-house. In-house sourcing made it possible for many empoloyees, who may have otherwise been laid off, to retain their jobs.

Harley's corporate staff was made very lean and the structure was simplified. Top executive officers were put in charge of functional areas. Under top management, the company was basically organized into two divisions-- motorcycles and defense. Holiday Rambler Corporation became a wholly owned subsidiary in 1986.

Top Management[16]

Vaughn L. Beals, Jr. was appointed as the Chief Executive Officer and Chairman of the Board of Directors of Harley-Davidson Motor Company following the buyout from AMF in 1981. He had originally earned an engineering degree from the Massachusetts Institute of Technology. He worked as a logging-machine manufacturer and as a diesel engine maker before joining AMF in 1975. In 1981, along with one of the grandsons of the founder and twelve other persons, he led the leveraged buyout of the Harley-Davidson Motor Company. He was known throughout the company for his devotion and enthusiasm for motorcycles. He owned a Harley deluxe Electra-Glide and rode it on business trips whenever possible.

Harley's top management always demonstrated their willingness to take a "hog" on the road for a worthy cause. On one occasion, in 1985, Beals and a product designer, William G. Davidson (known as "Willie G"), led a caravan of Harleys from California to New York in an effort to raise money for the Statue of Liberty renovation. At the conclusion of the ride, Beals presented a check for $250,000 to the Statue Foundation.

Beals claimed that his major responsibility was for product-quality improvements. On one occasion, during a business trip, Beals noticed a defect in a 1986 model's seat. He stopped long enough to call the factory about the problem. The workers and test riders, however, had already found and corrected the flaw.

Beals made an all-out effort to keep managerial levels in the company to a minimum. The Board of Directors was composed of six officers, four of whom were from outside the company. The CEO often communicated with everyone in the company through memos known as "Beals'-grams" (see Exhibits 2 and 3).

Because of the company's success, and in an effort to provide additional capital for growth, Harley went public with an offering of approximately 6 million shares in the summer of 1986. Beals owned nearly 16% of the Harley-Davidson stock, which was then increasing in value.

Human Resource Management[17]

Harley-Davidson employed approximately 2,336 people in 1986. This number was down from that of 3,840 in 1981. Under Chief Executive Beals, the company made great strides in developing a participative, cooperative, less hierarchical work climate. Employees wrote their own job descriptions and actively participated in on-the-job training. Employees learned that they were responsible for not only their own jobs, but for helping others learn as well. Performance was evaluated through a peer review program.

Exhibit 2   Board of Directors, Harley-Davidson, Inc.

Vaughn L. Beals, Jr.
Chairman, President and Chief
Executive Officer—Harley-Davidson,
Inc., Milwaukee, Wisconsin

Frederick L. Brengel
Chairman and Chief Executive
Officer—Johnson Controls, Inc.,
Milwaukee, Wisconsin

F. Trevor Deeley
Chairman and Chief Executive
Officer—Fred Deeley Imports,
Richmond, British Columbia, Canada

Dr. Michael J. Kami
President—Corporate Planning,
Inc., Lighthouse Point, Florida

Richard Hermon-Taylor
Management Consultant, South
Hamilton, Massachusetts

Richard F. Teerlink
Vice President, Treasurer
and Chief Financial Officer—
Harley-Davidson, Inc.,
Milwaukee, Wisconsin

Source: 1986 *Annual Report*

Exhibit 3   Harley-Davidson Executive Officers

	AGE	POSITION	YEARS WITH COMPANY[1]	ANNUAL COMPENSATION
Vaughn L. Beals	58	Chairman and CEO	10	$207,217
Richard F. Teerlink	49	Vice President, Chief Finance Officer	5	$143,375
Jeffrey L. Bleustein	46	Vice President, Parts and Accessories	15	$118,387
Thomas A. Gelb	50	Vice President, Operations	21	$132,666
James H. Paterson	38	Vice President, Marketing	15	$ 95,728
Peter L. Profumo	39	Vice President, Program Management	17	$129,521

[1]Years with Harley-Davidson or AMF, Inc.
Source: 1986 *Prospectus,* Dean Witter Reynolds

The company developed many career and placement opportunity programs as a response to employees' concern over job security. Harley also entered into a cooperative placement agreement with other Wisconsin unions. The company even developed a voluntary layoff program, in which senior workers voluntarily took themselves off in down times to protect the jobs of newer workers. Harley offered sophisticated health and retirement benefits, and has also developed employee wellness and college tuition funding programs.

Financial Performance

Harley was purchased from AMF through a leveraged buyout in 1981, for approximately $65 million.[18] The buyout was financed with a $30 million term loan and $35 million in revolving credit from institutional lenders. AMF also received $9 million of securities in the form of preferred stock. In 1984, the two companies reached an agreement whereby the preferred stock held by AMF was cancelled and subsequent payments were to be made directly to AMF from future Harley-Davidson profits.

In 1985, Harley negotiated an exchange of common stock for forgiveness of a portion of the loans. The company offered $70 million in subordinated notes and $20 million in stock for public sale in 1986. The proceeds from this sale were used to repay a portion of the debt to AMF, to refinance unfavorable loans, to provide financing for the Holiday acquisition, and to provide working capital.

Holiday Rambler Corporation was a privately held company until its acquisition by Harley in 1986. Holiday Rambler performed very well in its first year as part of Harley-Davidson. It had total sales of approximately $257 million through September of 1987, compared to $208 million for the same period in 1986; this was nearly a 24% increase.

Harley-Davidson's net sales and profitability improved during the years 1982 to 1986. Net income and earnings per share fluctuated in that period. The motorcycle division's sales as a percentage of total sales decreased, because of the rapid increase in the defense division. In the years following the 1981 buyout, the company relied greatly on credit for working capital (see Exhibits 4, 5, and 6).

Exhibit 4   Harley-Davidson, Inc.: Consolidated Balance Sheet
(Dollar Amount in Thousands)

Year Ended December 31	1984	1985	1986
Assets			
Current assets:			
Cash	$ 2,056	$ 9,070	$ 7,345
Temporary investments	--	4,400	20,500
Accounts receivable net of allowance			
for doubtful accounts	27,767	27,313	36,462
Inventories	32,736	28,868	78,630
Prepaid expenses	2,613	3,241	5,812
Total current assets	65,172	72,892	148,758
Property, plant and equipment, at cost,			
less accumulated depreciation and			
amortization	33,512	38,727	90,932
Deferred financing costs	--	2,392	3,340
Intangible assets	--	--	82,114
Other assets	523	81	2,052
	$99,207	$114,092	$327,196
Liabilities and Stockholders' Equity			
Current liabilities:			
Notes payable	$ --	$ --	$ 14,067
Current maturities of long-term debt	2,305	2,875	4,023
Accounts payable	21,880	27,521	29,587
Accrued expenses and other liabilites	24,231	26,251	61,144
Total current liabilities	48,416	56,647	108,821
Long-term debt, less current maturities	56,258	51,504	191,594
Long-term pension liability	856	1,319	622
Stockholders' equity			
Common stock 6,200,000 issued in 1986			
and 4,200,000 in 1985	42	42	62
Class B common stock, no shares issued	--	--	--
Additional paid-in capital	9,308	10,258	26,657
Deficit	(15,543)	(5,588)	(717)
Cumulative foreign currency translation			
adjustment	--	40	287
	(6,193)	4,752	26,289
Less treasury stock (520,000 shares)			
at cost	(130)	(130)	(130)
Total stockholders' equity	(6,323)	4,622	26,159
	$99,207	$114,092	$327,196

Sources: 1986 *Annual Report*; 1986 *Prospectus*--Dean Witter Reynolds

Exhibit 5   Harley-Davidson, Inc.: Consolidated Statement of Income
(Dollar Amount in Thousands Except Per-Share Data)

Year Ended December 31	1982	1983	1984	1985	1986
Income statement data:					
Net sales	$ 210,055	$ 253,505	$ 293,825	$ 287,476	$ 295,322
Cost of goods sold	174,967	194,271	220,040	217,222	219,167
Gross profit	35,088	59,234	73,785	70,254	76,153
Operating expenses:					
Selling and administrative	37,510	36,441	47,662	47,162	51,060
Engineering, research and development	13,072	9,320	10,591	10,179	8,999
Total operating expenses	50,582	45,761	58,253	57,341	60,059
Income (loss) from operations	(15,494)	13,473	15,532	12,913	16,096
Other income (expenses):					
Interest expense	(15,778)	(11,782)	(11,256)	(9,412)	(8,373)
Other	1,272	188	(311)	(388)	(388)
	(17,050)	(11,594)	(11,567)	(9,750)	(8,761)
Income (loss) before provision (credit) for income taxes, and extraordinary items, and cumulative effect of change in accounting principle	(32,544)	1,879	3,965	3,163	7,335
Provision (credit) for income taxes	(7,467)	906	1,077	526	3,028
Income (loss) before extraordinary items and cumulative effect of change in accounting principle	(25,077)	973	2,888	2,637	4,307
Extraordinary items and cumulative effect of change in accounting principle	-	7,795	3,578	7,318	564
Net income (loss)	$ (2,077)	$ 8,768	$ 6,466	$ 9,955	$ 4,871
Average number of common shares outstanding	4,016,664	3,720,000	3,680,000	3,680,000	5,235,230
Per common share:					
Income (loss) before extraordinary items and cumulative effect of change in accounting principle	$ (6.61)	.26	.79	.72	.82
Extraordinary items and cumulative effect of change in accounting principle	-	2.10	.97	1.99	.11
Net income (loss)	$ (6.61)	$ 2.36	$ 1.76	$ 2.71	$ .93

Source: 1986 Annual Report

Exhibit 6   Harley-Davidson, Inc.: Sales and Income by Business Segment
(Thousands of Dollars)

	1983	1984	1985
Net sales:			
Motorcycles and related products	$229,412	$260,745	$240,631
Defense and other businesses	24,093	33,080	46,845
	$253,505	$293,825	$287,476
Income from operations:			
Motorcycles and related products	$ 16,513	$ 15,489	$ 9,980
Defense and other businesses	3,566	7,012	9,390
General corporate expenses	(6,606)	(6,969)	(6,457)
	13,473	15,532	12,913
Interest expenses	(11,782)	(11,256)	(9,412)
Other	188	(311)	(338)
Income before income taxes, extra-ordinary items and cumulative effect of change in accounting principle	$ 1,879	$ 3,965	$ 3,163

Source: 1986 *Prospectus*--Dean Witter Reynolds

Marketing Strategy

Harley-Davidson's marketing efforts centered around the use of the Harley name. The company emphasized that its name was synonymous with quality, reliability, and styling. Company research indicated a 90% repurchase rate, or loyalty factor, by Harley owners.

Harley's marketing concentrated on dealer promotions, magazine advertising, direct mail advertising, sponsorship of racing activities, and the organization of the Harley Owners Group (HOG). The HOG club had enrolled 77,000 members by 1987, and permitted the company to have close contact with customers. Another major form of advertising was accomplished through the licensing of the Harley name, which was very profitable and served to promote the company's image.

In addition, Harley sponsored or co-sponsored organizations such as the Ellis Island Statue of Liberty Foundation and the Muscular Dystrophy Association.

The company was also the first motorcycle manufacturer to offer a national program of demonstration rides. Some dealers felt the program introduced in 1984, resulted in a large number of Harley motorcycle purchases.

The company also directed a portion of its marketing expenditures toward expanding the field sales force, in an effort to assist the domestic dealer network. In some areas the sales force developed local marketing programs to train dealers.

The Harley Image

Few companies could elicit the name recognition and brand loyalty of Harley-Davidson. Harley's appeal was based on the thrill and prestige of owning and riding the king of the big bikes. Harleys were known as sturdy, powerful, macho bikes: not for wimps and kids, they were true bikes for the open road, bikes for driving through brick walls!

A worrisome problem with the Harley image, however, was the perceptual connection of Harleys exclusively with "outlaw" groups. The negative "Road Warrior" image affected sales in some areas to such a degree that the company initiated a public relations campaign. They gently attacked the biker image by directing much of their advertising toward young professionals. The message was that Harley-Davidson represented fun, recreation, and reliability. The company heralded the fact that famous professionals such as Malcolm Forbes and Reggie Jackson rode Harleys, and advertisements picturing these celebrities atop their "hogs" further helped the company's image. The campaign seemed to work. More doctors, lawyers, and dentists began to purchase Harleys.

Harley also put tighter controls on licensing its name, ensuring that it was not used in obscene ways. Harley was careful not to alienate their loyal "biker" customers, however. And the company continued to promulgate, even enhance its tough image, through advertising in motorcycle magazines. For example, one ad pictured a group of rather tough looking bikers and had a caption which read: "Would you sell an unreliable bike to these guys? We Don't!" Another ad showed a junkyard filled with scrapped Japanese bikes. The caption was: "Can you find a Harley in here?"

A related problem with its image was that Harley could not attract very many women customers. This was due to the image and to the size of the bikes. Harleys were very big and heavy. The Harley low-rider series was attracting some women customers because the bikes were lower and easier to get on. Notwithstanding this partial success, some Japanese companies introduced smaller, lighter, low-riding, inexpensive, Harley look-alikes in a straightforward attempt to attract women buyers. Honda's "Rebel" (250cc) was one such bike that became fairly successful with women.

Perhaps the most objective indicator of the strength of the image came from an unlikely source--Japan itself! The Japanese made numerous attempts to copy Milwaukee designs.[19] For example, Suzuki's 1987 "Intruder" (1400cc) went to great lengths to hide the radiator--because Harleys were air cooled. Yamaha's "Virago" (1100cc) and Kawasaki's "Vulcan" (1500cc) were V-twin street bikes conspicuously styled in the Harley tradition. Nevertheless, some analysts felt that Japanese imitations only served to strengthen the mystique of the original. The more the Japanese tried to make look-alike bikes, the more the real thing increased in value. Beals agreed. He maintained that Harleys were built to last longer and have a higher resale than other bikes.

Diversification

Harley-Davidson competed in the heavyweight motorcycle market segment since the early years of the company. Heavyweight bikes were divided into three categories: touring/custom, standard street, and performance motorcycles. Harley was never totally successful in building smaller bikes, and at one time Beals was even quoted as saying that Harley would not attempt to build small bikes in the future.

Harley-Davidson had made attempts to diversify throughout its history. However, its current motorcycle product line was very narrow compared to those of its competitors. The company's management thought about breaking out of its narrow niche by expanding into international markets. The largest export markets for Harley were Canada, Australia, and West Germany.

In 1971, Harley attempted to diversify by manufacturing its own line of snowmobiles. The seasonal nature of the business and intense Japanese competition caused the company to abandon the product in 1975.

Another attempt at diversification was the company's purchase of a small three-wheeler firm named "Trihawk" in 1984. Shortly thereafter the company realized it could not make a go of it in this market because of high start-up costs, and the project was terminated.

Under Beals the company moved into the manufacturing of casings for artillery shells and rocket engines for military target drones. Beals set corporate goals to increase the level of defense-related business in an attempt to diversify the company. Thus, the company became very active in making bids for the design and development of defense products. The defense business was very profitable for Harley.

Accessories, bike parts, clothing, "leathers," even furniture associated with the Harley name were big businesses for the company. Brand-name licensing and related accessories generated about as much income as did the motorcycles.

But Beals wanted to move the company into other businesses not related to the rather narrow motorcycle line and not located in an industry with Japanese competitors. He felt Harley needed to diversify in order to be a truly stable performer. That is why Harley acquired the Holiday Rambler Company in December of 1986. Beals saw the fit as a good one because Holiday was a recreational vehicle producer and was what he called "manufacturing intensive" just as Harley was.

Holiday Rambler manufactured premium motorhomes, specialized commercial vehicles, and travel trailers. Holiday employed 2,300 people and was headquartered in Wakarusa, Indiana. Holiday was the largest privately owned maker of recreational vehicles at the time of the acquisition. The company was recognized as one of the leaders in the premium-class motorhome and towable-trailer markets. It ranked fourth, in 1986, in market share in the motorhome market and fifth in towable recreational vehicles. Its products were gaining share in the industry as a whole.

A Holiday subsidiary, Utilimaster, built truck trailers and bodies for commercial uses. The company had contracts with companies such as Purolator Courier and Ryder Truck Rentals. Other Holiday subsidiaries produced office furniture, custom wood products, custom tools, van conversions, and park trailers.

Even with the Holiday acquisition and with the success in defense, Harley looked for other means of diversifying. In September of 1986, a tobacco company purchased a license to test market Harley-Davidson brand cigarettes.

The Future

The Harley turnaround, in the face of stiff competition, caused the company to be viewed as an example of what can be accomplished by use of modern production and personnel-management techniques. Top management was committed to keeping the company lean and viable. Yet they knew they needed to diversify and change. Beals knew that his company needed to become as tough as its image.

Beals focused his turnaround effort on the internal operating efficiency of the company. Now he needed to provide leadership for a newly acquired subsidiary and plan for growth in the defense division.

He also faced the challenge of breaking the company out of its narrow market segment in its bread-and-butter division: motorcycles. Could he plan for growth and market penetration in the motorcycle industry? Or should he be content with maintaining Harley as a big bike company only?

Since 1903, 150 American motorcycle companies had come and gone. Harley-Davidson Motor Company, with Vaughn Beals at the helm, was the only one that survived. The eagle continued to soar alone.

References

1. Harley-Davidson, Inc., 1986 *Annual Report*.

2. David K. Wright, *The Harley-Davidson Motor Company: An Official Eighty-Year History,* Second Edition (Osceola, Wisconsin: Motorbooks International), 1987.

3. *Ibid.*, p. 17.

4. *Ibid.*, p. 17.

5. *Ibid.*, p. 35.

6. *Ibid.*, pp. 282-283.

7. "Uneasy Rider: Harley Pleads for Relief," *Time*, (December 13, 1982), p. 61.

8. David K. Wright, *The Harley-Davidson Motor Company: An Official Eighty-Year History,* Second Edition (Osceola, Wisconsin: Motorbooks International), 1987, pp. 244-262.

9. "Trade Protection: Mind My (Motor) Bike," *The Economist*, (July 2, 1977), p. 82.

10. David K. Wright, *The Harley-Davidson Motor Company: An Official Eighty-Year History*, Second Edition (Osceola, Wisconsin: Motorbooks International), 1987, p. 281.

11. *Ibid.*, pp. 244-262.

12. Dean Witter Reynolds, *Prospectus*, Harley-Davidson, Inc., July 8, 1986, p. 8.

13. Rod Willis, "Harley-Davidson Comes Roaring Back," *Management Review*, (October, 1986), pp. 20-27.

14. *Ibid.*

15. *Ibid.*

16. Jeff Baily, "Beals Takes Harley-Davidson On New Road," *Wall Street Journal*, (March 20, 1987), p. 39.

17. Rod Willis, "Harley-Davidson Comes Roaring Back," *Management Review*, (October, 1986), pp. 20-27.

18. Dean Witter Reynolds, *Prospectus*, Harley-Davidson, Inc., July 8, 1986, p. 10.

19. "Why Milwaukee Won't Die," *Cycle*, (June 1987), pp. 35-41.

Case 3

APPLE COMPUTER, INC., 1987 ... THE SECOND DECADE

On July 20, 1987, John Sculley, the CEO of Apple Computer Corporation is mulling over a report prepared for him by his marketing department. This report focuses on the computer industry's outlook for the late 1980s, with special emphasis on the recently announced IBM Personal System 2 or PS/2, and Intel's new 80386 microchip.

Apple is a $1.9 billion company that designs, manufactures, sells, and services personal computers (PCs) and related software and peripheral products. The major sources of Apple's customers are homes, businesses, and educational institutions. Although the company is best established in the education segment with the Apple II, it is trying, through its Macintosh product line, to become a more significant competitor in the business markets. Apple also competes internationally, and 26% of its revenues come from outside of the United States. The principal methods of distribution are the independent retail dealer, national retail accounts, and direct sales.

Until recently, experts questioned whether Apple would survive, because of the general slump in the computer industry and Apple's lackluster sales. Even though the company was successfully reorganized in 1985 into a leaner, more profitable organization, some pointed out that cutting costs is not a growth strategy, especially in an innovation-driven industry. Furthermore, it was doubtful that Apple could coexist with IBM, the dominant competitor, in the business market. In 1986, the first "open" Macintosh, designed to provide owners with ease in modification, was introduced. IBM PCs had always been "open."

This case was prepared by Ms. Phyllis Feddeler, MBA student, Professor Thomas L. Wheelen of the University of South Florida, and Professor David B. Croll of the McIntire School of Commerce at the University of Virginia. It was presented at the North American Case Research Association Meeting, 1988. All rights are reserved to the case authors and the North American Case Research Association. Copyright © 1987 and 1989 by Thomas L. Wheelen. Revised in 1989. Reprinted by permission.

HISTORICAL BACKGROUND

The company was founded in 1976 by Steve Jobs, who was then 21, and Stephen Wozniak, 26. With only $1,350, raised by the sale of a VW van and an HP programmable calculator, and an order for fifty computers with a selling price of less than $700, the two young men began their business by manufacturing the Apple I in Jobs' garage.

Not long afterward, a mutual friend helped recruit A.D. "Mike" Markkula to help market the company and give it a million-dollar image. Markkula had successfully managed the marketing departments of two semiconductor companies, Fairchild Semiconductor and Intel Corporation, that had experienced dynamic growth. Markkula's original business plan for Apple was the founders' dream and vision for the future of the new company (see Exhibit 1).[1] On January 3, 1977, Apple Computer, Inc., was incorporated. In December 1980 the company went public with an offering of 4.6 million shares of common stock. In May 1981 there was a secondary offering of 2.6 million shares of common stock by approximately 100 selling stockholders, all of whom had acquired their shares through the employee stock plan or private placement.

In the high-growth industry of personal computers, Apple did grow quickly, despite increasing numbers of business failures among competitors. In 1985, Apple was the second-largest competitor, next to IBM, in the PC industry. (See Exhibit 2.)

During the years of high growth, the company suffered internal turmoil because of disagreements as to the company's direction, especially in terms of product development (see Exhibit 3). Jobs' pet project, the Macintosh, was consuming an amount of funds disproportionate to the revenues it was bringing in. Internal rivalry grew between the Apple product department and the Macintosh product department. First Wozniak resigned (he now works as a consultant to Apple) and, in September 1985, Jobs resigned and took with him five key managers. Jobs intended to begin another company called Next, Inc. In its subsequent suit against Jobs, Apple accused him of "misappropriating Apple secrets and of breaching his fiduciary responsibility by plotting to form a new company and recruiting selected employees while still Chairman of Apple ... "[2]

When John Sculley (a former CEO of Pepsi-Cola Company, who started working at Apple in May 1983) took over full control, Apple had just suffered its first loss as a public company and had undergone a reorganization that included laying off 20% of its employees. Shipments of Macintosh PCs were only 10,000 per month but the manufacturing capacity was 80,000 per month.

**Exhibit 1   Mike Markkula's Original Business Plan:
Strategies and Objectives (November 18, 1976)**

MAJOR OBJECTIVES

1. Obtain a market share greater than or equal to two (2) times that of the nearest competitor.
2. Realize equal or greater than 20% pretax profit.
3. Grow to $500 million annual sales in 10 years.
4. Establish and maintain an operating environment conducive to human growth and development.
5. Continue to make significant technological contributions to the home computer industry.
6. (Possible) Structure company for easy exit of founders within five years.

KEY STRATEGIES

1. It is extremely important for Apple to be the first recognized leader in the home computer marketplace.
2. Continually market peripheral products for the basic computer, thereby generating sales equal to or greater than the initial computer purchase.
3. Allocate sufficient funds to R&D to guarantee technological leadership consistent with market demands.
4. Attract and retain absolutely outstanding personnel.
5. Rifle-shoot the hobby market as the first stepping stone to the major market.
6. Maintain significant effort in manufacturing to continually reduce cost of production.
7. Grow at the same rate that the market grows.
8. Design and market the computer to be more economical than a dedicated system in specific applications, even though all features of the Apple are not used.

Source: John Scully, *Odyssey* (New York: Harper and Row, 1987), pp. 387-388.

Exhibit 2 Market Share of PC Sales

		1986 (% Of Total Sales)	1985 (% Of Total Sales)
1.	IBM	29.5	40.5
2.	Apple	7.3	10.3
3.	Compaq	7.0	5.2
4.	Zenith	4.2	2.4
5.	Tandy	3.4	4.6
6.	Commodore	1.9	3.8
7.	Other	46.7	33.2

Source: Dataquest Inc.

Exhibit 3 The Rise of John Sculley and the Fall of Steven Jobs

Steve Jobs personally recruited John Sculley to be CEO of Apple. The initial job contact was between Gerry Roche, Chairman of Heidrick and Struggles, Inc., and John Sculley. Sculley asked, "How does Jobs feel about this?" Roche responded, "He wants to find someone who is really great who he can learn from. The chief executive will report directly to the board. Steve is focused largely on product development."[1] This meeting took place over the Thanksgiving Day holidays in 1982. The negotiations between Apple and Sculley lasted for approximately five months. Sculley joined the company in May, 1983. Jobs at one meeting told Sculley that "You can sell sugared water to children the rest of your career or you can change the world a little."[2] Sculley's original employment called for $1 million in annual pay (half in salary and half in bonus), $1 million up front to join Apple, and $1 million in severance pay if things did not work out. The contract also had a housing clause that cost Apple an additional million dollars. Sculley was also awarded stock options on 350,000 shares.[3]

At the hiring time, Sculley said of Jobs: "Steve is a great visionary." Jobs responded that "Sculley is someone I can learn from."[4] Sculley was hired to help Apple maintain its market share in the personal computer market. Since 1981, Apple's market share had been declining. The hiring also marked the beginning of the transition for Apple from an entrepreneurial corporate culture to a professional corporate culture. Jobs (age 28) and Sculley (age 44) quickly developed a remarkably close friendship. The relationship was part brotherly, part father-son. Sculley said, "Steve and I became soul mates and near-constant companions. We spoke with each other for hours throughout every day ... We had an unwritten understanding that either one could interrupt the other in whatever he was doing."[5] Their closeness provoked resentment among other top management executives at Apple. Sculley said of Jobs and himself, "Apple has one leader, Steve and me."[6]

In 1983, Sculley had consolidated the company's nine highly decentralized divisions organized along products lines into three divisions. The new organization had one division for the production of the Apple II family of products, another division for the development and production of the Macintosh (MAC) and the third division for sales of all Apple products. Jobs was named manager of the newly formed Macintosh Division.

In October 1984, the alliance between Jobs and Sculley started to deteriorate. Jobs had dual roles as Chairman of the Board and General Manager of the MAC division. He and Sculley, CEO, were faced with conflicting authority relationships--each was a subordinate to each other yet they both had authority over each other. This organizational structure caused many conflicts and much stress in their management partnership and friendship. The MAC division was not performing up to expectations, but Sculley felt awkward demanding better performance from Jobs because of his management roles. Some of Macintosh's major problems were (1) lagging sales--an automated plant to turn out 80,000 Macintoshes per month was built, but demand never exceeded 30,000; (2) Lisa (business version) had low acceptance by business corporations; (3) the closed architecture did not allow add-on options; (4) target market focused on business instead of Apple's traditional buyers in homes and schools, and (5) they were not delivering on a promised option that would make the Macintosh IBM compatible.[7]

Jobs treated the MAC division employees as the elite group of Apple employees. They were given special perks--free fruit juice and a masseur on call.[8] Steve felt that the Macintosh people represented the best of Apple. The company now consisted of two groups--Macintosh employees and others. The MAC group referred to everyone else in the company as "bozos." It got to the point that MAC people wore buttons with a line running through the face of Bozo the clown.[9]

In February 1985, Steven Wozniak severed all ties with Apple. He owned about 4% of the company's stock valued at approximately $70 million. Mr. Wozniak said that the Apple II division "... had been ignored in the hope that it will die and go away ...." He left to establish a new company.[10]

In early 1985, Sculley concluded that he had to remove Jobs as the General Manager. Sculley anguished for days over this problem. Finally, his responsibilities to the stockholders, the board, and the employees won out over strong friendship with Jobs. He went to Steve's office to inform him of his decision. He was going to present his decision at the next board meeting. What followed was a violent disagreement between Jobs and Sculley. At the April 10 board meeting, Sculley told the board,

> I'm asking Steve to step down and you can back me on it and I will take responsibility for running the company, or we can do nothing and you're going to have to find yourself a new CEO ... We've got enough problems and we've got to solve them right now.[11]

Sculley was fully prepared to resign. The board meeting was spread over two days. The board unanimously agreed to ask Steve to step down as executive vice-president, but continue as the chairman. It gave Sculley the authority to implement the reorganization.[12]

The next six weeks was a period of a bitter power struggle, as Sculley wrested control of the company from Jobs. There were many discussions between Jobs and Sculley. Jobs wanted to retain some day-to-day operating responsibilities. It was a time of power politics. Jobs lobbied informally with other executives and board members to ascertain if he could remove Sculley from the company. Sculley was advised by an Apple executive not to take a scheduled trip to China, because Jobs was planning to overthrow him while he was in China.

It all came to a head at the executive committee meeting on May 24. Sculley reiterated that he was the one running Apple. The round-table meeting lasted for three hours. The committee tried to find a future role for Jobs but failed. Jobs volunteered to take his scheduled vacation and return after the company reorganization was completed.

On May 31, Sculley signed the paperwork removing Jobs as Executive Vice President. It was also announced that the company had been reorganized along functional lines. Promotions and job responsibilities were also announced.[13] In a conversation with Mike Markkula, Sculley said, "When I got the board's authority to remove Steve, I shouldn't have waited around. I should have acted immediately. I was trying to make it easier on Steve and what I did was create a big mess. That was my mistake."[14] This year of chaos cost Mike almost $200 million in the value of his stock holdings.[15]

From the end of May to the middle of June, Sculley reorganized the company. On June 14, Sculley announced a cut in the permanent workforce by 20% (1,200 employees), eliminated almost all of the temporary workforce, and closed three factories; Apple produced its first-ever quarterly loss ($17.2 million). Later, the advertising budget of the company was reduced.

Jobs returned to the company. His new office was in an auxiliary building that he called "Siberia." Jobs held 7 million shares or 11.3% of the company's outstanding stock. His holdings were worth more than $400 million in 1983 and dropped to $120 million in June, 1984. He resigned in September 17, 1985.[16] About his new company, Next, Jobs said, "I have a certain degree of confidence that I can do it again." He is pretty certain that he can have another spectacular product and company. "I did it in the garage when Apple started, and I did it in the metaphorical garage when MAC started."[17]

Sources: J. Sculley, *Odyssey* (New York, Harper and Row Publishers, 1987)—cites: (1) p. 60; (3) p. 107; (5) p. 155; (6) p. 198; (7) pp. 227-297; (9) p. 241; (11) p. 242; (12) pp. 241-243; (13) pp. 245-261; (14) p. 275; (15) p. 272; and (16) p. 317.

(2) and (4), J. Dreyfuss, "John Sculley Rises in the West," *Fortune*, July 9, 1984, p. 183.

(8) B. Uttal, "Behind the Fall of Steven Jobs," *Fortune*, August 5, 1985, p. 22.

(10) P.A. Bellew, "Apple Computer Co-Founder Wozniak will Leave Firm, Citing Disagreements," *Wall Street Journal*, February 7, 1985, p. 38.

(17) "Showdown in Silicon Valley," *Newsweek*, September 30, 1985, p. 50.

Although the Macintosh was easy to use, it was criticized in the business world for being underpowered and overpriced. Sculley, who had no prior experience in the computer industry, knew marketing and personally pitched the Macintosh to large corporations such as GE and Eastman Kodak and to software manufacturers, before the improved Macintosh was introduced in January 1986.

MANAGEMENT

Apple is trying to centralize its operations and involve its senior management in day-to-day decisions. Recently, Sculley turned over responsibility of these decisions to Delbert Yocam, the Chief Operating Officer; Sculley could then spend his time on long-term planning. (See Exhibits 4 and 5 for the Board of Directors and top management.) New high-level management positions include Vice-President of Advanced Technology and Vice-President of U.S. Sales and Marketing. Between September 1986 and the end of 1986, the number of employees had grown from approximately 5,600 to 5,940.

In January 1986, an out-of-court settlement was reached with Steven P. Jobs. It allowed Apple to preview the first product from Job's new company, Next, for a specific period of time. It also restricted the hiring of additional Apple employees for at least six months.[4]

MICRO-COMPUTER INDUSTRY

There are two types of computer companies, those that follow and those that lead. Leaders are established by developing and producing the best-selling products. The followers wait for the leaders to build their products and then copy or "clone" them.

Since IBM first introduced its PC in 1981, many computer manufacturers have followed their lead. Marketing an innovative computer before IBM has presented its version is risky. If IBM later introduces a comparable machine with proprietary features, the earlier versions may be rendered obsolete and have to be redesigned.

For the past several years the technology industry has been in a slump, but increased earnings for the first quarter of 1987 (see Exhibit 6) might indicate that the entire industry is coming out of its recession. Dealer sales rose by 15% in the first two months of 1987 and PC shipments to computer stores rose 19% during the first quarter of 1987. Analysts believe that these strong first-quarter earnings, which contributed to the increases in the stock prices of companies such as IBM, Wang, Prime Computer, Inc., and Apple, also mean that sales will continue to increase.[5]

Important new developments in the personal computer industry include desktop publishing and the recent use of Intel Corporation's 80386 micro-chip. In desktop publishing, a PC is used to produce low-cost, high-quality printed

Exhibit 4 Board of Directors and Officers of Apple, Inc.

BOARD OF DIRECTORS

Peter D. Crisp
General Partner—Venrock
Associates; venture capital
investments

Albert A. Eisenstat
Senior Vice-President, Secretary,
and General Counsel—Apple
Computer, Inc.

A.C. Markkula, Jr.
Chairman—ADM Aviation, Inc.;
private flight service

Arthur Rock
Principal—Arthur Rock & Co.;
venture capital investments

Philip Schlein
Partner—U.S. Venture Partners;
venture capital investments

John Sculley
Chairman, President, and Chief
Executive Officer—Apple
Computer, Inc.

Henry Singleton
Chairman—Teledyne, Inc.;
diversified manufacturing company

OFFICERS

John Sculley
Chairman, President, and Chief
Executive Officer

Delbert W. Yocam
Executive Vice-President and Chief
Operating Officer

Albert A. Eisenstat
Senior Vice-President and General
Counsel

William V. Campbell
Executive Vice-President—U.S.
Sales and Marketing

Michael H. Spindler
Senior Vice-President—
International Sales and Marketing

David J. Barram
Vice-President—Finance and Chief
Financial Officer

Charles W. Berger
Vice-President—Business Development

Deborah A. Coleman
Vice-President—Operations

Jean-Louis Gassee
Vice-President—Product Development

Lawrence G. Tesler
Vice-President—Advanced
Technology

Roy H. Weaver, Jr.
Vice-President—Distribution

Robert W. Saltmarsh
Treasurer

Source: Apple Computer, Inc., *Annual Report 1986*

Exhibit 5   Executive Officers of Apple, Inc.

The following information was compiled December 15, 1986.

John Sculley (age 47) joined Apple as President and Chief Executive Officer and a Director in May 1983, and was named Chairman of the Board of Directors in January 1986. Prior to joining Apple, Mr. Sculley was President and Chief Executive Officer of Pepsi-Cola Company, a producer and distributor of soft drink products, from 1977 to 1983. Pepsi-Cola Company is a division of PepsiCo, Inc., of which Mr. Sculley was also a Senior Vice-President. Mr. Sculley is also a director of Communications Satellite Corporation.

Delbert W. Yocam (age 42) joined Apple in November 1979 as Director of Materials, was promoted to Vice-President and General Manager of Manufacturing in August 1981, to Vice-President and General Manager of Operations in September 1982, and in December 1983, was appointed Executive Vice-President and General Manager, Apple II Division. In May 1985, Mr. Yocam was named Executive Vice-President, Group Executive of Product Operations and in July 1985, he was appointed Executive Vice-President and Chief Operating Officer.

Albert A. Eisenstat (age 56) joined Apple in July 1980 as Vice-President and General Counsel; he has also served as Secretary of Apple since September 1980. In November 1985, Mr. Eisenstat was promoted to Senior Vice-President and was elected to the Board of Directors to fill the vacancy created by the resignation of Steven P. Jobs. Mr. Eisenstat is also a director of Adobe Systems, Inc., of Commercial Metals Company, and of Computer Task Group, Inc.

William V. Campbell (age 46) joined Apple as Vice-President of Marketing in June 1983; was appointed Vice-President, U.S. Sales, in January 1984; was appointed Executive Vice-President, Sales, in September 1984; and became Executive Vice-President, U.S. Sales and Marketing in June 1985. Before joining Apple, Mr. Campbell served as Director of Marketing for Eastman Kodak Company (a photographic equipment and supplies manufacturer) from May 1982 to June 1983, and as Account Director for J. Walter Thompson Advertising from January 1980 to May 1982. Mr. Campbell is also a director of Champion Parts Rebuilders.

Michael H. Spindler (age 44) joined Apple as European Marketing Manager in September 1980; was promoted to Vice-President and General Manager, Europe, in January 1984; was named Vice-President, International, in February 1985, and was promoted to Senior Vice-President of International Sales and Marketing in September 1986.

David J. Barram (age 42) joined Apple in April 1985 as Vice-President of Finance and Chief Financial Officer. Prior to his employment with Apple, he was the Vice-President of Finance and Administration and Chief Financial Officer of Silicon Graphics. Inc., a manufacturer of high-performance engineering workstations, from April 1983 to April 1985. From January 1970 to April 1983, Mr. Barram held various positions at Hewlett-Packard Company, a diversified electronics measurement and computer equipment manufacturer; his most recent position there was Group Controller of the Technical Computer Division.

Charles W. Berger (age 32) joined Apple in April 1982 as Treasurer and was appointed Director of Strategic Sales in June 1985. In September 1986, Mr. Berger was appointed Vice-President of Business Development. Prior to joining Apple, Mr. Berger served as Assistant Treasurer at Rolm Corporation, a wholly-owned subsidiary of IBM Corporation that manufactures computerized telephone switches and digital telephones, and President of Rolm Credit Corporation.

Deborah A. Coleman (age 33) joined Apple in November 1981, initially as Controller and subsequently as Director of Operations of the Macintosh Division. Ms. Coleman was promoted to Director of Manufacturing in June 1985, to Vice-President of Manufacturing in November 1985, and to Vice-President of Operations in October 1986. Before joining Apple, Ms. Coleman served as a financial manager and cost-accounting supervisor at Hewlett-Packard Company.

Jean-Louis Gassée (age 42) joined Apple in February 1981 as General Manager of Seedrin S.A.F.L., a wholly-owned subsidiary of the company. In May 1985, Mr. Gassee became Director of Marketing of the Macintosh Division, and in June 1985, he was named Vice-President, Product Development.

Lawrence G. Tesler (age 41) joined Apple in July 1980 as a senior member of the technical staff. Beginning in October 1980, he was appointed Project Supervisor, Lisa Applications Software; in August 1981, Section Manager, Lisa Applications Software; in February 1983, Consulting Engineering and Manager of Object-Oriented Systems. Prior to Mr. Tesler's promotion to Vice-President of Advanced Technology in October 1986, Mr. Tesler served as Director of Advanced Development from July 1986 to October 1986.

Roy H. Weaver, Jr. (age 54) joined Apple in September 1980 as U.S. Distribution Manager. In April 1981, he was Director of Distribution and Service Operations, and in April 1982, he was promoted to General Manager of Distribution and Service. In September 1982, he was appointed Vice-President and General Manager of the Distribution, Service, and Support Division; in September 1984, Vice-President, Field Operations; and in June 1985, Vice-President, Distribution.

Robert W. Saltmarsh (age 36) joined Apple as Assistant Treasurer in November 1982 and was promoted to Treasurer in October 1985. Between November 1978 and November 1982, Mr. Saltmarsh worked for Data General Corporation, a minicomputer manufacturer, first as European Treasury Manager and then as Corporate Treasury Manager.

Source: Apple Computer, Inc., *1986 10-K Report*

Exhibit 6 1987 First Quarter Sales

	SALES (MILLIONS OF DOLLARS)		PERCENT CHANGE
	1986	1987	
Apple	$ 409	$ 575	+41.0
Digital	1,928	2,410	+25.0
IBM	10,127	10,682	+5.5
Intel	280	395	+41.0
National Semiconductor	324	398	+23.0
NCR	961	1,122	+17.0

SOURCE: Quarterly reports of these companies.

documents in-house. It was Apple's innovation with the Macintosh. Since the introduction of the Macintosh, however, software developers have been creating desktop publishing programs for the IBM PC, and other companies will be soon to follow. The 80386 microchip, referred to as the 386, offers to increase the speed, memory, and multitasking capabilities of microcomputers.

In the summer of 1986, Compaq became the first company to market a personal computer with a 386; IBM began marketing its 386 models in April 1987. Both of these computers are proving to be quite popular. For instance, by December1986, Compaq had shipped 10,000 Deskpro 386s and was having trouble keeping up with orders. It is expected that 386 machines will make up around 10% of the entire PC market by the end of 1987, and 25% of the market by 1990. However, one problem with machines using the 80386 microchip is that the machines cannot take full advantage of its capabilities until software catches up with the new technology, which might take several years.[6]

Other than the microprocessor itself, software is becoming one of the most important parts of a computer. Companies such as Lotus and Microsoft develop software programs specifically for a particular computer model.

In April of 1987, IBM came out with its new product line, called the Personal System 2, or PS/2. Designed in part to discourage clonemakers, IBM incorporated custom microchips, and doubled the amount of software that will have to be written to make clone machines 100% compatible with PS/2. Those companies that use the Micro Channel to connect personal computers to mainframes (in other words IBM's top mainframe customers, or about half of the market) are expected to purchase the PS/2. However, sales of IBM compatibles were up more than 10% in the first five months of 1987, so many customers might not yet be inclined to switch over to the PS/2.[7]

FORECAST OF DEMAND

Overall computer sales are expected to grow in 1987. Some experts predict that the growth rate for microcomputers will range from 7% to 10%, as shown in Exhibit 7. Others expect the microcomputer market to grow by only 3% because of indecision in the business markets about IBM's new products. For example, PC unit growth in major corporations was 100% from 1981-1984, but this growth could slow to only 48% in 1987 because companies are waiting to see how good the IBM PS/2 products are.[8]

Currently, the hot topic in the personal computer market is the 80386 microchip, which is manufactured by Intel Corporation.

Exhibit 7   Projected World-Wide Sales
(in Billions of Dollars)

BUSINESS COMPUTERS		MICRO SALES		LAN EQUIPMENT	
Year	Sales	Year	Sales	Year	Sales
1990	50.0	1990	47.9	1991	3.02
1988	45.7	1988	38.9	1990	2.49
1986	40.6	1986	32.0	1989	2.05
1984	37.6	1984	24.4	1988	1.64
1982	28.1	1982	6.8	1986	.92

SOURCE: Kimball Brown, Dataquest.

The second hot issue, desktop publishing, is becoming so popular that dozens of companies are finding ways to adapt PCs to provide this option. It is expected that the sales of publishing systems for machines that are based on IBM and IBM-compatible computers will exceed the sales of the Macintosh in 1987. The market is growing very quickly, though, and Macintosh sales will probably grow by 70%.[9]

Corporate capital-equipment spending in the U.S. is projected to increase at an average annual rate of 8.8% in the last three quarters of 1987 compared to just 4.2% in 1986. However, the demand for Apple computers in the business environment depends on Apple's ability to convince its customer corporations' MIS managers and the people who actually buy computers, that the Macintosh line offers more than any competing machines can offer. In corporations, large multiple-computer sales are not awarded on price alone, but also on value and performance. Many business people think that Apple does not provide the necessary support to corporations but the company plans to improve their support before 1988. Buyers of large computers will also require a 25% increase in computing capacity in 1987.

The home computer market is projected to reach $34.5 billion wholesale in 1987. Twenty percent of consumers plan to purchase a computer in 1987 or

1988, and half of those intend to spend less than $1000. Currently, there are approximately 2.5 to 3 million units of IBM computers in homes. Many people, try as they might, cannot yet justify the purchase of a home computer, as evidenced by a 1985 survey that found that 76.7% of shoppers did not know what they would do with a home computer if they purchased one.

Networking is becoming increasingly important in the business market. Computer customers are being drawn to networks at an accelerating pace as software improves and technical difficulties subside. Access to a Local Area Network (LAN) makes computing easier for the average customer and places the complex issues on the shoulders of somebody more technically competent. Currently, only about 6% of the 13 million PCs installed in U.S. corporate offices are or were connected to a LAN. That percentage is expected to more than double by 1990. The number of networks installed worldwide is expected to be 220,000 by the end of 1987, up from 52,000 in 1984. As shown in Exhibit 7, worldwide sales of networks could hit $3.02 billion by 1990. The leaders in networking shipments in 1986 are shown below.

1986 Shipments

TERMINAL NETWORK, UNITS		PC NETWORK, UNITS	
Digital Equipment	3,750	Boyell	8,200
Proteon	1,220	3 Com	8,200
Wang	850	IBM PC Net	7,500
Xerox	750	Fox	3,800
Ungermann–Bass	450	Orchid	3,150
		IBM Token-Ring	1,200

DEC was the first computer giant to capitalize on network demand when they set up dozens of three-member teams with representatives from sales, service, and software, to push local networking. Many computer companies are now working on expanding their product lines to include networking. For example, in the past year DEC, AT&T, Hewlett-Packard, and Apple have all introduced new network products and regrouped their sales forces to go after the business market. Major computer makers are moving into this $1.5 billion market, which had been dominated by such independents as Ungermann-Bass, Novell, 3 Com, and Fox Research. Future network wars are possible. Tandem Computers, Inc., for example, has teamed with Boeing Company's computer services division, to sell factory networks. IBM also has joined with Microsoft Corporation, a software company, which is designing software to link the new PS/2 computers together. IBM's #1 corporate priority of late has been the networking market.

MARKET SEGMENTS

Apple's objectives are to excel in the business markets, where computer sales are growing fastest, but not get dragged into the low-priced end of the computer industry. To achieve these objectives, it plans to exploit and develop the communications talents of the Macintosh family.

There are three types of companies that use Apple computers. First are the technical and aerospace corporations (such as DuPont, Hughes Company, Chevron, Motorola, General Dynamics, and Plessey—British telecommunications), which use the Macintosh for computer-aided design and other technical uses. Second, there are service companies (such as Arthur Young; Peat, Marwick, Mitchell; and Seafirst Bank's Seattle branches), which have many employees who are computer illiterate. In these companies use of the Macintosh reduces training costs. Third are the groups (such as Knight—Ridder and marketing departments of GE) that need the desktop-publishing capabilities provided by the Macintosh and the LaserWriter.

Two-thirds of the one million Macintoshes that have been sold are in the business marketplace, and 27% of these units are in companies having fewer than 100 employees, 37% are in companies having 100-999 employees, and the remaining 36% are in companies with more than 1,000 employees.[10]

International markets are becoming more important as the computer revolution is just beginning in many countries. Apple's goal is to become multilocal by providing products tailored to each market, wherever it may be. In the United Kingdom, for example, Apple Centres, or satellite stores dedicated exclusively to selling Apple desktop solutions, provide business dealers with showcase locations in high-traffic areas. In Japan, Kanjitalk systems of software give Macintosh the three traditional Japanese alphabets, in addition to English, so Japanese users are provided immediate access to a powerful library of Macintosh software.

In the consumer segment, Apple has historically experienced increased sales during the Christmas season, especially with the Apple IIc.

At this time, no one customer of Apple accounts for 10% of net sales.

Apple currently has no significant U.S. government contracts, but plans to expand its sales efforts to the government. It has a separate thirty-person sales group that hopes to snare some of the estimated $1.6 billion federal microcomputer market.

COMPETITION

The market for the design, manufacture, sale, and servicing of personal computers and their related software and peripheral products is highly competitive. It has been characterized by rapid technological advances in both hardware and software development—advances that have substantially increased the capabilities and applications of personal computers. The principal competitive factors in this market are the product's quality and reliability, the relation of its price to its performance, the manufacturer's marketing and distribution capabilities, the quality of service and support, the availability of hardware and software accessories, and corporate reputation.

Many companies, such as IBM Corporation, Compaq Computer Corporation, AT&T Company, Tandy Corporation, Hewlett-Packard Company, Commodore Corporation, Atari Corporation, and various Japanese and Asian manufacturers, some of which have considerably greater financial resources than those of Apple, are very active in the personal computer market. In particular, IBM Corporation must be considered to be dominant in that market. In office automation and information processing, Apple competes directly with the companies mentioned and with other large domestic and foreign manufacturers, such as Digital Equipment Corporation and Wang Corporation.

IBM

Approximately 10 million IBM PCs and compatibles are in the business world, but for the first time since the PC was hatched in an obscure lab in Florida six years ago, the company is focusing its full technological and marketing expertise on its PCs. This focus could pose a critical threat to Apple. Before the introduction of the IBM PS/2, IBM's various PCs outsold the Macintosh by a 5 to 1 ratio in all businesses. In the largest corporations, IBM and IBM-compatible machines accounted for more than 75% of the PCs in use. If corporations perceive the new IBM PCs to be similar to the Macintosh, then the distinctive quality of the Macintosh will be reduced.

With its new PCs, IBM is aggressively attempting to regain its momentum in the PC industry. Evidence of a strong marketing approach is seen in the name "Personal Systems," which underscores the PCs' role as partners with IBM mainframes and midrange computers in corporate networks. Some competitors complain that in its marketing of the PS/2, IBM has implied that only they will perform such tasks as sharing complex software with IBM mainframes across companywide networks. IBM's commitment is also seen in research and development. About half of the technology being put into the new machines is being developed by IBM (vs. one-fifth in 1981). On the 32-bit machine, 80% is IBM technology.

IBM's market share went below 30% in 1986 because of the PC clonemakers, such as Compaq, Tandy, and Korea's Daewoo. For the PS/2, IBM did not switch to totally proprietary hardware and software, which would have made it harder for its competition to clone the products, because it also would have made it harder for customers to tailor the new PCs to their businesses and so would have limited PC sales. In an effort to stave off clonemakers, IBM did design a new way of sending graphic images to a screen and embedded that software in custom microchips. The machine's design also doubles the amount of software needed to make a clone 100% compatible with a new IBM PC. Thus, in the time it takes cloners to duplicate the PS/2, IBM will have put $50 million in ads behind its new machines and will keep the clones from reaching IBM's best corporate customers. Another competitive edge for the new PS/2 will be the efficiency of its manufacture. IBM PS/2 machines are based on circuit boards designed to be assembled at IBM's Austin, Texas, factory, a model of advanced automation, and are very cheap to make. Final assembly takes less than a minute.

The company introduced four new machines: two replacements for its PC/AT and one for its basic PC, plus a 32-bit machine that is as powerful as a small minicomputer. At the low end of IBM's new line is the Model 30, which in 1987 sold for $1,695. Like Apple's Macintosh, the Model 30 creates elaborate graphics, synthesizes music, and stores data on disks only 3 1/2 inches across. The new system, in fact, looks like a ringing endorsement of Apple's designs. But the price is no lower than that of a Macintosh and far above that of the Macintosh-like Apple IIGS. Experts feel that if IBM had priced the Model 30 at $1,000 or less that it would undoubtedly be successful. Higher up in the line are three machines, Models 50, 60, and 80, which cost from $3,600 to $11,000. All eventually will use new software and hardware accessories for easy communication with IBM mainframes. The best-received PS/2 appears to be the Model 50, which is a desktop system that is twice as fast as IBM's older, top-end PC/AT and, at $3,845, is regarded as competitively priced with the most powerful AT-compatibles.[11]

Some disadvantages of the new IBM Personal System/2 are that (1) it uses a different kind of floppy disk so it is difficult to transfer programs and files from previous IBMs to the new machines; (2) it can't use the add-in circuit cards designed for existing PCs (a new feature, called the Micro Channel, is used for connecting circuit cards and accepts only add-ons designed specifically for it, so existing PC circuit cards are obsolete); and (3) powerful software that will let the new PC use its power won't exist for a year after introduction.

The software for both the PC/AT and the new PS/2 is not sophisticated enough to take full advantage of the power of their chips—or to deliver the productivity that is promised with the new operating systems. Once these promised capabilities are realized, the machines will be able to perform several tasks at once and handle the voluminous software instructions and graphics needed to make PCs nearly as easy to use as typewriters.

Microsoft's new operating system for the three-year-old IBM PC/AT should be ready by 1988. Also ready in 1988 should be another operating system for a new generation of extremely powerful, 32-bit personal computers. Based on Intel Corp.'s new 386 microchip, these are now being introduced by IBM and others.

Windows, a Microsoft software program to be built into new operating systems, will be sold with every new IBM PC, except the most basic model. Windows uses graphics similar to those of Apple's Macintosh and will simplify the commands needed to operate the new PCs and therefore make them much easier to use.

Another software company, Lotus, will produce a spreadsheet, called 1-2-3/M, for IBM minicomputers and mainframes. Over the next decade, Lotus and IBM will jointly develop and market products for a full range of computers.

Dealers have complained that not only do they have to upgrade sales and support staffs (in the computer stores), but they are also required to invest the time and money needed for their staff members to gain expertise in at least one specialized computer application, such as accounting. Dealers can't offset such costs by selling the high-profit hardware upgrades that went with older IBM PCs. Many additional functions are built into the new models, and there is very little opportunity to add disk drives or monitors, which formerly were a major source of revenue.[12]

In May 1987, 15% of PC sales in U.S. computer stores were PS/2 models, but two-thirds of those were the PS/2 Model 30, which does not include the advanced PS/2 features.

International Data Corp. surveys show that 52% of corporate computer buyers may delay making major purchasing decisions immediately following the PS/2 introduction.[13]

AT&T

Another competitor in the PC business is AT&T, which has not been extremely successful of late. It has even been rumored that the $36 billion telephone giant might make its computer business a separate company to be jointly owned by its Italian computer partner, Olivetti. AT&T owns 23.5% of Olivetti, which supplies AT&T with its PCs and relies on the phone giant for its U.S. distribution. Although AT&T supposedly lost $800 million on its computer business in 1986, its strategy is to become a full-blown information-networking company. They dominate phone networking, but are the underdog in computers. The company's marketing presence has faded after an early success with Olivetti-built PCs. They didn't keep up with industry-wide price cuts in 1986, but have more recently cut prices to stay competitive. Dataquest estimates that AT&T PC shipments fell 25% to 172,000 units in 1987. The company will probably buy more products from outside vendors and spend development money on building computers with distinct advantages. One of AT&T's marketing tactics is called Selected International Accounts. In this approach, one team is sent to major multinational corporations and sells the entire product line for the office. New products to be launched in September 1987 include a new PC based on Intel Corp.'s 80386 microprocessor, which is claimed not to mimic the new IBM PS/2. Development money is being spent on operating systems and environment for the machine.[14]

Compaq

Compaq, founded in the early 1980s, is second only to IBM in the number of office PCs units it has sold. In 1986, its inexpensive clones sliced IBM's share of the worldwide PC market from 52% to 32%, while Compaq's share doubled from 7.5% to 15%. Compaq has a market valuation of $1.6 billion, and it got there by building IBM-compatible computers that cost about the same as IBM PCs but outperformed them or offered something extra. In 1986, Compaq's earnings were $43 million with sales of $625 million. In 1987 its first quarter earnings rose 142% to $20.2 million, while sales rose $210.94 million. Large companies accounted for 45% of Compaq's sales in 1986. Estimates for 1987 earnings are $98 million, or $2.50 per share on sales of $931 million, and estimates for 1988 earnings run from $3.00 to $3.50 per share. Analysts expect revenues for 1988 to reach $1.2 billion.

The company claims to have no plans to clone IBM's new product line, the PS/2, unless it becomes a widely accepted standard. Compaq sees an opportunity to succeed with potential purchasers who aren't delaying their purchasing decisions because of IBM's PS/2. Because customers have already sunk an estimated $80 billion into IBM PCs, PC clones, and the hardware options and software that work with them, and because there are some disadvantages to the PS/2 itself, the company is betting that even IBM will not be able to quickly get previous owners to trade up to the PS/2 line. Industry watchers, on the other hand, think that Compaq probably is cloning PS/2 as quickly as possible.

Compaq is, however, starting to assume more of a leadership role. For instance, in the end of summer 1986, it brought out the first IBM-compatible PC to use Intel's 386, a microchip with more than twice the power of the chips then used in IBM's most powerful model. In its PS/2 line, IBM did not introduce a product to compete directly with Compaq's model, the $6,500 Deskpro 386, and analysts say it will take some time for the company to fill that gap. About 20,000 Deskpro 386s were sold in the last quarter of 1986 and 25,000 in the first quarter of 1987. These sales added about $225-million to revenues. In fact, the company's desktop models are so popular that it hasn't been possible to fill all of the orders. Demand for Compaq's newest portable, the Portable III, is so strong, the company says, that it will be unable to fill all the orders until the fall of 1987.

With the international markets becoming so important in terms of potential sales, Compaq has made a goal to increase its sales outside the U.S. from 19% to 45% of revenues.[15]

Digital Equipment Corporation (DEC)

DEC is a full-line competitor with IBM. With its superior networking products, the company has been able to penetrate some of IBM's largest commercial accounts. DEC's net income increased approximately 80% to $1.1 billion in the year ending June 30, 1987. As a large company, DEC could pose an increasingly large threat to Apple in the years to come.

In 1986 DEC introduced an engineering workstation that directly competes with the Macintosh II and the IBM PS/2 Model 80, which both double as engineering workstations. DEC has reduced the price of its basic workstation by 50% to $4,600.

Other Competitors

Industry watchers feel that it should only take around six months for IBM PS/2 clones to start appearing. IBM's market share fell in 1986 because of the success of clonemakers such as Compaq, Tandy, and Korea's Daewoo. IBM is not the only company hurt by clonemakers. One can be sure that if IBM's success is impeded, then other less powerful companies in the industry are vulnerable, too. The biggest problem for rival computer makers may lie in the future. If IBM begins to upgrade its products more rapidly to take timely advantage of technological improvements, its rivals will be placed on a treadmill of shortened production cycles and increased capital investment.

Potential competition comes from the international arena, too. An example is Korea-based Daewoo Telecom Co. Daewoo kicked off the latest round in the low-priced computer battle in 1986; its Leading Edge model already has snared a 5% share of the home computer market. Another example is Multitech Industrial Corporation, a Taiwan-based firm that has been making computers for years and could become a legitimate rival to Japanese, Korean, and U.S. multinational corporations. The company's most recent offering is an IBM PC/AT compatible computer using Intel Corp's new 32-bit 80386 microchip. The machine hit the U.S. and European markets months before IBM brought out its first 80386-based machine. To successfully expand overseas, Multitech has adopted the name of Acer Technologies for its products and is launching a $5 million ad campaign to sell the name to consumers and computer distributors.[16]

Other companies that offer competition, especially in the less-than-$1,000 market, include Blue Chip, United Kingdom-based Amstrad (PC 1512), Commodore International (PC 10-1 and PC 10-2), Atari (PC), and Franklin Computer (PC 8000).[17]

PRODUCTION

The raw materials essential to Apple's business are generally available from multiple sources. Certain components, such as power supplies, integrated circuits, and plastic housings, are obtained from single sources, although Apple believes that other sources for such parts are available. New products often utilize custom components that are available only from a single source upon initial introduction of the product. Although Apple generally qualifies other sources after the product is introduced, the inability to obtain components fast enough to satisfy demand for the new product can cause significant delays in product delivery. The Apple IIGS encountered such delays during the fourth quarter of 1986.

Apple's foreign operations consist of three manufacturing facilities in Ireland and Singapore. In the United States, the company has four manufacturing facilities.

In general, Apple sells its products directly to customers, who typically purchase products on an as-needed basis and frequently change delivery schedules and order rates. For this reason, Apple's backlog of orders at any particular date might not represent its actual sales for any succeeding period.

MARKETING

William V. Campbell, Apple's Executive Vice-President for U.S. Sales and Marketing, says, "We've been dragged to our mission kicking and screaming. We've put together a business advisory panel. No longer do we put out technology for technology's sake." Marketing and distribution expenses were $477 million or 25% of sales in 1986. In 1986 more was spent in sales and marketing programs than in advertising and merchandising (excluding increases related to the Apple IIGS rollout and a new television campaign).

One goal is to increase international sales from 36% of total sales. There has been strong growth in newer markets, including Spain, Sweden, Holland, and Belgium. Sales in Japan are also rising to reflect the initial success with Kanjitalk. The largest international markets are France, Canada, and Australia.

PRODUCTS

Apple has two computer families, the Apple II and Macintosh families. The Apple II, the company's original line, has a large customer base in the education and home markets. There are three Apple II models, the IIC, IIE, and the IIGS. The Macintosh line has four models, the Macintosh 512K, Macintosh Plus, Macintosh SE, and Macintosh II. Macintosh is targeted towards the business markets.[19]

The Apple Line

Apple IIc

Introduced late in the 1986 fiscal year. the updated IIc can provide up to one megabyte of memory, which enables users to work with sophisticated software programs.

Apple IIGS and Apple IIe

The IIGS was introduced in September 1986 and is a high-end model, featuring a 16-bit microprocessor, high-resolution color graphics, advanced sound capabilities, and up to one megabyte of internal memory. Although the IIGS is praised for its speed and graphics, production problems slowed sales during the Christmas quarter of 1986, when the company usually earns more than one third of its annual profit. Some experts complain that what is being done on the GS can be accomplished just as well on a II Plus, IIe, or IIc. They say that about the only thing that can't be done with the old Apple II that can be done with the new GS is high-resolution color graphics. Color graphics are a bonus, but for routine, everyday tasks, they aren't really necessary. Apple IIe users can buy an upgrade kit that will give their computers all Apple IIGS capabilities.

The Macintosh Line

The Macintosh is an extremely user-friendly computer that makes use of graphic icons (pictorial representatives of function) and a mouse device, which allows a user to enter commands without touching the keyboard. Apple relies on the Macintosh for more than half of its revenues and earnings. In 1985, Apple sold 100,000 Macintoshes to businesses with annual revenues of more than $100 million. Sales of 175,000 surpassed Apple II sales for the first time in 1986. The prediction for 1987 is 325,000. As of 1986, the Macintosh had about 7% of total sales to the business market. Shipments of the Macintosh doubled in 1986, while worldwide PC shipments rose only 9%. Approximately one million Macintoshes have been sold; nearly two thirds of those sales were in the business marketplace. Companies with fewer than 100 employees comprise 27% of sales, 37% are in companies with 100-999 employees, and 37% in companies with more than 1,000 employees.

Desktop publishing, which Macintosh pioneered, is a method for printing typeset-quality documents. Approximately 50,000 Macintosh publishing systems were sold in 1986 and sales of accompanying printers grossed around $150 million.

Microsoft's Excel, a spreadsheet program, enables the Macintosh to go head-to-head with an IBM PC running Lotus's 1-2-3. In large companies, desktop-publishing enthusiasts have helped Apple sell the Macintosh for other uses. Since people began trying other Macintosh software, including the Excel spreadsheet, a lot of Lotus users have transferred their files. Some claim that the Macintosh increases productivity faster than do other computers because it is easier to use. Apple makes software developers conform to a single set of commands, so that once an operator has mastered those commands, it is relatively easy to learn another Macintosh software package.

Apple still owns the rights to Macintosh's built-in programs, so it can't be cloned the way the IBM PC can.

Macintosh Plus

Introduced in January 1986, the Mac Plus has a high-speed socket that limits the means by which hardware options can be connected. Thus Apple is courting companies whose add-on options can help sell the Macintosh-companies such as Radius Inc., whose 15-inch screen for the Macintosh Plus has scored big. Along with the LaserWriter Plus printer, this model opened the door for Apple in business. In fact, the two are seen as the standard for the rapidly growing desktop publishing market.

Macintosh 512K Enhanced

The 512K Enhanced was introduced in the early spring of 1986 and is a more affordable version of the Macintosh Plus. Now that the Macintosh Plus is selling to corporations and Apple has introduced a new model of the Macintosh, prices on the 512K Enhanced are falling to around $4,100. That makes it less expensive than the new IIGS and about the same price as the Atari 1040ST.

Macintosh SE

To get into the corporate MIS department, Apple has created Macintosh II and the Macintosh SE, which embrace MS/DOS, Unix, Ethernet, token ring, and all else dear to the heart of the corporate PC user. The new "open" Macintosh is designed to be flexible enough that its owners can customize it, and thus this Macintosh will eliminate one of business customers' largest objections to the old "closed" Macintosh. For instance, the machine has several card slots, so owners can customize a machine simply by plugging in circuit cards to give it new functions, such as high-resolution graphics.

The Macintosh SE, with prices ranging from $2,898 to $4,500, is intended to become the Macintosh line's staple for office use. It is an enhanced version of the flagship Macintosh Plus and uses the same, relatively slower Motorola 68000 microprocessor, but has room for the add-on features, such as extra speed or memory, demanded by customers.

SE stands for System Expansion. The Macintosh SE is equipped with an internal slot for add-in cards and with two internal disks, one of which can be a 20-megabyte SCSI (Small Computer Systems Interface) hard drive. With Dayna's DaynaFile, a disk drive that connects directly to the Macintosh via an SCSI port and acts as an external 5-1/4-inch drive, it is possible to access such IBM compatible files as Lotus 1-2-3, dBase III, or Wordperfect as though they had been created on a Macintosh disk.

MacIntosh II

The Macintosh II costs up to $12,000 and has a 13-inch color screen, four megabytes of internal memory, and an 80-megabyte hard disk. It combines advanced color graphics with computational muscle rivaling machines with three times the price. With this machine, Apple beat IBM to the 32-bit generation, because it features Motorola Corp.'s 68020 chip and thereby presents a direct challenge to the high-powered 385 PCs. Larry Magid, Senior Analyst at the Sybold, San Jose, California, says, "There no longer is an excuse for not buying a Mac. Now it's a matter of which machine is more suited to your application, to your environment. The Mac II is a credible second standard computer in the corporate area."

Other Products

The *AppleTalk* local-area network can link as many as thirty-two computers and peripheral devices. The company claims that *AppleTalk*, one of Apple's most successful new products in 1986, is the first and only network solution that is as easy to learn and use as Macintosh itself. There is an *AppleTalk* network connection built into every new Macintosh and Apple IIGS. This network "configures" itself so that linking computers, printers, and other peripherals becomes extremely simple and economical. As of 1986 there are over 200,000 *AppleTalk* networks in place. However, some people see LANs as the next bottleneck for Apple in the corporate world. *AppleTalk* is fine for small groups (eight or fewer machines) but might not be adequate if hundreds of machines need to be connected.

The *LaserWriter* and *LaserWriter Plus*, introduced January 1986, are high-resolution laser printers.

New peripherals include Hard Disk 20SC, Apple II-compatible UniDisk 3.5-inch 80K disk drive, ImageWriter II printer, and Apple Personal Modem.

The company announced in 1986 that it is creating a new software subsidiary to develop critical programs for its Apple II and Macintosh computers. This new subsidiary should also open up new areas of exploration for smaller vendors. William V. Campbell, who will be President of the new company, denies an anti-Microsoft strategy, but a highly placed Apple insider says one goal was to make Apple less dependent on Microsoft, which sells 50% of the software bought each year for Apple's Macintosh. Like IBM, Apple sees Microsoft aiding the enemy, because Microsoft's Windows program can turn another PC into a Macintosh look-alike. In 1986, the worldwide software sales were $27 billion.

One future worry about Apple's product line is that the Macintosh won't be unique for long. Graphics options for the IBM PC are moving fast, and dozens of companies are finding ways in which PCs can be adapted for desktop publishing. It is predicted that sometime in 1987, sales of desk top publishing systems based on IBM and IBM-compatible computers will start to exceed sales on the Macintosh. Even though the market is growing so quickly that Apple's own desktop publishing will increase by 70% in 1987, the Macintosh may lose some of its edge.

RESEARCH AND DEVELOPMENT

Apple's design principle is, "No matter how powerful or sophisticated the system, keep it simple to set up and operate." R&D expenses in 1986 increased to $128 million or 6.7% of sales, from $73 million or 3.8% of sales in 1985. The company plans to increase research budget by 30%, to $166 million, or about 7% of projected sales in fiscal 1987. These funds went to significant additions to the engineering staff, to increases in prototype materials and tooling, and to the purchase of other equipment and proprietary design software that can shorten product development cycles. In March 1986, the company installed a $15.5 million Cray X-MP/48 supercomputer from Cray Research Inc. One of the largest and most powerful scientific supercomputers in the world, the Cray can simulate new computer architectures and operating systems in three months to one year less than was ever before possible.

Current programs include a collaborative effort with the National Geographic Society and LucasFilm Ltd. to explore the effective use of optical technologies (video and compact disks) for the Apple II line in education. These devices can store vast amounts of information, including still and moving images and stereo sound, and still allow easy interaction.

Apple University Consortium brings universities and countries together to share and explore the integration of technology and education. The United States has 32 consortium members.

Apple's Office of Special Education represents the company's commitment to work with educational institutions and human services organizations, to identify and assist the computer-related needs of disabled persons.

PROMOTION

For the fiscal year 1986, advertising expenditures were $157,833. This figure is down from $187,457 in 1985 and $179,739 in 1984. This total includes both salaries and other costs of in-house advertising, graphic design, and public relations departments, as well as the costs of advertising in various media and employing outside advertising agencies.

Recent ads call the Macintosh "the computer for the rest of us." Another slogan, "The Power to be Your Best," focuses on people and how Apple products help them realize their full potential. Consumers who are a bit more educated about computers now want to know precisely how a computer will solve real problems in their work and their lives. In response to these consumers, image ads are are no longer being used.

DISTRIBUTION

Apple has distribution facilities in the U.S., Europe, Canada, and Australia. In 1986 the U.S. dealer organization was trimmed by 25% and sales per dealer location increased by 15%. A field sales force gave the best service to those dealers with the best performance.[20]

Apple's strategy is to carefully select its dealers and restrict distribution of the more complex products to the most sophisticated outlets, which will attract business customers. For example, Businessland Inc. sells both IBM and Apple products to large corporations. The dealer's most important characteristic is that it markets Apple machines effectively.

However, Apple is up against the direct-sales forces of IBM and DEC, and many experts think that it's not possible to sell in the business market without a direct-sales force. Through a national accounts program, Apple has been trying to convince the heads of information services and data processing departments of how Apple products differ and why those differences are important to business. Between 1985 and 1987, more than twenty companies have put Apple on their approved vendor list.

Exhibit 8   Consolidated Statements of Income
Nine-Year Summary, Apple Computer
(Dollars and Shares in Thousands, Except Per Share Amounts)

	1986	1985	1984	1983	1982	1981	1980	1979	1978
Net Sales	$1,901,898	$1,918,280	$1,515,876	$982,769	$583,061	$334,763	$117,126	$47,867	$ 7,883
Costs and expenses:									
Cost of sales	891,112	1,117,864	878,586	505,765	288,001	170,124	66,490	27,450	3,960
Research and development	127,758	72,526	71,136	60,040	37,979	20,956	7,282	3,601	597
Marketing and distribution	476,685	478,079	398,463	229,961	119,945	55,369	12,619	8,802	1,170
General and administrative	132,812	110,077	81,840	57,364	34,927	22,191	7,150	2,080	609
Total costs and expenses	1,628,367	1,778,546	1,430,025	853,130	480,852	268,640	93,541	41,933	6,336
Operating income	273,531	102,768	85,851	129,639	102,209	66,143	23,585	5,933	1,547
Interest and other income, net	36,187	17,277	23,334	16,483	14,563	10,400	567	0	0
Income before taxes on income	309,718	120,045	109,185	146,122	116,772	76,543	24,152	5,933	1,547
Provision for income taxes	155,755	58,822	45,130	69,408	55,466	37,123	12,454	860	754
Net income	$ 153,963	$ 61,223	$ 64,055	$ 76,714	$ 61,306	$ 39,420	$ 11,698	$ 5,073	$ 793
Earnings per common and common equivalent share	$ 2.39	$ .99	$ 1.05	1.28	1.06	.70	.24	.12	.03
Common and common equivalent shares used in the calculations of earnings per share	64,315	61,895	60,887	59,867	57,798	56,181	48,412	43,620	31,544

SOURCE: Apple Computer, Inc., *Annual Report*, 1986, p. 38; *Annual Report*, 1984, p. 38; *Annual Report*, 1983, p. 16; and *Annual Report*, 1981, p. 16.

NOTE: The financial data was expanded to include the years 1981–1978.

Mass merchants, such as Target Stores, The Wiz, Toys 'R' Us, Wal-Mart, K-Mart, and Jamesway Corp., have been selling home computers since the late 70s and early 80s ushered in Commodore's 64 and Atari's 600 XL and 130 XE. This competition may cause some concern to Apple's retailers. It is most likely, though, that the middle market outlets such as Radio Shack will suffer more than will the specialty retailers at the hands of the discounters selling clones, since the specialty retailers are geared toward businesses.[21]

Approximately 4.500 dealers sell computers. During 1985, about 7% dropped out of the business because their profit margins were down. Apple and IBM (51% of computer store sales) requalify their dealers to be sure that only the best carry products such as the Macintosh II and the most powerful models of the new IBM PS/2 line. Of Apple's 2000 dealers, 300 have been chosen to carry the top-of-the-line Macintosh II. Apple is expected to allow 800 more to carry the Macintosh II. Apple feels that the fewer the stores carrying the product, the higher the profit margins. Dealers who aren't allowed to carry the best products will have to compete in the high-volume discount business—almost a guarantee of thin margins for these retailers.

FINANCIAL POSITION

Apple relies on funds from operations ($273 million in 1986; $102 million in 1985) to meet its liquidity needs. It also uses proceeds from the sale of common stock ($46 million in 1986 vs. $22 million in 1985) under the company's stock-option and employee stock-purchase plans, and related tax benefits ($9 million in 1986 vs. $23 million in 1985). In 1986, Apple had $576,215,000 in cash and no debt. See Exhibits 8 and 9 for detailed information.

Apple stock was the most active OTC issue of 1986; it rose 18 1/2 points on $7.71 billion of volume and finished the year at 40 1/2. Prior to 1987 its record price was 63 1/4—that level was reached in 1983 after its all-time low of 10 3/4 only a year earlier. Apple's stock traded over the counter on the NASDAQ. Officers and directors control about 11% of the outstanding common, while institutions hold approximately 60%. The largest investor (as of December, 1986) is Citicorp with 4.7 million shares, followed by Atalanta/Sosnoff Capital, which has 2.2 million. There are about 35,000 shareholders of record. As of 1986 there were about 65 million shares outstanding. Apple stock has risen to close to $80 in 1987.

On April 23, 1987, Apple announced its first-ever quarterly dividend of $.12 per share. The company also announced a 2-for-1 stock split. This makes Apple one of the first Silicon-Valley-based computer and electronics concerns to pay a dividend. Mr. Sculley called the dividend "an expression of our confidence" in Apple's long-term future. Apple plans to continue paying this dividend quarterly.

Exhibit 9   Apple Computer, Inc.: Consolidated Balance Sheets
(Dollar Amounts in Thousands)

	SEPT. 26, 1986	SEPT. 25, 1985	SEPT. 28, 1984
Assets			
Current assets:			
Cash and temporary cash investments	$ 576,215	$337,013	$114,888
Accounts receivable	263,126	220,157	258,238
Inventories	108,680	166,951	264,619
Prepaid income taxes	53,029	70,375	26,751
Other current assets	39,884	27,569	23,055
Total current assets	1,040,934	822,065	687,551
Net Property, plant and equipment	107,315	90,446	75,868
Other assets	11,879	23,666	25,367
Total assets	1,160,128	936,177	788,786
Liabilities and Shareholders' Equity			
Current liabilities	328,535	295,425	255,184
Deferred income taxes	137,506	90,265	69,037
Shareholders' equity	694,087	550,177	464,565
Total liabilities and shareholders' equity	1,160,128	935,867	788,786

SOURCE: Apple Computer, Inc., *Annual Report*, 1986.

NOTES

1. J. Sculley, *Odyssey*, (New York: Harper and Row, 1987, p. 388.

2. *Ibid.*, pp. 387-388.

3. "Jobs Calls Apple's Suit 'Absurd Shock,'" *Tampa Tribune*, September 26, 1985, p. 2F.

4. P. Watt, "Out-of-Court Settlement Allows Apple to Preview Next Products," *Computerworld*, January 27, 1986, pp. 100-123.

5. G. Lewis, "The First Sign of Spring for IBM and Its Rivals," *Business Week,* April 27, 1987, pp. 35-36.

6. J. Steinberg, "Computer Marketing: Technology Drives Industry Down a New Path," *Advertising Age*, April 6, 1987, pp. S-3-S-10.

7. "Who's Afraid of IBM?" *Business Week*, June 29, 1987, pp. 68-74.

8. J. Steinberg, p. S-5.

9. K.M. Hafner, "Apple's Comeback," *Business Week*, January 19, 1987, pp. 84-89.

10. E.D. Meyer, "Waiting Impatiently at the Gates of MIS Kingdom," *Datamation*, April 15, 1987, pp. 37-38.

11. P. Nulty, "IBM, Clonebuster," *Fortune*, April 27, 1987, p. 225; and R. Brandt, "The Billion-Dollar Whiz Kid," *Business Week*, April 13, 1987, pp. 68-76.

12. Brandt, "The Billion-Dollar Whiz Kid," pp. 68-76; and "Computer Retailers: Things Have Gone from Worse to Bad," *Business Week*, June 8, 1987, pp. 104-109.

13. "Who's Afraid of IBM," p. 69.

14. "AT&T May Be Ready to Cut Its Losses in Computer," *Business Week*, June 6, 1987, p. 30.

15. "Who's Afraid of IBM," pp. 68-74.

16. C. Wilder, "IBM, Industry Clouds Break Away," *Computerworld*, April 20, 1981, p. 125.

17. F. Brookman, "Clones Tap into Mass Retail with Mixed Results," *Advertising Age*, June 6, 1987, p. 5.

18. Apple Computer, Inc. *1986 Annual Report*, p. 8.

19. Hafner, "Apple's Comeback," pp. 84-89; *1986 Annual Report*, pp. 1-12; C.H. Gajeway, "Machine Specifics: Apple," *Family Computing*, April 1987, p. 28; J. Schwartz, "Apple's Big Mac Attack," *Newsweek*, March 19, 1987, p. 48; and Meyer, "Waiting Impatiently at the Gates of MIS Kingdom," pp. 37-38.

20. Apple Computer, Inc. *1986 Annual Report*, p. 10.

21. Brookman, "Clones Tap into Mass Retail with Mixed Results," p. 5.

Case 4

DEERE AND COMPANY: INTO THE 1990S

> Worldwide net sales to our dealers increased 30 percent to
> $5.4 billion in 1988, the highest level since 1981. Net income
> totaled $315.4 million, a record level of earnings for the
> company. ...We view the future, then, with a sense of
> optimism... (Shareholder letter, Annual Report, Deere and
> Company, 1988)

> **Retail Sales Start the Year With A Thud**. (Headline in
> *Implement & Tractor*, March, 1989, p.5)

> **Deere & Co. Posts Profit Rise of 51% for Its 2nd Period**
> (Headline in the *Wall Street Journal*, July 1989)

Through most of the 1980s Deere and Company did not experience the success
it had in 1988 and 1989. From 1982-1987 the firm was battling the impact of
the worst recession in the farm belt since the 1930s, suffering six straight years
of depressed earnings. Although Deere took a number of steps to diversify, cut
costs, and reduce its inventories and break even point, its continued heavy
reliance on sales to the farm sector produced heavy losses in 1986 and 1987 of
$229 million and $99 million, respectively.

The long recession of the 1980s resulted in the financial restructuring of farm
assets and the winnowing of the weaker farmers. Those that remained seemed
ready to buy new equipment in a search for increased productivity. However,
early in 1988 it looked like disaster would strike again as the entire Farm Belt
suffered from the most serious drought since the dust bowl days. In spite of the
drought, however, Deere produced record earnings as high farm prices, record
government subsidies, and drought payments protected farm income. Further,
the drought reduced carryover stocks of feed grains to their lowest levels of the
decade, portending higher prices in 1989. The only cloud on this otherwise

sunny horizon is the fact that the drought continued through the winter of 1988-89. This left soil moisture levels critically low and dramatically reduced the winter wheat crop. Spring and early summer rains continued at only half of normal levels through July. In spite of this threat to the otherwise fragile farm recovery, Deere enjoyed record profits in the first half of 1989. Did this mean that the firm's efforts at restructuring had finally begun to pay dividends or would the next recession in the 1990s again plunge them into a series of massive losses?

DEERE AND COMPANY STRATEGY IN THE 1980S

In the 1970s the management of Deere and Company reacted to growing strength in the farm belt in two ways. First, it made a number of large capital improvements. Manufacturing facilities were reorganized and several new factories were constructed. The firm built an automated engine plant and an automated tractor assembly plant which was widely hailed as one of the most modern manufacturing plants in the world. It also doubled the size of its large research facility. In addition to providing what management felt was a necessary expansion of capacity, these capital projects greatly increased Deere's efficiency. As a result the sales per employee rose from $56,700 in 1976 to $140,200 in 1988. Through this efficiency Deere sought not only to increase in size, but also to establish itself as the industry's low cost producer. Moreover, as the 1970s came to a close, Deere's major competitors were struggling, producing much of their output in old, inefficient plants. Case, International Harvester, Massey-Ferguson, and Allis-Chalmers were all in trouble and Deere saw its opportunity to emerge as the clear industry volume leader as well. What it apparently did not see was the danger that the failure of these other competitors would pose to the whole industry in a severe recession.

The second part of Deere's strategy involved diversification. Two new business lines were given increasing attention in the 1970s, industrial equipment and later, home and garden tractors and equipment. Both of these product lines were logical extensions of Deere's expertise in manufacturing and its reputation for quality. Industrial equipment shared many design and marketing characteristics with agricultural equipment. Both are based heavily on engine, power train, and hydraulic technology. Quality and reliability, as well as a strong dealer network and the availability of financing, are also important for both types of products. All of these characteristics represent traditional strengths for Deere.

Deere and Company also extended its existing product lines into home and commercial lawn care products, although these lines naturally share less of the firm's expertise than do its other extensions. This lawn and garden product group marked Deere's entrance into consumer markets. Dealer requirements in this market are much different than for agricultural and industrial equipment. More dealers are required and they must be located in suburban rather than rural locations. Although these dealers must also service their customers, repairs and parts represent a smaller part of sales and profits for these dealers than for tractor dealers. Further, consumers are generally less knowledgeable about the product and less willing to engage in necessary maintenance.

As the farm crisis of the 1980s unfolded both the lawn tractor and industrial equipment product lines were developed with even more urgency to offset steady declines in the agricultural equipment business. This activity was complemented by diversification in Deere's financial subsidiary, including the addition of insurance products and an expansion of the scope of lending activities to include production loans to farmers. In addition, in 1984 and 1985, Deere was operating at such a low level of capacity utilization (less than 25%) that it embarked on a number of new manufacturing ventures designed to take advantage of its highly integrated structure by selling up to $100 million of parts annually to original equipment manufacturers (OEMs). The firm began producing engine blocks and diesel engines for various divisions of General Motors and motor home chassis for Winnebago. Further diversification involved the purchase of the world rights to aviation applications for the rotary engine and a major agreement to provide tractor technology to the Peoples Republic of China. Finally, in its biggest move, Deere signed an agreement to develop a jointly-owned diesel engine firm with GM's Detroit-Allison Division. Deere was to provide its engine plant and engineering capability and Allison was to add its plants and products, ultimately producing a firm with expected sales of $1.5-$2 billion dollars a year.

AGRICULTURAL EQUIPMENT INDUSTRY ENVIRONMENT

Although the sales mix of Deere and Company has changed in the last decade, the majority of the firm's revenues are still provided by farm equipment sales. (See Table 7). The farm environment is complex and volatile. The 1970s were largely a period of increasing prosperity in the farm economy, based in large part on rising land prices and farm receipts. However, the prosperity did not last. Prolonged inflation in the economy led to higher interest rates and eventually, two recessions. Ultimately, the high interest rates increased the burden on farmers who had borrowed heavily to expand production in the previous decade, forcing many of them into bankruptcy.

An important trend influencing the farm belt of the 1980s was the expansion of farm production in the 1970s. This expansion resulted in a complex chain of events. Governmental policy had encouraged planting "from fence row to fence

Table 1

Selected Farm Price Data
Index #'s — 1977 = 100

	All Farm Receipts	All Farm Inputs	Equip. Expend.	Agricul. Land & Bldgs.	Value of Interest Paid	Consumer Prices
1980	134.0	138.0	131.0	145.0	174.0	136.0
1981	139.0	150.0	145.7	158.0	211.0	150.1
1982	133.0	157.0	157.2	157.0	241.0	159.3
1983	134.0	160.0	164.9	148.0	250.0	164.4
1984	142.0	165.0	169.8	146.0	251.0	171.4
1985	128.0	163.0	170.5	134.3	250.0	177.5
1986	123.0	159.0	171.8	112.0*	211.0	180.9
1987	127.0	161.0	171.5	105.0*	190.0	192.4
1988E	138.0	170.0	187.6	108.0*	186.0	195.2

Sources: Farm price data from U.S. Department of Agriculture
Consumer prices from U.S. Department of Labor

*Estimated from graphs produced by U.S. Department of Agriculture

row." Land values increased, causing the book values of farm properties toincrease, creating many paper millionaires. However, because the prices received by farmers for their products are determined by supply and demand, they are largely beyond the control of any individual producer. Thus, as Table 1 shows, higher domestic production, coupled with increasing overseas productivity, resulted in increased supplies of farm outputs and reduced growth in the demand for U.S. exports. In addition, the inflation and energy shortages of the 1970s caused the prices of inputs to the farm sector to rise faster than the prices received by farmers, exceeding them for the first time in 1980. This cost-price squeeze further encouraged farmers to increase production to raise revenues and profits through productivity. Tables 1 and 2 illustrate how all these trends collectively caused grain stocks to rise to all time highs by 1986, depressing prices for receipts far below the price levels of inputs. High interest rates, falling farm product prices, and falling values for farm property combined to reduce farm equity and resulted in high numbers of farm bankruptcies in the mid-1980s (see Table 2).

Collectively, all these trends encouraged a dramatic rise in governmental subsidies and a reduction in the sales of expensive farm equipment (see Table 3). This decline was even more dramatic when viewed in real terms (exclusive of price increases). As Table 3 illustrates, the real value of customer expenditures on agricultural equipment in 1988 was estimated at only 40% of its

Table 2

Selected Farm Financial Data
Index #'s — 1977 = 100

	Net Farm Inc.	Net Cash Inc. ($bil.)	Farm Assets	Farm Debt $bil.	Ave. Farm Size Acres	. . . . . . Grain & Feed Stocks . . . . . . (mils met. tons) Domes. Supply			
						Supply	Use	Exprt.	Endg.
1980	18.8	34.2	996.1	166.8	427	357.7	171.0	114.9	71.8
1981	28.6	32.8	996.7	182.3	425	400.6	178.6	110.8	111.2
1982	23.5	37.8	961.2	189.5	428	442.6	193.1	96.3	153.2
1983	12.2	36.9	945.3	192.7	432	360.1	183.0	97.7	79.4
1984	30.0	38.7	848.5	190.8	438	393.1	197.0	97.3	98.8
1985	28.9	46.6	749.0	175.2	446	444.3	200.8	62.8	180.9
1986	32.8	51.4	691.6	155.3	456	497.0	217.0	76.0	204.0
1987	39.5	57.1	708.9	142.7	461	483.0	215.0	98.0	169.0
1988E	33.0	58.0	743.0	139.0	465*	368.0	206.0	94.0	68.0
1989E	38.0	50.0	757.0	143.0	—	—	—	—	—

Source: U.S. Department of Agriculture

*Estimated from graphs prepared by the U.S. Department of Agriculture

Table 3

Agricultural Equipment Sales
($ in billions, Index #'s — 1977 = 100)

	Total Customer Expenditures			Indus. Shipments to Dealers		
Year	Total Expend.	Price Ind. Ag. Equip. Expend.	Real Expend. 1 ÷ 2	Value of Shipments	Price Ind. Industry Shipments	Real Indus. Sales
1980	$10.64	131.0	$8.12	$12.84	132,9	$9.66
1981	10.22	145.7	7.01	13.95	148.5	9.39
1982	7.67	157.2	4.88	10.74	160.5	6.69
1983	7.34	164.9	4.45	8.98	164.8	5.45
1984	7.22	169.8	4.25	9.86	169.5	5.82
1985	5.60	170.5	3.28	8.21	169.8	4.84
1986	4.61	171.8	2.68	6.74	171.0	3.94
1987	5.76	171.5	3.36	6.95	171.6	4.05
1988E	6.05	187.6	3.22	7.09	174.8	4.06

Source: Expenditures from U.S. Department of Agriculture
        Shipments from U.S. Department of Commerce

1980 level. This means that on a constant dollar basis the purchase of farm equipment units has declined 60% in the decade of the 1980s. Industry shipments to dealers show a similar trend, falling 58% during the same time period.

This reduction in real equipment sales had a dramatic effect on the industry's dealer network. Dealers failed in record numbers. As a result dealers have adopted numerous strategies to survive. Parts sales and service have become increasingly important. Price pressures have forced dealers to become more aggressive marketers, focussing more closely on selected customer groups. Dealers will probably seek inventory reductions by encouraging their customers to plan ahead and order equipment in advance of their needs. This action will lower dealer investments and carrying costs, as well as the markdowns which go along with high stock levels.[1] Finally, it is expected many dealers have begun to abandon their traditionally exclusive approach to producers by broadening the number of product lines they carry. To combat this trend Deere has announced that beginning May 1, 1990, it will amend its dealer agreement to allow it to demand that dealers separate their non-Deere business if, in the company's opinion, they conflict with the dealers' fulfillment of their obligations to the company. This proposal has been met with nearly universal objection.[2]

The behavior of the agricultural environment and the resulting trend in industry sales have caused significant changes in the industry. J.I. Case and International Harvester [Navistar] are now owned by Tenneco. Tenneco and Deere are the only remaining firms producing tractors in the U.S. Massey-Ferguson has been reorganized as Varity Corporation (Canada) and farm equipment accounts for less than half its sales. Ford, the leading producer of tractors in unit volume, purchased the New Holland equipment division of Sperry Corporation and moved all tractor production overseas. The farm equipment business of Allis-Chalmers is now owned by Germany producer Deutz. Although exact figures are not available, the market shares of these producers are estimated in Table 4.

At the present time most, if not all, of the tractors below 100 horsepower (hp.) are produced outside the U.S., largely by subsidiaries of U.S. firms and by the Japanese. These tractors are designed primarily for smaller farms and are considerably lower in price than the higher horsepower and large four wheel drive (4 WDr) models. Deere, especially, has concentrated on the larger models because they feel that for farmers to achieve satisfactory productivity it is inevitable that they will be forced to work on large farms and utilize powerful equipment.[3]

Table 4

Estimated Market Shares
Agricultural Equipment Industry

Company	Overall Share 1984	1988 Farm Tractor Sales ....Estimated Market Share............			
		< 40 hp.	40-99 hp.	>100 hp.	4WDr.
Deere and Co.	32.4%	17%	27%	45%	30%
Case-IH (Tenneco)	19.8	8	18	31	36
Ford-New Holland	15.0	18	22	7	27
Varity	11.1	12	11	4	1
Deutz-Allis	4.0	4	5	5	3
Kubota (Japan)	9.0	33	10	—	—
Others	8.7	8	7	8	3
Unit Sales 1987		{ 30,718 }		15,911	1,653
Unit Sales 1978		{ 66,836 }		65,257	8,744

Sources: Wertheim & Co. (1984 shares); *Implement & Tractor*, January, 1989,
pp. 6-7, 30 (1988 shares); Standard and Poor's (unit sales).

This trend toward rising farm size is illustrated in Table 2. In 1980, there were more than 2.4 million farms in the U.S. By 1987 that number had dropped to less than 2.2 million. In addition, the U.S. Department of Labor estimates that the number of farmers and farm workers will drop by nearly 30% by the year 2000.[4] Although these trends point to a rise in the capital intensity of farming, there are reasons why the trend may not continue indefinitely. As farm size increases and heavy equipment must be used, there are some negative consequences. Large tractors use a great deal of energy and there have been few improvements in efficiency recent years.[5] Heavy equipment also causes soil compaction which has negative environmental consequences. Heavy equipment may also destroy valuable top soil which cannot be replaced in any reasonable time frame.

In addition to environmental problems, heavy equipment is very expensive. The typical 4 WDr tractor costs over $100,000 and purchases have been subject to high interest rates. In 1987, only 14% of the farms in the U.S. even had annual sales exceeding $100,000.[6] Although these "high revenue" farms accounted for 76% of the total cash receipts and 89% of the net income received by all farms, they had less than half the farm assets. Also, a considerable number of the most prosperous farms in the U.S., for example, are less than 40 acres in size, too small to need heavy equipment.[7] Finally, a tractor is not enough to run a farm. Plows, cultivating and planting equipment, and some means of harvesting the crop are also needed. Harvesting equipment can also cost in excess of $100,000. The net effect of these factors is illustrated in Table 4 which shows that while unit sales of tractors under 100 hp. have declined 54% in the last decade, unit sales of over 100 hp. tractors and four wheel drive models have declined 76% and 81%, respectively, from 1978-1987. Self-propelled combine sales declined 77% during the same period.

CONSTRUCTION EQUIPMENT INDUSTRY ENVIRONMENT

Although the market for industrial and construction equipment is not affected by exactly the same factors which influence farming, there are similarities. Users of this equipment require reliable products, high levels of service in the field, and financing for product purchases. There are also many technological similarities between the two types of equipment. The market for industrial equipment is strongly influenced by interest rates for two reasons. High interest rates influence the ability to finance new construction as well as the ability to purchase the equipment. As a result of the influence of interest rates and overall economic activity, the sale of construction equipment tends to be cyclical. This is illustrated in Table 5 which shows industry sales for the decade of the 1980s in current dollars and in real terms. For comparison, the Table also presents Deere and Company sales for both its heavy equipment product lines for the same period.

Table 5

Construction Equipment Data
Deere and Company Sales Summary
($ in billions, Index #'s—1977 = 100)

| | Construction Equipment Industry Shipments to Dealers | | | | Deere & Co. Sales* | |
Year	Index of Constr. Activity	Value of Shipments	Price Ind. Industry Shipments	Real Industry Sales	Agric. & Garden Equipment	Indust. & Const. Equip.
1980	133.9	$15.99	135.2	$11.82	$4.488	$0.981
1981	138.4	16.93	151.1	11.20	4.665	.782
1982	131.1	11.66	157.0	7.42	4.034	.575
1983	149.6	10.31	161.8	6.37	3.314	.654
1984	174.8	12.69	164.5	7.71	3.505	894
1985	189.3	12.80	166.4	7.69	3.118	.942
1986	206.8	12.99	167.8	7.74	2.649	.868
1987	207.3	13.77	170.2	8.09	3.223	.911
1988E	210.6	14.45	175.0	8.26	4.203	1.162

Source: Shipments from U.S. Department of Commerce

*Sales for Deere and Company are for fiscal years ended 10/31.

The decade of the 1980s has been characterized by a more or less continuous rise in the general level of construction activity. Although growth in new construction has slowed since 1986, growth has been continuous since 1982. The real sales of construction equipment, however, have not kept pace with the level of activity. Uncertainty over interest rates in 1987-88, the latest two years of a prolonged economic expansion, and the resulting impact on housing starts may be one major reason for declining construction growth. In addition, budget pressure on public works and defense spending may also be a major factor influencing current conditions.

The markets for industrial and construction equipment are distinctive and highly segmented. Industrial equipment includes such product groups as fork lift trucks and other types of material handling equipment such as overhead cranes, conveyors, and automated inventory storage and retrieval systems. This market is not included in the sales data in Table 5 because Deere does not participate in it. The product segments in the construction equipment market include: earthmoving and excavation equipment, logging equipment, mining machinery, paving machines, and other related products. This industry and its various segments are dominated by a few large firms.

Deere and Company participates in many of these product segments, although its primary emphasis is on earthmoving and smaller types of excavating equipment, markets traditionally dominated by Caterpillar. Deere also produces some specialized logging equipment and, through its OEM product lines, it produces original equipment (OEM) parts for many of the market leaders such as Caterpillar and Dresser Industries.

Because of its fundamental role in the building of an infrastructure and the production of natural resources, construction equipment plays a major role in economic development, especially in less developed nations. For this reason the industry has traditionally been heavily involved in exporting its products. Historically, approximately 20% of U.S. production has been exported. Caterpillar has typically exported about half of its output. Although the industry contains over 700 firms, six of these provide over 70% of the total value of all worldwide production and two-thirds of the U.S. exports.[8] Caterpillar is the clear world leader in the industry, with roughly a 35% worldwide market share. Other large broad-line producers include: Case (Tenneco), Deere, Ingersoll-Rand, Dresser Industries, Clark Equipment, and Komatsu.

The market segments dominated by these major producers include:

1. Earthmovers-Caterpillar, Komatsu, Deere
2. Excavators and cranes - American Hoist and Derrick, PMC, Manitowoc

3. Mining Machinery - Joy Manufacturing
4. Paving, Road-building - Barber-Greene, Ingersoll-Rand, Koehring, Dresser Industries, Rexnord.

As was the case in the agricultural equipment industry, the decade of the 1980s has been a period of industry consolidation. Many older plants have been closed and more efficient ones constructed. Breakeven points have been lowered dramatically. Caterpillar, in order to be more competitive internationally, closed nine plants from 1983-1987 in an attempt to save $250 million and lower overall costs 15-20% by 1991. Deere has also proceeded in much the same way, cutting the labor content of its industrial equipment by 50% in the mid-1990s. To combat the falling dollar, Komatsu, a leading Japanese producer, built a major plant in Tennessee and entered into a joint venture with Dresser Industries. In spite of all these changes, however, the overall outlook for real growth in the industry is not expected to be greater than 2-3% per year for the next few years.[9]

OTHER MARKETS SERVED BY DEERE

In addition to its domestic agricultural and industrial equipment markets, Deere and Company serves several other markets with lesser amounts of output.

Lawn Care Products:

A significant proportion of Deere's agricultural product sales (see Table 7, for example) results from the sales of small garden tractors, lawnmowers and other lawn care equipment, and snow removal equipment for both the consumer and commercial markets. Although reliable figures are not available, these sales probably range between $700 and $750 million.[10] In the few years since it has been in the commercial lawn care market Deere has become the market leader and has added a new golf course turf care line. Deere's lawn care products are sold through a network of over 5000 dealers, nearly 100 of which have sales in excess of one million dollars annually. Overall, the consumer segment of this market is estimated at $3.75 billion in 1988. The market is tied closely to consumer income growth and new housing construction. Accordingly, annual real growth is expected to average 1.5-2% through 1993.[11] Sales in this market are also affected by the weather and the level of interest rates.

Deere's lawn care lines have achieved strong market positions for many of the same reasons as its other products. The products in the lawn care line are characterized as well designed, among the safest, reliable, and reasonably priced. *Consumer Reports* recently rated Deere's line among the safest and most effective.[12] Although riding mowers and lawn tractors can easily cost from

$1000-4000, Deere's equipment also rates well on price compared to some of its lower quality competitors.

OEM Parts:

As part of its industrial sales, Deere sells a variety of parts and products to original equipment manufacturers (OEMs). The OEM product line was originally developed as a way of offsetting low capacity utilization. Although reliable figures are not available, this segment of the firm has grown dramatically in recent years. A major product group in this segment is a line of diesel engines and power trains for off-road vehicles. The proposed joint venture with Detroit-Allison was broken off in 1987 for undisclosed reasons. Allison then formed a joint venture with the Penske Company, a firm managed by the famous race team manager, Roger Penske. In spite of this setback, however, Deere reported that its own diesel engine group sold in excess of 25,000 units in 1988, an increase of 38% over the previous year. The engine group has also been successful in achieving a modest level of diesel sales to the government and plans to expand its rotary engine product to operate in land vehicles such as assault craft.

Financial Services and Health Care:

As a result of its need to finance the sales of its products, Deere maintains a number of financially-related subsidiaries. Through these operations (currently not consolidated for financial reporting purposes) Deere provides customer financing, loans, leases, and insurance. On January 1, 1989, the credit and leasing subsidiaries were reorganized to form the John Deere Credit Company which, in turn, became the owner of the other finance subsidiaries. This was ostensibly done to coordinate the activities of the finance group and give it greater emphasis in corporate strategic planning. It may also have been done in anticipation of the rising trend toward consolidation of such activities into the regular financial statements. The primary function of this group is to purchase customer loans from dealers. (These receivables appear only in the non consolidated balance sheet shown in Table 9.) Loans to dealers for the purchase of equipment are carried on the regular balance sheet (Table 8). The operation of this group closely resembles other such subsidiaries such as General Motors' GMAC. In addition, this subsidiary also purchases loans on boats and recreational vehicles from various dealers of these products. Further, the group also makes farm production and related loans to customers through the Farm Plan division and provides significant amounts of lease financing for equipment (over $355 million was outstanding in 1988).

The other major part of Deere's financial services business centers on insurance. Initially offered to employees and customers, this subsidiary now produces about $350 million in revenues annually (see Table 9). In an effort to control its health care costs, Deere established its own HMO. Its success in this effort encouraged it to sell health care management expertise to other firms. Established in 1985, the firm's health care services subsidiary now generates $140 million in annual revenues.

International Markets:

Although Deere produces most of its output in the U.S., it also has significant operational capacity outside the U.S. Manufacturing plants for tractors, engines, and other equipment are operated in Canada, Spain, France, Germany, South Africa, Australia, and Argentina. In addition, the firm has industrial affiliates in Brazil and Mexico. Sales branches are operated in all the countries where manufacturing is done as well as Sweden, Italy, and England. As Table 6 shows, the sales in these overseas markets is approximately 25% of the total sales of the firm's foreign operations. As noted earlier, the production of small tractors is almost entirely outside the U.S. However, the world market shares shown in Table 4 also show that this production is dominated by U.S. based firms. Deutz and Kubota are the only major foreign-based producers. As a side note, however, the Russians, shipped around 2500 small tractors to the U.S. in 1988.[13] Because of its existing presence in Europe, Deere should be in a good position to take advantage of the changes in the Common Market in 1992.

RECENT EVENTS AND PROSPECTS

Since 1985, the return of Deere and Company to profitability has been marked by a number of critical events. Although small profits were reported in 1985, negative operating profits were offset only by profits in the financial services segment. While operating at extremely low levels of capacity utilization in late 1986 and early 1987, the firm suffered from a costly strike. This reduced operations to less than 10% of capacity and created huge operating losses.[14] Although the growth in 1987 and 1988 did raise utilization considerably, Deere's state-of-the-art tractor assembly plant still has the capacity to produce more than twice as many tractors as the whole industry sold in the 100 hp. and four wheel drive markets in 1988. Some of this capacity has been absorbed by new products, increases in market share, and the production of chassis for motor homes. Although Deere may never utilize all of its available capacity, cost cutting and increased productivity have allowed the firm to break even on manufacturing operations at only 35% of capacity.[15]

Deere's lawn and garden and industrial lines have been expanded since 1985 and have provided increasing profits to the firm, as has the financial service segment. Some of the prospects for the OEM group were reduced when the GM joint venture was dropped and a major GM engine block contract was lost in 1989. Some chassis production has also been sold to a Wisconsin truck manufacturer. However, engine sales have been improved in spite of these setbacks. Further, the firm acquired Funk Manufacturing, a small ($50 million in sales) producer of off-road transmission equipment. In addition, Deere introduced a broad line of new products in its agricultural equipment group in 1989. This was the largest package of new products in the firm's history.

Deere and Company faces the 1990s having diversified, cut costs, and restructured itself to emphasize new products. However, its sales are still dominated by dealer financing in heavy equipment markets. OEM sales are promising, but do not yet provide material revenues. Further, these sales are competitive, as the loss of the engine block contract illustrates, and many of the firm's largest customers are also its competitors. How long can the firm afford to sell its technology to its competitors? Further, Deere still has considerable excess capacity it must eventually utilize.

Table 6

Overseas Activity
Deere and Company
(Dollars in millions)

	1988	1987	1986	1985
Net Sales				
U.S. & Canada	$4,418	$3,308	$2,821	$3,432
Overseas	1,574	1,209	1,077	1,070
Less: Interarea	(627)	(382)	(382)	(441)
	$5,365	$4,135	$3,516	$4,061
Operating Profits*				
U.S. & Canada	325	(114)	(403)	33
Overseas	61	(7)	5	45
	$ 386	$ (121)	$ (398)	$ 78
Assets				
U.S. & Canada	$3.203	$2,782	$2,838	$3,677
Overseas	920	869	768	680
Corporate	1,122	1,109	1,368	1,105
	$5,245	$4,760	$4,974	$5,462
Employees				
U.S. and Canada	28,200	27,700	26,700	29,600
Overseas	10,100	10,200	11,100	10,900

*Includes equity investments in non-consolidated subsidiaries and affiliates.

Note: Canadian sales are historically about 11% of total U.S. and Canada sales. About 82% of these are made in the U.S. and 79% of Canadian production is exported to the U.S.

Table 7
Deere and Company
Income Statements
Years Ending October 31, ($ millions)

Item	1985	%	1986	%	1987	%	1988	%	Ave. % Growth /year
Sales:									
Farm Equipment	3,118	76.8	2,648	75.3	3,223	77.9	4,203	78.3	10.5
Indus. Equip.	943	23.2	868	24.7	912	22.1	1,162	21.7	7.2
Net Sales	4,061	100.0	3,516	100.0	4,135	100.0	5,365	100.0	9.7
—Cost of Sales	3,355	82.6	3,271	93.0	3,669	88.7	4,367	81.4	9.2
Gross Profit	706	17.4	245	7.0	466	11.3	998	18.6	12.2
Less:									
G & A Expense	508	12.5	317	9.0	304	7.3	315	5.9	-14.7
Other Oper. Exp.	54	1.3	225	6.4	214	5.2	216	4.0	58.7
Depreciation	184	4.5	191	4.7	184	4.4	180	3.4	-.7
Operating Profit	(40)	-1.0	(488)	-13.1	(235)	-5.7	287	5.4	NA
+Other Income	206	5.1	188	5.4	213	5.2	225	4.2	3.0
—Inter. & Other	199	4.9	214	6.1	189	4.6	164	3.1	-6.3
Income Bef. Tax	(33)	-.8	(513)	-13.9	(211)	-5.1	349	6.5	NA
—Income Tax	(65)	-1.6	(284)	-8.1	(113)	-2.7	33	.6	NA
Net Income	32	.8	(230)	-5.8	(98)	-2.4	316	5.9	114.5
Per Share:									
Income	.46		-3.38		-1.46		4.32		
Dividends	1.00		.75		.25		.65		
Cap. Expend. (mil)	144		173		171		185		
R & D (mil)	223		225		214		180		
# of Employees	40,509		37,793		37,931		38,268		
Sales/Employ ($)	100,249		93,033		109,014		140,195		
Segment Data									
Farm Equipment:									
Sales	3,118		2,648		3,223		4,203		
Operat. Profit	65		(392)		(136)		284		
Ident. Assets	3,625		2,960		2,909		3,207		
Indus. Equip.:									
Sales	943		868		912		1,162		
Operat. Profit	22		4		9		97		
Ident. Assets.	732		646		742		916		
Corp. & Subsid.:									
Pretax Inc.	-120		-125		-84		-32		
Ident. Assets	4787		5330		4657		5173		
% Foreign Sales	22.0		25.1		24.7		24.1		

Table 8

Deere and Company
Balance Sheets
Years Ending October 31, ($ millions)

Item	1985	%	1986	%	1987	%	1988	%	Ave. % Growth /year
Assets									
Current Assets:									
Cash & M.S.	88	1.6	182	3.7	116	2.4	49	.9	-17.7
Acct's Rec.	2,749	50.3	2,079	41.8	2,111	44.3	2,308	44.0	-5.7
Inventory	447	8.2	483	9.7	465	9.8	708	13.5	16.6
Other	150	2.7	218	4.4	45	1.0	50	1.0	-30.7
Total C/A	3,434	62.9	2,961	59.5	2,737	57.5	3,115	59.4	-3.2
Fixed Assets:									
Plant & Equip.	2,629	48.1	2,767	55.6	2,943	61.8	3,056	58.3	5.1
-Accum. Deprec.	1,613	29.5	1,816	36.5	1,960	41.2	2,063	39.3	8.6
Other F/A Net	1,012	18.5	1,062	21.3	1,040	21.9	1,137	21.7	3.9
Total F/A	2,028	37.1	2,013	40.5	2,023	42.5	2,130	40.6	1.6
Total Assets	5,462	100.0	4,974	100.0	4,760	100.0	5,245	100.0	-1.3
Liabilities & Owners Equity									
Current Liabil.:									
Acct's Pay.	1,044	19.1	1,003	20.2	1,037	21.8	1,122	21.4	2.4
Notes Pay.	521	9.5	383	7.7	342	7.2	455	8.7	-4.4
Curr Pay. LTD	16	.3	12	.2	13	.3	21	.4	9.7
Taxes Pay.	333	6.1	111	2.2	58	1.2	84	1.6	-36.8
Other					79	1.7	46	.9	-41.8
Total C/L	1,914	35.0	1,509	30.3	1,529	32.1	1,728	33.0	-3.3
Long Term Debt:									
Bonds & Notes	1,130	20.7	1,290	25.9	1,062	22.3	817	15.6	-10.2
Def. Tax & Pens.	160	2.9	176	3.5	248	5.2	244	4.6	15.1
Total LTD	1,290	23.6	1,466	29.5	1,310	27.5	1,061	20.2	-6.3
Equity:									
Common Stock	491	9.0	492	9.9	497	10.4	760	14.5	15.7
Retained Earn.	1,767	32.4	1,507	30.3	1,424	29.9	1,696	32.3	-1.4
Total Equity	2,258	41.3	1,999	40.2	1,920	40.3	2,456	46.8	2.8
Total L & OE	5,462	100.0	4,974	100.0	4,760	100.0	5,245	100.0	-1.3

Table 9

Deere and Company
Financial Results—Finance Subsidiaries
Years Ending October 31, ($ millions)

INCOME STATEMENTS

	Finance Subsidiary				Insurance Subsidiary			
	1985	1986	1987	1988	1985	1986	1987	1988
Net Revenues	335	324	306	385	260	308	313	356
Less: Expenses	63	58	68	80	227	259	266	306
Operating Profit	272	266	238	305	33	49	47	50
Less: Interest	172	176	153	180				
Income Bef. Tax	100	90	85	125	33	49	47	50
—Income Tax	40	36	33	35	7	12	9	13
Net Income*	60	54	52	90	26	37	38	37

BALANCE SHEETS

	Finance Subsidiary				Insurance Subsidiary			
	1985	1986	1987	1988	1985	1986	1987	1988
Cash					40	42	45	31
Notes Rec.	2624	2540	2374	2620				
Investments	443	740	690	521	410	485	539	652
Other Assets	94	72	108	132	71	83	93	95
Total Assets	3161	3352	3172	3273	521	610	677	778
Notes Pay	1288	1344	1628	1720				
Due JD & Co.	76	193	17	37				
Policy Reserves					218	254	292	350
Unearn. Premium					57	70	74	88
Other	370	362	270	218	32	45	46	50
LT Debt	818	813	598	590				
Total Debt	2552	2712	2513	2565	307	369	412	488
Owners Equity	609	640	659	708	214	241	265	290
	3161	3352	3172	3273	521	610	677	778

*Income from both these subsidiaries is entered on the income statement (Table 7) under "Other Income."
Balance sheet items above are not included on the consolidated balance sheet (Table 8).

ENDNOTES

1. J. Ecker, "Dealers of the '90s." *Implement & Tractor*, April, 1989, pp. 24-26.

2. R. Rose, "Deere, Dealers Cross Swords Over Plows." *Wall Street Journal*, November 7, 1989, p. B2.

3. A. Anderson Jr., "Future Farming." *Omni*, June, 1979, pp. 90-94ff.

4. J. Rachlin, "Best Jobs in the Future." *U.S. News and World Report*, April 25, 1988, pp. 60-62.

5. F. Buckingham, "Why Doesn't Fuel Efficiency get any Better?" *Implement & Tractor*, April, 1989, pp. 22-23ff.

6. U.S. Department of Commerce, *Statistical Abstract of the U.S.*, 1988, Table 1070, p. 614.

7. D. Kendall, "'Superfarm' Numbers have Grown Rapidly in the Past Decade." *Waterloo Courier*, February 16, 1986.

8. "Steel and Heavy Machinery." *Standard and Poor's Industry Surveys*, July 7, 1989, pp. S35-37.

9. U.S. Department of Commerce, *1989 U.S. Industrial Outlook*, pp. 21-1 - 21-2.

10. K. Deveny, "As John Deere Sowed, So Shall It Reap." *Business Week*, June 6, 1988, pp. 84-85.

11. U.S. Department of Commerce. *1989 Industrial Outlook*, pp. 43-8 - 43-9.

12. "Lawn Tractors: Can They Cut It?" *Consumer Reports*, June, 1989, p. 368-373.

13. J. Zweig, "'It was a matter of economics'." *Forbes*, February 22, 1988, pp. 106-107.

14. K. Deveny, "Thinking Ahead Got Deere in Big Trouble." *Business Week*, December 8, 1986, p. 69.

15. K. Deveny, ob.cit., 1988, p. 84.

INDEX

Abell, Derek F. 131
Accounts receivable, management of 37
Acquisitions 132
Advertising
 and promotion 33, 168
 budget 61
 effectiveness 142, 143
Alternative grand strategies,
 evaluating 46, 159, 162
American Express 132
Analysis, definition of 16
Appendix 181
Apple Computer, Inc. 314-344
Approach
 semi-structured 46, 160, 163
 structured 46, 161, 162, 163
 unstructured 46, 159, 163
Area, functional 174
Barriers
 entry 82
 entry/exit 145, 146
 exit 83
BCG growth/share matrix 135, 136, 138
Board of directors 25, 39, 95
 composition of 39
Boards
 catalyst 40
 constitutional 39
 oversight 40
 rubber stamp 39
 types of 39
Boston Consulting Group
 (BCG) 135
Budget 35, 167, 170, 171
Budgetary allocations 27
Business domain 42, 156
Business strength 139, 141, 142, 149, 150, 158
Business-strength index 145
Capital 160, 162
Capital budgeting 38

Case analysis 1
Case method 1
 communication dimensions
  of 173
 popularity of 1, 2
 rationale of 2
Cash cows 136-138, 141, 159
Cash, management of 37
Causal treatment 116, 117
Cause 112, 120, 124, 126
 as independent variable 106
 meaning of 105
 untreatable 116
Cause-tracking question 108, 110
 limits 109
Centralization 57
CEO's decision-making style 41
 autocratic 41
 participative 41
CEO's managerial modes 40
 adaptive 40
 entrepreneurial 40
 strategic planning 40
Checklists 23, 25
 definition of 23
 subcomponents of
  environmental analysis
  25
 subcomponents of finance/
  accounting 37
 subcomponents of human
  resources 35
 subcomponents of marketing
  32
 subcomponents of
  production 34
 subcomponents of public
  affairs 36
 subcomponents of research
  and development 35
 subcomponents of strategic
  managers 25
 subcomponents of strategy

control 28
subcomponents of strategy
    formulation 26
subcomponents of strategy
    implementation 27
Checklists and factors 78
Communication 28, 171, 172
Communication skills 173
    avoiding overparticipation
        173, 180
    expressing criticism 173,
        178
    handling criticism 173, 177
    oral report 173, 184
    overcoming nonparticipation
        173, 179
    written report 173, 180
Compensation 36
Competitive position 140, 142,
    143, 149, 150
Competitive strategies 27, 46,
    165
    cost leadership 27
    focus 27
    product differentiation 27
Competitor intelligence 41
Competitors 75
    major weakness of 150
    reaction of 162
    sources of information on
        84
Constraint 128, 130, 134, 141,
    149, 158, 161, 162
    definition of 128
    illustration 128
Control mechanism 169
Corporate culture 28, 60, 142,
    143, 160, 162, 172
    dysfunctional 60
    functional 60
Corporate objectives 26,
    43, 154, 156
    good 43
    poor 43
Corporate/business level 20,
    29, 171
    combined 21
    major components of 23

profiling 21
strengths 93
weaknesses of 98
Corporate/business policy 174
    illustrating 174
Cost leadership 46, 165
Creativity 13
Crisis management 37
Criticism 177
Culture 77, 146, 147, 161,
    162
    dysfunctional 28, 61
    functional 28, 61
    sources of information on
        86
Curran 19
Customers 42, 76, 156
Cyclicality 145, 146
Date
    completion 169
    starting 169
Debt, management of 38
Decentralization 57
Decision-making
    process 10
    style 25
Deere and Company 345-361
Demographics 77, 146, 147,
    161, 162
    sources of information on
        86
Descriptive phase 3, 16, 72
    benefits of 6
    definition of 16
    observations on 80
    purpose of 6
Deviations, correction of 29
Diagnosis 90
Diagnostic labels 7
Diagnostic phase 7, 128
    definition of 90
    objective of 90
Diagnostic process, steps of 91
Directors
    affiliated nonmanagement
        39
    independent 39
    management 39

Distinctive competency 96,
        150, 160, 162
Distribution 33, 168
Distribution channels 42, 156
Dogs 136, 138, 141
Dysfunctional culture, features
        of 28, 61
Economies of scale 82
Economy 77, 146, 147, 161,
        162
Economy, sources of
        information on 86
Entry and exit barriers 82, 83,
        145
Environmental analysis 5, 22,
        24, 25, 40, 94, 98, 99,
        119, 122, 124, 126
Ethics 36
Evaluation criteria 145, 146,
        161
Experience curve 75, 84, 142,
        143
Express Mail 130
External analysis 26
External environment
        profiling of 72
        scanning of 26, 41
Eye contact 184
Facial expressions 184
Facilities
        layout of 34
        location of 34
        newness of 34
Factor, meaning of 79
Factoring 12, 16, 18
Factors
        favorable 80
        unfavorable 80, 121
Fear barrier 179
Finance/accounting 175
Firm
        multi-business 149
        single-business 149
Focus 35, 62, 165
Footnotes 181, 182
Forecasting 41
Framework 3, 4
        objectives of 11

three phases of 3
Functional culture, features of
        29, 61
Functional level 20, 29, 31
        major components of 32
        profiling 29
        strengths of 96
        weaknesses of 98
GE planning grid 138, 139,
        141
        three zones of 140, 141
General Electric Co. 138, 164
General environment 74
        checklists 77
        definition of 77
General profit picture 38
Gestures 184
Glueck 20
Government regulations 76,
        146, 147
        sources of information on 85
Grand strategies 21, 26, 43,
        156
        alternative 156, 157, 161,
                162
        concentration 26, 43, 157,
                161, 162
        concentric diversification
                27, 43, 44, 158, 159
        conglomerate diversification
                27, 43, 45, 158, 159
        divestiture 27, 43, 45, 157,
                158, 159
        entrepreneurial 171
        evaluating alternative 46,
                159
        functional 171
        geographic 171
        harvest 27, 43, 45, 157,
                158, 159
        horizontal diversification
                157
        horizontal integration 27,
                43, 44
        innovation 43, 44
        joint venture 27, 43, 45,
                159
        liquidation 27, 43, 45,

157, 158, 159
market development 26,
        43, 157
matrix 171
product 171
product development 26,
        43, 157, 159
product innovation 26, 158
project structure 171
retrenchment/turnaround
        27, 43, 45, 158, 159
strategic business unit 171
vertical integration 26, 43,
        44, 157, 158, 161, 162
Gut feeling 160
Harley-Davidson, Inc. 293-313
Hofer 18
Human resources 35, 160,
        162, 175
IBM 133
Industrial espionage 41
Industry 75
attractiveness 139, 140, 145,
        146
average 37
growth 145, 146
ratios, observations on use of
        67
ratios, sources of information
        on 66
sources of information on 83
Information-gathering skills 12
Intermediate factor 107, 108
definition of 107
one-level 108, 109
two-level 109, 110
Internal analysis 25
Internal environment 16, 19,
        20
profiling 19
scanning 26
Intuition, definition of 159
Inventories 35
management of 37
Jauch 20
Joint venture 157
Labor
availability of 76

availability, sources of
        information on 85
unions 76, 146, 147, 161, 162
Leadership 28, 58, 59, 172
authority-compliance 28,
        58, 59, 172
country-club management
        28, 58, 59, 172
grid 58, 59
impoverished management
        28, 58, 59
middle-of-the-road
        management 28, 58,
        59, 172
style 28, 58, 172
team management 28, 58,
        59, 172
Leverage 128, 130, 134, 141,
        149, 158
definition of 131
List of illustrations 181
Logan 18
Logical thinking 12
Maintenance 128, 130, 132,
        134, 141, 149, 158, 159
definition of 132
Major and subordinate problems
        126
causes 105
diagnosing 105
difference between 118
process of diagnosing 121
symptoms 105
Major components 22, 29
functional level 32
profiling 23
Major problem, as critical gap
        118
diagnosing 125
Management
authority-compliance 28,
        58, 59, 172
beliefs and values of 42,
        156
country-club 28, 58, 59,
        172
familiarity 162
impoverished 28, 58, 59

middle-of-the road 28, 58, 59, 172
  participative 172
  team 28, 58, 59, 172
Management familiarity 160
Managerial mode 25
Manuscript speech 184
Market growth 135
  definition of 135
Market share 33, 135
Marketing 167, 175
Marketing research 32, 167
Martin Marietta Corp. 131
Mary Kay Cosmetics, Inc. 264-292
Matrix 136
McCarthy 18
McKinsey and Co. 138
Mergers 132
Miner 164
Minichiello 19
Mission 26, 42, 174
  elements of 42
  statement 154, 156
Motivation 28, 171, 172
Multi-business organizations 20
Nabisco, RJR 137
Newman 18
No information (N/I) 93-95, 101
Not available (N/A) 93-95, 101
NutraSweet 137
Objectives
  functional 154, 165
  long-term 156, 167
  short-term 156, 167, 169
Observations
  on opportunities 104
  on strengths 104
  on threats 104
  on weaknesses 104
Opportunities 134, 141, 145, 154
  definition of 99
  diagnosing 99
  in task and general environments 101
  key 101

Optima 132
Organization 112
Organizational structure 27, 47, 171
  entrepreneurial 27, 47, 48
    advantages 48
    disadvantages 48
  functional 27, 47, 49
    advantages 49
    disadvantages 49
  geographic 27, 47, 50
    advantages 50
    disadvantages 50
  matrix 27, 47, 55
    advantages 55
    disadvantages 55
  product 27, 47, 52
    advantages 52
    disadvantages 52
  project management 47, 56
  strategic business unit 27, 47, 53
    advantages 53
    disadvantages 53
Osborne Computer Corporation 132
Osborne, Adam 132, 133
Percolation effect 112
  and intermediate factors 112
  definition of 112
Performance
  appraisal 36
  evaluation of 29
Philip Morris Cos. 138
Policies 27, 57, 171, 174-176
  changing 176
  corporate/business 174
  functional 174
  purposes of 57
Politics 78, 146, 147, 161, 162
  sources of information on 87
Porter, Michael 46
Portfolio planning
  definition of 133
  techniques 133, 138
Positive attitude 179
Posture 35, 62

catch-up 35
    innovative 35
    protective 35
Premier 137
Prescriptive phase 9, 110, 154,
        171
    and healthy organizations 9
    functions of 154
    two objectives of 9
Pressure groups 78, 146, 147,
        161, 162
    sources of information on 88
Pricing 33, 168
Probable cause, determination
        of 123
Problem 120
    definition of 116
    statement of 119
Problem-solving skills 10
Procedures 176
Product
    differentiation 82, 165
    quality 142, 143
Production 34, 175
    capacity 34, 142, 143
Products 32, 42, 156
Profiling process 16
Profitability 156
Public affairs 36, 63, 175
    crisis management 64
    ethics 63
    social responsibility 64
Quality control 34
    techniques 62
Question marks 136, 137, 141,
        157
Ranking 146, 147
Rating 142, 144, 162
Ratio
    activity 65
    collection-period 38
    current 37
    debt-to-total-assets 38
    inventory-turnover 37
    leverage 66
    liquidity 64
    profit-margin 38
    profitability 66, 142, 143

quick (acid-test) 37
    return-on equity 38
    times-interest-earned 38
    total-assets 38
Ratios, meaning and
        computation of 64
Reaction, of competitors 160
Recommendations 111, 166
    specificity of 169
Recruitment and selection 36
Regulations 160, 162
Relative market share, definition of
        135
Research and development 35,
        62, 142, 143, 175
Rewards
    financial 172
    nonfinancial 172
Risk 160, 162
Root cause 110
Rules 176, 177
Sales 168
    volume 33
Sanctions 172
Savings 167, 170, 171
Scenarios 164
    optimistic 165
    pessimistic 165
Schendel 18
Searle, G.D. 137
Seasonality 145, 146
Semi-structured approach 27
Services 42, 156
Social responsibility 36
Speaking rate 185
Standards, establishment of 28
Stars 136, 137, 141
Steiner 164
Strategic business unit (SBU)
        20, 21, 46, 133, 137, 138,
        149
    plotting 140
Strategic choice 154, 156
Strategic management 1
    cases 2
    definition of 18
Strategic managers 25
    strengths of 95

Strategic match 128
   definition of 128
   dimensions of 128
   matrix 141, 148, 149
   primary position 133, 141
   process of determining
        primary position 141
   value of dimensions 133
Strategic option 163
Strategic plan 150, 154, 156,
   171
   implementation of 171
Strategic windows, examples of
   131
Strategies 154
   alternative 162
   annual 166
   clusters of 141, 157, 158
   combination 164
   constraint 141, 157
   contingency 164, 165
   decline 157
   evaluation of 163
   formulation 26
   functional 165, 166, 167,
      170
   growth 157, 158
   leverage 141, 157
   maintenance 141, 157
   selecting 163
   structure of short-term 167
   vulnerability 141, 157
Strategy control 5, 22, 24, 25,
     28, 81, 94, 98, 99, 119,
     122, 124, 126
Strategy formulation 26
Strengths 23, 134, 141
   definition of 91
   diagnosing 91
   examples of 93
Structure
   centralized 27
   decentralized 27
   entrepreneurial 47
   functional 47
   geographic 47
   matrix 54
   product 51

   project management 54
   strategic business unit 51
Structure follows strategy 57
Structured approach 27, 162
Subcomponents 23
Subordinate problem 126
   as minor gap 118
   diagnosing 125
Success factors 142, 143
Succession planning 35, 63
Suppliers 146, 147
   capital 76
   labor 76
   raw materials 75
Symptom 112, 120, 121, 124,
   126
   as dependent variable 106
   major 123
   meaning of 105
   minor 123
Symptomatic relief 116, 117
Symptoms and causes
   differences between 106
   illustration of 107
System 112
Table of contents 180
Target marketing 32, 60, 167
   concentrated 60
   differentiated 60
   undifferentiated 60
Task environment 74
   checklists 72
   definition of 72
Technology 78, 146, 147, 161,
   162
   sources of information on 87
Text 181
Threats 134, 141, 145
   definition of 102
   examples of 102
   diagnosing 102
   in task and general
        environments 103
   key 104
Time table 167, 169-171
Timing 160, 162
Title page 180
Top management 25, 40, 95

    caliber of 142, 143
Total assets, management of 38
Training and development 36
U.S. Postal Service 128
Unstructured approach 27
Visa 132
Voice pitch 185
Vulnerability 128, 130, 132,
        141, 149, 150, 158, 159
    definition of 132
Weaknesses 23, 134, 141
    critical 150
    definition of 96
    diagnosing the 96
    examples of 98
    key 98
Weight 142, 144, 146, 147,
        161, 162
Weighted score 142, 144, 146,
        148, 162
    composite 163
Weighting process 144
    subjectivity of 163
Xerox Corporation 130
Zone
    green 140
    red 140
    yellow 140